COMPARATIVE ADVANTAGE, TRADE POLICY AND ECONOMIC DEVELOPMENT

COMPARATIVE ADVANTAGE, TRADE POLICY AND ECONOMIC DEVELOPMENT

Bela Balassa

New York University Press

WASHINGTON SQUARE, NEW YORK

HF
1411
.B22192
1989

© 1989 by Bela Balassa

Manufactured in Great Britain

First published in 1989 in the U.S.A. by
NEW YORK UNIVERSITY PRESS
Washington Square
New York, NY 10003

Library of Congress Cataloging-in-Publication Data

Balassa, Bela A.
    Comparative advantage, trade policy and economic development/
Bela Balassa.
    p.   cm.
    ISBN 0–8147–1129–4
    1. Comparative advantage (Commerce)   2. Commercial policy.
3. Tariff.   4. Economic development.   5. Developing countries—
Economic policy.   I. Title.
HF 1411.B22192   1989
382'.1042—dc 20   89–3437 CIP

1 2 3 4 5   93 92 91 90 89

4/8/91 RB

To the memory of my parents

CONTENTS

PREFACE

This book contains a selection of my writings on comparative advantage, tariffs and trade, and development strategies, exports, and economic growth. Space limitations have not permitted to cover other areas of my research interest, such as the history of economic thought, Soviet-type economies, comparative systems, project evaluation, and international monetary issues. Nor does the book include my oft-cited paper on purchasing power parities.

I have also omitted my papers on development policy that have been published in separate volumes. They include *Policy Reform in Developing Countries* (1977), *The Newly Industrializing Countries in the World Economy* (1981), *Change and Challenge in the World Economy* (1985), and *New Directions in the World Economy* (1989).

I am indebted to publishers of professional journals and collective volumes who have given permission to the reprinting of my articles in this volume. They are indicated in the autobiographical essay which follows.

Bela Balassa

TABLES

FIGURES

INTRODUCTION –
AN AUTOBIOGRAPHICAL
ESSAY

A BRIEF LIFE HISTORY

I was born in Budapest, Hungary on 6 April 1928. My father was an officer in the Hungarian army. This meant high social standing on a very small income. None the less, I was sent to the best schools and the education I received at the Cistercian Gymnasium was a major asset in my professional life.

Having finished high school in 1946, I enrolled at both the Law and Political Science Faculty of the University of Budapest and at the Foreign Trade Academy, completing both with honors. At the University, my interest soon turned to economics. I was much influenced in this by my mentor, Professor István Varga, with whom I worked at the University as well as at an Institute he directed. This work, but not our relationship, ended in 1949 when Varga was pensioned under the Stalinist regime. In view of the changes at the University, it appeared safer for me to write my doctoral dissertation on sampling theory rather than on economics.

With my newly minted doctorate, I went to the Construction Trust in Miskolc, the third largest city in Hungary, as a planner in May 1951. I was soon noticed by the director, József Bondor, who wanted to appoint me head of planning. However, deportation from Budapest (which had remained my domicile) was ordered for people of a particular social or political background, of whom I was considered to be one. I was not in Budapest on the night the deportation was to take place but, when I appeared next day at police headquarters armed with a laudatory letter from Bondor, this was rejected and I was summarily taken to the train just before it departed for the eastern part of Hungary.

This introduction will appear in a slightly different form under the title 'My Life Philosophy' in a collective volume provisionally entitled *The Life Philosophy of Eminent Economists* to be published by the Cambridge University Press.

There followed three months of working in the cotton fields, a crop that represented a misuse of land in Hungary's climatic conditions. Fortunately, my parents were living and working on our land in the western part of Hungary, hence they escaped deportation, and I was allowed to join them while being confined to their village. I soon found a job as head of finances in an alcohol factory and stayed there until it was discovered that as a deportee I was not to do intellectual work.

The next year and a half was a period that greatly strengthened my physique through work in the fields, in the forest and in construction. It also brought a deepening of my intellectual interests. István Varga provided me with books on economics (Keynes was proscribed at the time in Hungary). I tried my hand at writing papers on economics, including comparisons of Karl Marx and John Stuart Mill as well as Marx and Keynes; the former subsequently saw the light of day in a revised form. My first published paper in English (in 1959) was also on John Stuart Mill.

During the deportation, I learnt Italian (in order to read Pirandello and to listen to the Italian radio). Eight years of learning Latin at the Gymnasium helped me in this task. I also acquired a life-long taste in music, in particular opera. (I still remember chancing on *Pelléas et Mélisande* on the radio and recognizing it immediately for what it was.)

Deportation came to a sudden end in June 1953 under the first Nagy government. By that time József Bondor was heading a large construction trust in Sztalinváros (subsequently renamed Dunaujváros) and he hired me as organizer of the Trust. I was later to become what might be called business manager. This was a unique opportunity since few former deportees were able to return to their old, or equivalent, jobs.

There followed a very pleasant period of three years, which included interesting work and considerable travel to the enterprises supervised by the Trust and weekends in Budapest on a relatively high income. I also wrote two books, both of them on the construction industry.

There was a fly in the ointment, however. I had nowhere to go, in terms of advancement, because of my social background. Thus, at 28 years of age, I had an excellent job without any possibility of further advancement.

On 23 October 1956 the Revolution broke out. With four engineers, I became a member of a committee that took over the Ministry of Construction and I was also to teach economics at the University with my mentor, István Varga.

At the Ministry, we started to think how to proceed. On 2 November, we called the Prime Minister's office and asked for a meeting at the weekend. We were told that the Prime Minister wanted to rest for the first time in weeks and we could see him on Monday. It was too late; on Sunday, 4 November Russian troops regained Budapest. The rest is history.

On 18 November I left Budapest for Austria, where I arrived travelling by truck, bicycle and boat. It was the last night before the lake froze over and I spent it under some cornstalks on the Austrian side of the border.

Armed with a letter of introduction from István Varga I went to Vienna, where I visited the Institute for Economic Research. There I met Professor Gottfried Haberler, who was spending his sabbatical in Vienna and who helped me to write an application to the Rockefeller Foundation. Haberler became a fatherly friend who cheered me on in my subsequent career.

I received one of the Foundation's postgraduate grants for Hungarian refugees and applied to Yale for graduate studies in economics. Haberler advised me to go to the United States and to choose Yale rather than the Institute for Graduate Studies in Geneva which had offered me a place. My reason for selecting Yale among the American universities was that Willy Fellner, a friend of István Varga, taught there. It turned out to be a good choice and Fellner became a guiding light in my studies and subsequently my daughter's godfather.

From Vienna I went to Salzburg and to Frankfurt, where I wrote and lectured on the Hungarian economy in German, a language that has since been largely pushed out by English and French. However, I had little chance to extend my knowledge of economics although I badly needed to.

I had a curious background in economics, having been taught successively by a member of the German historical school, a follower of Veblen and Commons (István Varga), and a Marxist. I had no access to books published after the war and had never read Chamberlin or Joan Robinson. I knew practically no microeconomics and Keynes was my only source for macro-economics.

It was not surprising that, on reading Samuelson's introductory textbook, I found it very advanced. I consoled myself that, since my interest was in international economics, I did not have to know the theoretical chapters. . .

LIFE IN THE UNITED STATES

It was with such naivety that I arrived at Yale on 1 April 1957. Then came the cold shower and an understanding of what was required of me. Fortunately, Keynes helped in the macro course and in May I successfully passed the examinations for the second semester.

In the summer I took courses in microeconomics and in statistics at the Harvard summer school. As luck would have it, I had as my professor of microeconomics Franco Modigliani, later to be a Nobel Prize winner, whose rapid-fjre Italian-accented English I understood better than my American fellow students. Statistics was taught by a young professor with a French-sounding name, Louis Lefeber. One day, however, I could read from his lips that he was counting the number of students in Hungarian. Thus at Harvard I found also a Hungarian connection.

Returning to Yale I completed a full year of studies and passed the comprehensives with distinction, an honor I shared with Sidney Winter who is now professor at Yale. At Yale I specialized in international economics. I learned the subject by myself as I had an impossible teacher, a visitor for the year, in whose class I took only half a page of notes. But, going through the readings, I developed lecture notes myself that I used two years later when I began teaching.

But first the dissertation had to be written. My original intention was to write my thesis on economic integration. But I wanted to write what became my first book in English on the *Hungarian Experience in Economic Planning* (1959). Having finished the book in about six months and having it accepted for publication by the Yale University Press, the idea occurred to me to use it as a dissertation. This was agreed to, and a committee was set up consisting of Willy Fellner, Lloyd Reynolds and Robert Triffin who accepted the finished product. It received the Addison Porter prize of Yale University.

This meant that I completed the requirements for the PhD in economics in less than two years and in June 1959 I received the degree. My children would like to have this certified as a world record but they have yet to contact the Guinness outfit to receive confirmation.

I stayed on at Yale as assistant professor to teach international trade and microeconomics, where my notes from Modigliani's course were of great help. I continued at Yale the following year, although I received an invitation from MIT, in the hope that I could teach the PhD course in international economics (at the time I was teaching the course in the masters' program in international economic administration). This happened soon afterwards when I returned from a year's leave at Berkeley. I was accompanied there by my wife, the former Carol Levy, a graduate student in international relations, whom I married in June 1960. She received her PhD at Johns Hopkins many years (and two children) later and has become an international economist with the Office of the US Trade Representative.

Before going to Berkeley I finished my book on *The Theory of Economic Integration* (1961), which was translated into Spanish, Portuguese, Japanese and Czech, and seems to have remained the standard book in the field. At Berkeley, I embarked on a large research project that became my *Trade Prospects for Developing Countries* (1964), also published in Spanish and Portuguese.

I edited *Changing Patterns in Foreign Trade and Payments* (1964), with two subsequent editions (1970 and 1978). I also gave a series of lectures at the Centro de Estudios Monetarios Latinoamericanos that was published under the title *Economic Development and Integration* (1965) simultaneously in English and Spanish.

After my return to Yale as associate professor, I wrote chiefly on international economics. Then came, in rapid succession, a paper on Ricardian comparative advantage (Chapter 1);[1] the introduction of the concept of 'revealed' comparative advantage (Chapter 4);[2] a paper on effective protection (Chapter 10),[3] simultaneously with Max Corden and Harry Johnson; the introduction of the concepts of intra-industry vs inter-industry trade and horizontal vs vertical specialization (Chapter 8);[4] and a new method of measuring trade creation and trade diversion (Chapter 7).[5]

My next large research project was at the Council on Foreign Relations where I directed a group of studies on international trade policy. They were published under the title *Studies in Trade Liberalization* (1967), while my own book on the subject appeared under the title *Trade Liberalization among Industrial Countries: Objectives and Alternatives* (1967). When these books were published, I was already at Johns Hopkins where I was appointed Professor of Political Economy in 1966.

There came a period of dual existence as professor at John Hopkins and consultant to the World Bank over the next 21 years. I found this arrangement, combining teaching at Hopkins with research and policy advising at the World Bank, a happy one. Each of the two institutions may have benefited as my experience at the World Bank helped my teaching of international trade, development policy and comparative systems at Hopkins, while keeping up with the economic literature for my teaching helped my work at the Bank.

THE DEVELOPMENT EXPERIENCE

At the World Bank I divided my time between my own research, research and policy advising, and advising developing countries. I particularly enjoyed the latter as it meant applying economic principles to practical situations. My first experience was in the Dominican Republic, followed by advising in Argentina, Chile, Mexico, Venezuela, Portugal, Turkey, Egypt, Morocco, Tunisia, Korea and Taiwan.

My advice to developing countries was influenced by my liberal economic philosophy. I advocated liberalizing trade and reducing state interventions in economic life. This came at a time when a *dirigiste* philosophy still held sway. Acclaimed writers like Gunnar Myrdal, Raul Prebisch and Hans Singer called for import protection and state intervention.

In the older generation, Gottfried Haberler alone espoused a liberal economic philosophy in the development field. In 1966, when I wrote my first paper on development, I was practically alone with such a philosophy among economists of my generation. At the World Bank protection and state intervention were also the order of the day.

Things changed slowly in subsequent years as more and more economists recognized the need for import liberalization and for reducing the extent of state intervention. Changes occurred also at the World Bank, which has come to be regarded as one of the mainstays of a liberal economic philosophy in development.

In 1969 I was first asked to head a Bank economic mission. This led to the preparation of a report under the title *Policies for Economic Growth in*

Portugal (1970). There followed a hiatus of nearly a decade but afterwards I led a Bank mission every two years. The reports of three of my missions, *Industrial Development Strategy in Thailand* (1980), *Turkey: Industrialization and Trade Strategy* (1982) and (originally written in French) *Morocco: Industrial Incentives and Export Promotion* (1984), were published by the Bank; two – *Tunisia: Industrial Sector Report* (1986) and *Development Strategy in Venezuela* (1988) – remained confidential.

At the World Bank, I also directed several research projects. The findings of the first of these projects appeared under the title *The Structure of Protection in Developing Countries* (1971), also published in Spanish; those of the second were published under the title *Development Strategies in Semi-Industrial Economies* (1982). Other research projects on Western Africa and on export incentives resulted in articles and short monographs.

My work at the World Bank on development strategies led to the publication of several journal articles (Chapters 13 and 16)[6] and I also examined the relationship between exports and economic growth (Chapters 17 and 18).[7] Furthermore, I analyzed issues of developed country protection (Chapters 11 and 12)[8] and employed again the concept of 'revealed' comparative advantage (Chapters 5 and 6).[9]

'The Process of Industrial Development and Alternative Development Strategies' was the subject of my Frank D. Graham Memorial Lecture at Princeton, while the topic of my V. K. Ramaswami Memorial Lecture in New Delhi was 'Policy Making for Economic Development'. International trade and economic development were combined in my work on the 'stages approach' to comparative advantage that represented the application of the Heckscher-Ohlin theory in a dynamic context (Chapters 2 and 3)[10] and again on policy responses to external shocks (Chapters 14 and 15).[11]

My teaching also increasingly moved in the direction of development economics. On the graduate level, I continued with my international economics course but added a new course on development policies and programming. Subsequently, I also taught a graduate course on the theory of development.

My interests in development again came to the fore when I joined the Institute for International Economics as a visiting fellow while on sabbatical from Johns Hopkins. My first project there, carried out with three outstanding Latin American economists, was to write a book entitled *Toward Renewed Economic Growth in Latin America* (1986), simultaneously published in English, Spanish and Portuguese, in which the adoption of an outward-oriented development strategy with less government intervention was recommended. I stayed on at the Institute on a part-time basis afterwards, which lead to the publication of *Adjusting to Success: Balance of Payments Policy in the East Asian NICs* with John Williamson (1987), translated into Chinese.

THE FRENCH CONNECTION

For centuries Hungarians looked to Paris as the center of the universe. Apart from French culture, they were attracted to French political philosophy, and they regarded France as a counterweight to Germany. (After the Second World War it was reported in the newspapers that Hungarians looked to Moscow but this was not taken seriously.)

My own interest in France goes back to reading French literature while in high school. I prepared an anthology of French poetry – in the original and in a Hungarian translation – during my first year at the University. From François Villon onwards all major French poets were represented in the anthology.

Not surprisingly, soon after arriving in the United States, I explored the possibility of visiting France. The opportunity presented itself in 1959 when I obtained travel documents to go to France in the summer. While I did some travelling, I spent most of my time in Paris which has become my favorite city. I had an office at the Institut d'Economie Appliquée that published one of my first papers in its journal.

In 1960 I spent my honeymoon in France, with a sidetrip to Italy. We visited friends of my wife whom she met under the Experiment in International Living Program a few years earlier. At 18 years of age she wrote on the application form that she liked to play tennis and was chosen by a family that had a tennis court – a rare thing in France. They became her French family and subsequently also acquired a swimming pool.

I was well received by Carol's French family and we went back there every year; first by ourselves and later with our children, Mara born in 1970 and Gabor born in 1972. We stayed with the family who originally welcomed Carol; Aymé Bernard, now 94 and an amazingly intelligent and knowledgeable man, and his charming wife. We also developed lifelong friendships with people of our own age who had summer homes on the same property. We bought a house there ourselves in 1985, helped by a dollar worth 9.50 French francs at the time.

But France was not all vacation for me. In 1963 I spent a sabbatical semester in Paris at CEPREL, a research institute, where I studied French planning. This led to the publication of a paper entitled 'Whither French Planning?' where I correctly predicted its demise following entry into the Common Market. In another paper, 'Planning in an Open Economy,' I emphasized the incompatibility of planning and full participation in international trade.

Paris was not only a place of intellectual pursuits for me. It was also a culinary delight. After exploring many bistros with my wife and discussing their merits with my friends, it was suggested that I write a culinary guide. This I did under the title 'A Primer in Culinary Economics or How to

Maximize the Culinary Utility of the Dollar in Paris.' The first edition, prepared in 1969, covered 20 restaurants with one page each; in the subsequent seven editions 25 restaurants were covered with two pages each. An eighth edition of the guide also appeared in print.

In 1970 I returned to Paris on sabbatical to teach at the Université de Paris IX (Dauphine). I also started writing on the French economy and in 1979 the French translation of my paper 'The French Economy under the Fifth Republic, 1958–1978' received the Prix Rossi of the Académie des Sciences Morales et Politiques, which gave me the title Lauréat de l'Institut. In subsequent years I wrote annually a paper for the French review *Commentaire*, the English versions of which were published in *The Tocqueville Review*.

In my papers, I emphasized the need to liberalize the French economy which has been the direction taken in subsequent years. I also called for improved competitiveness, using the exchange rate and incentives to investment activity, as well as research and development, as instruments.

At the same time, I started teaching mini courses in France. I began at the Institut d'Etudes Politiques (customarily called Sciences-Po) and continued at the Université de Paris I (Sorbonne-Panthéon) and at the Université de Clérmont-Ferrand. My subjects were international trade and development economics.

In 1984 I travelled to Kiel in Germany to receive the Bernhard Harms Prize in International Economics at the Institute for World Economics of the University of Kiel. My prize lecture was entitled 'The Economic Consequences of Social Policies in the Industrial Countries', a subject that is of particular importance for France. In fact, my paper was translated into French.

MY HUNGARIAN RELATIONS

I did not return to Hungary between 1956 and 1968. During this period my mother died in an automobile accident but my father was still alive during subsequent visits there. He died in 1988.

In 1968 I was invited officially to Budapest. I gave a public lecture at the Karl Marx University of Economics that was chaired by two former ministers. The lecture was announced in the Communist Party newspaper and was well attended.

In subsequent years I returned to Hungary at least once a year to lecture and to participate in conferences. On these occasions I usually met with the Ministers of Planning and of Finance and had discussions with leading academic and governmental economists. I published several papers in Hungarian economic journals, which also appeared in English.

In my discussions and papers I emphasized the need for continuing with the reform effort and for carrying out adjustment measures to reduce Hungary's large external debt. The taking of such measures was unfortunately postponed so that a much larger adjustment effort has become necessary.

My trips to Hungary provided opportunities to meet relatives and friends. Apart from seeing my father, I particularly cherished the meetings with my economist friends and with my former co-workers in Dunaujváros for whom my visit provided an occasion to get together.

Every two years I took my children to Hungary to visit Budapest and to spend a few days at Lake Balaton with my father. My wife also came with us when her work permitted.

My children very much enjoyed these trips. While they had no common language with my father (the children speak English and French and my father Hungarian, German and Italian), they were linked by strong feelings that obviate the need for verbal communication. In fact, just like the yearly stays in France, the trips to Hungary became part of my children's life.

EPILOGUE AND PROLOGUE

This is an epilogue as my 30-year career in economics came to an end with my cancer operation on 5 August 1987. It is also a prologue because it describes my activities as they have developed after the operation.

On 30 July 1987 I was diagnosed as having neck and head cancer. This came as a complete surprise. Not only did I not have any warning signs but I had a complete physical check-up in June 1987. Also, I gave up the sporadical smoking of my youth a long time ago and was a moderate consumer of alcohol.

The cancer was very far advanced. I overheard an intern saying that I was on the very limit where an operation was still possible. In fact, because of the advanced stage of the cancer, I was admitted to the Johns Hopkins University Hospital on an emergency basis and was operated on two days later. It involved removing part of my jaw, my palate and part of my tongue. It necessitated putting a piece of steel in my jaw and transplanting a flap from my left breast. My neck was also operated on and I often have the feeling of having a collar inside it.

The operation, which took 13 hours, was performed by Dr John Price, an outstanding surgeon at the Johns Hopkins Hospital, who considers it his masterwork. I spent five weeks at the hospital, partly because I contracted pneumonia. During my stay I had the daily visits of my wife and children whose support has been of immense benefit since the operation.

My wife and daughter also often accompanied me on my daily visits for radiotherapy to the Johns Hopkins Hospital over a seven-week period. On

other visits friends and students drove me there. The radiotherapy necessi-
ated removing one-third of my teeth, fortunately from the back of my
mouth. It also left me with a dryness of the mouth that requires using
artificial saliva on a regular basis.

I cannot swallow and have to take nourishment through a gastro-ostomy
tube. I was also given a tracheostomy tube that was removed in December
1987 but reinstated a few days afterwards as I developed a life-threatening
breathing problem. It was removed on the first anniversary of my operation.

My inability to swallow brings to an end my writing of the culinary guide
and removes one of the pleasures of life. Because of the danger of infection
around the tube I cannot swim either, thus ending another of my pleasures –
the daily kilometer-swim which I rarely ever missed. Also, movement in my
left arm is impaired so that I have some difficulty in putting on a coat.

More important for my professional career, my speech is impaired. This
brings to an end leading Bank missions to developing countries, creates
difficulties in day-to-day contacts and does not permit me to lecture. I have,
however, continued directing a dissertation seminar at Johns Hopkins and
next year I am to give a graduate seminar on development policies, relying on
notes distributed to the students and having students make presentations.

Despite my disabilities following the operation, I started my professional
life again. At the World Bank I completed the report on Venezuela referred
to above. I also finished a book, written with Luc Bauwens, on *Changing
Patterns of Trade in Manufactured Goods: An Econometric Investigation*
(1988) which incorporated papers on comparative advantage and on intra-
industry trade (Chapter 9).[12] I also collected my comparative papers and
country advisory reports written between 1985 and 1987 in a volume entitled
New Directions in the World Economy (1989). Furthermore I wrote several
papers on varied subjects in development.

My work at the World Bank involves writing papers and commenting on
papers written by others as well as reports by the economics staff. I was also
given responsibility for reviewing submissions to the new Working Paper
series at the Bank.

I continue part time at the Institute for International Economics. Following my operation I completed, with Marcus Noland, a book on *Japan in the
World Economy* (1988). I also started work on a Pacific project that deals
with the developing countries of the area. I am organizing a conference on
Europe 1992 to examine the measures to be taken to complete the internal
market of the European Community.

I am also resuming travel, although this is made difficult by having to carry
cans of liquid food and a variety of paraphernalia necessary for mouth care.
Consultations at the OECD and OECD Development Centre in June will be
followed by trips to Middlebery, Geneva and New York to deliver papers. In
fact, the papers will be read by my wife while I will intervene in the discussion
stage.

The continuation of these activities will depend on future developments regarding my health. At the time of the operation, I was told that the probability of recurrence of the cancer was 80 percent. This probability, however, declines rapidly as time progresses. It is 50 percent one year after the operation and 35 percent two years later. I sometimes feel as if I am living on borrowed time.

Bela Balassa

REFERENCES

1. 'An Empirical Demonstration of Classical Comparative Cost Theory', *Review of Economics and Statistics*, August 1963, pp. 231–8.
2. 'Trade Liberalization and "Revealed" Comparative Advantage', *Manchester School*, May 1965, pp. 99–123.
3. 'Tariff Protection in Industrial Countries: An Evaluation', *Journal of Political Economy*, December 1965, pp. 573–94.
4. 'Tariff Reductions and Trade in Manufactures among the Industrial Countries', *American Economic Review*, June 1966, pp. 466–73.
5. 'Trade Creation and Trade Diversion in the European Common Market', *Economic Journal*, March 1967, pp. 1–21.
6. 'Growth Strategies in Semi-Industrial Countries', *Quarterly Journal of Economics*, February 1970, pp. 24–47 and 'Export Incentives and Export Performance in Developing Countries: A Comparative Analysis', *Weltwirtschaftliches Archiv*, Band 114, Heft 1, 1978, pp. 24–60.
7. 'Exports and Economic Growth: Further Evidence', *Journal of Development Economics*, June 1978, pp. 181–9 and 'Exports, Policy Choices, and Economic Growth in Developing Countries After the 1973 Oil Shock', *Journal of Development Economics*, May–June 1985, pp. 23–35.
8. 'Industrial Protection in the Developed Countries' (jointly with Carol Balassa), *The World Economy*, June 1984, pp. 179–96 and the 'The Extent and the Cost of Protection in Developed-Developing Country Trade' (jointly with Constantine Michalopoulos) in *New Protectionist Threat to World Welfare* (Dominick Salvatore, ed.). Amsterdam, North Holland, 1987, pp. 482–504.
9. '"Revealed" Comparative Advantage Revisited: An Analysis of Relative Export Shares of the Industrial Countries, 1953–1971', *Manchester School*, December 1977, pp. 327–44 and 'The Changing comparative Advantage of Japan and the United States' (jointly with Marcus Noland), *Journal of the Japanese and International Economies* (forthcoming).
10. 'The Changing Pattern of Comparative Advantage in Manufactured Goods', *Review of Economics and Statistics*, May 1979, pp. 259–66 and 'Comparative Advantage in Manufactured Goods: A Reappraisal', *Ibid*, May 1986, 315–19.
11. 'The Adjustment Experience of Developing Economies After 1973', in *IMF Conditionality* (John Williamson, ed.) Washington, DC, Institute for International Economics, 1983, pp. 145–74 and 'Policy Responses to Exogenous Shocks in Developing Countries', *American Economic Review, Papers and Proceedings*, May 1986, pp. 75–8.
12. 'Intra-industry Specialization in a Multi-country and Multi-industry Framework' (with Luc Bauwens), *Economic Journal*, December 1987, pp. 923–39.

PART I

COMPARATIVE ADVANTAGE

1 · AN EMPIRICAL DEMONSTRATION OF CLASSICAL COMPARATIVE COST THEORY

Economic theory can be regarded as consisting of a number of models designed to explain economic phenomena and to yield predictions for the future. Any choice among alternative models should be based on their explanatory value – a model (or hypothesis) can be regarded as superior to another if it explains actual phenomena better and it is more helpful in predicting future events.

The theory of international trade abounds in theoretical models, some of them complementary, others conflicting. Alternative approaches towards explaining the causes of international specialization are followed, for example, by classical economists on the one hand, and by Heckscher and Ohlin on the other. While the hypothesis advanced by the former presupposes the existence of inter-country differences in production functions, the latter assume identical production functions and qualitatively identical factors of production in the trading countries and attribute international specialization to differences in factor endowments. The empirical testing of the Heckscher-Ohlin hypothesis by Leontief led to inconclusive results, and the interpretations and explanations given to the Leontief paradox have demonstrated that the assumptions of this model require modification.[1] In this chapter, we will not attempt to test the Heckscher-Ohlin hypothesis, but will rather inquire into the validity of the classical model.

According to the original formulation of the classical theory, comparative advantage based on relative productivity differentials determines international specialization. It has subsequently been realized that inter-country differences in the wage structure and in the capital–labor ratios of various industries may compensate for productivity differentials; a country

This chapter was prepared during the tenure of a research grant from the Economic Growth Center at Yale University in the summer of 1961. The author wishes to express his appreciation to Marnie Mueller who has cheerfully borne the burden of data collecting and computations and also made helpful comments on an earlier version of the chapter. Further thanks are due to Michael Lovell for valuable suggestions and criticism. First published in *Review of Economics and Statistics*, August 1963.

possessing a relative productivity advantage in a particular industry may still import the commodity in question if it paid relatively higher wages and/or had higher capital costs per unit of output in that industry.[2] Still, the defenders of classical theory – among others, Taussig – expressed the opinion that the latter factors are not sufficiently important to warrant significant changes in the trade pattern as determined by relative differences in productivity.[3]

Let us adopt the following notation:

C = unit cost
A = labor input per unit of output
W = wage rate
T = ratio of capital plus labor costs to labor costs

Subscripts I and II refer to country I and country II, respectively.
Capital letters refer to commodity X, small letters to commodity Y.
The modified classical hypothesis can now be written:
If

$$\frac{A_I}{A_{II}} < \frac{a_I}{a_{II}} \tag{1}$$

it is likely also that

$$\frac{C_I}{C_{II}} < \frac{c_I}{c_{II}} \tag{2}$$

when the latter expression is equivalent to

$$\frac{A_I W_I T_I}{A_{II} W_{II} T_{II}} < \frac{a_I w_I t_I}{a_{II} w_{II} t_{II}}. \tag{3}$$

Consequently, country I will export commodity X, and country II will export commodity Y.

In order to test the classical hypothesis, MacDougall compared relative export volumes and relative productivity differences for American and British manufacturing industries, and found that in 20 out of the 25 industries examined, 'where American output per worker was more than twice the British, the United States had, in general, the bulk of the export market, while for products where it was less than twice as high the bulk of the market was held by Britain.'[4] At the same time, relying on data of 13 industries MacDougall concluded that although we can, to some extent, better explain differences in export shares if considering unit labor costs instead of productivity, productivity differentials are but scarcely modified by wage disparities.[5]

This chapter can be regarded as a continuation of MacDougall's work, with differences in the choice of data and in methodology. Whereas MacDougall relied on Rostas' productivity estimates for the 1930s,[6] we will make use of Paige and Bombach's more inclusive observations that refer to 1950.[7] At the same time, we will attempt to reach some conclusions as to the relative importance of productivity, wages and capital costs in determining the pattern of exports.

PRODUCTIVITY AND EXPORTS

American and British productivity comparisons have been made by Paige and Bombach for 44 selected industries that include about one-half of manufacturing production in the two countries.[8] Productivity is measured as net output (gross output minus purchased inputs other than labor) per worker.[9] The index numbers for productivity (UK = 100) are calculated separately at US and UK prices and a geometric average of these figures is taken.

For the purposes of the present investigation, it was necessary to exclude several industries from the sample. First, industries whose output did not exceed one-third of 1 percent of the value of manufacturing production in the two countries have not been included since these industries are not representative of manufacturing as a whole. In the absence of the necessary information, the same procedure was followed with regard to industries processing agricultural raw materials, such as grain milling, canning and breweries, because easy access to such materials affects export possibilities but not the net output per worker. Finally, we had to disregard electrical household equipment and passenger automobiles since in the period under investigation third countries discriminated against American consumer durables as compared with British. Our sample thus covers 28 industries which produced 43.1 percent of manufacturing output in Britain and 41.4 percent in the United States.

Relative productivity differences in these industries are compared with their export performance in the two countries.[10] In comparing American and British exports we exclude trade between the two countries themselves since this is obviously greatly influenced by the relative height of American and British tariffs. In other words, we ask the question, to what extent do productivity differences determine the success of US and UK industries in exporting to third countries. No attempt will be made, however, to correct for the differential effects of Commonwealth preference, discrimination against American goods other than consumer durables and locational factors. It would be difficult to give numerical expression to these influences in the present context; they should therefore be used as qualifications to the results derived from the model.

Further problems arise in determining the ratio of American to British exports. Theoretically, one should deal with export quantities rather than export values. This is what MacDougall attempted to do. However, he ran into difficulties in regard to heterogeneous commodity groups that comprise by far the larger part of his sample in terms of production value. In some cases, he used value data (machinery, outer clothing), in others, a system of weighting (motor cars, leather footwear, hosiery). Both of these solutions entail errors, and one could also question the advisability of mixing quantity and value data in the same sample.

Because of the unreliability of quantity comparisons in most of the industries included in our sample, we have chosen to work with export values. In other words, we propose to investigate the impact of productivity differences on export shares in third markets. By doing this we implicitly assume that the elasticity of substitution between American and British exports of the same commodity (or commodity group)[11] exceeds unity, since substitution elasticities equal to or less than unity would lead to inconclusive results. To give an example, if productivity ratios were equal to price ratios, and the elasticity of substitution between the two countries' exports were unity, *export values* would be identical. The findings of Kubinski, MacDougall, and Zelder indicate, however, that elasticities of substitution significantly exceed unity.[12] Therefore, it can be expected that, if a positive correlation between productivity and export quantities exists, relative productivity advantages will lead to larger export shares.[13]

The export data used in the calculations refer to 1951. This year has been chosen partly because we can expect a lag between changes in productivity and changes in export shares, partly because export values in 1950 do not yet reflect the full effect of the 1949 devaluation. Separate calculations were made for the years 1954–6.

The relevant data are found in columns (1) and (2) of Table 1.1. The scatter diagram, plotted on a natural scale (Fig. 1.1) gives indication of a definite relationship between the two variables. As a first approximation, a straight line regression was fitted to the data, reflecting the hypothesis that there is a linear relationship between productivity ratios and export ratios. Introducing the symbols, E for export value and $P = 1/A$, the regression equation will assume the following form:

$$\frac{E_I}{E_{II}} = -53.32 + 0.721 \frac{P_I}{P_{II}} \qquad (4)$$
$$(0.103)$$

Thus, on the average, an increase in the US/UK productivity ratio from 200 to 220 would lead to an increase of the ratio of export values to third countries from 91 to 105, and the value of American and British exports would become equal in an industry where American productivity exceeded British productivity by 113 percent.

The correlation coefficient between productivity ratios and export ratios is 0.80; in other words, 64 percent of the variance in export shares can be

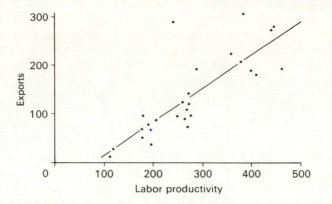

Figure 1.1 US/UK export and productivity ratios 1950 and 1951 (normal scale).

explained by differences in productivity. Since the coefficient of linear correlation might be influenced by extreme values, we also calculated the Spearman rank correlation coefficient. This gives the value of 0.81, indicating that extreme values did not have an appreciable influence on r.

The next question concerns the reliability of the results. We have calculated the confidence interval for the linear correlation coefficient with the use of Fisher's z-transformation. This gives the limits of 0.60–0.90 for r, at the 5 percent confidence level. However, we should note that, for the purposes of the present investigation, statistical methods are of limited usefulness in determining what significance can be attached to the estimates, since these presuppose random sampling from a bivariate normal distribution of the variables in question. Although we can assume that the underlying distributions approach a normal curve, the group of industries investigated cannot be regarded as a random sample.

Approaching the problem of reliability in a different way, we note that our sample includes 40–45 percent of manufacturing production and exports in the two countries; hence it may give a reasonably good approximation for manufacturing as a whole for the period under consideration. It is a different problem whether the same relationship would apply to years other than the ones chosen since the results are affected by errors due to variables not included in the analysis and by observational errors in the independent variable. Productivity data are available only for 1950, but these can be compared with trade figures for later periods. Surely, the comparison has only limited validity since we disregard possible changes in productivity, but it will still be of some interest if we can assume that year-to-year changes in productivity are small or that export trade follows variations in productivity with a comparatively long time lag. We have proceeded to calculate the correlation between the variables in question using export data for 1954–6,[14] and arrived at $r = 0.73$. Considering the differences in the two time periods, the

Table 1.1 American and British productivity, wages, unit costs and exports

Industries	Export value UK = 100 (1)	Output per worker UK = 100 (2)	Wage ratio $ per £ UK = 100 (3)	Unit labor cost $ per £ UK = 100 (4)	Net unit cost ratio $ per £ UK = 100 (5)
1. Woolen and worsted	2.7	185	1017	550	335
2. Shipbuilding and repairing	20.9	111	899	810	802
3. Cement	31.4	116	756	652	572
4. Structural clay products	40.9	197	804	408	498
5. Tanneries	48.9	168	904	538	370
6. Footwear, except rubber	66.5	171	805	471	440
7. Cotton spinning and weaving	68.4	249	928	373	280
8. Tools and implements	77.3	190	1041	548	570
9. Tires and tubes	84.9	241	1014	421	438
10. Knitting mills	86.3	187	914	489	359
11. Rayon, nylon and silk	87.8	226	958	424	354
12. Iron and steel foundries	92.6	202	928	459	398
13. Bolts, nuts, rivets, screws	94.7	256	1223	478	523
14. Wirework	103.4	244	1042	427	409
15. Outerwear and underwear	110.9	170	1016	598	535
16. Soap, candles and glycerine	114.8	249	1101	442	581
17. Generators, motors, transformers	117.6	239	998	418	466
18. Rubber products, except tires and footwear	136.3	250	1013	405	393

19. Blast furnaces	186.9	408	828	203	370
20. Radio	191.4	400	948	237	291
21. Steel works and rolling mills	196.6	269	879	327	338
22. Automobiles, trucks and tractors	205.7	466	942	202	247
23. Basic industrial chemicals	213.2	372	947	255	322
24. Pulp, paper and board	233.9	338	1021	302	297
25. Metal-working machinery	277.5	221	1108	501	459
26. Containers, paper and card	290.4	428	1146	268	229
27. Agricultural machinery, except tractors	291.8	429	958	223	224
28. Paint and varnish	320.1	363	980	270	255

Sources:
Column 1:
Great Britain, Customs and Excise Department (1956) *Annual Statement of the Trade of the United Kingdom, 1954. Compared with the years 1951–1953* III. (London: Her Majesty's Stationery Office).
United Nations, Statistical Office (1952) *Commodity Trade Statistics, January–December 1951* (New York).
United Nations, Statistical Office (1953) *Yearbook of International Trade Statistics, 1952* (New York)
United States, Bureau of the Census, Report No. FT 410 (1952) *United States Exports of Domestic and Foreign Merchandise, Calendar Year 1951.* Parts I and II (Washington).

Columns 2, 3, 4 and 5:
Paige, Deborah, and Gottfried Bombach (1959) *A Comparison of National Output and Productivity of the United Kingdom and the United States* (Paris, OEEC).

results are remarkably close and suggest the relative constancy of the observed relationship.

In the above discussion we have assumed the existence of a linear relationship between the variables considered. However, the scatter diagram of Fig. 1.1 indicates increasing deviations from the regression line as the values of observations increase, suggesting that a logarithmic relationship may provide a better fit. If this were so, a 1 percent increase in productivity ratios would be associated with a given percentage change in export ratios.

The observations – with one exception – are plotted on a logarithmic scale in Fig. 1.2 and show a close relationship. The exception is the wool industry in which American exports amount to only a small fraction of British exports. The deviation of the data of this industry from the observed pattern is explained by the fact that Britain has differential advantages over the United States in manufacturing woolens inasmuch as she can procure wool at a lower price from Commonwealth countries (Australia and New Zealand) and also the quality of British wool products is greatly superior to the American. The difference in quality suggests that the reliability of the comparison is greatly reduced by the differentiation of the product.

If we exclude the wool industry from the investigation, the regression equation takes the form,

$$\log \frac{E_I}{E_{II}} = -1.761 + 1.594 \log \frac{P_I}{P_{II}} \tag{5}$$
$$(0.181)$$

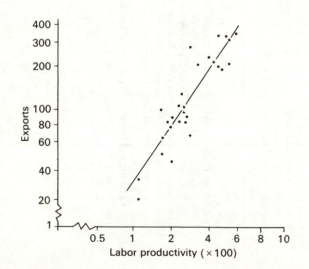

Figure 1.2 US/UK export and productivity ratios 1950 and 1951 (logarithmic scale).

Thus, a 1 percent change in productivity ratios leads to an approximately 1.6 percent change in the ratio of export values between the two countries. The coefficient of correlation is 0.86, with confidence limits of 0.73–0.94 at the 5 percent level of significance. The coefficient of determination is 0.74; that is, 74 percent of the variance in export ratios can be explained by relative productivity differences.[15]

PRODUCTIVITY, WAGES AND EXPORTS

The next question to be answered is whether the explanation of export ratios given here can be improved upon if we consider not only productivity differences but also wage ratios as the determinants of export shares. Wage ratios (US/UK) are found in column (3) of Table 1.1. A multiple regression equation can be fitted using productivity ratios and wage ratios as independent, and the ratio of export values as dependent, variables, since no multicollinearity is present. (The coefficient of linear correlation between productivity ratios and wage ratios is 0.20.)

Assuming additivity in the effect of the independent variables on export shares, the regression equation will take the form,

$$\frac{E_\mathrm{I}}{E_\mathrm{II}} = -181.2 + 0.691\frac{P_\mathrm{I}}{P_\mathrm{II}} + 0.140\frac{W_\mathrm{I}}{W_\mathrm{II}} \qquad (6)$$
$$\quad\quad\quad\quad\quad (0.167)\quad\quad (0.102)$$

The multiple correlation coefficient is 0.81, compared with 0.80 for the simple correlation coefficient. The two values become equal if the adjustment suggested by H. Theil for specification analysis is made.[16] The partial coefficient of correlation between productivity and exports is 0.77, between wages and exports 0.24. The latter coefficient is not significant at the 5 percent confidence level.

The explanatory value of wage differentials with regard to differences in export values changes but little if we fit a logarithmic equation to the data.

$$\log\frac{E_\mathrm{I}}{E_\mathrm{I}} = -5.164 + 1.457\log\frac{P_\mathrm{I}}{P_\mathrm{II}} + 1.250\log\frac{W_\mathrm{I}}{W_\mathrm{II}} \qquad (7)$$
$$\quad\quad\quad\quad\quad (0.328)\quad\quad (0.566)$$

Again, there is no significant difference between the multiple correlation coefficient ($R = 0.88$) and the simple correlation coefficient ($r = 0.86$). The partial coefficients of correlation are: between productivity and exports, 0.84; between wages and exports, 0.11 – the latter is not significant at the 5 percent level.[17]

These results indicate that a definite relationship between wage ratios and export shares cannot be established. Productivity advantages are not counterbalanced by higher wages paid in industries with higher productivity, and productivity differences continue to account, in a large measure, for differences in export shares. Actually, there is some – although largely inconclusive – evidence that higher relative wages might be associated with higher export shares.[18] If this were so, a possible explanation would be that greater success in exportation may lead to higher wages. This implies that the relationship between wages and export shares is by no means uni-directional; while lower wages could conceivably lead to higher export shares, higher export shares may also make possible paying higher wages.

UNIT COSTS AND EXPORTS

We come now to the question of whether our results could be improved upon by including capital costs in the estimates. At this point we encounter statistical difficulties, however. The available data do not provide information on capital cost per unit of output but only on 'net costs,' inclusive of profits. Net costs as defined by Paige and Bombach are equivalent to net output so that net costs per unit of output refer to value added plus depreciation per quantity of output. We will make use of these figures in the following (see Table 1.1, col. (5)), while the implications of this procedure will be noted at a later point.

Fig. 1.3 shows the tendency of export shares to favor the country with the lower relative net unit costs. As a first approximation, we have again fitted a straight line regression of the form

$$\frac{E_I}{E_{II}} = 299.8 - 0.410\,\frac{N_I}{N_{II}} \tag{8}$$
$$(0.103)$$

when N refers to net unit costs as defined above. The correlation coefficient between the two variables is -0.60, with confidence limits of -0.28 to -0.80 at the 5 percent level of significance.

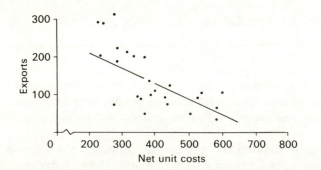

Figure 1.3 US/UK export and net unit costs ratios 1950 and 1951 (normal scale).

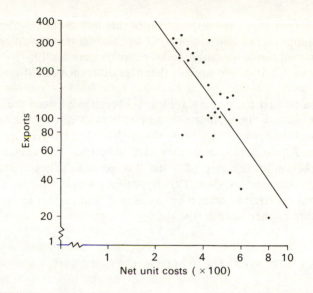

Figure 1.4 US/UK export and net unit costs ratios 1950 and 1951 (logarithmic scale).

We find a closer relationship between net unit costs and export values if the relevant data are plotted on a logarithmic scale (Fig. 1.4).[19] Fitting a logarithmic regression to the observations, this will assume the form

$$\log \frac{E_I}{E_{II}} = 6.162 - 1.590 \log \frac{N_I}{N_{II}} \tag{9}$$
$$(0.301)$$

Thus, a 1 percent increase in the ratio of net unit costs would lead to an approximately 1.6 percent reduction in the ratio of export values. The coefficient of correlation is -0.71, with confidence limits -0.44 to -0.86 at the 5 percent level of significance. Thus, a little over 50 percent of the variance in export values can be explained by differences in net unit costs.

The results show that a 1 percent increase in productivity ratios *or* in net unit cost ratios leads to a 1.6 percent change in the ratio of export values. At the same time, the correlation coefficient between productivity ratios and export shares appears to be higher than between net unit cost ratios and export shares.

The first question to be answered is whether the difference between the two coefficients (taken without sign) is significant. For the normal regression, the correlation coefficients are 0.80 and -0.60, respectively; for the logarithmic regression, 0.86 and -0.71. The value of T is 1.44 in the first case and 1.51 in the second.[20] Deviations of such magnitude could occur in a normal distribution 13–15 times in 100 cases. Hence, the differences between the observed values of the coefficients do not appear to be significant. However, doubts may arise about the application of this test to the problem at hand, since it presupposes random sampling. If we consider that the difference in the correlation coefficients is maintained if export values for 1954–6 are used in the calculations,[21] it would appear that this difference might not be due to random factors.

If we assume that there is a significant difference between the correlation coefficients, we face the further problem of indicating why the relationship between productivity and exports is closer than that between net unit costs and exports. A possible explanation is that industries with greater success in export markets enjoy higher profits and this reduces the negative correlation between net costs and exports. This hypothesis would take care of market imperfections that lead to different rates of profits in various industries, but it would require further justification.

EVALUATION OF THE EMPIRICAL RESULTS

The evidence presented indicates that there is a high correlation between productivity ratios and export shares, and the introduction of further explanatory variables only slightly modifies the results. On the one hand, there is inconclusive evidence that inter-industry wage differences would appreciably affect export shares; on the other, differences in capital cost per unit of output do not seem to have a significant influence on export performance. These results may be surprising to many, although they appear by no means implausible.

Two possible explanations can be given for the absence of a correlation between wage ratios and export shares. Taussig advanced the proposition that the hierarchy of wages in different countries is largely similar because there is little competition between the labor force of various industries (non-competing groups) *and* inter-industry wage differences are determined by the disutility and regularity of work, the required strength and skill and other factors, all of which act in basically the same way in all countries.[22] On the other hand, I. B. Kravis argued that the labor groups in various occupations do compete with each other and, consequently, in any one country, wage differences are considerably smaller than productivity differences.[23]

As to the first explanation, Stanley Lebergott has shown that, in the years immediately following the Second World War, inter-industry wage patterns were almost identical between the United States, the United Kingdom, and Canada, and differed only slightly for Sweden.[24] Similar results have been reached for the United States and Japan by I. B. Kravis.[25] At the same time, it has been shown that, compared with productivity differences, wages paid in different industries tend to cluster around the national average.[26]

In our sample, the coefficient of variation is 37.1 for productivity ratios and 10.7 for wage ratios. This result is in conformity with the arguments of both

Taussig and Kravis, since the low degree of dispersion in wage ratios may be due to similarities in the wage patterns of the two countries, to small inter-industry wage differences in the individual countries, or to a combination of both. Under the latter alternative, one would argue that although different occupational groups are to some extent in competition with one another, the inter-industry wage pattern is still determined by factors, such as the skills required in particular industries, that act in a similar fashion in every country. In other words, there is no need for assuming the existence of non-competing groups in order to explain the similarity of the inter-industry wage pattern in various countries.

The absence of correlation between wage ratios and export shares appears to refute the arguments of those who believe that cheap wages have played an important part in determining export patterns in manufacturing industries.[27] At the same time, our results do not establish the frequently argued correlation between productivity and wages either, considering that the correlation coefficient between productivity ratios and wage ratios is 0.20.

With respect to the relationship between capital costs and export performance, a frequent misunderstanding should be noted. Bertil Ohlin asserted that the classical economists were guilty of neglecting the capital factor, and in his criticism Ohlin referred to the existing large inter-industry differences of capital–labor ratios. In the United States, for example, the amount of capital per worker was said to vary between $10,000 in the chemical industry and $1,700 in tobacco manufacturing.[28] However, in determining the competitive position of any industry, capital costs per unit of output rather than capital–labor ratios are relevant. And it is by no means necessary that high capital costs per unit of output would be accompanied by high productivity, considering that the application of more advanced technological methods associated with higher capital intensity may reduce rather than increase the cost of capital per unit of output in modern plants. In other words, a high capital – labor ratio may correspond to high productivity of labor *and* capital as well. In fact, this result has been reached by Marvin Frankel, who found a slight association between low unit labor costs and low unit capital costs in a cross-section study of American and British industries.[29] Finally, even if we assumed a negative correlation between labor productivity and capital costs, the importance of the capital factor in determining trade patterns would be reduced if the hierarchy of industries with regard to capital intensity were similar in individual countries.

In conclusion, we can state that our results are in conformity with the classical hypothesis: the evidence presented indicates that the consideration of differences in wage patterns and capital costs offers little improvement over the results reached by relating export shares to productivity differences. On the other hand, productivity differentials cannot give a full explanation of export shares, so that we also have to take account of transportation costs as well as non-economic factors (Commonwealth preference, trade and exchange restrictions, good will, etc.) in order to provide a more comprehensive explanation of international specialization. The latter considerations fall outside the confines of this chapter, however.

NOTES

1. W. W. Leontief (1954) 'Domestic Production and Foreign Trade: The American Capital Position Re-examined', *Economia Internazionale*, (February), pp. 9–38; (1956) 'Factor Proportions and the Structure of American Trade: Further Theoretical and Empirical Analysis', *Review of Economics and Statistics*, XXXVIII (November), pp. 386–407. Also, P. T. Ellsworth (1954) 'The Structure of American Foreign Trade: A New View Examined', *Review of Economics and Statistics*, XXXVI (August), pp. 279–85; Stefan Valavanis-Vail (1954) 'Leontief's Scarce Factor Paradox', *Journal of Political Economy*, LXII (December), pp. 523–8; N. S. Buchanan (1955) 'Lines on the Leontief Paradox', *Economia Internazionale* (November), pp. 791–4; and the discussion in the supplement to the February 1958 issue of *Review of Economics and Statistics* by Stefan Valavanis-Vail, Romney Robinson, G. A. Elliott, Beatrice Vaccara, and W. W. Leontief, pp. 111–22.
2. For references, see Jacob Viner (1937) *Studies in the Theory of International Trade* (New York), pp. 493–512.
3. F. W. Taussig (1927) *International Trade* (New York), pp. 43–68.
4. G. D. A. MacDougall (1951) 'British and American Exports: A Study Suggested by the Theory of Comparative Costs', Part I *Economic Journal* LXI (December), pp. 697–8.
5. *Ibid.*, pp. 706–7.
6. L. Rostas (1948) *Comparative Productivity in British and American Manufacturing* (Cambridge).
7. Deborah Paige and Gottfried Bombach (1959) *A Comparison of National Output and Productivity of the United Kingdom and the United States* (Paris: Organisation for European Economic Co-operation).
8. The industries were selected on the basis that productivity comparisons for these are considered reliable inasmuch as the inter-country output comparison is relatively good and employment data are not likely to be subject to substantial errors resulting from differences in classification.
9. Depreciation is not deducted from the net output figures, hence net output also equals value added plus depreciation.
10. The sample includes 48 percent of British and 41 percent of American manufacturing exports.
11. The elasticity of substitution between American and British exports of a given commodity is

$$\frac{d \log(q_\text{I}/q_\text{II})}{d \log(p_\text{I}/p_\text{II})}$$

when I and II refer to American and British, respectively.
12. A. Kubinski (1950) 'The Elasticity of Substitution between Sources of British Imports, 1921–38', *Yorkshire Bulletin of Economic and Social Research* (January), pp. 17–29: MacDougall, *op. cit.*; R. E. Zelder (1955) 'The Elasticity of Demand for Exports, 1921–38' (unpublished doctoral dissertation, University of Chicago), cited in A. C. Harberger, 'Some Evidence on the International Price Mechanism', *Journal of Political Economy* LXV (December 1957), pp. 506–21.

13. Still, our results will be influenced by inter-commodity differences as regards the elasticity of substitution.
14. The choice of these years was given by the availability of the data for purposes of a different investigation. Since discrimination against American consumer durables abated by 1954, electrical household equipment and automobiles were included in our sample.
15. If the wool industry were included in the calculations, the correlation coefficient would be 0.78.
16. See his *Economic Forecasts and Policy* (revised edition: Amsterdam 1961), pp. 210 ff.
17. The wool industry was excluded in estimating the regression equation.
18. See also I. B. Kravis (1956) 'Wages and Foreign Trade', *Review of Economics and Statistics*, XXXVIII (February), p. 30.
19. As in all logarithmic regressions, the wool industry is excluded from the data.
20. For a description of this test, see F. C. Mills (1955) *Statistical Methods* (New York), pp. 506–7.
21. The correlation coefficient between productivity and exports is 0.73, while between net unit costs and exports this is −0.44, if export data for 1954–6 are used and the variables are expressed on a normal scale.
22. *op. cit.*, pp. 43 ff.
23. '"Availability" and Other Influences on the Commodity Composition of Trade', *Journal of Political Economy*, LXIV (April 1956), p. 146.
24. 'Wage Structures', *Review of Economics and Statistics*, XXIX (November 1947), pp. 274–85.
25. '"Availability" and Other Influences on the Commodity Composition of Trade', *Journal of Political Economy*, LXIV (April 1956), p. 145.
26. 'Wages and Foreign Trade', *Review of Economics and Statistics*, XXXVIII (February 1956), pp. 14–30.
27. Cf., e.g., Karl Forchheimer (1947) 'The Role of Relative Wage Differences in International Trade', *Quarterly Journal of Economics*, LXII (November), pp. 1–30.
28. *Interregional and International Trade* (Cambridge, Mass., 1933), p. 572.
29. *British and American Manufacturing Productivity*, Bulletin No. 49, University of Illinois, Bureau of Economic and Business Research (Urbana, 1957), p. 45.

2 · THE CHANGING PATTERN OF COMPARATIVE ADVANTAGE IN MANUFACTURED GOODS

This chapter analyzes the changing pattern of comparative advantage in manufactured goods in the process of accumulation of physical and human capital that characterizes economic development. Section I of the chapter describes the model to be estimated while Section II defines the explanatory variables employed. The empirical results are presented in Section III, and the policy implications of the results are analyzed in Section IV.

I

In investigating the determinants of trade between developed and developing countries, Lary (1968), Kojima (1970), Fels (1972) and Mahfuzur Rahman (1973) considered developing countries as a group. In turn, Hufbauer (1970) attempted to explain differences in the average product characteristics of the exports of individual countries in an inter-country framework, but his sample of 24 countries included only 9 countries that may be considered developing and they were all at the upper end of the distribution in terms of per capita incomes.

Herman and Tinbergen (1970), and subsequently Herman (1975), suggested a scheme of 'ideal' export composition allegedly reflecting the physical and human capital endowments of countries classified into 11 groups, but did not subject their scheme to statistical testing. Finally, Hirsch (1974) correlated

This chapter was prepared while the author was at the Johns Hopkins University and the World Bank. It draws on a presentation made at the 5th World Congress of the International Economic Association held in Tokyo on 29 August–3 September 1977. It was prepared in the framework of a consultant arrangement with the World Bank but it should not be interpreted to reflect the Bank's views. The author is indebted to Dominique de Crayencour, Jonathan Levy and especially to Kishore Nadkarni for research assistance. He has benefited from comments on an earlier version of the chapter by T. N. Srinivasan and other participants of a seminar held at the World Bank. First published in *Review of Economics and Statistics*, May 1979.

export performance and value added per worker in the non-agricultural sector in an inter-country framework for each of 18 industry groups and also correlated export–output ratios with the average product characteristics of the 18 industry groups for each of 29 countries without, however, attempting to establish a statistical relationship between the two sets of estimates.

A different approach is followed in this chapter. Thirty-six countries have been chosen for the investigation, of which 18 are developed and 18 developing. For each country, regression equations have been estimated relating their 'revealed' comparative advantage in 184 manufactured product categories to the relative capital intensity (capital–labor ratio) of the individual product categories. The regression coefficients thus obtained have in turn been correlated with particular country characteristics in an inter-country framework. In this way, results obtained in 'commodity space' have been transposed into 'country space', so as to indicate the effects of country characteristics on international specialization in manufacturing goods.

Following earlier work by the author (1965, 1977), a country's relative export performance in individual product categories has been taken to reflect its 'revealed' comparative advantage within the manufacturing sector. Relative export performance has been used as an indicator of comparative advantage in preference to export–import ratios or net exports, since inter-country differences in the commodity pattern of imports are greatly influenced by the system of protection applied. This is in particular the case in developing countries, where import barriers are high and vary from commodity to commodity.

The investigation is limited to manufactured goods that play an increasingly important role in domestic production and exports as the accumulation of physical and human capital proceeds. Natural resource products have been excluded, since trade in these products largely depends on the country's resource endowment that cannot be easily quantified. The choice has entailed limiting the sample to countries that export manufactured goods in appreciable quantities.

Relative export performance in individual product categories has been expressed as the ratio of a country's share in the world exports of a particular product category to its share in the world exports of all manufactured goods. Thus, a ratio of 1.10 (0.90) means that the country's share in the particular product category is 10 percent higher (lower) than its share in all manufactured exports.[1]

For each of the 36 countries, ratios of 'revealed' comparative advantage, calculated for the individual product categories, have been regressed on variables representing relative capital intensity, defined alternatively using a stock and a flow measure. The regression equations, shown in (1), have been estimated in a double-logarithmic form, so that the value of the β coefficient for country j indicates the percentage change in the country's comparative advantage ratio (x_{ij}) associated with a 1 percent change in capital intensity

(k_i):[2]

$$\log x_{ij} = \log \alpha_j + \beta_j \log k_i, \tag{1}$$

A positive (negative) β coefficient thus shows that a country has a comparative advantage in capital (labor) intensive products while the numerical magnitude of the β coefficient indicates the extent of the country's comparative advantage in capital (labor) intensive commodities.[3]

Next, we have tested the hypothesis that inter-country differences in the β coefficients can be explained by differences in country characteristics. This test has been carried out by regressing the β coefficients estimated for the individual countries on variables representing their physical and human capital endowments in an inter-country framework. The basic estimating equation used is shown in (2),

$$\beta_j = f(GDICAP_j, HMIND_j) \tag{2}$$

where $GDICAP$ refers to per capita physical capital endowments and $HMIND$ to per capita human capital endowments. We have further experimented with explanatory variables representing the level of development.

II

Capital intensity has been defined as the sum of physical and human capital per worker.[4] Technological variables used in recent work on US comparative advantage (Baldwin, 1971; Morall, 1972; Branson and Junz, 1971; and Goodman and Ceyhun, 1976) have not been introduced in the analysis because of their limited relevance to developing countries that engage in research and development to a small extent, if at all. Rather, investment in research and development has been assumed to be part of physical capital (e.g. laboratories) or human capital (e.g. scientists and engineers engaged in R&D).

Capital intensity has been expressed in terms of stocks (the value of the capital stock plus the discounted value of the difference between the average wage and the unskilled wage, divided by the number of workers) and in terms of flows (value added per worker). The former approach has been used by Kenen (1965) and, more recently, by Fels (1972) and Branson (1973); the latter approach has been employed by Lary (1968).

The stock measure of capital intensity (k^s) is expressed in (3) for industry i:

$$k_i^s = p_i^s + h_i^s = p_i^s + \frac{\bar{w}_i - w_i^u}{r^h} \tag{3}$$

where p_i and h_i, respectively, refer to physical and human capital per worker, $\bar{w}_i$ is the average wage rate, w_i^u the wage of unskilled labor, and r^h the discount rate used in calculating the stock of human capital. In turn, the flow measure of capital intensity (k^f) is expressed in (4),

$$k_i^f = va_i = p_i^f + h_i^f = (va_i - \bar{w}_i) + \bar{w}_i \tag{4}$$

where va_i refers to value added per worker. Now, non-wage value added per worker $(va_i - \bar{w}_i)$ is taken to represent physical capital intensity and wage value added per worker $(\bar{w}_i)$ human capital intensity.

As far as physical capital intensity is concerned, the two measures would give identical rankings in risk-free equilibrium in the event that product, capital and labor markets were perfect and non-wage value added did not include any items other than capital remuneration. In turn, the stock and the flow measures of human capital would give identical rankings if unskilled wages were the same in every industry.

Both the stock and the flow measures have their advantages and disadvantages. The usefulness of the stock measure would be greatly impaired in an inflationary situation, where historical values of physical capital shown in the accounts differ from replacement values and the magnitude of these differences varies with the age of equipment. And while the benchmark years used for estimating capital intensity (1969 and 1970) are part of a long non-inflationary period, error possibilities remain due to inter-industry differences in depreciation rates. In turn, the usefulness of the flow measure is limited by reason of the fact that profit rates show considerable variation over time and inter-industry differences in profit rates cannot be fully explained by reference to risk factors.

In order to indicate the stability of the results derived under alternative assumptions, we have made estimates by the use of both measures. The necessary data on capital intensity have been obtained from US statistics as data for other countries are not available in a sufficiently detailed commodity breakdown.[5]

For purposes of the investigation, we have used the definition of the manufacturing sector (SIC 19 to 39) in the US Standard Industrial Classification (SIC), excluding foods and beverages (SIC 20), tobacco (SIC 21) and primary non-ferrous metals (SIC 333), where the high cost of transportation favors the producers of the basic material, as well as ordinance (SIC 19), for which comparable trade data are not available. Under this definition, the 184 product category classification scheme has been established on the basis of four-digit SIC categories, with some further aggregation in cases when the economic characteristics of the products in question were judged to be very similar and when comparable data did not exist according to the UN Standard International Trade Classification, which has been used to collect trade figures.[6]

Data on the capital stock, employment, value added and wages used in calculating capital intensity originate from the US Census of Manufacturing. Data for unskilled wages have been taken from the *Monthly Labor Review*, published by the US Bureau of Labor Statistics; they relate to two-digit industries, thus involving the assumption that unskilled wages are equalized at this level. Finally, the value of human capital under the stock measure has been estimated by discounting differences between the average wage and the unskilled wage for the individual product categories at a rate of 10 percent.

As noted earlier, the sample of 36 countries used in the investigation is evenly divided between developed and developing countries; countries in the first group had per capita incomes above $1,800 in 1972; incomes per head did not exceed $1,400 (more exactly, $1,407) in the second group. The variability of per capita incomes is 1:3 in the developed country subsample, 1:13 in the developing country subsample, and 1:56 in the entire sample. The distinction between developed and developing countries has been introduced in the econometric analysis through the use of a dummy variable for developed countries.

In the absence of data on the physical capital stock in the individual countries, we have taken the sum of gross fixed investment over the period 1955–71, estimated in constant prices and converted into US dollars at 1963 exchange rates, as a proxy for physical capital endowment, reflecting the assumption that physical capital has a life of 16 years.[8] In turn, we have used the Harbison-Myers index of human resource development as a proxy for human capital endowment. While this index is a flow measure,[9] the use of estimates pertaining to 1965 (Harbison, Maruhnic, and Resnick, 1970, pp. 175–6) permits us to provide an indication of a country's general educational level, and thus its human capital base, in 1972, the year for which trade data have been obtained. We have also experimented with the skill ratio (the ratio of professional, technical and related workers shown in Group 0/1 of the International Standard Classification of Occupations to total employment), which has been employed by Hufbauer (1970). The use of this variable may be objected to, however, on the grounds that Group 0/1 includes personnel in liberal occupations, such as jurists, preachers, artists and athletes and includes production supervisors, foremen and skilled workers who are important in the manufacturing sector. Note further that this variable does not give statistically significant results in any of the regressions.

III

The β coefficients estimated by the use of equation (1) are reported in Table 2.1. It is shown there that, in the regression equations utilizing the stock measure of capital intensity, the β coefficient is statistically significant at the 5 percent level in the case of 22 countries and at the 10 percent level for 26 countries. In turn, in regression equations utilizing the flow measure, the β coefficient is significant at the 5 percent level in the case of 29 countries, with no additional countries included at the 10 percent level. In interpreting these results, it should be added that coefficient values near to zero have an

Table 2.1 Country characteristics and regression coefficients obtained in estimates for individual countries

	Country characteristics				Regression coefficients	
	Dummy	*GNPCAP*	*GDICAP*	*HMIND*	β_j^s	β_j^f
Argentina	0	1139.65	2013.68	122.0	0.32	0.19
Australia	1	3271.69	6675.24	183.3	0.34[b]	0.78[a]
Austria	1	2741.26	5129.79	112.9	−0.31[a]	−0.93[a]
Belgium	1	3701.15	5441.70	140.5	0.11	0.04
Brazil	0	511.27	1016.00	29.3	−0.69[a]	−1.48[a]
Canada	1	4691.51	7970.65	179.9	0.75[a]	0.87[a]
Colombia	0	357.08	751.59	32.3	−1.31[a]	−2.48[a]
Denmark	1	4187.67	6259.56	139.2	−0.40[a]	−0.12
Finland	1	2877.73	6999.27	109.9	−0.26	−0.62[a]
France	1	3841.68	7211.24	138.8	−0.07	−0.08
Germany	1	4218.84	7102.15	114.3	0.20[a]	0.43[a]
Greece	0	1407.20	2196.43	93.7	−0.27	−1.05[a]
Hong Kong	0	1048.88	1370.61	60.7	−2.30[a]	−2.84[a]
India	0	102.03	214.25	50.2	−1.10[a]	−2.30[a]
Ireland	1	1840.20	2701.89	110.7	−0.48[a]	−0.80[a]
Israel	1	2416.28	4280.96	148.9	−0.37[b]	−0.70[a]
Italy	1	2176.52	3366.47	91.3	−0.33[a]	−0.46[a]
Japan	1	2740.95	4765.11	146.2	−0.31[b]	−0.52[a]
Korea	0	301.03	402.89	66.7	−1.67[a]	−3.02[a]
Malaysia	0	408.62	494.56	34.5	−0.88[a]	−2.32[a]
Mexico	0	745.41	1067.02	41.1	−0.91[a]	−1.48[a]
Morocco	0	279.13	293.08	27.9	−1.18[a]	−2.95[a]
Netherlands	1	3466.90	5375.15	158.6	0.28[a]	0.44[a]
Norway	1	3786.91	7806.11	107.4	0.22	0.01
Pakistan	0	104.11	197.76	33.1	−1.56[a]	−3.11[a]
Philippines	0	223.50	448.72	134.2	−1.34[a]	−2.28[a]
Portugal	0	1084.26	1154.43	68.1	−0.81[a]	−2.09[a]
Singapore	0	1354.41	1189.84	97.6	−1.47[a]	−2.35[a]
Spain	0	1333.76	2049.09	63.4	−0.43[a]	−0.56[a]
Sweden	1	5141.10	9452.90	129.6	0.21	0.15
Switzerland	1	4810.02	8852.63	112.6	0.04	−0.10
Taiwan	0	481.94	629.88	103.5	−1.56[a]	−2.61[a]
Turkey	0	431.16	581.22	37.5	−0.42	−1.62[a]
UK	1	2765.25	4844.68	136.2	0.13	0.46[a]
USA	1	5679.47	7616.20	325.0	0.84[a]	1.47[a]
Yugoslavia	0	798.30	1162.06	110.0	−0.47[b]	−1.41[a]

Note: Country characteristics: *Dummy* = 1 for developed. 0 for developing countries
GNPCAP = GNP per capita in 1972, $US
GDICAP = Cumulated gross fixed investment per capita, 1955–71, $US
HMIND = Harbison-Myers index.
   Regression coefficients have been obtained by regressing for each country the ratio of 'revealed' comparative advantage, estimated for 184 product categories, on measures of capital intensity. Coefficients β^s and β^f have been estimated by regressing the comparative advantage ratio on the stock and the flow measures of capital intensity, respectively.
[a] Significant at the 5 percent level.
[b] Significant at the 10 percent level.

Table 2.2 Inter-country regression equations for the total capital intensity measure

Dependent variable	Equation number	Coefficient of determination	Explanatory variables				
			GDICAP	HMIND	Dummy	GNPCAP	Constant
β_j^s	1.1	0.65	1.46 (4.24)	0.34 (1.92)			−1.37 (−8.78)
	1.2	0.65	1.39 (2.40)	1.34 (1.83)	0.05 (0.15)		−1.36 (−8.44)
	1.3	0.65	1.39 (1.20)	0.33 (1.52)		0.14 (0.06)	−1.36 (−8.46)
β_j^f	2.1	0.78	2.57 (5.37)	0.77 (3.12)			−2.72 (−12.54)
	2.2	0.78	2.11 (2.66)	0.74 (2.91)	0.33 (0.71)		−2.69 (−12.05)
	2.3	0.78	1.79 (1.11)	0.68 (2.25)		1.66 (0.51)	−2.70 (−12.06)

Note: For explanation of symbols, see Table 2.1. In the estimating equations, GDICAP and GNPCAP have been expressed in units of 10,000 dollars and HMIND in units of 100: t-values are shown in parentheses.

economic interpretation even if they are not significantly different from zero; they indicate that a country is at the dividing line as far as comparative advantage in capital- and labor-intensive products is concerned.

The β coefficients estimated by using the stock and the flow measures of capital intensity are highly correlated, with a Spearman rank correlation coefficient of 0.96. This finding is in part explained by the relatively high degree of correspondence in the ranking of product categories by the two measures of capital intensity. The Spearman rank correlation coefficient between the two is 0.78.

The results pertaining to the stock and the flow measures of capital intensity are also broadly similar in the second stage of the estimation procedure, where we regress the coefficients on physical and human capital endowment variables in an inter-country framework. Thus, in equation (2), statistically significant results have been obtained for both the physical and the human capital endowment variables, regardless of whether the dependent variable originated in country regressions utilizing the stock or the flow measure of capital intensity.[10] In both regressions, the physical as well as the human capital endowment variables are significant at the 5 percent confidence level while the coefficient of determination is 0.65 using the stock measure, and 0.78 using the flow measure, of capital intensity (equations 1.1 and 2.1 in Table 2.2).[11]

The level of statistical significance of the regression coefficients for the physical and human capital endowment variables is hardly affected if we introduce a dummy variable (*Dummy*) representing the level of economic development. At the same time, the dummy variable is not statistically significant and its introduction does not increase the coefficient of determination.

We have further estimated Spearman rank correlation coefficients for pairs of country characteristics in the 36 country sample (Table 2.3). The correlations between per capita GDI and the Harbison-Myers index, on the one hand, and per capita GNP, on the other, point to the effects of investment in physical and in human capital on incomes per head. The existence of this

Table 2.3 Spearman rank correlation coefficients for country characteristics in the 36 country sample

	GNPCAP	GDICAP	HMIND
GNPCAP	1.000	0.984	0.754
GDICAP	0.984	1.000	0.730
HMIND	0.754	0.730	1.000

Note: For explanation of symbols, see Table 2.1. All coefficients are statistically significant at the 1 percent level.

correlation also explains that the inclusion of all three variables in the regression equation raises the standard error of the coefficients of the physical and human capital endowment variables. Nevertheless, the fact that the level of statistical significance of these two variables much exceeds that for incomes per head can be taken as an indication of the 'primacy' of the former (Table 2.2).

IV

This chapter has investigated the changing pattern of comparative advantage in the process of the accumulation of physical and human capital that characterizes economic development. Comparative advantage has been defined in terms of relative export performance, thus neglecting the composition of imports that is greatly affected by the structure of protection.

For each country, export performance has been related to the capital intensity of the individual product categories, using a stock as well as a flow measure of capital, inclusive of physical and human capital. Next, the regression coefficients thus obtained have been correlated with country characteristics, such as physical and human capital endowments and the level of economic development, in an inter-country framework.

The empirical estimates show that inter-country differences in the structure of exports are in a large part explained by differences in physical and human capital endowments. The results lend support to the 'stages' approach to comparative advantage, according to which the structure of exports changes with the accumulation of physical and human capital.[12] The approach is also supported by inter-temporal comparisons for Japan, which indicate that Japanese exports have become increasingly physical capital and human capital intensive over time (Heller, 1976).

These findings have important policy implications for the developing countries. To begin with, they warn against distorting the system of incentives in favor of products in which the country has a comparative disadvantage. The large differences shown among product categories in terms of their capital intensity point to the fact that there is a substantial penalty for such distortions in the form of the misallocation of productive factors. This will be the case in particular when the system of incentives is biased in favor of import substitution in capital-intensive products and against exports in labor-intensive products.

Possible magnitudes of the economic cost of distortions are shown in Table 2.4. The table provides comparisons for seven capital-intensive and seven labor-intensive products between production costs in the United States and in a hypothetical developing country where unskilled wages are one-third of US wages[13] and the cost of capital is commensurately higher.[14] In the hypothetical developing country, the estimated cost of the capital-intensive

Table 2.4 Hypothetical production costs calculated under alternative assumptions ($US)

Product category	United States				Developing country				Ratio of total costs
	Physical capital	Human capital	Unskilled labor	Total costs	Physical capital	Human capital	Unskilled labor	Total costs	
Capital-intensive									
1. Petroleum refining and products	37,833	6,563	5,342	49,738	54,215	9,405	1,781	65,401	1.315
2. Wood pulp	26,400	4,747	6,382	37,529	37,831	6,802	2,127	46,760	1.246
3. Organic chemicals	22,635	4,875	6,632	34,142	32,436	6,986	2,211	41,633	1.219
4. Synthetic rubber	20,826	5,121	6,632	32,579	29,844	7,338	2,211	39,393	1.209
5. Carbon black	18,669	3,893	6,632	29,194	26,753	5,579	2,211	34,543	1.183
6. Inorganic chemicals	16,044	3,928	6,632	26,604	22,991	5,629	2,211	30,831	1.159
7. Paper	14,778	3,983	6,382	25,143	21,177	5,707	2,127	29,011	1.154
Labor-intensive									
8. Games and toys	1,521	359	5,436	7,316	2,180	514	1,812	4,506	0.616
9. Vitreous china food utensils	1,608	186	6,082	7,876	2,304	267	2,027	4,598	0.584
10. Costume jewelry	978	533	5,436	6,947	1,401	764	1,812	3,977	0.572
11. Leather bags and purses	711	311	5,096	6,118	1,019	446	1,699	3,164	0.517
12. Earthenware food utensils	1,056	0	6,082	7,138	1,513	0	2,027	3,540	0.496
13. Woolen yarn and thread	486	160	4,228	4,874	696	229	1,409	2,334	0.479
14. Footwear	660	156	5,450	6,266	946	224	1,817	2,987	0.477
All categories	6,155	2,828	5,831	14,815	8,818	4,052	1,944	14,815	1.000

Note: US production costs have been calculated by adding 30 percent of the gross value of physical capital, assumed to reflect pre-tax earnings and depreciation, to observed labor costs. In turn, for the hypothetical developing country it has been assumed that unskilled wages are one-third of US wages and the cost of capital is correspondingly higher. The latter has been estimated to exceed US costs by 43.3 percent under the assumption that value added in the entire manufacturing sector is the same in the two cases. All data are expressed per worker.

products is 15 percent to 32 percent higher, and that of the labor-intensive products 38 percent to 52 percent lower, than in the United States, so that differences in relative costs between capital and labor-intensive products range from 1.87 to 2.76.[15]

The results can further be utilized to gauge the direction in which a country's comparative advantage is moving. This may be done by substituting projected future values of a country's physical and human capital endowments in the inter-country regressions, so as to estimate the prospective values of the β coefficients.[16] In turn, these coefficients can be used to derive the hypothetical structure of exports corresponding to the country's future physical and human capital endowments. Comparing the projected export structure with the actual structure of exports, one may then indicate prospective changes in export flows.[17]

The stages approach to comparative advantage also permits one to dispel certain misapprehensions as regards the foreign demand constraint for manufactured exports under which developing countries are said to operate. With countries progressing on the comparative advantage scale, their exports can supplant the exports of countries that graduate to a higher level. Now, to the extent that one developing country replaces another in the imports of particular commodities by the developed countries, the problem of adjustment in the latter group of countries does not arise. Rather, the brunt of adjustment will be borne in industries where the products of newly graduating developing countries compete with the products of the developed countries. A case in point is Japan, whose comparative advantage has shifted towards highly capital-intensive exports and is now competing with the United States and European countries in these products.

NOTES

1. An alternative measure would involve relating exports to output in each country. In the absence of output figures, however, this measure could not be utilized in the present study. At any rate, it would require adjusting for country size (Balassa, 1969) while the measure used here does not require such an adjustment.
2. Since the logarithm of zero is undefined, in the estimating equations an export ratio of 0.001 has been used to represent cases when the exports of a country in a particular product category were nil. We have also experimented with the use of a 0.01 ratio and have obtained practically the same results. Nor are the results materially affected if we drop the zero observations from the regressions. This and other estimates not reported in the chapter are available from the author on request.
3. Alternatively, use may be made of non-parametric tests involving the calculating of the Spearman rank correlation coefficient between the 'revealed' comparative advantage ratio and the individual factor intensity measures. This test has the disadvantage, however, in that it cannot handle more than one explanatory variable and that it does.not permit one to indicate the implications of the inter-country results for a country's further comparative advantage (on the last point, see Section IV.)

4. Branson observes that the aggregation of various forms of capital assumes that they are perfect complements or perfect substitutes (1973, p. 11). We have also experimented with separate variables for physical and human capital. The results are available from the author.

5. The use of US data in the investigation will be appropriate if factor substitution elasticities are zero or they are identical for every product category. While these assumptions are not fulfilled in practice, Lary has shown variations to be small in US–UK, US–Japan and US–India comparisons as regards the flow measure of capital (1968, Appendix D). For lack of information, similar comparisons could not be made for the stock measure and the further investigation of this question had to be left for future research.

6. Appendix tables providing information on the capital intensity of the 184 product categories and the SIC and SITC categories corresponding to these product categories are available from the author. In order to reduce the effects of variations due to the business cycle and non-recurring events, we have used simple averages of data for the two latest years (1969 and 1970) for which information was available.

7. This is in between the discount rates of 9.0 percent and 12.7 percent used by Kenen (1965); the same discount rate was used by Fels (1972) and Branson (1973).

8. The data, derived from *World Tables, 1976*, published by the World Bank, are shown together with other country characteristics in Table 2.1. A similar procedure was employed by Hufbauer (1970), who used data for an earlier and shorter period (1953–64).

9. It is derived as the secondary school enrollment rate plus five times the university enrollment rate in the respective age cohorts.

10. Note that, with variations in the standard errors of the β coefficients derived in equation (1), the regression results obtained in equation (2) will be subject to heteroscedasticity, which tends to raise the standard error of the coefficients. However, the estimates are little affected if we weight the estimates for the individual countries by the reciprocals of the standard errors of the β coefficients to reduce heteroscedasticity.

11. Regressing the rank correlation coefficients calculated as between the 'revealed' comparative advantage ratios and the factor intensity measures on factor endowment variables has generally confirmed the reported results, although the level of statistical significance of the coefficients was somewhat lower.

12. The expression 'stages' is used here to denote changes over time that occur more or less continuously rather than discrete, stepwise changes. It is thus unrelated to economic stages described by Marx, the exponents of the German historical school and Rostow.

13. In 1974 average wages in manufacturing in Korea were 9 percent, and in the Philippines 6 percent, of US wages (ILO, *Yearbook of Labor Statistics*).

14. The difference in the cost of capital has been estimated at 43.3 percent under the assumption that average value added in the manufacturing sector was the same in the two cases. It has further been assumed that the absolute difference between skilled and unskilled wages remained the same.

15. As elsewhere in the chapter, the calculations do not allow for factor substitution in response to inter-country differences in factor prices.

16. In line with the stages approach to comparative advantage, this is done on the assumption that new countries exporting manufactured goods continuously enter at the lower end of the spectrum. It is further assumed that the relative importance of capital-intensive goods in world exports will continue to increase over time.

17. These projections further need to be adjusted in cases when observed values of the β coefficients differ from values estimated from the inter-country regression. The results are also subject to the usual projection error.

REFERENCES

Balassa, Bela (1965) 'Trade Liberalization and "Revealed" Comparative Advantage', *Manchester School* 33 (May), pp. 99–123.
Balassa, Bela (1969) 'Country Size and Trade Patterns: Comment', *American Economic Review* 59 (Mar.), pp. 201–4.
Balassa, Bela (1977) ' "Revealed" Comparative Advantage Revisited: An Analysis of Relative Export Shares of the Industrial Countries, 1953–1971', *Manchester School* 45 (Dec.), pp. 327–44.
Baldwin, Robert E. (1971) 'Determinants of the Commodity Structure of US Trade', *American Economic Review* 61 (Mar.), pp. 126–46.
Branson, William H. (1973) 'Factor Inputs, US Trade, and the Heckscher-Ohlin Model', Seminar Paper No. 27, Institute for International Economic Studies, University of Stockholm.
Branson, William H., and Helen Junz (1971) 'Trends in US Comparative Advantage', *Brookings Papers on Economic Activity* 2, pp. 285–345.
Fels, Gerhard (1972) 'The Choice of Industry Mix in the Division of Labor between Developed and Developing Countries', *Weltwirtschaftliches Archiv*, Band 108, Heft 1, pp. 71–121.
Goodman, Bernard, and Fikret Ceyhun (1976) 'US Export Performance in Manufacturing Industries: An Empirical Investigation', *Weltwirtschaftliches Archiv*, Band 112, Heft 3, pp. 525–55.
Harbison, Frederick H., Jan Maruhnic and Jane R. Resnick (1970) *Quantitative Analyses of Modernization and Development*, Industrial Relations Section, Department of Economics, Princeton University.
Heller, Peter S. (1976) 'Factor Endowment Change and Comparative Advantage', *Review of Economics and Statistics* 58 (Aug.), pp. 283–92.
Herman, Bohuslav (1975) *The Optimal International Division of Labor*, International Labor Office, Geneva.
Herman, Bohuslav, and Jan Tinbergen (1970) 'Planning of International Development', *Proceedings of the International Conference on Industrial Economics*, Budapest, April 15–17.
Hirsch, Seev (1974) 'Capital or Technology? Confronting the Neo-factor Proportions and the Neo-technology Accounts of International Trade', *Weltwirtschaftliches Archiv*, Band 110, Heft 4, pp. 535–63.
Hufbauer, Gary C. (1970) 'The Impact of National Characteristics and Technology on the Commodity Composition of Trade in Manufactured Goods', in R. Vernon (ed.), *The Technology Factor in International Trade* (New York, Columbia University Press for the National Bureau of Economic Research).
Kenen, Peter B. (1965) 'Nature, Capital and Trade', *Journal of Political Economy* 73 (Oct.), pp. 437–60.
Kojima, Kiyoshi (1970) 'Structure of Comparative Advantage in Industrial Countries: A Verification of the Factor-Proportions Theorem', *Hitotsubashi Journal of Economics* 11 (June), pp. 1–29.
Lary, Hal B. (1968) *Imports of Manufactures from Less-Developed Countries* (New York, Columbia University Press for the National Bureau of Economic Research).
Mahfuzur Rahman, A. H. M. (1973) *Exports of Manufactures from Developing Countries*, Centre for Development Planning, Rotterdam University Press.
Morall, J. F. (1972) *Human Capital. Technology and the Role of the US in International Trade* (Gainesville, University of Florida Press).

3 · COMPARATIVE ADVANTAGE IN MANUFACTURED GOODS: A REAPPRAISAL

I

In setting out to explain the pattern of international trade by reference to inter-industry differences in factor intensities and inter-country differences in factor endowments, the Heckscher-Ohlin theory posits the existence of a well-defined relationship among trade flows, factor intensities and factor endowments. In his *Sources of International Comparative Advantage: Theory and Evidence*, Edward E. Leamer correctly notes that 'the way to measure the accuracy of the theory is to obtain direct and independent measures of all three concepts' (1984, p. 49).

Rather than introducing all three elements in their empirical investigations, a long list of researchers, including Baldwin (1971 and 1979), Branson (1973), Stern (1976), Branson and Monoyios (1977), Stern and Maskus (1981), Maskus (1983) and Urata (1983), attempted to infer the relative factor endowments of a single country *vis-à-vis* the rest of the world from the factor intensity of its trade. However, following on the work of Leamer and Bowen (1981), Aw (1983) has proved that inferences about relative factor abundance from cross-section results obtained for the trade of a particular country cannot be made, unless very stringent conditions are met.

An alternative approach, utilized by Leamer (1974), Bowen (1983) and, again, Leamer (1984), attempted to test the Heckscher-Ohlin theory by

This chapter was written while the author was at the Johns Hopkins University and the World Bank. It was prepared in the framework of the World Bank's research project 'Changes in Comparative Advantage in Manufactured Goods' (RPO 672-41). The author is greatly indebted to Luc Bauwens for suggesting the application of alternative econometric techniques and for making useful comments on the previous drafts. He is also grateful to Carl Christ, Tatsuo Hatta and Masahiro Kawai for valuable comments and to the referees for helpful suggestions. Further thanks are due to Linda Pacheco and Marcus Noland for data collection, to Jerzy Rozanski for generating the trade data, and to Shigeru Akiyama for carrying out the arduous task of estimation. However, the author alone is responsible for the opinions expressed in the chapter that should not be interpreted to represent the views of the World Bank. First published in *Review of Economics and Statistics*, May 1986.

relating trade flows to factor endowments. However, as Bowen, as well as Leamer, has admitted, there is no necessary relationship between the coefficients estimated in regard to factor endowments and the factor intensity of trade. Correspondingly, this method will not provide an appropriate test for the Heckscher-Ohlin theory either.

Following an earlier study by the author (Balassa, 1979, Chapter 2 in this volume), this chapter sets out to test the Heckscher-Ohlin theory by simultaneously introducing trade flows, factor intensities and factor endowments in an empirical investigation of the pattern of comparative advantage in manufactured goods in a multi-country model. Following Deardorff's theoretical analysis of the Heckscher-Ohlin theorem, the chapter utilizes data on net exports to test the hypothesis that countries relatively well endowed with capital (labor) will export relatively capital-intensive (labor-intensive) commodities.[1]

The chapter makes use of a three-factor model (physical capital, human capital and labor), with labor as the numeraire. Thus, factor intensities are expressed in terms of physical and human capital per worker while factor endowments are defined by relating the endowment of physical and human capital to the size of the labor force.

Section II of the chapter describes the data used in the investigation. Section III provides the derivation of the estimating equation and the empirical results obtained. The effects of additional variables on the pattern of trade in manufactured goods are examined in section IV while section V contains a brief conclusion.

II

The investigation covers altogether 167 commodity categories in the manufacturing sector as defined by the United States Standard Industrial Classification (SIC), after the exclusion of natural resource products whose manufacture is importantly affected by the availability of natural resources in a particular country.[2] The classification scheme has been established by merging four-digit SIC categories in cases when the economic characteristics of particular products have been judged to be very similar, the principal criteria being high substitution elasticities in production and in consumption. The individual commodity categories have further been matched against the three- and four-digit categories of the United Nations Standard International Trade Classification (SITC), which provides the breakdown for the trade data.

The net exports of individual countries in particular commodity categories had to be normalized in order to avoid size effects. Normalization has been done by expressing the net exports of country j in industry i $(X_{ij} - M_{ij})$ as a ratio of the sum of country j's exports and imports in industry i $(X_{ij} + M_{ij})$.[3] This ratio, taking values between -1 and 1, is denoted by NNX_{ij}.

Physical (p_i) as well as human (h_i) capital intensity is defined in terms of both stocks and flows. The stock measures of physical and human capital intensity, respectively, are the value of the physical capital stock per worker and the discounted value of the difference between the average wage and the unskilled wage, using a discount rate of 10 percent. The corresponding flow measures are the non-wage value added divided by the number of workers and the difference between the average wage and the unskilled wage.[4]

The use of the US industrial classification scheme has involved utilizing US input coefficients. As is well known, this will be appropriate if factor substitution elasticities are zero or they are identical for every industry. The non-fulfillment of this assumption introduces error possibilities in the estimation without, however, necessarily biasing the results.

The estimates have been made by utilizing trade data as well as data on capital intensities for the year 1971. They pertain to 38 countries, in each of which manufactured exports accounted for at least 18 percent of total exports and surpassed $300 million in 1979.[5]

Physical capital endowments (G_j) have been estimated as the sum of gross fixed investment over the preceding 17-year period, expressed in constant prices and converted into US dollars at the 1963 exchange rate. Investment values have been assumed to depreciate at an annual rate of 4 percent a year, so as to reflect the obsolescence of capital; such an adjustment was not made in the earlier chapter. Physical capital endowments have been expressed in per capita terms.

The Harbison-Myers index of education has been used as a proxy for human capital (H_j). This index, derived as the secondary school enrollment rate plus five times the university enrollment rate in the respective age cohorts, is a flow measure. It has been used with a six-year lag, as an indicator of the country's general educational level.

III

The estimating equation has been derived in the two-stage framework utilized in the earlier chapter by the author. In (1) a positive (negative) coefficient is taken to indicate that a country has a comparative advantage in capital (labor) intensive industries while the numerical magnitude of the β-coefficient has been interpreted to express the extent of the country's comparative advantage in capital (labor) intensive industries. In turn, in (2) the hypothesis is tested that inter-country differences in the β coefficient can be explained by differences in relative factor endowments.

Estimating equation (3), used in the present chapter, involves combining (1) and (2). This permits directly testing the hypothesis that relatively capital (labor) abundant countries tend to export relatively capital (labor) intensive commodities. A modified form of (3) has also been estimated by aggregating the two forms of capital, with k_i being the sum of p_i and h_i. This permits testing the hypothesis as to the appropriateness of aggregation, which assumes that the two forms of capital are perfect complements or substitutes (Branson, 1973).

$$NNX_{ij} = \alpha_j + \beta_{pj} \ln p_i + \beta_{hj} \ln h_i + u_{ij} \tag{1}$$

$$\beta_{pj} = a_p + b_p G_j + v_{pj} \tag{2a}$$

$$\beta_{hj} = a_h + b_h H_j + v_{hj} \tag{2b}$$

$$NNX_{ij} = \alpha_j + a_p \ln p_i + a_h \ln h_i + b_p G_j \ln p_i + b_h H_j \ln h_i + \varepsilon_{ij},$$

$$\varepsilon_{ij} = v_{pj} \ln p_i + v_{hj} \ln h_i + u_{ij}. \tag{3}$$

A comparison of (2) and (3) shows that one can interpret the coefficients of $\ln p_i$ and $\ln h_i$ in one-pass estimation as the constants of the second-stage equation and the coefficients of $G_j \ln p_i$ and $H_j \ln h_i$ as the coefficients of G_j and H_j in the second-stage equation. Under certain assumptions the two sets of estimated coefficients will have equal values (Amemiya, 1978), although their levels of statistical significance will differ owing to differences in the number of observations.

In the equations, u_{ij} is the error term in (1), v_{pj} and v_{hj} are the error terms in (2),[6] and ε_{ij} the error term in (3). The latter term will be heteroscedastic even if u_{ij}, v_{pj} and v_{hj} are assumed to be homoscedastic. In estimating (3) by ordinary least squares (OLS), adjustment has been made for heteroscedasticity by the use of a procedure proposed by White (1980).

In estimation by OLS, α_j is considered as a country-specific intercept term. Alternatively, α_j may be treated as a country-specific error term. One may further introduce an industry-specific error term (w_i) to parallel the country-specific error term. This has been done in the present chapter by making alternative estimates by applying the error component model (ECM) to (3). In making estimates by ECM, it can be assumed that α_j and w_i are homoscedastic; for ease of estimation, the same assumption has been made in regard to ε_{ij}.

The OLS results are reported in Table 3.1. The regression coefficients of the capital endowment variables have the expected sign and all the coefficients, as well as the constants of the regression equations, are statistically significant at the 1 percent level. Very similar results have been obtained with the error component model; in order to economize with space, they are not reproduced here. Rather, the ECM method is utilized in reporting the estimates obtained by the use of the enlarged model in Table 3.2.

The aggregation of capital does not affect the statistical significance of the estimated coefficients; nor does aggregation affect the explanatory power of the regression equations, with the coefficients of determination being in the 0.46–0.47 range in both cases. This result contrasts with that obtained by several authors (Branson, 1973; Stern, 1976; Branson and Monoyios, 1977;

Table 3.1 Explanation of inter-country differences in the pattern of specialization in manufactured goods: basic model (OLS estimates, corrected for heteroscedasticity with t-values in parentheses)

Equations	$\ln k_i$	$\ln p_i$	$\ln h_i$	$G_j \ln k_i$	$H_j \ln k_i$	$G_j \ln p_i$	$H_j \ln h_i$	$\bar{R}^2$	$\hat{\sigma}^2$
Stock	0.47 (−18.74)[a]			0.68 (9.89)[a]	0.10 (3.72)[a]			0.4704	0.2619
Flow	−0.46 (−16.32)[a]			0.60 (8.05)[a]	0.12 (4.11)[a]			0.4626	0.2657
Stock		−0.21 (−12.64)[a]	−0.26 (−11.74)[a]			(0.45 (10.28)[a]	0.17 (10.21)[a]	0.4675	0.2633
Flow		0.21 (−9.16)[a]	0.29 (−12.56)[a]			0.43 (7.80)[a]	0.18 (11.01)[a]	0.4618	0.2661

Note: For explanation of symbols, see text. $\hat{\sigma}^2$ is the variance of the residuals of the estimating equation.
[a] Significant at the 1 percent level.

Table 3.2 Explanation of inter-country differences in the pattern of specialization in manufactured goods: extended model (ECM estimates, with t-values in parentheses)

Equations	$\ln k_i$	$G_j \ln k_i$	$H_j \ln k_i$	BTO $\ln k_i$	$XCON$ $\ln k_i$	FDI $\ln k_i$	$\hat{\sigma}^2$
Stock	−0.42 (−10.10)[a]	0.43 (7.55)[a]	0.08 (4.13)[a]	−0.02 (−1.34)	−0.45 (−2.23)[b]	0.01 (2.71)[a]	0.2280
Flow	−0.42 (−9.51)[a]	0.37 (6.29)[a]	0.09 (4.56)[a]	−0.01 (2.71)[a]	−0.48 (−2.33)[b]	0.01 (2.71)[a]	0.2303

Note: See Table 3.1.
[a] Significant at the 1 percent level.
[b] Significant at the 5 percent level.

and Stern and Maskus, 1981). However, in the latter studies differences in the signs of physical and human capital were shown for two industrial countries at the upper end of the distribution – the United States and Germany. Also, as noted above, the interpretation of the estimates of these authors is open to question because capital endowments were inferred from estimates pertaining to capital intensities.

IV

The estimates reported in the preceding section aimed at explaining the pattern of international specialization in manufactured goods by reference to inter-industry differences in capital intensities and inter-country differences in factor endowments. In the following, additional influences will be introduced that may explain why some countries export (import) more – and others less – capital-intensive products than may be expected on the basis of their physical and human capital endowments. These additional country-specific variables are introduced in (2) and are utilized in estimating an extended form of (3).

A possible explanatory factor is the trade policies applied by the individual countries. Following estimation done elsewhere by the author (1985), trade orientation has been measured in an indirect way, defining it as the difference between actual and hypothetical values of per capita exports. Hypothetical values have been derived from a cross-section regression equation that, in addition to the per capita income and population variables utilized in early work by Chenery (1960), includes variables representing the availability of mineral resources and propinquity to foreign markets.

Downward deviations from the regression line, with actual exports falling short of hypothetical exports, are considered as a manifestation of protectionist policies that tend to reduce imports as well as exports. Conversely, upward deviations, with actual exports exceeding hypothetical exports, are taken to reflect the application of liberal trade policies.

Deviations from the trade orientation regression, whether in an upward or a downward direction, are by far the largest for the developing countries, where trade policies vary to a much greater extent than in the developed countries. Deviations from the regression line estimated by (3) are also considerably larger for the developing countries than for the developed countries.[7] In devising a statistical test, then, we will focus on the results obtained for the former group of countries.

In the case of the developing countries, upward (downward) deviations in the net export equations are expected to be associated with the application of protectionist (liberal) trade policies. This is because protectionist policies do not permit specialization according to comparative advantage, thereby raising the capital-intensity of exports, while the capital-intensity of exports is lowered as a result of the application of liberal trade policies. In fact, the largest upward deviations in the net export equations are shown for developing countries with relatively high protection, such as Argentina, Brazil and Mexico, and the largest downward deviations in developing countries with relatively low protection, such as Hong Kong and Korea.

It is hypothesized, then, that upward (downward) deviations in the trade orientation equation will be associated with downward (upward) deviations in the net export equations. Correspondingly, in an extended form of (3), which includes the trade orientation variable, the sign of this variable is expected to be negative.

Deviations between the actual and the predicted capital intensity of trade may also depend on the commodity concentration of exports in the countries concerned. It is hypothesized that export concentration (diversification) will favor (retard) the exploitation of a country's comparative advantage. With protection in developing countries hindering specialization in products in which a country has a comparative advantage, it may be expected that export concentration would give rise to negative (positive) deviations in the net export equations.[8]

Another variable used to explain differences between actual and predicted values is foreign direct investment. It has been suggested that foreign direct investment in developing countries is biased towards capital-intensive activities. Correspondingly, it is hypothesized that foreign direct investment will give rise to positive deviations in the net export equations.[9] The foreign investment variable has ben measured by cumulating balance-of-payments data deflated by the price index of world export unit values for a ten-year period preceding the year of estimation.

Table 3.2 reports the results obtained with the enlarged equations, incorporating the trade orientation (*BTO*), export concentration (*XCON*) and foreign direct investment (*FDI*) variables. The equations have been estimated by the use of ECM for the case when capital intensity is introduced in an aggregated form.

All three newly introduced variables have the expected sign while their level of statistical significance varies. The trade orientation variable is significant at the 1 percent level in the flow but not in the stock equations, and the export concentration and the foreign direct investment variables are significant at the 5 percent and the 1 percent levels, respectively, in both equations. At the same time, the introduction of these variables in the estimating equation does not affect the statistical significance of the factor endowment variables or of the constants of the regression equations.

V

This chapter has shown that differences in physical and human capital endowments explain a substantial part of the observed differences in the pattern of trade in an inter-country framework. This conclusion holds irrespective of whether capital intensity is introduced in an aggregated form or is disaggregated into physical and human capital and whether a stock or a flow measure of capital is used.

In extending the basic equation, it has been shown that the pattern of specialization in manufactured goods is further influenced by the extent of trade orientation, the concentration of the export structure and foreign direct investment. At the same time, their introduction in the estimation does not affect the statistical significance of the factor endowment variables.

The chapter has provided a test for the Heckscher-Ohlin theory for manufactured goods by simultaneously introducing trade flows, factor intensities, and factor endowments in the framework of a multi-country and multi-product model. The findings confirm the hypothesis in indicating that relatively capital (labor) abundant countries export relatively capital (labor) intensive commodities. It has also been shown that the pattern of trade is further affected by the policies applied.

Transposing the results obtained in a cross-section into a time-series framework, it would appear that as countries accumulate physical and human capital their manufactured trade pattern correspondingly changes. At the same time, in interfering with international specialization according to comparative advantage, protection imposes an economic cost on the countries concerned. A cost also appears to be associated with foreign direct investment, which is biased towards capital-intensive activities, thereby reducing the benefits it otherwise provides.

NOTES

1. For a generalized formulation of the relationship among the three variables, see Deardorff (1982).
2. The sensitivity of the empirical results to the inclusion of natural resource industries is noted by Stern and Maskus, who suggest that 'the results reported by Branson and Monoyios (1977) may reflect the importance of physical capital in some natural resource industries that were included in their cross sections' (1981, p. 212).
3. Lack of data for the individual countries did not permit scaling by the value of shipment as done by Branson and Monoyios (1977) in their investigation of the determinants of the US trade pattern. On the importance of scaling, see Stern and Maskus (1981), p. 211.
4. This contrasts with the earlier chapter, where the average wage was used to represent the flow coefficient of human capital. For a description of the data, the reader is referred to Balassa (1979), which also considers the advantages and disadvantages of the stock and flow measures of capital.
5. While the trade data refer to 1971, the year 1979 has been chosen as the benchmark in determining the choice of countries for the present investigation in order to include all countries with a potential to export manufactured goods.
6. Attempts made to introduce cross-terms, H_j in (2a) and G_j in (2b) have not been successful due to multicollinearity between the two endowment variables.

7. In the trade orientation equation, the standard deviation of the unweighted residuals is three times, in the export equation two-and-a-half times, greater for the developing than for the developed countries.
8. Export concentration has been measured for the 167 industries covered in the sample by utilizing the so-called Herfindahl index.
9. While direct foreign investment is used here as an explanatory variable, Baldwin has attempted to explain the pattern of US direct foreign investment using the same explanatory variables as those employed in explaining the US pattern of trade (1979).

REFERENCES

Amemiya, Takeshi (1978) 'A Note on a Random Coefficients Model', *International Economic Review* 19 (Oct.), pp. 793–6.
Aw, Bee-Yan (1983) 'The Interpretation of Cross-Section Regression Tests of the Heckscher-Ohlin Theorem with Many Goods and Factors', *Journal of International Economics* 14 (Feb.), pp. 163–7.
Balassa, Bela (1979) 'The Changing Pattern of Comparative Advantage in Manufactured Goods', *Review of Economics and Statistics* 61 (May), pp. 259–66. Reprinted as Chapter 2 in this volume.
Balassa, Bela (1985) 'Exports, Policy Choices, and Economic Growth in Developing Countries After the 1973 Oil Shock', *Journal of Development Economics* 18 (May–June), pp. 23–36.
Baldwin, Robert E. (1971) 'Determinants of the Commodity Structure of US Trade', *American Economic Review* 61 (Mar.), pp. 126–46.
Baldwin Robert E. (1979) 'Determinants of Trade and Foreign Investment: Further Evidence', *Review of Economics and Statistics* 61 (Feb.), pp. 40–8.
Bowen, Harry P. (1983) 'Changes in the International Distribution of Resources and their Impact on US Comparative Advantage', *Review of Economics and Statistics* 65 (Aug.), pp. 402–14.
Branson, William H. (1973) 'Factor Inputs, US Trade and the Heckscher-Ohlin Model', Seminar Paper No. 27, Institute for International Economic Studies, University of Stockholm.
Branson, William H. and Nikolaos Monoyios (1977) 'Factor Inputs in US Trade', *Journal of International Economics* 7 (May), pp. 111–31.
Chenery, Hollis B. (1960) 'Patterns of Industrial Growth', *American Economic Review* 50 (Sept.), pp. 624–54.
Deardorff, A. V. (1982) 'The General Validity of the Heckscher-Ohlin Theorem', *American Economic Review* 72 (Sept.), pp. 683–94.
Leamer, Edward E. (1974) 'The Commodity Composition of International Trade in Manufactures: An Empirical Analysis', *Oxford Economic Papers* 26 (Nov.), pp. 350–74.
Leamer, Edward E. (1984) *Sources of International Comparative Advantage: Theory and Evidence* (Cambridge, Mass., MIT Press).
Leamer, Edward E., and Harry P. Bowen (1981) 'Cross-Section Tests of the Heckscher-Ohlin Theorem: Comment', *American Economic Review* 71 (Dec.), pp. 1040–3.
Maskus, Keith E. (1983) 'Evidence on Shifts in the Determinants of the Structure of US Manufacturing Foreign Trade, 1958–76', *Review of Economics and Statistics* 65 (Aug.), pp. 415–23.
Stern, Robert M. (1976) 'Some Evidence on the Factor Content of West Germany's Foreign Trade', *Journal of Political Economy* 84 (Feb.), pp. 131–41.

Stern, Robert M., and Keith E. Maskus (1981) 'Determinants of the Structure of US Foreign Trade, 1958–76', *Journal of International Economics* 11 (May), pp. 207–24.

Urata, Shujiro (1983) 'Factor Inputs and Japanese Manufacturing Trade Structure', *Review of Economics and Statistics* 65 (Nov.), pp. 678–84.

White, Halbert (1980) 'A Heteroskedasticity-Consistent Covariance Matrix Estimator and a Direct Test for Heteroskedasticity', *Econometrica* 48 (May), pp. 817–38.

4 · TRADE LIBERALIZATION AND 'REVEALED' COMPARATIVE ADVANTAGE

I

In discussions on the possible effects of trade liberalization in the framework of the Kennedy-round, attention has been focused on the short-run problems of adjustment and the consequences for the balance of payments of the countries participating in the negotiations. At the same time, little attention has been paid to the enduring effects of trade liberalization: the reallocation of resources following the freeing of trade barriers. In the present chapter, we propose to examine the latter problem.

Since the reallocation of resources depends on comparative advantage, we have to ascertain where the comparative advantage of industrial countries lies in their trade with each other. One possible solution would be to make comparisons on the basis of a production census undertaken simultaneously – and using identical methods of investigation – in all countries. In practice, production censuses have been conducted at different times, using different methods of inquiry, and sufficient information for making inter-country cost-comparisons has not been made available.

An exception is the case of the United States and the United Kingdom where inter-industry cost-comparisons have been made for the year 1950 in a study prepared for the Organization for European Economic Co-operation.[1] But 1950 can hardly be regarded as a 'normal' year in any sense and, at any rate, the long time elapsed since this inquiry has reduced the value of the comparisons. For present purposes, a further deficiency of the estimates is that costs have been defined as value added inclusive of depreciation, so that material costs are excluded while profits are comprised in the 'cost' figures.

Data collection and calculations were carried out in the framework of the Atlantic Trade Project, directed by the author and sponsored by the Council on Foreign Relations. The writing of this chapter was undertaken while the author was a Social Science Research Council fellow. First published in *Manchester School*, May 1965.

Alternatively, we may utilize the results of industry studies that provide cost comparisons for the manufacturing industries of developed countries. A study of this nature has been prepared for the National Industrial Conference Board, which has relied on information supplied by 147 companies conducting operations in the United States and abroad.[2]

The NICB report provides much interesting material on production costs in the domestic and foreign operations of American firms but, in the absence of a cross-classification according to countries and industries, the comparative advantage of foreign countries, taken individually, is not indicated. Further, the industry-breakdown used in the report is not detailed enough for our purposes and the sample does not include domestic companies of foreign countries.

In the absence of appropriate data on production costs in the manufacturing industries of individual countries, it may be proposed to rely on prevailing theories of international specialization for determining the pattern of comparative advantage. Among these doctrines, the Heckscher-Ohlin theory and the classical theory of comparative advantage can claim our attention.

II

In a two-country, two-factor world where production functions are identical internationally, and the elasticity of substitution among the factors of production is zero or unity, the relative factor intensities of individual commodities will be uniquely determined, and international specialization will correspond to inter-country differences in factor endowments. If allowance is made for differences in tastes, relative factor endowments can be expressed in terms of relative factor prices, i.e. the country with the lower relative price of labor will be considered labor-abundant, and his trade partner capital-abundant.

In a comparative study of 19 countries, Arrow *et al.* have claimed to establish, however, that substitution elasticities are generally lower than unity, and also differ among industries, implying that relative factor intensities would not be independent of factor prices.[3] As wage rates rise compared to the price of capital, the capital-intensity of the industry with the higher elasticity of substitution will increase relative to the industry with the lower elasticity; now, if the latter industry was capital intensive at lower wage levels, a switch in factor intensities will occur and relative factor endowments will not uniquely determine comparative advantage.

But irrespective of the possibility of factor reversal, a calculation of direct *plus* indirect labor and capital coefficients will not provide an appropriate indication of comparative advantage if inter-country differences in efficiency exist. Under the assumption that these differences pertain equally to all industries; the countries at a higher level of efficiency will possess advantages in industries that utilize intermediate products in larger quantities. It may then be suggested to consider separately direct labor and capital requirements and material inputs (intermediate products), when inter-country differences with regard to the latter will reflect relative efficiencies in intermediate stages of manufacturing.[4]

Difficulties arise in attempting to apply the Heckscher–Ohlin theory to the three-factor case, however. Whereas – in the absence of factor reversals – we can provide a unique ranking of industries according to their relative factor intensities in the case of two factors, in the three-factor case a unique ranking may be possible only with regard to pairs of factors. Thus we may rank industries, e.g. with respect to their labor and material requirements, but not necessarily with regard to labor, materials and capital.[5] And we can hardly speak of a homogeneous material input since the comparative advantages of industries utilizing material inputs will also depend on the number of the preceding stages of transformation. A consideration of differences in natural endowments will increase the number of factors, and compound the difficulties of establishing a unique ranking.

Similar difficulties arise if more than two countries are considered. In the two-factor case, some conclusions can now be derived with regard to national economies at the opposite ends of the scale, such as the United States and Japan among the industrial countries, but less can be said concerning the countries of Western Europe that inhabit the middle ground. The introduction of more countries *and* more factors further complicates the problem and if we also take account of inter-industry differences in efficiency among the industrial countries, the Heckscher–Ohlin theory will hardly offer a guide in evaluating comparative advantages.

In turn, the consideration of inter-country differences in the efficiency of individual industries underlies the explanation given by the classical theory of comparative advantage when data on labor productivity have been used as a proxy for efficiency. The explanatory value of this hypothesis has been indicated in United States–United Kingdom comparisons,[6] but comparable data on productivity are not available for all industrial countries, and in US–UK relationships, too, in addition to the observed productivity differences in a single year (1950), changes over time would be of interest.

At any rate, the lack of consideration given to inter-industry differences in capital costs and non-price factors reduce the usefulness of the classical doctrine for the present purposes. Non-price variables have often suffered neglect in theoretical discussions and in empirical studies, although quality differences, goodwill, servicing, the existence of repair facilities and differences in weights and measures all bear influence on the pattern of international trade among the industrial countries. Cost considerations will not be sufficient to explain the widespread use of British woolen goods and the success of Volkswagen, for example, and, more generally, a complete explanation of comparative advantage could not leave out of consideration the non-price variables.

III

But is it necessary explicitly to take account of all influences that determine comparative advantage? This would be a rather laborious exercise and, in view of the difficulties of assigning numerical values to these variables, it might bring disappointing results. Instead, for purposes of indicating the possible consequences of trade liberalization, it appears sufficient to provide information on 'revealed' comparative advantage.

It is suggested here that 'revealed' comparative advantage can be indicated by the trade performance of individual countries in regard to manufacturing products, in the sense that the commodity pattern of trade reflects relative costs as well as differences in non-price factors. For one thing, comparative advantage would be expected to determine the structure of exports;[7] for another, under the assumption of uniformity in tastes and a uniform incidence of duties in every industry within each country, export-import ratios would reflect relative advantages. Thus, while the heterogeneity of statistical commodity groups allows for exports and imports within the same category, the greater a country's advantage in producing the commodities in question, the higher the ratio of the fob value of exports to that of imports is likely to be.

The assumption of the uniformity of tastes and uniform incidence of duties is not fulfilled in the real world, however. Rather, imports will be affected by inter-country differences in tastes, as well as by inter-industry disparities in the degree of protection. Moreover, in the case of intermediate products, export–import ratios are influenced by demand for purposes of further transformation in producing for export. To take account of these influences, separate consideration has to be given to the special circumstances relating to individual products, which fact reduces the generality of the comparisons.

On the other hand, as long as all exporters are subject to the same tariff, data on relative export performance are not distorted by differences in the degree of tariff protection. Correspondingly, in evaluating 'revealed' comparative advantage, we have given greater weight to export performance than to export–import ratios, and, in order to exclude extra-area trade, we have regarded the European Common Market as a unit.[8] Other areas included in the investigation are the United States, Canada, the United Kingdom, Sweden and Japan. These countries, the largest exporters of manufactured goods, account for over four-fifths of world exports of manufactures.

The inquiry has been limited to manufactured goods, partly because these provide the lion's share in trade among industrial countries, and partly because a large number of primary products are subject to subsidies, quotas and special arrangements, so that the ensuing trade pattern can hardly reflect comparative advantage. Manufactured goods have been defined to include the products classified in commodity catagories 5 to 8 of the Standard International Trade Classification, the exception being unwrought metals which – following the customs of international organizations – we have regarded as primary products.

With respect to manufactured goods, we have attempted to establish a commodity classification based on the elasticity of substitution in production, i.e. commodities with high substitution elasticity have been included in one category. Our point of departure has been the three-digit breakdown of the SITC, which we have supplemented by a four-digit breakdown whenever this appeared necessary and was made possible by the availability of statistical information.

Altogether, we have distinguished 74 categories, having excluded from the investigation commodities that are not easily transportable, such as lime, cement and fabricated building materials (SITC 661), clay construction materials (662), and mineral manufacturers n.e.s. (663), as well as commodities where the countries under consideration, taken together, have an import surplus. This solution has been chosen because in such instances other exporters are likely to benefit from an overall tariff reduction; less developed countries in regard to mineral tar and crude chemicals (521), dyeing and tanning extracts (532), wood and cork manufacturers (631), jute fabrics (653.4), pearls and precious stones (667), silver (681), and miscellaneous metals (688.9), and Switzerland in the case of watches and clocks (864). Further, for obvious reasons, we have excluded developed cinematographic film (863), printed matter (892), as well as the motley collection of other miscellaneous manufactured articles, n.e.s. (893–6, 898).

IV

The export performance of individual industries in a particular country can be evaluated by (a) comparing the relative shares of a country in the world exports of individual commodities, and (b) indicating changes in relative shares over time. In both instances, the data have to be made comparable through appropriate 'normalization.' This we have accomplished by dividing a country's share in the exports of a given commodity by its share in the combined exports of manufactured goods of the ten industrial countries under consideration, and expressing the result in index number form. Thus, for a given export commodity of a particular country, an index number of 110 will mean that the country's share in this commodity's exports is 10 percent higher than its share in the total exports of manufactured goods. Similar calculations have been made for changes in shares between the two three-year periods (1953–5 and 1960–2) that have been chosen as representative of the mid-1950s and the early 1960s.

Correspondingly, we have calculated the following:

1. The relative share of country i's exports of commodity j in the years 1953–5.
2. The relative share of country i's exports of commodity j in the years 1960–2.
3. The ratio of the relative share of country i's exports of commodity j in the second period to that in the first period.

In all cases, the expression 'relative share' refers to the ratio of the share of country i in the exports of commodity j to the share of country i in the exports of all manufactured goods. In symbols,[9]

$$\frac{X_{ij}^o}{X_{nj}^o} \bigg/ \frac{X_{it}^o}{X_{nt}^o} = \frac{x_{ij}^o}{x_i^o} \tag{1}$$

$$\frac{X_{ij}^l}{X_{nj}^l} \bigg/ \frac{X_{it}^l}{X_{nt}^l} = \frac{x_{ij}^l}{x_i^l} \tag{2}$$

$$\frac{x_{ij}^l}{x_i^l} \bigg/ \frac{x_{ij}^o}{x_i^o} \tag{3}$$

In evaluating relative advantages in the exportation of manufactured goods, various assumptions may be made. We may assume, for example, that relative shares observed in the most recent period will pertain also to the future, or we may take relative growth rates as an indicator. Both of these methods have their advantages and disadvantages. On the one hand, in considering relative export performance in a certain year, or an average of several years, we neglect the trend factor; on the other, relative growth rates can give a misleading impression of comparative advantage since high growth rates are compatible with small exports in absolute terms, while a country that has a large segment of the export market in a given commodity can hardly be expected to increase its share further.

These considerations indicate the need for using some combination of the two indicators for expressing comparative advantage. One possible solution would be to project the continuation of past trends in relative shares by multiplying equations (2) and (3). We have decided against using this formula since it involves the questionable assumption that changes in relative shares take the form of a geometrical progression which can be extrapolated into the future. Instead, a compromise solution has been chosen by calculating the arithmetical average of equations (2) and (4). This choice reflects the presumption that while past trends in relative shares can be expected to continue, this will take place at a declining pace as compared to the past. The reader will observe that any other average of the two figures could have been taken, and our choice is based on the assumption that it is appropriate to give equal

Table 4.1 Indices of export performance

SITC		US Index	US Rank	Canada Index	Canada Rank	EEC Index	EEC Rank	UK Index	UK Rank	Sweden Index	Sweden Rank	Japan Index	Japan Rank
512	Organic chemicals	109.9	27	418.8	4	116.7	26	69.4	55	39.0	50	51.3	51
513, 4, 5	Inorganic chemicals	126.7	21	186.5	12	96.1	48	94.0	38	41.0	49	62.7	46
531	Synthetic organic dyestuffs	50.0	50	651.3	72	128.8	13	145.7	14	1.6	73	30.9	63
533	Pigments, paints and varnishes	107.4	29	28.7	45	90.8	59	239.8	3	32.7	52	20.3	65
541	Medical and pharmaceutical	144.2	16	34.3	41	95.6	49	127.7	23	26.6	55	38.5	58
551	Essential oils and perfumes	187.3	8	10.2	60	114.2	28	84.4	44	5.5	67	7.0	70
553, 4	Perfumery and cosmetics	128.0	20	17.9	54	93.1	56	160.5	11	44.2	45	42.2	56
561	Fertilizers, manufacture	87.6	33	240.1	8	127.9	15	6.8	75	2.5	71	107.0	35
571	Explosives and pyrotechnic	72.6	44	6.5	65	95.5	51	217.3	4	113.8	21	73.4	45
581	Plastic materials	142.8	18	29.2	44	104.0	39	86.1	43	84.7	31	77.2	43
599	Chemical material and products	288.6	2	43.7	33	67.4	69	119.0	26	35.4	51	7.2	69
611	Leather	84.4	35	120.8	18	112.8	31	136.1	19	43.5	46	32.5	62
612	Manufactures of leather	57.5	48	200.2	11	125.2	20	105.2	32	74.1	33	94.2	32
613	Fur skins	221.1	4	92.6	20	96.8	47	87.6	42	47.7	42	7.3	68
621	Materials of rubber	26.5	63	36.6	40	112.9	30	136.8	17	155.4	15	139.0	26
629.1	Rubber tires and tubes	78.1	40	40.0	36	100.6	43	133.9	21	102.2	25	163.5	23
629.0	Other rubber articles	209.1	6	18.3	53	50.9	72	115.4	29	323.5	6	118.1	31
641	Paper and paperboard	76.0	42	1430.2	1	29.4	73	28.9	71	502.3	2	47.3	53
642	Articles made of paper	118.9	23	50.5	30	95.6	50	118.0	28	87.6	29	135.4	28
651.2	Yarn of wool	0.7	74	5.5	66	157.7	2	98.1	34	13.8	64	54.8	50
651.3	Cotton yarn, unbleached	18.1	66	—	72	103.0	40	43.8	67	0.5	74	545.9	2
651.4	Cotton yarn, bleached	16.6	68	4.2	67	136.2	7	118.6	27	22.8	56	243.4	16
651.6	Yarn of synthetic fibers	124.7	22	40.4	35	105.1	37	80.9	48	8.6	65	107.1	34
652	Cotton fabrics	61.9	46	78.3	22	79.5	62	54.7	65	45.6	43	442.0	5
653.2	Woolen fabrics	1.0	73	21.1	49	120.6	23	200.1	6	4.5	70	137.9	27
653.5, 6, 8	Synthetic fabrics	50.3	51	18.7	52	92.4	58	21.4	72	43.5	47	469.9	3
653.0	Other woven textile fabrics	36.0	58	58.9	23	110.9	33	78.2	49	53.8	40	361.9	7
654	Tulle, lace, embroidery	37.5	55	10.0	61	111.4	32	88.6	40	22.4	58	312.6	11
655	Special textile fabrics	60.2	47	57.4	24	94.1	54	139.4	16	68.9	35	184.2	21
656.6	Blankets	14.5	69	6.7	64	127.1	16	63.0	60	22.5	57	250.3	14

Table 4.1 (continued)

SITC		US		Canada		EEC		UK		Sweden		Japan	
		Index	Rank	Index	Rank	Index	Rank	Index	Rank	Index	Rank	Index	Rank
656.0	Made up textiles	165.5	11	33.5	42	79.5	63	74.2	52	51.7	41	157.2	24
657	Floor coverings	21.8	64	4.0	68	118.7	25	136.6	18	30.7	54	190.2	19
664	Glass	49.4	53	9.1	62	147.1	5	72.2	54	18.9	61	55.1	49
665	Glassware	102.4	30	2.9	69	115.8	27	66.4	57	102.8	24	77.5	42
666	Pottery	2.6	72	—	72	76.0	65	135.5	20	31.9	53	458.8	4
671	Pig iron	31.4	60	258.6	7	148.2	3	32.6	70	149.9	17	50.2	47
673	Iron and steel bars	17.3	67	40.0	37	133.3	10	59.1	62	114.8	20	99.9	37
674	Universals, plates and sheets	49.8	52	172.3	14	125.1	21	82.5	46	91.8	27	126.5	30
675	Hoops and strips	37.1	57	—	72	135.2	8	57.6	63	227.2	8	103.1	36
676	Railway construction material	75.2	43	396.2	5	95.4	52	83.5	45	558.1	1	153.2	25
678	Tubes, pipes and fittings	37.3	56	51.9	29	127.0	17	94.1	37	178.4	12	116.6	32
682.2	Copper, wrought	19.6	65	281.7	6	108.0	34	169.7	9	223.2	9	33.3	61
683.2	Nickel, wrought	174.7	9	160.4	16	60.5	71	180.4	8	116.6	19	2.0	74
684.2	Aluminum, wrought	78.6	39	214.6	10	119.5	24	110.9	31	101.2	26	33.9	60
685.2	Lead, wrought	48.5	54	852.7	2	128.6	14	97.2	35	411.7	4	45.2	54
686.2	Zinc, wrought	118.7	24	48.6	31	107.6	35	146.7	13	2.4	72	2.8	73
687.2	Tin, wrought	270.1	3	—	72	129.5	12	149.7	12	17.8	62	50.2	52
691.8	Manufactures of metal	81.5	37	46.8	32	101.8	42	111.9	30	106.6	23	128.7	29
711	Power generating machinery	99.0	31	228.0	9	64.9	70	248.0	2	78.2	32	40.2	57
712.0	Agricultural machinery	139.4	19	476.9	3	87.3	61	76.5	51	151.2	16	11.8	67
712.5	Tractors	214.7	5	53.7	26	25.9	74	301.3	1	42.9	48	3.8	71
714	Office machinery	157.0	14	132.8	17	92.5	57	62.1	61	170.8	13	77.0	44

Code		Item												
715	Metal working machinery	173.2	10	20.9	50	97.2	46	72.3	53	56.6	39	22.5	64
717.1	Textile machinery	85.9	34	26.8	47	113.9	29	128.7	22	21.1	59	83.4	41
718.9	Other machinery	143.6	17	40.0	38	93.4	55	99.5	33	149.9	18	35.4	59
722.1	Electric generators	113.6	25	52.6	28	99.9	44	120.7	25	91.7	28	98.2	38
72.0	Other electric machinery	109.3	28	57.1	25	94.9	53	92.1	39	72.7	34	309.6	12
731	Railway vehicles	200.2	77	30.9	43	71.5	68	65.5	59	166.8	14	215.8	18
732.1, 6	Automobiles	28.8	62	17.8	55	162.5	1	124.7	24	317.8	7	42.7	55
732.2, 5, 7	Buses, lorries and trucks	110.4	26	17.1	56	87.9	60	205.1	5	183.7	11	385.0	6
732.0	Bodies, chassis and frames	164.4	12	37.7	39	79.2	64	140.7	15	63.8	36	226.9	17
733	Bicycles	52.8	49	53.3	27	98.7	45	191.9	7	62.5	37	113.3	33
734	Aircraft	331.4	1	169.0	15	72.0	67	55.9	64	4.7	68	3.5	72
735	Ships and boats	14.5	70	13.0	59	102.0	41	82.4	47	423.6	3	347.1	8
812	Sanitary, plumbing and heating	97.3	32	100.6	19	104.2	38	77.4	50	407.1	5	92.9	40
821	Furniture	63.5	45	43.1	34	134.7	9	88.3	41	210.8	10	57.7	48
831	Travel goods and handbags	31.6	59	8.2	63	124.7	22	42.6	69	59.0	38	321.9	10
841	Clothing	29.5	61	20.0	51	136.6	6	43.3	68	87.2	30	245.9	15
842	Fur clothing	77.5	41	88.6	21	122.6	18	163.7	10	109.7	22	262.7	13
851	Footwear	7.2	71	26.5	48	147.4	4	47.9	66	15.9	63	601.4	1
861	Scientific, medical and optical	159.6	13	184.8	13	75.7	66	68.5	56	45.1	44	189.7	20
862	Photographic and cinematographic	148.1	15	28.1	46	106.5	36	95.3	36	4.7	69	20.3	66
891	Musical instruments	80.0	38	13.4	58	130.7	11	66.3	58	19.1	60	329.5	9
897	Jewelry and goldsmith	83.5	36	14.5	57	126.5	19	15.8	73	6.8	66	169.1	22

Table 4.2 Indices of export–import ratios

SITC		US Index	US Rank	Canada Index	Canada Rank	EEC Index	EEC Rank	UK Index	UK Rank	Sweden Index	Sweden Rank	Japan Index	Japan Rank
512	Organic chemicals	324.3	15	1478.6	3	83.0	55	68.3	60	37.3	37	46.4	59
513, 4, 5	Inorganic chemicals	113.3	34	109.1	9	106.6	33	123.4	39	16.2	57	184.8	50
531	Synthetic organic dyestuffs	109.1	36	0.0	72	121.5	19	201.1	26	1.2	72	20.7	66
533, 4	Pigments, paints and varnishes	545.4	10	7.3	51	66.9	66	773.6	8	14.2	60	45.2	60
541	Medical and pharmaceutical	169.6	24	16.7	32	82.6	58	686.0	9	13.1	62	43.1	61
551	Essential oils and perfumes	166.1	25	7.2	52	112.8	26	76.3	56	13.5	61	5.5	69
553	Perfumery and cosmetics	241.0	18	4.7	60	75.5	60	474.8	13	23.8	51	592.3	34
561	Fertilizers, manufacture	93.0	39	174.1	7	176.8	4	6.2	74	1.5	71	61.8	56
571	Explosives and pyrotechnic	63.1	48	2.0	64	146.0	12	6627.5	2	31.9	45	495.0	37
581	Plastic materials	1683.6	4	8.2	47	95.2	42	82.7	53	39.4	35	76.0	55
599	Chemical material and products	1367.8	5	7.8	49	76.3	59	104.7	46	23.3	52	4.6	71
611	Leather	88.4	41	107.4	10	104.6	34	100.0	47	43.4	32	241.9	46
612	Manufactures of leather	49.5	56	80.2	12	165.8	8	64.7	61	59.3	21	307.9	43
613	Fur skins	163.1	26	46.1	17	108.8	30	64.1	62	34.0	42	87.4	54
621	Materials of rubber	1879.8	3	16.8	31	112.2	27	109.9	44	49.5	25	313.1	42
629.1	Rubber tires and tubes	74.6	43	22.2	26	88.1	46	279.4	19	28.6	47	2093.1	21
629.0	Other rubber articles	91.1	40	4.3	61	64.5	68	1216.5	6	403.3	4	375.6	41
641	Paper and paperboard	36.6	59	1498.0	2	38.4	73	22.0	72	2683.1	2	2386.6	18
642	Articles made of paper	153.3	28	11.1	44	90.4	45	179.5	31	54.6	22	1109.2	31
651.2	Yarn of wool	2.0	72	7.8	48	102.5	37	251.0	22	15.8	58	1320.8	29
651.3	Cotton yarn, unbleached	50.3	54	—	72	110.1	28	22.1	71	0.2	74	—	1
651.4	Cotton yarn, bleached	35.3	60	0.3	69	146.0	11	186.2	29	12.8	63	10766.3	9
651.6	Yarn of synthetic fibers	504.6	11	35.6	20	72.0	62	219.9	25	2.7	69	1121.2	30
652	Cotton fabrics	65.9	46	22.7	25	139.8	13	22.6	70	50.9	24	11142.8	8
653.2	Woolen fabrics	1.1	73	11.7	42	64.1	68	424.5	16	4.1	68	449.4	38

Code	Commodity												
653.5, 6, 8	Synthetic fabrics	152.0	29	7.0	53	72.0	63	26.2	69	17.6	56	674.5	33
653.0	Other woven textile fabrics	22.3	63	20.4	28	83.8	51	123.3	41	77.0	18	5876.2	11
654	Tulle, lace and embroidery	51.9	52	3.2	62	100.1	38	75.2	51	34.8	40	3252.8	16
655	Special textile fabrics	49.9	55	12.7	40	104.2	36	232.5	24	38.6	36	2008.2	23
656.6	Blankets	50.7	53	1.9	65	84.6	50	119.1	42	40.6	33	3581.6	14
656.0	Made up textiles	156.0	27	6.9	54	104.3	35	56.9	64	45.1	30	2193.5	20
657	Floor coverings	18.0	66	3.0	63	108.1	31	145.6	36	21.1	55	3989.2	13
664	Glass	23.4	62	1.8	67	172.1	6	258.4	21	10.8	64	283.2	45
665	Glassware	103.9	38	0.5	68	129.6	17	73.5	58	155.3	7	417.4	40
666	Pottery	—	74	—	72	130.0	16	94.4	40	48.5	26	∞	2
671	Pig iron	68.3	45	622.4	4	114.4	24	84.7	51	131.5	10	11.5	68
673	Iron and steel bars	10.8	70	27.2	21	114.6	23	434.5	15	141.9	9	1638.1	25
674	Universals, plates and sheets	150.9	30	170.8	8	82.8	57	276.6	20	40.1	34	5018.8	12
675	Hoops and strips	53.1	51	—	72	87.1	48	2756.0	4	175.9	5	125.8	53
676	Railway construction material	424.4	12	569.0	5	54.6	69	5633.1	3	2749.4	1	177.4	52
678	Tubes, pipes and fittings	17.7	67	24.3	24	139.3	15	347.4	17	77.8	17	1516.3	27
682.2	Copper, wrought	14.1	69	212.7	6	91.2	44	576.1	10	98.4	13	417.5	39
683.2	Nickel, wrought	2671.2	2	26.9	22	87.8	47	77.1	55	21.8	54	2.8	73
684.2	Aluminum, wrought	61.0	50	89.9	11	154.4	9	95.3	48	47.1	28	13.5	67
685.2	Lead, wrought	40.6	58	35212.1	1	93.4	43	234.2	23	105.3	12	2442.3	17
686.2	Zinc, wrought	299.3	16	19.2	30	68.3	65	298.2	18	14.6	59	36.6	63
687.2	Tin, wrought	1340.1	6	0.0	72	83.3	54	∞	1	4.5	67	500.0	36
691.8	Manufactures of metal	62.9	49	8.6	45	121.0	20	187.2	28	74.7	20	787.4	32
711	Power generating machinery	403.7	14	46.4	16	71.6	64	182.5	30	44.3	31	51.1	57
712.0	Agricultural machinery	119.0	32	52.4	15	107.6	32	168.4	32	168.1	6	184.2	51
712.5	Tractors	194.4	22	4.9	58	34.6	74	2054.6	5	26.5	49	24.5	64
714	Office machinery	219.2	20	62.4	14	109.7	29	81.1	54	79.2	16	40.9	62
715	Metal working machinery	780.9	8	15.2	34	98.8	39	111.9	43	34.6	41	5.0	70
717.1	Textile machinery	147.1	31	12.8	39	97.5	41	144.0	37	26.7	48	10444.2	10
718.9	Other machinery	807.5	7	8.5	46	83.4	53	108.2	45	94.6	14	48.4	58
722.1	Electric generators	224.2	19	15.0	35	83.5	52	199.8	27	45.2	29	200.8	49
72.0	Other electric machinery	112.9	35	22.1	27	86.1	49	160.8	34	36.2	38	1397.2	28
731	Railway vehicles	648.8	9	11.7	43	43.3	71	147.9	35	51.5	23	557.5	35
732.1, 6	Automobiles	15.1	68	4.8	59	789.8	2	508.7	12	33.6	43	0.3	74
732.2, 5, 7	Buses, lorries and trucks	4209.3	1	5.2	56	72.7	61	1030.3	7	33.0	44	11177.5	7
732.0	Bodies, chassis and frames	284.4	17	13.2	37	39.2	72	451.4	14	93.0	15	21329.9	5

Table 4.2 (*continued*)

SITC		US		Canada		EEC		UK		Sweden		Japan
		Index	Rank	Index	Rank	Index	Rank	Index	Rank	Index	Rank	Index	Rank
733	Bicycles	29.6	61	14.0	36	120.8	21	527.3	11	35.5	39	1997.3	24
734	Aircraft	405.3	13	37.6	19	53.2	70	166.1	33	6.8	66	3.6	72
735	Ships and boats	104.0	37	13.0	38	124.1	18	43.1	66	153.9	8	222.7	48
812	Sanitary, plumbing and heating	212.2	21	24.8	23	82.9	56	89.1	50	412.4	3	2083.2	22
821	Furniture	68.4	44	15.6	33	114.1	25	127.2	40	126.8	11	3541.6	15
831	Travel goods and handbags	18.6	65	1.9	66	210.2	3	42.5	67	48.4	27	1609.8	26
841	Clothing	18.7	64	12.0	41	175.8	5	39.8	68	76.1	19	32751.2	4
842	Fur clothing	74.9	42	63.0	13	115.9	22	83.6	52	22.7	53	16686.4	6
851	Footwear	3.6	71	20.1	29	895.4	1	47.5	65	10.4	65	194489.9	3
861	Scientific, medical and optical	189.3	23	41.6	18	98.5	40	58.5	63	25.5	50	223.3	47
862	Photographic and cinematographic	114.5	33	7.7	50	139.5	14	140.7	38	2.2	70	22.7	65
891	Musical instruments	65.7	47	5.2	57	149.8	10	70.0	59	30.2	46	2311.4	19
897	Jewelry and goldsmith	44.4	57	6.2	55	170.3	7	16.2	73	0.8	73	306.4	44

weights to the two indicators.

$$\frac{x_{ij}^l}{x_i^l} \cdot \frac{x_{ij}^l}{x_i^l} \Big/ \frac{x_{ij}^o}{x_i^o} \tag{4}$$

$$\frac{1}{2}\left[\frac{x_{ij}^l}{x_i^l} + \frac{x_{ij}^l}{x_i^l} \cdot \frac{x_{ij}^l}{x_i^l} \Big/ \frac{x_{ij}^o}{x_i^o} \right] \tag{5}$$

In the case of export–import ratios, too, indices of relative level and relative growth have been calculated, when the procedure of 'normalization' has taken the form of dividing the export–import ratio of a country for a given commodity by that of the ten countries, taken together. After appropriate transformation, carried out on the basis of considerations similar to those relating to export shares, the following indicator has been derived:[10]

$$\frac{1}{2}\left[\frac{x_{ij}^l}{m_{ij}^l} + \frac{x_{ij}^l}{m_{ij}^l} \cdot \frac{x_{ij}^l}{m_{ij}^l} \Big/ \frac{x_{ij}^o}{m_{ij}^o} \right] \tag{6}$$

V

Export-performance indices provide an indication of relative advantages (and disadvantages) for individual countries but the dispersion of these indices – representing the 'markedness' of comparative advantage – is likely to differ from country to country. In general, one would expect that large countries, as well as countries that occupy a middle position in terms of technological development, would produce a great variety of commodities and hence show relatively small differences in export-performance indices. On the one hand, large countries usually possess a more balanced resource endowment and will have a home market sufficiently wide to permit the production of most industrial goods; on the other, countries that are in the middle of the range among industrial economies are likely to export technologically less developed products to economies at higher levels of industrialization and more sophisticated products to countries at lower levels of industrial development.

These expectations are by and large confirmed by empirical evidence. We find that the standard deviation of the export-performance indices is the smallest in countries that fulfill both conditions, such as the European Common Market (26.5) and the United Kingdom (55.5), while it is somewhat higher in the United States (70.2) which is at the upper end of the range in terms of technological advance. Further, the standard deviation of the export-performance indices is 119.6 in Sweden, the smallest of the countries under consideration in terms of home market for manufactured goods, 136.8 in industrially less developed Japan, and 205.1 in Canada – a country small in terms of domestic market and a relative newcomer among the industrial nations.

In the case of the European Common Market, the indices also reflect the lack of complete integration in this area. Despite the tariff reductions undertaken during the second period under consideration, the trade pattern of the countries participating in the EEC is still determined to a large extent by their comparative advantages, taken individually and, with the aggregation of national data, the dispersion of the indices is necessarily reduced. Nevertheless, differences in the relative position of Common Market industries are indicated by the fact that in the case of one-half of the 74 commodities under review the export-performance indices fall outside the 80 to 120 range.

The next problem concerns the similarities and dissimilarities shown in the inter-industry pattern of export performance and export–import ratios for the individual countries. In the case of the majority of these countries, there appears to be a considerable degree of correspondence between the two sets of indices: the rank correlation coefficients are 0.92 for Canada, 0.87 for Sweden, 0.78 for the United States, 0.75 for Japan, while lower values have been obtained for the United Kingdom (0.62) and the European Common Market (0.57). Various factors explain the observed differences in the correlation coefficients: the 'markedness' of comparative advantage, inter-industry differences in the degree of protection and, in the case of the Common Market, the problems related to the aggregation of national data.

Other things being equal, the more marked are inter-industry differences in trade performance, the greater will be the correspondence between the indices of export performance and of export–import ratios since the random error in the two sets of indices will be relatively small. The results will be further affected by the degree of skewness in the pattern of protection; in general, a high degree of protection of selected industries will reduce the correlation between the export performance and the export–import indices. Finally, the aggregation of data for the six Common Market countries will diminish the correspondence between the two indicators.

	Standard deviation of export-performance indices	Rank correlation coefficient between indices of export performance and of export–import ratios
United States	70.2	0.776
Canada	205.1	0.902
European Common Market	26.5	0.567
United Kingdom	55.5	0.621
Sweden	119.6	0.829
Japan	136.8	0.753

Among the countries under consideration, Canada shows the greatest dispersion of the export-performance indices as well as the highest correlation coefficient between the two sets of indices. With the exception of shipbuilding, there is little evidence of the distorting effects of protection on export–import ratios; this result is explained by the fact that, while tariffs are generally high in Canada, large inter-industry disparities in duties are not observed.

Japan, the country with the second highest standard deviation of export-performance indices, occupies fourth place as far as the correlation coefficient between the two indicators is concerned. The explanation lies in the high degree of protection applied to selected manufacturing industries that has distorted the ranking of the export–import ratios. The effects of protection are manifest in the case of perfumery and cosmetics, paper, furniture, woolen yarn and textile machinery, as well as in regard to wrought lead and tin, where high tariffs and/or quotas have virtually excluded all imports.

In turn, low tariffs contribute to the high correlation observed between indices of export performance and of export–import ratios in Sweden, and the distorting effects of protection on export–import ratios are observable only in a few industries in the United States. The US tariff appears to be nearly prohibitive for synthetic rubber material and synthetic fabrics, while subsidies to domestic production reduce the imports of ships.

High tariffs on imports of selected commodities have contributed to the relatively low degree of correlation between the two sets of indicators in the United Kingdom, however. The 19 percent tariff on glass and the 24 percent, duty on synthetic yarn are largely responsible for the small imports of these commodities; more important, the wide differences shown between indices of export performance and of export–import ratios for all kinds of steel products appear to be due to the fact that, among the industrial countries, Britain has the highest tariffs on steel.

Tariffs and quotas account for the relatively high export–import ratios for cotton fabrics and a few other products in the European Common Market, too. Nevertheless, a consideration of individual commodities indicates that, in the case of the EEC, the error possibilities introduced by the aggregation of national data have had a greater influence on the observed differences between the two sets of indices than did protection. The export–import ratio was reduced by large German imports of woolen yarn and fabrics, for example, while after integration an increasing part of German demand may be satisfied by production in the partner countries.

VI

Despite the observed differences between indices of export performance and of export–import ratios, the ranking of products at the top and at the bottom of the list is reasonably clear for all the countries under consideration. Taking account of import tariffs and other influences affecting export–import ratios, the 'revealed' comparative advantage of the countries in question can then be indicated.

The United States appears to have relative advantages with respect to chemical materials and products, aircraft, wrought tin and nickel, as well as with regard to railway vehicles, metal-working machinery and plastic materials. On the other hand, the US is at a disadvantage in the production of woolen yarn and fabrics, cotton yarn,[11] footwear and pottery, followed by blankets, carpets, simple forms of steel (bars, rods, sections and wire) and ships.

Cotton and woolen yarns, floor coverings and pottery also appear on the list of products in which Canada has a comparative disadvantage; further commodities on this list are hoops and strips of iron and steel, wrought tin, synthetic dyes and glassware. At the same time, Canadians possess relative advantages in the manufacturing of paper, organic chemicals, lead, copper, aluminum, pig iron, railway construction material and fertilizers.

While the 'aggregation problem' makes the evaluation of comparative advantage more difficult in the case of the EEC countries, it appears clear that the Common Market has relative advantages in manufacturing passenger cars, footwear, clothing, glass and musical instruments, and disadvantages in producing paper, rubber goods, tractors, power generators, railway equipment and aircraft. In turn, tractors, buses and trucks, pigments and paints, and explosives are on the top of Britain's list, followed by woolen fabrics, bicycles, wrought tin and copper. At the same time, Britain appears to be at a comparative disadvantage in the manufacture of fertilizers, jewelry, travel goods, paper, cotton and synthetic fabrics, and clothing.

By comparison, Sweden possesses relative advantages with regard to railway construction material, paper, ships, plumbing and heating fixtures, lead, copper and rubber goods, and disadvantages in cotton and synthetic yarns, woolen fabrics, synthetic dyes, fertilizers and photographic equipment. Finally, we find the Japanese ahead in exporting footwear, cotton yarn and fabrics, clothing, pottery, and – surprisingly – buses and trucks, while they appear to be at a disadvantage in the manufacture of aircraft, tractors, wrought nickel and zinc, essential oils and chemical products.

The reader will note that the commodities at the two ends of the comparative scales are, with few exceptions, standardized products or non-durable consumer goods. This is hardly surprising since, in the case of homogeneous products, national product differentiation plays a relatively small role and trade patterns are determined largely by inter-country differences in relative costs, while low labor costs (Japan) and high labor quality (EEC) are of importance in regard to non-durable consumer goods. On the other hand, medical and pharmaceutical products, scientific and optical instruments, as well as electrical and much of non-electrical machinery, are characterized by specialization within commodity categories, and most industrial countries export *and* import them. Still, we can provide an indication of the pattern of comparative advantages in these commodity groups if we examine the relative position of the countries in question with regard to the various groups of products.

In the chemical group, Canada appears to have comparative advantages with respect to organic and inorganic chemicals and manufactured fertilizers, the United Kingdom in synthetic dyes, paints and varnishes, medical and pharmaceutical preparations, perfumes and cosmetics, and explosives, while the United States has a leading position in the exportation of medical and pharmaceutical preparations, plastic materials and other chemical materials and products. In turn, Sweden and Japan are at a comparative disadvantage in most chemicals, and Canada in the highly processed products of this group.

Among material-intensive commodities, Canada leads in leather and leather goods, with the United States at the bottom of the list. At the same time, the United Kingdom and Japan have relative advantages in the manufacture of rubber tyres, while in other rubber goods they are surpassed by Sweden. In both instances, Canada is at a disadvantage. In turn, Canada and Sweden are in a leading position with regard to paper, in the production of which the European Common Market and the United Kingdom have a decided disadvantage. Finally, the EEC is in the most favorable position in the case of glass, Sweden leads in the exportation of glassware, and Japan in pottery.

Turning to textile products, we find Japan possesses relative advantages in manufacturing cotton yarn and thread, cotton and synthetic fabrics, tulle and lace, made-up textile fabrics, blankets and floor coverings; however, she cedes first place to the European Economic Community in the case of wool yarn, to the United States in synthetic yarns, and to the United Kingdom in woven woolen fabrics. On the other hand, Sweden and Canada appear to be at a comparative disadvantage with respect to most textile products, the United States in cotton yarn, woolen yarns and fabrics, tulle and lace, blankets and floor coverings, and the United Kingdom in cotton yarn and thread, while the European Common Market occupies the middle position in most cases.

By and large, the United States and the United Kingdom are at a disadvantage in iron and steel products, when export–import ratios in Britain are often raised as a result of high tariffs. Within this group of products, Sweden leads in the highly manufactured forms of iron and steel (hoops and strips, tubes, pipes and fittings) and shares first place with the Common Market in iron and steel bars and with Canada in railway construction material. In turn, Canada has the lead in the case of pig iron and also in universals, plates and sheets of iron and steel.

As to wrought ferrous metals, our previous discussion has indicated relative advantages for Canada and Britain in copper, the United States in nickel, Canada in aluminum and lead, the United Kingdom in zinc, and the United States and the United Kingdom in tin. Countries at a comparative disadvantage in these metals are the United States with regard to copper and lead, Japan in nickel, aluminum and zinc, Sweden in zinc and tin, and Canada also in tin.

We find further that the United Kingdom and the United States are in a favorable position with regard to much non-electrical machinery. The United Kingdom occupies first place in the exportation of power-generating machinery, textile machinery, as well as tractors, although Canada is ahead in other agricultural machinery. At the same time, the United States leads in metal-working machinery, office machinery and other non-electrical machinery, with Sweden occupying the second place in the last two instances. Finally, with the exception of textile and office machinery, Japan and the EEC appear to be at a comparative disadvantage in this category of products and Canada is also behind in several commodity groups.

The classification employed in this study with regard to electrical machinery is rather aggregated; by reason of the unavailability of statistical information in a more detailed breakdown, we have been able to distinguish only two commodity groups: electrical generators and other electrical machinery. The United Kingdom and the United States appear to have a comparative advantage with regard to the first while Japan is ahead in the second – rather heterogeneous – category. In both instances, Canada and Sweden are at a disadvantage.

Turning to transport equipment, we find the United States in the lead in the case of aircraft and railway vehicles, she falls behind Japan in the exportation of bodies and frames of automotive vehicles, and is at a decided disadvantage in shipbuilding, bicycles and passenger automobiles. In turn, the countries of the Common Market have a strong lead in car exports, but are behind in regard to most other types of transportation equipment. Finally, Sweden and Japan appear to have a comparative advantage in shipbuilding while the United Kingdom and Japan share in first place in the case of buses and trucks, as well as in bicycles.

Among household accessories, Sweden possesses relative advantages in sanitary and plumbing equipment and furniture, the United Kingdom being at a disadvantage in the former case, and the United States and Canada in the latter. Turning to non-durable consumer goods, we find the United States, the United Kingdom and Canada at a comparative disadvantage in regard to clothing, footwear and leather goods; in all three instances Japanese producers have a leading position. with the European Common Market a close second in the case of clothing and footwear.

In turn, the United States has comparative advantages in the manufacture of different types of precision instruments, such as scientific, medical and optical equipment, as well as photographic and cinematographic equipment. The United Kingdom appears to be at a disadvantage in the former case, Canada, Sweden and – surprisingly – Japan, in the latter. Finally, Japan and the Common Market countries lead in the exportation of musical instruments and the EEC in jewelry; Canada, Sweden and the United Kingdom are far behind.

VII

We have set out to examine the 'revealed' comparative advantage of the main industrial countries in manufactured goods by utilizing available information on their trade performance (export shares and export–import ratios) with regard to 74 commodity categories. This method appears to be the most satisfactory in its application to standardized products and non-durable consumer goods but has given less clearcut results in the case of machinery and precision instruments.

It appears that cost differences largely determine the export performance of industries manufacturing standardized products that are usually found at the extremes of the comparative range, although non-price factors bear influence on trade in steel and non-ferrous metals. Considerations of the continuity of shipments and international differences in specifications seem to restrict the imports of steel into the United States, for example, while ownership relations affect the pattern of trade in non-ferrous metals. At the same time, inter-industry disparities in tariff levels have a differential impact on export–import ratios.

Cost differences often find their origin in the availability and cost of raw materials in the case of material-intensive commodities while labor costs appear to be the main factor determining relative advantages with regard to textile products. Exceptions are woolen fabrics and synthetic yarns where, respectively, quality differences and technological advance play an important role. Labor costs and quality differences are of importance in the case of other non-durable consumer goods, too.

In turn, specialization within commodity categories is observable with regard to machinery and precision instruments. While differences in the level of technology are often of considerable importance, and labor costs greatly affect the determination of comparative advantage in the case of light electrical equipment, most industrial countries export *and* import these commodities and relative advantages are generally less pronounced. This conclusion may be objected to on the grounds that these commodity groups could be made more homogeneous if an adequately detailed statistical breakdown were available. A consideration of the pattern of trade in countries that publish a more detailed trade classification suggests, however, that intra-group specialization exists within any meaningful commodity category.

At any rate, although in the presence of product differentiation, comparative advantages with regard to machinery and precision instruments are not indicated as clearly as with regard to standardized products and non-durable consumer goods, this should not mean that a reduction or elimination of tariffs would not lead to an expansion of trade in the former group of products. Rather, whereas the observed differences in relative advantages provide an indication of cost savings obtainable through the reallocation of resources after a reduction of tariffs for standardized products, decreases in duties would give rise to a more extended differentiation and specialization in machinery and precision instruments.

It appears, then, that the benefits of international specialization are of a different character depending on the category of products under consideration. While the traditional gains derived from substituting cheaper imports for more expensive domestic merchandise are relevant with regard to simple manufactures, economies of scale obtainable through specialization within commodity categories are likely to provide the main benefit of tariff reductions in the case of more sophisticated products.[12] It goes without saying that the dividing line between the two groups of products is not clearcut; it is difficult to classify transport equipment, for example, and national product differentiation is of importance in the case of non-durable consumer goods, too. In connection with the latter, mention should also be made of improvements in consumer welfare due to the increased exchange of consumer goods following a reduction in tariffs.

This discussion indicates some of the deficiencies of the traditional theories of international trade that attempt to explain international specialization, and to indicate the gains from specialization, by the use of a single classifying principle – should this be inter-country differences in factor proportions or in production functions. Comparative advantages appear to be the outcome of a number of factors, some measurable, others not, some easily pinned down, others less so. One wonders, therefore, whether more could not be gained if, instead of enunciating general principles and trying to apply these to explain actual trade flows, one took the observed pattern of trade as a point of departure, and subsequently attempted to find the main influences that have determined the pattern.

This chapter may be considered as a step in the application of the latter alternative. Its limited scope permitted but a censory survey of the possible determinants of comparative advantages, and it may be usefully followed by more detailed investigations. It would appear desirable to explore the principal influences determining trade flows in more detail and one may also wish to examine the stability of the trade performance indices, the effects of changes in relative prices on these indices, or the relationship between the level of technological development and comparative advantage.

Finally, note should be taken of various limitations of the analysis that affect the results to a lesser or greater extent. Mention has already been made of the often arbitrary choice of the commodity groups that has been imposed upon us by the availability of statistical data. The restriction of the investigation to manufactured goods also creates certain inconveniences in comparing the relative position of the industrial countries with regard to individual commodities, given that the United States and Canada appear to have comparative advantages *vis-à-vis* Western Europe in a number of agricultural products and raw materials. Also, it has not been possible to take account of the advantages provided by Commonwealth preference to British exports of various manufactured goods. It is hoped, however, that the chapter in its present form may also be of some interest to students of international trade.

NOTES

1. Deborah Paige and Gottfried Bombach (1959) *A Comparison of National Output and Productivity of the United Kingdom and the United States*, Paris, OEEC.
2. Theodore R. Gates and Fabian Linden (1961) *Costs and Competition: American Experience Abroad*, New York, National Industrial Conference Board.
3. K. J. Arrow, H. B. Chenery, B. S. Minhas and R. M. Solow (1961) 'Capital–Labour Substitution and Economic Efficiency', *Review of Economics and Statistics*, August, pp. 225–50.
4. On the importance of inter-country differences in the cost of intermediate products for determining relative costs, see Arrow *et al.*, *op. cit.*, p. 244, and *Costs and Competition: American Experience Abroad*, Ch. III and VIII.
5. Take, for example, the case when in industries A, B and C, labor requirements per unit of output are 1, 1, 1, capital requirements 4, 3, 2 and material requirements 2, 6, 5. The ranking of industries with respect to capital and labor inputs will be A, B, C, for material and labor inputs B, C, A and for material and capital inputs C, B, A.
6. G. O. D. MacDougall (1951) 'British and American Exports: A Study Suggested by the Theory of Comparative Costs', Part I, *Economic Journal*, December, pp. 694–8, and Bela Balassa (1963). 'An Empirical Demonstration of Classical Comparative Cost Theory', *Review of Economics and Statistics*, August, pp. 231–8.
7. Relative export performance has been used as an indicator of comparative advantage by H. H. Liesner in examining the possible effect of entry into the Common Market on British industry (H. H. Liesner (1958) 'The European Common Market and British Industry', *Economic Journal*, June, pp. 302–16). By comparison, in the present inquiry we have extended the scope of investigation to cover the main industrial countries which has necessitated a reappraisal of the methodology used by Liesner.
8. Note, however, that inasmuch as in the first period under consideration the trade pattern of the EEC countries was determined by their comparative advantage, taken individually, a certain degree of 'aggregation bias' has been introduced in the results.
9. Explanation of symbols:
   X = exports
   x = relative share of exports
   Superscripts: o = average for the years 1953–5
   l = average for the years 1960–2
   Subscripts: i = country i
   n = ten industrial countries taken together
   j = product j.
10. In the equation, m stands for relative export–import ratios.

11. For purposes of the analysis, unbleached and bleached cotton goods have been considered together.
12. Economies of scale are understood here in a broader sense to include cost reductions obtained through the lengthening of production runs obtainable by consequence of the reduction of product variety in individual plants.

5 • 'REVEALED' COMPARATIVE ADVANTAGE REVISITED

An analysis of relative export shares of the industrial countries, 1953–71

THE CONCEPT AND ITS APPLICATION

The concept of 'revealed' comparative advantage, introduced by the author over a decade ago (1965, reproduced as Chapter 4 in this volume),[1] pertains to the relative trade performances of individual countries in particular commodities. On the assumption that the commodity pattern of trade reflects inter-country differences in relative costs as well as in non-price factors, this is assumed to 'reveal' the comparative advantage of the trading countries.

In the earlier chapter, data on exports and on export–import ratios were used to indicate the 'revealed' comparative advantage of the major industrial countries (United States, Canada, European Common Market, United Kingdom, Sweden and Japan) in manufactured goods. It was noted, however, that data on relative export performance are more appropriate for the purpose at hand, since export–import ratios are affected by tariffs and other protective measures whose incidence on individual commodities varies from country to country (1965, p. 104).

In the present chapter, exclusive reliance has been placed on export performance and 'revealed' comparative advantage indices have been derived from data on relative export shares. The indices have been calculated by dividing a country's share in the exports of a given commodity category by its share in the combined exports of manufactured goods of the 13 industrial countries under consideration. Thus, an index number of 110 will mean that the export share of the particular country in the commodity category in question is 10 percent higher than its share in the total exports of manufactured goods of the group.

Calculations have been made in the 73 product-group breakdown used in the earlier chapter for the years 1953, 1962, and 1971.[2] The results are

Research on this chapter was carried out under contract with the US Department of Commerce, Contract No. 6-28705. The author is indebted to Wendy Takacs, Ifzal Ali and André Sapir for assistance at various stages of the work. First published in *Manchester School*, December 1977.

reported in Appendix Table 5.1 in the form of rankings of 'revealed' comparative advantage indices for the United States, Canada, the European Common Market, the United Kingdom, the Continental member countries of EFTA, and Japan. Rankings for the individual EEC countries (Belgium, France, Germany, Italy, and the Netherlands) and the Continental EFTA countries (Austria, Denmark, Norway and Sweden), and the underlying comparative advantage indices are available from the author. Appendix Table 5.2 contains the product classification scheme utilized in the chapter.

The first part of the chapter will examine the 'revealed' comparative advantage of the 11 industrial countries in research-intensive products. This will be followed by an analysis of the structure of comparative advantage in the individual countries, and the extent of specialization and diversification in their manufactured exports. Throughout the discussion, the situation exist-ing in 1971 as well as changes over time will be considered.

'REVEALED' COMPARATIVE ADVANTAGE IN RESEARCH-INTENSIVE PRODUCTS

The product cycle hypothesis endeavors to explain the pattern of US trade as a dynamic process, in which the United States starts to produce and to export new goods embodying advanced techniques, and the place of production gradually shifts to other countries of the world. Erik Hoffmeyer (1958) suggested that the ever-renewing technological advantage of the United States provides an explanation for the dollar shortage in the early post-war period; in turn, Albert Hirschman (1960) expressed the view that the shortening of the US technological lag accounts for the end of the dollar shortage and the emergence of the dollar glut.

These contributions, as well as the formalization of the product cycle hypothesis by Raymond Vernon (1966), explicitly or implicitly raise questions as to the length of the product cycle and the ability of US industry continuously to generate new products. Another question, much neglected in the literature, is whether and to what extent the United States can re-establish its superiority in regard to particular products through product or process innovations. A case in point is the computer industry, where new generations of computers have made their appearance by the time the US comparative advantage might have been lost in the previous ones.

While these questions can be fully dealt with only in product level studies,[3] data on the changing pattern of comparative advantage in research-intensive industries can shed some light on the ability of the United States to renew its technological lead. This approach is followed in the present chapter, which considers changes in relative advantages in research-intensive industries during the post-war period.

Following earlier studies, research-intensity has been defined in terms of the share of research and development expenditures in total sales and the ratio of R&D scientists and engineers to all employees (Gruber *et al.*, 1967, and Keesing, 1967). Industries where R&D expenditures accounted for more than 3.5 percent of total sales *and* R&D scientists and engineers accounted for more than 3.5 percent of all employees in 1967 in the United States have been considered research intensive.[4] In terms of the trade classification scheme utilized in this chapter, the industries (product groups) in question include organic chemicals (SITC 512), inorganic chemicals (51.0), medical and pharmaceutical products (541), office machinery (714), miscellaneous electrical machinery (72.0), electrical power equipment (722), aircraft (734), scientific, medical and optical instruments (861), and photographic and cinemato-graphic supplies (862).

As the results of Table 5.1 indicate, the United States has not only maintained but has increased its relative advantage in research-intensive products during the period under consideration. To begin with, apart from inorganic chemicals in 1953, all research-intensive industry groups had higher than the median rank among the 73 product groups in all the three years under consideration.[5] Moreover, the average rank of research-intensive products, taken as a group, has increased over time. It was 18 in 1953, increased to 15 in 1962, and was just under 10 in 1971.

Among individual industries, aircraft manufacture continued to occupy first place on the US comparative advantage scale during the period under consideration. Office machinery moved up from ninth to third place, while electrical power equipment maintained its place among the first ten. Also, considerable improvements are shown in the relative positions of organic chemicals, inorganic chemicals, scientific, medical and optical instruments, and photographic and cinematographic supplies.

Exceptions are medical and pharmaceutical products and miscellaneous electrical machinery which have lost ground over time. In the first case, Denmark, Germany, the Netherlands and the United Kingdom have emerged as major competitors. In turn, the second category includes radios and television sets that have low research intensity and the United States has a low share in their exports. However, radios and television sets could not be shown separately for lack of data.

All in all, six research-intensive industries rank among the first ten in terms of the 'revealed' comparative advantage of the United States among the 73 product groups. The other four product groups in the first ten also have above-average research intensity. They include, with their 1971 ranks on the scale of 'revealed' comparative advantage in parentheses, agricultural machinery (No. 7), power generating machinery (No. 4), railroad vehicles (No. 7), and automobile bodies, chassis and frames (No. 9).

The evidence provided points to the strong, and increasing, comparative advantage of the United States in research-intensive products. By contrast, with few exceptions, research-intensive industries do not rank among the first

Table 5.1 Ranking of 'revealed' comparative advantage indices of the industrial countries in research-intensive products

SITC	United States			Canada			Common Market			United Kingdom			Continental EFTA			Japan		
	1953	1962	1971	1953	1962	1971	1953	1962	1971	1953	1962	1971	1953	1962	1971	1953	1962	1971
512	16	26	11	53	17	43	48	45	41	53	54	49	61	55	60	57	35	24
51.0	46	25	6	6	9	12	28	39	47	43	35	53	22	23	31	38	38	41
541	7	12	19	29	36	40	49	53	38	48	26	9	53	60	54	44	49	62
714	9	10	3	21	19	18	54	57	40	54	57	40	46	64	69	63	67	35
72.0	15	20	23	23	24	22	46	50	48	38	31	47	35	38	42	53	22	8
722	8	6	8	44	40	15	72	65	68	28	30	45	69	51	53	66	33	40
734	1	1	1	14	10	13	73	64	70	65	69	55	73	70	70	71	73	71
861	32	15	10	39	16	54	62	69	69	56	52	29	30	57	55	14	15	14
862	30	16	5	12	35	32	8	10	21	42	40	24	66	71	71	58	58	46
Average	18	15	10	27	23	28	49	50	49	47	44	39	51	54	56	52	43	38

SITC	Belgium			France			Germany			Italy			Netherlands		
	1953	1962	1971	1953	1962	1971	1953	1962	1971	1953	1962	1971	1953	1962	1971
512	49	57	31	49	28	53	7	10	29	33	23	45	41	12	9
51.0	24	33	29	25	22	37	17	23	42	19	27	50	29	41	27
541	47	54	46	24	25	24	45	42	21	36	34	27	37	21	24
714	66	71	67	52	37	39	31	40	44	13	12	29	46	31	46
72.0	39	45	51	55	48	56	32	28	40	44	44	31	16	13	23
722	70	61	66	73	51	42	12	18	6	63	52	56	73	52	47
734	71	62	70	71	45	61	73	73	73	68	48	62	57	49	56
861	60	68	69	44	56	58	2	6	22	40	54	55	49	44	26
862	6	7	11	47	47	45	46	46	41	42	35	54	62	55	45
Average	48	51	49	49	40	46	29	32	35	40	37	45	46	35	34

SITC	Austria			Denmark			Norway			Sweden		
	1953	1962	1971	1953	1962	1971	1953	1962	1971	1953	1962	1971
512	59	54	54	20	16	31	29	24	46	31	39	53
51.0	35	41	55	50	57	60	5	8	7	19	38	43
541	61	52	53	3	4	8	18	49	52	37	45	42
714	66	67	66	28	40	47	13	33	62	5	9	21
72.0	29	28	38	18	21	24	33	42	23	17	18	19
722	64	43	51	8	20	22	72	41	45	6	4	48
734	71	68	68	71	65	68	55	50	58	54	69	47
861	27	45	52	36	23	33	38	55	55	21	36	38
862	62	64	67	62	64	63	60	71	68	40	64	54
Average	53	51	56	33	34	40	36	42	46	26	36	41

512 Organic chemicals
51.0 Inorganic chemicals
541 Medical and pharmaceutical products
714 Office machinery
72.0 Miscellaneous electrical machinery
722 Electrical power equipment
734 Aircraft
861 Scientific, medical and optical instruments
862 Photographic and cinematographic supplies

Source: See Appendix Table 5.1.

ten on the comparative advantage scale of the other industrial countries. The exceptions are electrical power equipment in Germany, medical and pharmaceutical products in Denmark and the United Kingdom, inorganic chemicals in Norway, and miscellaneous electrical equipment in Japan. In the latter case, radios and television sets dominate, which, as noted above, have relatively low research intensity.

Canada occupies second place in terms of the average ranking of research-intensive products on its comparative advantage scale (28 in 1971). Its relatively favourable position is explained by the existence of a considerable intra-industry specialization and the exchange of parts, components and accessories in machinery and transport equipment within the North American area.

Among European countries, average ranks for research-intensive products in 1971 were the highest in the Netherlands (34), Germany (35) and the United Kingdom (39). These countries, however, show different trends over time. The Netherlands has greatly improved its position in the exports of research-intensive products. An improvement is shown also in the United Kingdom, while Germany's relative position in these products has deteriorated. These results do not correspond to expectations, at least as far as the latter two countries are concerned, and require explanation.

Among research-intensive exports, the Netherlands has lost ground only in the miscellaneous electrical machinery category. In turn, considerable improvements are shown in the relative position of organic chemicals, inorganic chemicals, medical and pharmaceutical products, scientific, medical and optical instruments, and photographic and cinematographic supplies. A contributing factor may have been the importance of multinational corporations in the Netherlands that carry out research on a large scale.

The operations of multinational corporations may also account for the fact that medical and pharmaceutical products, office equipment, and scientific, medical and optical instruments have moved up on the comparative advantage scale in the United Kingdom. In turn, organic chemicals, inorganic chemicals, and scientific, medical and optical instruments, which used to be among the top performers in Germany, have lost ground in German exports, and these changes have been only partly offset by the improvements experienced in regard to medical and pharmaceutical products and electrical power equipment. Rather, as noted below, Germany has increasingly assumed a comparative advantage in metal products and machinery, which have lower research intensity.

Among the other European countries, the average ranks of research-intensive exports range between 40 (Denmark) and 56 (Austria), i.e. in all cases below the median on the comparative advantage scale. A deterioration in the position of research-intensive products is shown in Austria, Denmark, Norway and Sweden and, to a lesser extent, Italy, with little change indicated in Belgium and France.

Finally, the average rank of research-intensive products increased in Japan from 52 in 1953 to 43 in 1962 and, again, to 38 in 1971. In a large part, these results are explained by the substantial changes occurring in the position of miscellaneous electrical machinery, dominated by radio and television sets which, as noted above, have relatively low research intensity. Nevertheless, the relative position of organic chemicals, office equipment, electrical power equipment, and photographic and cinematographic supplies has also improved in Japan.

THE 'REVEALED' COMPARATIVE ADVANTAGE OF THE INDIVIDUAL COUNTRIES

The counterpart of the improved performance of research-intensive industries has been a decline in the US comparative advantage in non-durable goods and their inputs which have low research intensity. These products, including woolen yarn, synthetic yarn, textile fabrics, blankets, pottery, furniture, travel goods and handbags, clothing, fur clothing, and footwear ranked between 60 and 73 on the US comparative advantage scale in 1971.

Among the lowest-ranking products, two do not fit this classification. They are iron and steel bars (65) and ships and boats (68). In the first case, technological advances have been made mostly in foreign countries; in the second, the labour intensity of the production process has created a comparative disadvantage for the United States.

Within the manufacturing sector, Canada's comparative advantage lies in the processing of its abundant raw materials. Paper maintained first place throughout the period under consideration; in 1971, it was immediately followed by fertilizers and fur clothing. With the increased processing of metals that had earlier been exported in an unwrought form, wrought zinc and wrought lead also rank high on the scale of 'revealed' comparative advantage in Canada. After placing low in earlier years, automobiles and automobile bodies, chassis, and frames, too, ranked high in 1971 as a result of Canada's participation in an automotive agreement with the United States. Finally, exports to the United States in the framework of specialization within multinational firms may largely account for the improved position – and the high rank – of tractors and power generators.

The 'revealed' comparative advantage of the European Common Market mirrors the US disadvantage in a variety of non-durable consumer goods and their inputs. The highest-ranking products include woolen and cotton yarn, woolen fabrics, blankets, floor coverings, glass, travel goods, and handbags, clothing, footwear, and jewelry. Apart from the improvement in the relative position of the last-mentioned two categories, these product groups show little change in their ranking indicating that, within the industrial country group, the Common Market traditionally had a comparative advantage in their exports. The same conclusion applies to iron and steel bars, which ranked eighth in 1971.

Among the Common Market countries, however, there are considerable differences in ranking according to 'revealed' comparative advantage. Of the afore-mentioned products, Belgium's comparative advantage is concentrated in woolen yarn, cotton yarn, floor coverings, glass, and iron and steel bars; woolen yarn and cotton yarn rank high in France; cotton yarn, blankets, and floor coverings in the Netherlands; and travel goods and handbags, clothing, and footwear and jewelry in Italy.

A conspicuous omission is Germany; none of the first ten product groups on the EEC list is among the first 15 in Germany's comparative advantage rankings. Rather, the first ten in Germany include paints (synthetic organic dyestuffs and pigments, paints and varnishes), metal products (steel tubes, pipes, and fittings, wrought lead, and metal manufactures), machinery (metal working, textile and miscellaneous machinery), buses, lorries, and trucks; and furniture.

Among the other EEC countries, France appears to have comparative advantage mainly in non-durable consumer goods and their inputs, including perfumes (essential oils and perfumes and perfumery and cosmetics), cotton products (unbleached and bleached yarn and tulle, lace and embroidery), leather, rubber tyres and tubes, glassware and fur clothing. Italy's comparative advantage also seems to lie in non-durable consumer goods and their inputs, chiefly those made of leather (leather manufactures, travel goods and handbags, and shoes), and textiles (cotton yarn, woolen fabrics, blankets, and clothing), as well as jewelry.

In turn, in conformity with the hypotheses put forward by Linder (1961) and Drèze (1960), the smaller EEC member countries tend to specialize in standardized products.[6] In Belgium's case these include fertilizers, textiles (wool yarn, floor coverings), glass, iron and steel products (bars, universals, plates and sheets, and hoops and strips), and non-ferrous metals (wrought copper, lead, and zinc) while in the Netherlands chemicals (organic chemicals, pigments, paints, and varnishes, essential oils and perfumes, and miscellaneous chemical products), paper articles, textile products (cotton yarn, synthetic yarn, cotton fabrics, and floor coverings), and wrought tin predominate.

Standardized commodities predominate also in the exports of the small Continental EFTA countries. In Austria, Norway and Sweden their production largely entails the transformation of domestic materials such as hides and skins (leather manufactures), fur (fur manufactures), wood (paper and paper manufactures), and iron ore (pig iron and steel products). One can include in this category aluminum that makes use of cheap hydro-electricity.

Among these product groups, fertilizers, fur manufactures, pig iron, and aluminum rank high in Norway; leather manufactures occupy first place and steel products are also high in Austria's comparative advantage ranking;

Austria, Norway and Sweden have a strong comparative advantage in paper and paper products; and fur skin manufactures and pig iron are high on Sweden's list.

The 'revealed' comparative advantage of the three countries is explained by the availability of a variety of raw materials and energy. In turn, Denmark, a country poor in natural resources, has a higher share of consumer goods in its exports, including sanitary, plumbing, and heating equipment, furniture, clothing and fur clothing. Finally, ships and boats rank high in the exports of the Nordic countries while tulle, lace and embroidery are traditional Austrian exports.

In line with its long-standing role in the marketing of processed non-ferrous metals, made from imported ores or metal, the United Kingdom appears to have a comparative advantage in the exports of wrought copper, nickel and tin. It also maintained its predominance in woolen fabrics while losing its comparative advantage in other woven fabrics, cotton yarn and floor coverings. Finally, the data show the United Kingdom to have a comparative advantage in a variety of disparate products, including explosives, fur skin manufactures, pottery, power generating machinery, and agricultural machinery.

Japan maintained its comparative advantage in two disparate product groups, pottery as well as ships and boats, during the period under consideration. It also established a comparative advantage in miscellaneous electrical machinery (mainly radios and TV sets), travel goods and handbags, and musical instruments. Finally, within the textile category, Japan's comparative advantage shifted from cotton to synthetic products. One may add that, among the countries under study, Japan showed the largest changes in the pattern of its comparative advantage.

SPECIALIZATION AND DIVERSIFICATION IN MANUFACTURED PRODUCTS

The next question concerns the degree of specialization and diversification of manufactured exports. This can be indicated by the standard deviation of the 'revealed' comparative advantage indices and may be explained by reference to the size of domestic markets, the level of technological development, natural resource endowments, and the effects of economic integration. These will be taken up in turn.

It can be expected that large countries will tend to have a more diversified export structure, mainly because their large domestic markets permit the exploitation of economies of scale in a wide range of industries. The results for 1953 tend to confirm these expectations. Thus, the United States had the smallest standard deviation of the comparative advantage indices, followed

Table 5.2 Standard deviations of 'revealed' comparative advantage indices

	1953	1962	1971
United States	52.5	56.5	60.7
Canada	150.5	166.3	104.7
Common Market	128.5	90.3	84.6
United Kingdom	56.3	52.3	67.7
Continental EFTA	210.9	159.4	157.9
Japan	141.7	120.3	78.5
Belgium	169.1	159.4	123.0
France	102.3	79.1	70.6
Germany	75.3	45.8	47.7
Italy	189.4	115.9	128.9
Netherlands	178.1	92.9	78.8
Austria	200.8	202.8	165.3
Denmark	114.8	130.6	135.9
Norway	317.3	283.3	304.3
Sweden	101.1	93.4	130.4

Source: See Appendix Table 5.1.

by the United Kingdom and Germany, with France slightly behind. At the other end of the spectrum, Austria, Belgium, the Netherlands and Norway had the largest standard deviations of these indices (Table 5.2).

There are several exceptions to the association between size and diversification, however, for which explanations based on a knowledge of those countries' economic structure can be tentatively suggested. For example, the lack of natural resources may explain the relatively high degree of diversification enjoyed by Denmark, while the availability of raw materials and energy resources, conversely, may explain the relatively high degree of specialization evident in the cases of Austria, Canada and Norway. Among the larger industrial countries, exceptions were Italy and Japan, where the relatively low level of technological development during the period under consideration may explain the high extent of specialization in exports.

The time pattern of the standard deviations is of further interest. In the United States, the results show a slight decline in the extent of export diversification in conjunction with increased reliance on research-intensive exports. By contrast, with growing industrial sophistication, the Japanese export structure has become increasingly diversified. These results are consistent with the hypothesis, advanced in the earlier chapter, that the extent of export diversification tends to increase with the degree of technological development but a reversal takes place at higher levels (Balassa, 1965).

In turn, the increased degree of diversification in the EEC countries is consistent with the results obtained by the author that show the predominance of intra-industry specialization within the Common Market. This tendency is not apparent in the European Free Trade Association where integration through trade has progressed much less than in the Common Market (Balassa, 1974).

CONCLUSION

In this chapter, evidence has been provided on the pattern of comparative advantage of the industrial countries in manufactured products as indicated by the product composition of their exports. It has been shown that the United States has a strong and increasing 'revealed' comparative advantage in research-intensive products. These results confirm and extend the findings of other authors on trade in research-intensive products and indicate the continuous renewal of the product cycle, with the United States maintaining and even increasing its technological lead.

The US comparative disadvantage in non-durable consumer goods and their inputs contrasts with the comparative advantage in these products of France, Italy and Japan among the larger countries of the group. In turn, Germany's comparative advantage appears to lie in machinery and metal products, while, apart from processed non-ferrous metals, the comparative advantage of the United Kingdom does not show a clearcut pattern.

In line with the hypothesis advanced by Linder and Drèze, the comparative advantage of the smaller European countries appears to lie in standardized commodities. Among these countries, the transformation of domestic materials and energy dominates the exports of Austria, Norway and Sweden. Canada's comparative advantage, too, lies in natural resource-based products.

Finally, it would appear that the extent of specialization and diversification of manufactured exports depends on a variety of factors, including the size of domestic markets, the level of technological development, natural resource endowments, and the effects of economic integration. Large countries tend to have more diversified exports and, if the explanations suggested are correct, it seems that increased industrial sophistication leads to export diversification, although the technologically leading country tends to specialize in research-intensive products; the availability of natural resources also seems to contribute to specialization. Finally, in conformity with earlier results of the author, the establishment of the European Common Market appears to have contributed to the increased diversification of manufactured exports in the member countries through intra-industry specialization.

Appendix Table 5.1 'Revealed' comparative advantage in manufactured goods: industrial countries (rankings for 73 commodity categories)

	SITC	United States			Canada			Common Market			United Kingdom			Continental EFTA			Japan		
		1953	1962	1971	1953	1962	1971	1953	1962	1971	1953	1962	1971	1953	1962	1971	1953	1962	1971
1	512	16	26	11	53	17	43	48	45	41	53	54	49	61	55	60	57	35	24
2	51.0	46	25	6	6	9	12	28	39	47	43	35	53	22	23	31	38	38	41
3	531	48	46	59	69	70	70	64	72	72	34	21	33	68	73	72	31	51	55
4	533	6	30	35	47	47	57	41	63	62	27	6	19	38	32	13	49	57	51
5	541	7	12	19	29	36	40	49	53	38	48	26	9	53	60	54	44	49	62
6	551	22	7	13	60	60	62	24	43	57	67	55	20	55	69	67	47	62	68
7	55.0	41	19	29	59	58	61	65	62	58	17	10	15	64	63	56	60	53	59
8	561	66	39	16	8	6	2	11	15	19	71	73	73	4	6	8	11	29	56
9	571	31	33	25	69	57	24	51	47	34	5	3	4	18	19	10	41	43	60
10	599	24	5	17	5	27	48	53	58	49	55	38	35	7	53	44	45	50	38
11	611	51	43	47	11	15	30	35	41	26	19	20	13	39	29	43	68	70	50
12	612	26	45	55	49	21	38	17	19	14	31	36	30	23	13	7	39	32	27
13	613	53	17	31	18	18	45	19	21	20	18	39	7	31	7	14	65	69	73
14	621	54	61	21	33	32	35	25	54	37	10	27	16	33	1	28	52	36	45
15	629.1	25	31	50	19	26	39	31	37	28	23	19	27	40	15	17	36	25	11
16	629.0	5	3	27	26	48	53	56	67	59	50	29	25	14	40	39	37	34	31
17	641	63	47	28	1	1	1	68	71	63	72	71	68	5	4	3	56	55	63
18	642	11	55	32	37	55	46	50	22	46	39	22	34	28	16	5	43	59	37
19	651.2	72	73	73	64	66	63	10	11	8	21	37	22	20	21	20	21	31	13
20	651.3	64	56	46	69	70	70	3	5	10	12	53	37	29	27	32	5	5	67
21	651.4	52	66	51	63	68	70	20	16	13	6	5	18	59	67	62	20	20	20
22	651.6	49	27	61	27	51	56	14	17	31	59	43	46	16	25	37	6	23	10
23	652	44	41	30	56	46	37	32	44	35	24	58	59	50	48	30	2	2	9
24	653.2	70	72	72	61	54	64	12	3	5	2	4	3	43	45	49	34	26	42

Obs	V1	V2	V3	V4	V5	V6	V7	V8	V9	V10	V11	V12	V13	V14	V15	V16	V17	V18	Value
25	1	3	67	33	36	6	72	44	52	33	31	7	58	33	69	63	28	73	653.5
26	7	6	42	35	43	56	23	34	3	32	20	13	52	49	58	67	64	65	653.0
27	19	16	17	2	3	3	50	47	41	61	57	45	59	53	69	49	59	59	654
28	34	11	3	25	22	19	39	15	15	30	35	29	20	23	13	39	50	47	655
29	36	10	12	48	52	71	17	59	62	2	1	1	28	61	48	68	68	57	656.6
30	15	19	9	22	56	51	52	60	29	24	40	30	21	52	42	26	18	20	656.0
31	52	14	13	40	50	47	12	14	9	4	7	2	49	62	62	56	67	67	657
32	48	40	28	58	58	32	43	46	46	7	4	6	66	59	31	22	49	45	664
33	57	41	19	11	5	2	44	65	69	23	27	34	36	64	51	34	22	17	665
34	4	1	1	61	61	58	6	13	13	52	55	54	70	70	28	70	71	68	666
35	39	44	27	1	2	1	71	70	73	66	66	69	11	3	3	57	63	69	671
36	12	24	35	16	11	10	58	66	70	11	12	4	26	41	40	66	65	60	673
37	54	65	7	21	9	11	38	33	49	16	23	16	17	20	34	58	48	33	674
38	16	37	40	24	17	42	61	62	57	17	13	15	70	70	69	54	54	36	675
39	32	18	30	9	20	21	14	49	51	44	38	18	14	4	55	42	40	39	676
40	5	21	23	45	44	65	57	41	22	55	36	67	33	42	57	44	51	56	678
41	29	42	32	36	35	57	5	18	44	15	24	22	10	8	10	52	58	12	682.2
42	70	68	25	66	33	52	10	9	1	73	73	66	19	5	69	14	8	58	683.2
43	53	47	29	6	8	9	66	24	7	18	26	39	41	11	7	18	44	62	684.2
44	61	54	55	68	41	36	42	56	64	27	14	9	9	7	50	20	24	61	685.2
45	30	64	50	47	46	67	26	25	60	29	6	5	8	14	69	36	70	42	686.2
46	66	72	69	65	65	72	1	1	37	39	8	21	70	70	69	48	36	71	687.2
47	23	28	26	34	24	15	36	23	25	40	32	37	27	34	32	38	21	38	69.0
48	44	52	54	52	49	25	8	8	14	67	49	44	7	13	35	4	2	27	711
49	69	71	59	64	68	60	8	2	61	51	68	70	31	28	2	2	14	10	712.0
50	35	63	73	38	47	37	41	51	35	53	59	59	5	2	25	15	10	3	712.5
51	47	67	63	69	64	46	40	57	54	54	33	36	18	19	21	3	11	9	714
52	28	60	62	50	54	44	32	50	63	45	51	43	42	44	30	24	29	13	715
53	49	27	16	59	66	54	21	16	8	42	34	38	55	45	46	43	13	40	717.1
54	8	56	48	41	37	34	31	32	26	50	56	55	29	31	36	12	20	18	718.0
55	40	33	53	42	38	35	47	31	38	48	50	46	22	24	23	23	6	15	72.0
56	21	12	66	53	51	69	45	30	20	68	65	72	15	40	44	8	9	8	722.0
57	18	61	33	46	62	27	65	42	16	40	48	27	16	30	24	7	53	35	731
58	17	45	70	73	72	70	60	17	68	36	30	40	6	70	15	45	32	21	732.1
59	25	39	61	57	31	63	62	11	30	25	25	71	70	70	20	53	4	2	732.2
60			64	63	59	49	28	28		65	60	57	4	37	16	9		4	732.0

Appendix Table 5.1 (*continued*)

	SITC	United States 1953	1962	1971	Canada 1953	1962	1971	Common Market 1953	1962	1971	United Kingdom 1953	1962	1971	Continental EFTA 1953	1962	1971	Japan 1953	1962	1971
61	733	55	52	40	54	25	50	47	46	43	4	7	11	24	28	19	18	30	22
62	734	1	1	1	14	10	13	73	64	70	65	69	55	73	70	70	71	73	71
63	735	28	62	69	22	39	60	42	61	71	58	67	70	12	10	4	4	7	2
64	812	14	23	41	43	22	25	63	52	22	32	48	51	41	30	18	22	46	58
65	821	23	42	62	9	38	23	52	29	12	40	45	64	48	34	27	51	48	64
66	831	50	60	64	52	63	47	61	28	9	47	68	67	62	42	51	15	8	6
67	841	37	57	60	41	43	34	23	9	6	36	64	56	17	18	23	8	9	26
68	842	19	37	65	4	12	3	'60	70	56	45	12	48	13	26	29	73	66	72
69	851	43	69	71	17	29	51	33	2	1	11	61	63	26	39	12	24	4	33
70	861	32	15	10	39	16	54	62	69	69	56	52	29	30	57	55	14	15	14
71	862	30	16	5	12	35	32	8	10	21	42	40	24	66	71	71	58	58	46
72	891	29	34	33	45	56	65	26	42	60	33	63	54	45	12	15	46	13	3
73	897	34	35	37	38	50	44	58	18	3	66	72	69	8	14	26	10	17	65

Note: For explanation of SITC Code, see Appendix Table 5.2.
Source: National and international trade statistics.

Appendix Table 5.2 SITC product categories used in calculations of 'revealed' comparative advantage

512	Organic chemicals	675	Hoops and strips
51.0	Inorganic chemicals	676	Railway construction material
531	Synthetic organic dyestuffs	678	Tubes, pipes and fittings
533	Pigments, paints and varnishes	682.2	Copper, wrought
541	Medicinal and pharmaceutical	683.2	Nickel, wrought
551	Essential oils and perfumes	684.2	Aluminum, wrought
55.0	Perfumery and cosmetics	685.2	Lead, wrought
561	Fertilizers, manufactured	686.2	Zinc, wrought
571	Explosives and pyrotechnics	687.2	Tin, wrought
599	Chemical material and products	69.0	Manufactures of metal
611	Leather	711	Power generating machinery
612	Manufactures of leather	712.0	Agricultural machinery
613	Fur skins	712.5	Tractors
621	Materials of rubber	714	Office machinery
629.1	Rubber tires and tubes	715	Metal working machinery
629.0	Other rubber articles	717.1	Textile machinery
641	Paper and paperboard	718.0	Other machinery
642	Articles made of paper	72.0	Other electric machinery
651.2	Yarn of wool	722	Electrical power equipment
651.3	Cotton yarn, unbleached	731	Railway vehicles
651.4	Cotton yarn, bleached	732.1	Automobiles
651.6	Yarn of synthetic fibres	732.2	Buses, lorries and trucks
652	Cotton fabrics	732.0	Bodies, chassis and frames
653.2	Woolen fabrics	733	Bicycles
653.5	Synthetic fabrics	734	Aircraft
653.0	Other woven textile fabrics	735	Ships and boats
654	Tulle, lace, embroidery	812	Sanitary, plumbing and heating
655	Special textile fabrics	821	Furniture
656.6	Blankets	831	Travel goods and handbags
656.0	Made up textiles	841	Clothing
657	Floor coverings	842	Fur clothing
664	Glass	851	Footwear
665	Glassware	861	Scientific, medical and optical
666	Pottery	862	Photographic and cinematographic
671	Pig iron	891	Musical instruments
673	Iron and steel bars	897	Jewelry and goldsmith
674	Universals and steel plates		

Source: Standard International Trade Classification.

NOTES

1. One of the first uses of the concept was in M. E. Kreinin (1966). For recent applications, see M. Panić and A. H. Rajan (1971); Seev Hirsch (1974); T. G. Parry (1975) and Juergen B. Donges and James Riedel (1976).
2. 1971 has been chosen as the terminal year, in part to exclude the effects of the currency upheavals in subsequent years, and in part to show the situation existing before British entry into the European Common Market. Correspondingly, the Common Market is defined to include the original member countries. Within the EEC, the combined exports of Belgium and Luxemburg will be referred to as Belgian exports.

3. Examples of studies on particular products and product groups are Hufbauer (1966) and Tilton (1971).
4. The averages for all manufacturing were 0.26 and 0.19 percent, respectively. The results pertaining to all firms in an industry, irrespective of whether they engage in research, have been derived from the National Science Foundation (1973) and the Bureau of Census (1967). The numerical estimates are provided in Bela Balassa (1977).
5. Low numbers indicate high ranks, and high numbers low ranks – by 1971, inorganic chemicals had assumed a rank of 6.
6. According to this explanation, small countries have a comparative advantage in standardized products for which success in exportation does not depend on the availability of a large market as for finished manufactures.

REFERENCES

Balassa, B. (1965) 'Trade Liberalization and "Revealed" Comparative Advantage', *The Manchester School*, Vol. XXXIII, No. 2, pp. 99–123. Reprinted as Chapter 4 in this volume.

Balassa, B. (1974) 'Trade Creation and Trade Diversion in the European Common Market: An Appraisal of the Evidence', *The Manchester School*, Vol. XLII, No. 2, pp. 93–125.

Balassa, B. (1977) 'US Export Performance: A Trade Share Analysis', *Working Papers in Economics*, No. 24, Baltimore, Maryland, Johns Hopkins University.

Drèze, J. (1960) 'Quelques reflexions sereines sur l'adaptation de l'industrie belge au Marché Commun', *Comptes Rendus des Travaux de la Société Royale d'Economie Politique de Belgique*, pp. 4–26.

Donges, J. B., and Riedel J. (1976) 'The Expansion of Manufactured Exports in Developing Countries: An Empirical Assessment of Supply and Demand Issues', *Kiel Working Paper*, No. 49, Kiel, Institute of World Economics.

Gruber, W., Mehta, D., and Vernon, R. (1967) 'The R&D Factor in International Trade and International Investment of United States Industries', *Journal of Political Economy*, Vol. LXXV, No. 1, pp. 20–37.

Hirsch, S. (1974) 'Capital or Technology? Confronting the Neo-Factor Proportions and the Neo-Technology Accounts of International Trade', *Weltwirtschaftliches Archiv*, Band 110, Heft 4, pp. 535–63.

Hirschman, A. O. (1960) 'Invitation to Theorizing about the Dollar Glut', *Review of Economics and Statistics*, Vol. XLII, No. 1, pp. 100–2.

Hoffmeyer, E. (1958) *Dollar Shortage*, Amsterdam, North-Holland.

Hufbauer, G. C. (1966) *Synthetic Materials and the Theory of International Trade*, London, Duckworth.

Keesing, D. B. (1967) 'The Impact of Research and Development on U.S. Trade', *Journal of Political Economy*, Vol. LXXV, No. 1, pp. 38–48.

Kreinin, M. E. (1966) 'On the Restrictive Effect of the Tariff: A Note on the Use of the Balassa Index', *The Manchester School*, Vol. XXXIV, No. 1, pp. 75–80.

Linder, S. B. (1961) *An Essay on Trade and Transformation*, Stockholm, Almqvist and Wiksell.

National Science Foundation (1973) *Research and Development in Industry*, 1973, Washington, DC, National Science Foundation.

Panić, M. and Rajan, A. H. (1971) *Product Changes in Industrial Countries' Trade: 1955–1968*, NEDO Monograph 2, London, National Economic Development Office.

Parry, T. G. (1975) 'Trade and Non-trade Performance in US Manufacturing Industry – Revealed Comparative Advantage', *The Manchester School*, Vol. XLIII, No. 2, pp. 158–72.

Tilton, J. E. (1971) *International Diffusion of Technology: The Case of Semiconductors*, Washington, DC, The Brookings Institution.

US Bureau of Census (1967) *Census of Manufactures*, Volume 1, Washington, DC, Bureau of the Census.

Vernon, R. (1966) 'International Investment and International Trade in the Product Cycle', *Quarterly Journal of Economics*, Vol. LXXX, No. 2, pp. 190–207.

6 · THE CHANGING COMPARATIVE ADVANTAGE OF JAPAN AND THE UNITED STATES

INTRODUCTION

This chapter analyzes the changing comparative advantage of Japan and the United States. This will be done through the examination of indices of 'revealed' comparative advantage, (Balassa, 1965, 1977) derived for 57 primary and 167 manufactured product categories and aggregated for 20 commodity groups. The structure of 'revealed' comparative advantage in manufactured goods in the two countries will be estimated econometrically as a function of inter-industry differences in factor intensities. Finally, changes in the commodity pattern of trade in high-technology products in the overall trade of the two countries will be discussed.

In this study, two indices of trade specialization have been employed. The export index of revealed comparative advantage (XRCA) has been defined as the ratio of a country's exports in a particular commodity category to its share in total merchandise exports:

$$\text{XRCA}_{ij} = \frac{X_{ij}}{\sum_j X_{ij}} \bigg/ \frac{\sum_i X_{ij}}{\sum_i \sum_j X_{ij}}, \tag{1}$$

where X stands for exports, and the subscripts i and j refer to industry (product category) and country, respectively. The net export index has been defined as net exports divided by the sum of exports and imports for a particular industry.

$$NX_{ij} = \frac{X_{ij} - M_{ij}}{X_{ij} + M_{ij}}, \tag{2}$$

where M refers to imports.

Written with Marcus Noland. The authors would like to thank participants at the MITI US/Japan symposium, held 26–7 January 1987 in Tokyo, for helpful comments on an earlier version of this chapter. Published simultaneously in *Journal of the Japanese and International Economies* (forthcoming).

The net export index of revealed comparative advantage is, however, affected by the country's overall trade balance. To facilitate inter-temporal comparisons, the net export index has been normalized using the formula:

$$NX'_{ij} = NX_{ij} + [NX_{ij} * NX_{Tj}] \qquad \text{if } NX_{Tj} < 0,$$

$$NX'_{ij} = NX_{ij} - [NX_{ij} * NX_{Tj}] \qquad \text{if } NX_T > 0, \tag{3}$$

where NX_{Tj} is the net export index of total trade for country j. This normalization imposes equiproportional adjustment to an aggregate trade balance surplus or deficit across all industries.[1]

The use of the net export index is superior to the export index of revealed comparative advantage on trade-theoretical grounds. This is because the former indicates the effects of comparative advantage on the relationship between exports and imports rather than on exports alone.

However, the net export index has the practical disadvantage of being affected by the idiosyncrasies of national import protection; in the extreme, prohibitive protection will give rise to a net export index of 100 for a differentiated product, some of which is exported. Also, in the case of intermediate products, net exports are influenced by demand for purposes of further transformation in production for export.

These considerations have led to the use of both export and net export indices in the following discussion of the changing pattern of revealed comparative advantage. However, in the econometric investigation of the determinants of comparative advantage, exclusive use has been made of the net export index, owing to its trade-theoretical advantages over the export index.[2]

Revealed comparative advantage indices have been calculated for 57 primary and for 167 manufactured product categories. The results have been aggregated into 20 commodity groups, of which three represent primary products and 17 manufactured goods. They are presented in Table 6.1 for the export index and in Table 6.2 for the net export index.

Estimates have been made for the years 1967, 1971, 1975, 1979 and 1983, to permit examination of changes in revealed comparative advantage in four-year intervals. The 'comparator' countries chosen for the estimation include 18 industrial countries[3] and 19 developing countries in whose exports manufactured goods accounted for at least 18 percent of total exports and exceeded $300 million in 1979.[4]

THE REVEALED COMPARATIVE ADVANTAGES
OF JAPAN AND THE UNITED STATES

The results reported in Tables 6.1 and 6.2 show the transformation of the structure of Japan's comparative advantage over time. At the beginning of the

Table 6.1 Export index of revealed comparative advantage

Industry	Japan					United States				
	1967	1971	1975	1979	1983	1967	1971	1975	1979	1983
Food, beverages and tobacco	50	48	23	22	18	211	195	262	260	264
Agricultural raw materials	15	11	9	7	5	237	332	331	406	396
Non-oil mineral products	15	18	17	26	20	221	244	284	301	286
Textile mill products	486	337	258	196	198	63	55	65	94	72
Clothing and other finished textile products	372	190	64	31	42	68	54	55	57	40
Lumber and wood products	96	50	20	11	7	105	110	143	130	122
Furniture and fixtures	94	64	30	28	37	85	49	57	57	79
Paper and allied products	70	73	80	74	63	125	149	133	110	130
Printing and publishing	57	59	44	56	82	225	218	198	204	232
Chemical and allied products	168	158	163	122	100	209	207	180	200	206
Rubber and plastic products	307	272	274	254	291	141	118	116	112	119
Leather and leather products	280	164	68	44	40	42	28	40	37	42
Stone, clay and glass products	333	211	183	192	196	128	120	101	105	104
Primary metal and allied products	354	393	429	390	318	98	94	92	81	76
Fabricated metal products	262	240	226	209	210	187	147	156	149	142
Non-electrical machinery	115	135	157	215	247	263	263	260	272	289
Electrical machinery	421	392	334	404	433	210	193	187	210	210
Transportation equipment	273	300	365	368	370	258	266	242	230	213
Instruments and related products	323	286	314	439	432	238	242	212	186	193
Miscellaneous manufactured products	355	238	164	145	206	95	111	111	103	103

Source: GATT tapes.

Table 6.2 Net export index of revealed comparative advantage

Industry	Japan					United States				
	1967	1971	1975	1979	1983	1967	1971	1975	1979	1983
Food, beverages and tobacco	−61.7	−67.9	−82.5	−81.2	−89.4	0.4	−11.4	25.0	14.3	16.6
Agricultural raw materials	−91.2	−105.6	−94.9	−94.0	−105.0	27.0	49.0	48.4	62.3	67.8
Non-oil mineral products	−91.7	−10.5	−93.9	−88.9	−100.5	3.8	15.3	33.0	32.7	48.0
Textile mill products	90.7	67.9	56.9	27.5	45.0	−34.8	−48.2	16.1	−4.0	−30.6
Clothing and other finished textile products	96.5	69.0	−12.2	−60.2	−30.4	−53.2	−63.8	−57.1	−60.6	−71.2
Lumber and wood products	−30.9	−58.0	−86.0	−88.8	−100.2	−45.5	−52.2	−20.7	−40.4	−40.6
Furniture and fixtures	86.8	61.6	−15.7	−32.6	−13.8	−26.7	−63.4	−40.8	−45.9	−47.5
Paper and allied products	70.3	64.0	60.5	44.0	20.4	−41.9	−28.3	−14.5	−32.0	−27.8
Printing and publishing	−16.7	0.6	−27.8	−12.9	24.1	38.6	34.4	36.3	32.1	19.9
Chemical and allied products	13.8	24.8	37.2	13.1	3.7	43.1	38.0	35.7	35.4	25.3
Rubber and plastic products	96.5	82.4	88.0	78.2	74.2	25.6	−10.4	−2.5	−28.9	−29.8
Leather and leather products	86.5	61.1	6.3	−34.9	−16.2	−76.2	−84.2	−78.4	−72.7	−70.5
Stone, clay and glass products	88.9	71.9	73.1	68.4	66.4	3.4	−8.0	−0.3	−16.3	−23.1
Primary metal and allied products	54.9	75.9	87.5	79.8	66.1	−23.4	35.6	−19.5	−37.1	−40.8
Fabricated metal products	79.7	65.3	82.3	84.9	73.3	47.5	25.4	45.8	31.9	15.1
Non-electrical machinery	21.6	29.8	56.8	69.0	70.0	48.1	43.1	47.6	38.6	28.4
Electrical machinery	79.3	70.0	75.2	77.9	73.8	20.7	−1.0	12.1	2.4	−12.3
Transportation equipment	83.2	71.9	89.7	89.0	79.3	25.0	2.7	17.7	−1.3	−14.4
Instruments and related products	63.5	53.0	57.9	67.1	65.0	30.2	28.3	29.6	4.5	−3.9
Miscellaneous manufactured products	55.6	24.4	9.6	10.8	35.9	−39.6	−35.3	−22.9	−31.7	−41.3
Total net exports as percentage of trade	−5.5	9.8	−1.8	−3.7	8.1	7.5	−1.6	5.2	−8.9	−14.4

Source: GATT tapes.
Note: The index measures net exports as a percentage of trade flow, corrected for aggregate net exports as a proportion of aggregate trade flow.

period, Japan's comparative advantage was in unskilled labor-intensive commodities, including textile mill products (for short, textiles), clothing and other finished textile products (for short, clothing), rubber and plastic products, leather and leather products, and stone, clay and glass products.

All these commodity groups had capital–labor ratios, calculated by including physical as well as human capital, less than three-fifths of the average for the manufacturing sector (Table 6.1).[5] At the same time, they had export indices of revealed comparative advantage ranging from 486 (textiles) to 280 (leather and leather products) and net export indices between 96 (clothing and rubber and plastic products) and 87 (leather and leather products).

Lumber and wood products are also unskilled labor intensive but Japan is at a disadvantage in their production because of the lack of natural resources, which explains why its export index was less than 100 and the net export index was negative. Furniture, another unskilled labor-intensive product affected by the availability of natural resources, gives a mixed picture, with a low export index and a high net export index, possibly reflecting the existence of trade barriers in Japan.

Miscellaneous manufactured products also represent a special category. They are unskilled labor-intensive products, where Japan had a high export index but a net export index below the median for manufacturing industries. This is because the exports of musical instruments, games and toys, and clothing accessories were partly offset by the importation of jewelry and silverware, children's vehicles and floor coverings.

The next category includes non-electrical machinery, electrical machinery, transportation equipment, as well as instruments and related products. All these commodity groups are relatively skilled labor- (human-capital) intensive, as indicated by the fact that the ratio of physical to human capital in their production is between one-third (electrical machinery) and three-fifths (transportation equipment) of the average for the manufacturing sector (Table 6.1).

Apart from non-electrical machinery, the export index was between 421 (electrical machinery) and 273 (transportation equipment), with net export indices ranging from 79 (electrical machinery) to 64 (instruments and related products). While non-electrical machinery represents an exception, with the two indices being 115 and 22, this may be explained by Japan's technical inability at the time to manufacture advanced computers and office machinery, as well as certain specialized machines.

Among physical capital-intensive products, for which the ratio of physical capital to labor is at least double the average for the manufacturing sector (Table 6.1), Japan had low export and net export indices for paper and allied products, while export indices exceeded 100 but net export indices were below the median for chemicals and primary metals. In the case of chemicals, the divergence of the two indices is explained by Japan's trade deficit in synthetic rubber, biological and medicinal products, and various chemical preparations. Among primary metals, Japan exported steel, where it had transportation cost advantages owing to the use of the sea route to import coking coal and iron ore, while it imported specialized steel products.

Finally, in accordance with its poor land and mineral endowment, Japan had by far the lowest export indices for the three primary product groups and net export indices for these groups are also strongly negative. Thus, already in 1967 Japan was exchanging manufactured goods for primary products while its manufactured exports were unskilled labor intensive and, to a lesser extent, human-capital intensive.

Japan's comparative advantage was much transformed during the period under consideration. The largest change occurred with regard to clothing which is by far the most unskilled labor-intensive commodity group. Between 1967 and 1979, the export index for clothing decreased from 372 to 31 while the net export index shifted from 97 to − 60, with a slight reversal in 1983 to 42 in the first case and to − 30 in the second. Leather and leather products underwent comparable developments. The export and net export indices were 280 and 87 in 1967 and 40 and − 16 in 1983.

Similar changes occurred in the case of textiles, stone, clay and glass products, and miscellaneous manufactured products. But these changes were of smaller magnitude, with the export indices remaining above 100 and exports continuing to exceed imports. There were practically no changes with regard to rubber and plastic products. This compares with a shift of total Japanese trade from a net import to a net export position, the relevant index numbers being − 5 for 1967 and 8 for 1985.

In turn, Japan greatly strengthened its comparative advantage in human capital-intensive products. The export indices of electrical machinery, transportation equipment and instruments were about 400 in 1983 while the net export indices were in the 70–80 range. But the largest increase occurred with regard to non-electrical machinery, with the export index rising from 115 to 247, and the net export index from 22 to 72, between 1967 and 1983.

Increased specialization in human capital-intensive products contrasts with reduced specialization in physical capital-intensive products in Japan. Export indices declined in every case as did the net export indices, except for primary metals where the imports of steel products decreased.

Finally, Japan's comparative disadvantage increased further in natural resource products, whether in a primary form (food, beverages, and tobacco and agricultural raw materials) or in a transformed state (lumber and wood products and furniture). And while no change occurred with regard to non-oil mineral products, Japan had a pronounced comparative disadvantage in the commodity group already in 1967.

The results for Japan may be contrasted with those for the United States. In 1967 the US comparative advantage was in three categories: primary products, physical capital-intensive products, and human capital-intensive products. Apart from primary metals, the export index of revealed comparative advantage exceeded 200 and the United States had a large export surplus in all these commodity groups.

By contrast, the export index was less than 100 and the United States had an import surplus in all unskilled labor-intensive commodity groups, except for rubber and plastic products and stone, clay and glass products. Finally, an intermediate category consisted of transformed natural resource products, such as lumber and wood products and furniture, in which the US had the benefit of the availability of natural resources, although some of them required the use of unskilled labor.

Between 1967 and 1983, with the exception of primary metals, the United States increased its comparative advantage in primary products. It also improved or, at least, maintained its comparative advantage in transformed primary products (lumber and wood products and furniture).

The picture for other manufactures was less clear. The export index of comparative advantage for transportation equipment and instruments fell between 1967 and 1983, that for electrical machinery remained unchanged, and the index for non-electrical machinery increased slightly. Further, the deterioration of the net export index in all these commodity groups exceeded that of the overall average, although this may be related, in part, to increased intra-industry trade in these products.

Overall, Tables 6.1 and 6.2 are useful for highlighting the contrasts between Japan and the US. Two points stand out. The first is the differing position of natural resource-based products in the two countries. Japan had a comparative disadvantage in natural resource products which continued to deteriorate over the sample period. The United States, on the other hand, increased its comparative advantage in these products during this time. Second, Japan exhibited dramatic shifts in specialization within the manufacturing sector, moving from specialization in unskilled labor-intensive products to human capital-intensive products. These shifts stand out in comparison with the US, where major changes in specialization within manufacturing were not observed.

THE DETERMINANTS OF REVEALED COMPARATIVE ADVANTAGE

Having established the broad contours of specialization in the above section, a more disaggregated commodity breakdown has been utilized to analyze econometrically the factors determining the structure of comparative advantage in the two countries. Because of the complete specialization in some natural resource products (hence an absence of production data for the non-producing country), the empirical investigation has been limited to 167 manufactured goods. Correspondingly, the econometric results are not fully comparable to those shown in Table 6.1 and 6.2 which include primary products.

The net export index, NX_{ij}, is used as the dependent variable in the regression results presented in Tables 6.3 to 6.6. Since this index is defined over the range $[-1, 1]$ ordinary least squares (OLS) estimation will not be appropriate, as it could lead to fitted values of the dependent variable outside its defined range. In fact, since the residuals are truncated at the values -1 and 1, they are heteroscedastic.

One way of addressing this problem is to redefine the dependent variable so that it takes values between $-\infty$ to ∞. A customary way of doing so is to use a logistic transformation of the variable:

$$N\hat{X}_{ij} = \frac{(NX_{ij}+1)}{2} \tag{4}$$

$$NXADJ_{ij} = \ln(N\hat{X}_{ij}/1 - N\hat{X}_{ij}) \tag{5}$$

The regressions have been estimated using both the unadjusted (NX) and adjusted ($NXADJ$) measures as dependent variables. The results were virtually identical. The estimates reported in Tables 6.3 to 6.6 have been obtained using the theoretically preferable adjusted index.[6] The data used to construct these variables originate from the GATT trade tapes.

In constructing the explanatory variables, factor intensity has been defined as that factor's share of value added. The share specification has been adopted since it yields an unambiguous ranking of industries by factor intensity in the multifactor model and has a straightforward interpretation in terms of the multifactor Heckscher-Ohlin model. For both countries, the relative shares of unskilled labor, physical capital and human capital in value added, and the share of research and development (R&D) expenditure in output have been derived from the country's own industrial statistics. This allows production techniques to differ across countries in response to differences in relative factor prices, and avoids the econometric mis-specification (errors-in-variables) caused by incorrectly imposing one country's pattern of factor usage on the other.

The unskilled labor share has been defined as

$$\text{LABOR}_{ij} = (W_{ij}^u \cdot L_{ij})/VA_{ij} \tag{6}$$

where W_{ij}^u is the industry unskilled wage, L_{ij} is full-time employment in the industry, and VA_{ij} is value added. The unskilled wage is defined on an industry-by-industry basis since differences in market structure, union power, etc., will cause the renumeration of unskilled workers to vary across industries. In turn, the human capital share is defined as wage payments in excess of those attributed as returns to unskilled labor:

$$HCAP_{ij} = (W_{ij} - W_{ij}^u) \cdot L_{ij}/VA_{ij} \tag{7}$$

Table 6.3 The determinants of comparative advantage: Japan (explanatory variables in natural units)

	Year	N	Constant	LABOR	PFLOW	PSTOCK	HCAP	RD	$\bar{R}^2$
(3.1)	1967	161		6.308 (5.168)[a]	1.374 (2.173)[b]		−7.077 (−2.714)[a]		0.097
(3.2)	1967	161	136.372 (2.161)[b]	4.989 (2.991)[a]		0.024 (2.008)[b]	−8.690 (−2.857)[a]		0.093
(3.3)	1971	159		2.691 (2.527)[b]	1.902 (3.142)[a]		−2.971 (−1.041)		0.009
(3.4)	1971	159	188.778 (3.131)[a]	0.873 (0.609)		0.038 (3.003)[a]	−5.271 (−1.611)		0.008
(3.5)	1975	160		−1.626 (1.275)	1.753 (2.851)[a]		4.154 (1.282)		0.021
(3.6)	1975	160	173.491 (2.835)[a]	−3.274 (−2.009)[b]		0.048 (3.083)[a]	1.913 (0.523)		0.024
(3.7)	1979	161		−2.246 (−1.680)[c]	1.077 (1.746)[c]		8.396 (2.425)[b]		0.053
(3.8)	1979	161	105.667 (1.725)[c]	−3.212 (−1.925)[c]		0.048 (3.545)[a]	6.829 (1.754)[c]		0.056
(3.9)	1983	161		−0.845 (−0.604)	1.344 (2.001)[b]		6.864 (1.905)[c]		0.019
(3.10)	1983	161	132.935 (1.984)[b]	−2.109 (−1.192)		0.034 (2.562)[b]	5.171 (1.261)		0.017
(3.11)	1967	161		6.309 (5.261)[a]	1.731 (2.733)[a]		−6.169 (−2.341)[b]	−17.963 (−1.565)	0.103

	Year	N							R²
(3.12)	1967	161	171.817 (2.719)[a]	4.632 (2.895)[a]		0.022 (1.840)[c]	−8.129 (−2.677)[a]	−17.765 (−1.552)	0.100
(3.13)	1971	159		2.691 (2.547)[b]	2.085 (3.389)[a]		−2.509 (−0.849)	−9.200 (−0.807)	0.006
(3.14)	1971	159	205.459 (3.369)[a]	0.695 (0.497)		0.037 (2.759)[a]	−4.993 (−1.500)	−8.890 (−0.782)	0.005
(3.15)	1975	160		−1.705 (−1.351)	1.274 (2.090)[b]		2.844 (0.872)	23.946 (2.139)[b]	0.042
(3.16)	1975	160	124.388 (2.054)[b]	−2.858 (−1.793)[c]		0.050 (3.953)[a]	1.030 (0.284)	24.488 (2.199)[b]	0.046
(3.17)	1979	161		−2.334 (−1.796)[c]	0.329 (−0.505)		6.060 (1.780)[c]	38.680 (3.452)[a]	0.111
(3.18)	1979	161	28.823 (0.448)	−2.520 (−1.535)		0.055 (4.900)[a]	5.130 (1.339)	39.569 (3.562)[a]	0.116
(3.19)	1983	161		−1.079 (−0.821)	0.257 (0.382)		3.495 (1.008)	45.651 (5.404)[a]	0.136
(3.20)	1983	161	23.464 (0.352)	−1.241 (−0.750)		0.039 (2.531)[b]	2.832 (0.709)	45.881 (5.449)[a]	0.135

Note: *t*-statistics in parentheses; the superscript a indicates a coefficient estimate significantly different from 0 at the 1 percent level in a two-tail test; b indicates significance at the 5 percent level; c at the 10 percent level.

Explanation of symbols:

LABOR = unskilled labor share of value added
PFLOW = physical capital flow share of value added
PSTOCK = physical capital stock share of value added
HCAP = human capital share of value added
RD = research and development expenditures as a percentage of value output.

Table 6.4 The determinants of comparative advantage: Japan (explanatory variables in logs)

	Year	N	Constant	LABOR	PFLOW	PSTOCK	HCAP	RD	$\bar{R}^2$
(4.1)	1967	161	-1486.182 (-3.040)[a]	234.737 (4.237)[a]	234.089 (3.014)[a]		-26.570 (-0.943)		0.089
(4.2)	1967	161	-27.079 (-0.163)	124.787 (3.037)[a]		-16.163 (-1.202)	-60.132 (-2.054)[b]		0.079
(4.3)	1971	159	-1036.440 (-1.802)[c]	110.421 (1.805)[c]	196.315 (2.131)[b]		11.913 (0.406)		0.000
(4.4)	1971	159	169.263 (1.009)	18.873 (0.481)		-9.210 (-0.627)	-17.064 (-0.563)		-0.012
(4.5)	1975	160	-1135.301 (-1.404)	36.310 (0.504)	224.067 (1.627)		89.251 (2.789)[a]		0.039
(4.6)	1975	160	198.991 (1.204)	-68.158 (-1.638)		3.182 (0.251)	51.402 (1.707)[c]		0.022
(4.7)	1979	161	-1352.347 (-2.316)[b]	51.824 (0.925)	234.951 (2.328)[b]		137.342 (4.172)[a]		0.085
(4.8)	1979	161	53.838 (0.348)	-58.425 (-1.419)		2.145 (0.180)	97.510 (2.949)[a]		0.067
(4.9)	1983	161	-1202.154 (-1.680)[c]	67.100 (1.028)	208.604 (1.677)[c]		113.874 (3.295)[a]		0.043
(4.10)	1983	161	96.876 (0.580)	-30.763 (-0.704)		-14.747 (-1.032)	84.349 (2.417)[b]		0.034
(4.11)	1967	161	-1447.907 (-3.018)[a]	228.891 (4.216)[a]	228.833 (2.989)[a]		-22.670 (-0.804)	-18.367 (-1.006)	0.88

(4.12)	1967	161	−16.524 (−0.102)	120.860 (3.010)[a]		−17.519 (−1.256)	−54.301 (−1.843)[c]	−21.301 (−1.151)	0.079
(4.13)	1971	159	−1022.114 (−1.777)[c]	108.272 (1.784)[c]	194.348 (2.098)[b]		13.251 (0.445)	−6.540 (−0.364)	−0.006
(4.14)	1971	159	172.787 (1.044)	17.344 (0.448)		−9.336 (−0.639)	−14.957 (−0.484)	−8.121 (−0.445)	−0.018
(4.15)	1975	160	−1233.125 (−1.636)	51.627 (0.733)	237.511 (1.895)[c]		75.403 (2.301)[b]	56.513 (2.799)[a]	0.082
(4.16)	1975	160	173.068 (0.999)	−59.214 (−1.400)		6.106 (0.475)	34.554 (1.116)	55.759 (2.724)[a]	0.063
(4.17)	1979	161	−1464.959 (−2.690)[a]	68.437 (1.262)	251.919 (2.737)[a]		118.593 (3.697)[a]	74.700 (4.941)[a]	0.168
(4.18)	1979	161	30.888 (0.189)	−49.858 (−1.211)		6.250 (0.492)	74.692 (2.322)[b]	74.029 (4.768)[a]	0.148
(4.19)	1983	161	−1337.820 (−2.190)[b]	85.309 (1.455)	223.995 (2.145)[b]		89.783 (2.712)[a]	100.711 (6.287)[a]	0.176
(4.20)	1983	161	41.449 (0.224)	−19.953 (−0.480)		−10.470 (−0.772)	56.614 (1.659)[c]	99.137 (6.084)[a]	0.162

Note: t-statistics in parentheses; the superscript a indicates a coefficient estimate significantly different from 0 at the 1 percent level in a two-tail test; b indicates significance at the 5 percent level; c at the 10 percent level.

Explanation of symbols: See Table 6.3.

Table 6.5 The determinants of comparative advantage: United States (explanatory variables in natural units)

	Year	N	Constant	LABOR	PFLOW	PSTOCK	HCAP	RD	$\bar{R}^2$
(5.1)	1967	158		−5.542 (−4.590)[a]	1.598 (3.876)[a]		5.868 (3.067)[a]		0.140
(5.2)	1967	158	173.926 (3.638)[a]	−7.143 (−5.306)[c]		−0.158 (−0.673)	4.098 (1.861)[c]		0.136
(5.3)	1971	162		−6.329 (−4.979)[a]	1.549 (3.263)[a]		5.719 (3.002)[a]		0.154
(5.4)	1971	162	135.729 (2.596)[a]	−7.869 (−5.402)[a]		0.212 (0.824)	4.404 (2.000)[b]		0.152
(5.5)	1975	162		−5.263 (−4.304)[a]	1.611 (4.176)[a]		5.252 (2.905)[a]		0.156
(5.6)	1975	162	126.542 (2.993)[a]	−6.857 (−5.158)[a]		0.323 (1.645)[c]	4.063 (1.998)[b]		0.161
(5.7)	1979	162		−4.521 (−3.836)[a]	1.284 (3.996)[a]		3.432 (2.115)[b]		0.125
(5.8)	1979	162	84.707 (2.293)[b]	−5.791 (−4.638)[a]		0.495 (1.851)[c]	2.639 (1.515)		0.145
(5.9)	1983	163		−4.950 (−4.243)[a]	0.635 (1.862)[c]		4.442 (2.624)[a]		0.112
(5.10)	1983	163	4.556 (0.113)	−5.566 (−4.604)[a]		0.667 (2.237)[b]	4.469 (2.518)[b]		0.146
(5.11)	1967	158		−5.098 (−4.196)[a]	1.318 (3.010)[a]		5.153 (2.666)[a]	9.642 (2.032)[b]	0.147

	Year	N							
(5.12)	1967	158	146.051 (3.051)ᵃ	−6.418 (−4.694)ᵃ		−0.160 (−0.683)	3.660 (1.663)ᶜ	9.657 (2.040)ᵇ	0.143
(5.13)	1971	162		−5.891 (−4.590)ᵃ	1.279 (2.540)ᵇ		5.009 (2.623)ᵇ	9.496 (1.679)ᶜ	0.160
(5.14)	1971	162	108.917 (2.040)ᶜ	−7.162 (−4.775)ᵃ		0.210 (0.836)	3.963 (1.803)ᶜ	9.481 (1.671)ᶜ	0.157
(5.15)	1975	162		−4.858 (−4.665)ᵃ	1.363 (2.372)ᵇ		4.597 (2.494)ᵇ	8.750 (1.515)	0.162
(5.16)	1975	162	101.846 (1.644)	−6.206 (−4.572)ᵃ		0.381 (1.454)	3.657 (1.672)ᶜ	8.732 (1.515)	0.168
(5.17)	1979	162		−3.938 (−3.312)ᵃ	0.937 (2.758)ᵃ		2.517 (1.531)	11.940 (2.727)ᵃ	0.149
(5.18)	1979	162	49.833 (1.303)	−4.859 (−3.812)ᵃ		0.496 (2.050)ᵇ	2.071 (1.187)	11.971 (2.856)ᵃ	0.169
(5.19)	1983	163		−4.406 (−3.678)ᵃ	0.307 (0.816)		3.592 (2.076)ᵇ	11.306 (2.174)ᵇ	0.129
(5.20)	1983	163	−28.457 (−0.663)	−4.691 (−3.729)ᵃ		0.668 (2.564)ᵇ	3.946 (2.233)ᵇ	11.350 (2.318)ᵇ	0.164

Note: t-statistics in parentheses; the superscript a indicates a coefficient estimate significantly different from 0 at the 1 percent level in a two-tail test; b indicates significance at the 5 percent level; c at the 10 percent level.

Explanation of symbols: see Table 6.3.

Table 6.6 The determinants of comparative advantage: United States (explanatory variables in logs)

	Year	N	Constant	LABOR	PFLOW	PSTOCK	HCAP	RD	$\bar{R}^2$
(6.1)	1967	158	-1192.164 (-1.368)	-64.090 (-1.067)	267.092 (1.655)[c]		132.871 (3.507)[a]		0.130
(6.2)	1967	158	248.782 (2.626)[a]	-164.044 (-5.217)[a]		15.313 (0.822)	92.560 (2.740)[a]		0.122
(6.3)	1971	162	-1714.959 (-1.897)[c]	-43.886 (-0.722)	361.012 (2.134)[b]		152.445 (3.938)[a]		0.150
(6.4)	1971	162	170.701 (1.088)	-181.284 (-5.164)[a]		40.007 (1.769)[c]	94.799 (2.498)[b]		0.148
(6.5)	1975	162	-1516.748 (-1.743)[c]	-32.166 (-0.561)	324.302 (2.008)[b]		129.308 (3.255)[a]		0.145
(6.6)	1975	162	143.519 (1.458)	-156.823 (-4.985)[a]		46.281 (2.704)[a]	75.916 (2.181)[b]		0.155
(6.7)	1979	162	-904.118 (-1.233)	-55.323 (-1.233)	209.485 (1.536)		90.534 (2.423)[b]		0.117
(6.8)	1979	162	100.786 (1.189)	-134.701 (-4.999)[a]		51.110 (2.836)[a]	48.129 (1.655)[c]		0.157
(6.9)	1983	163	-951.984 (-1.317)	-56.950 (-1.229)	198.315 (1.484)		114.684 (3.126)[b]		0.106
(6.10)	1983	163	-56.935 (-0.693)	-133.881 (-5.179)[a]		65.812 (3.627)[a]	71.346 (2.478)[b]		0.169
(6.11)	1967	158	-605.701 (-0.661)	-68.220 (-1.110)	145.079 (0.851)		39.095 (2.654)[a]	9.800 (3.018)[a]	0.162

	Year	N							
(6.12)	1967	158	163.007 (1.770)c	−119.857 (−3.642)a		10.184 (0.538)	81.050 (2.403)b	30.879 (3.141)a	0.160
(6.13)	1971	162	−1137.143 (−1.222)	−46.011 (−0.741)	239.993 (1.376)		122.855 (3.120)a	30.622 (3.319)a	0.182
(6.14)	1971	162	81.299 (0.808)	−135.150 (−3.871)a		34.733 (1.751)c	82.696 (2.429)b	32.092 (3.391)a	0.186
(6.15)	1975	162	−1096.443 (−0.568)	−33.712 (−0.568)	236.272 (1.377)		107.784 (2.608)b	22.275 (2.550)b	0.167
(6.16)	1975	162	78.291 (0.772)	−123.164 (−3.761)a		42.432 (2.431)b	67.087 (1.906)c	23.414 (2.706)a	0.180
(6.17)	1979	162	−478.261 (−0.618)	−58.074 (−1.259)	121.212 (0.837)		68.658 (1.791)c	21.302 (2.514)b	0.143
(6.18)	1979	162	43.258 (0.497)	−105.970 (−3.740)a		47.947 (2.748)a	40.997 (1.380)	20.688 (2.613)a	0.183
(6.19)	1983	163	−467.741 (−0.599)	−60.086 (−1.254)	97.868 (0.669)		89.949 (2.404)b	24.345 (2.573)b	0.136
(6.20)	1983	163	−120.969 (−1.336)	−102.056 (−3.756)a		62.311 (3.673)a	63.575 (2.165)b	23.004 (2.750)a	0.198

Note: t-statistics in parentheses; the superscript a indicates a coefficient estimate significantly different from 0 at the 1 percent level in a two-tail test; b indicates significance at the 5 percent level; c at the 10 percent level.

Explanation of symbols: see Table 6.3.

In a previous study of Japan (Urata, 1983) two measures of human capital intensity were used. One was the wage differential measure described above, and the other was the share of technical and administrative workers. In this study, the wage differential approach has been adopted for a variety of reasons. First, this is an economically more appealing measure based on market information rather than an arbitrary classification of occupations. Second, the wage differential approach coincides with the share of value added specification, while the skill index does not. Finally, the estimated coefficients Urata obtained using the skill index were generally insignificant. In turn, Balassa (1979, 1986) reached highly significant results in a cross-country investigation of comparative advantage with the use of the wage differential variable.

Physical capital intensity has been defined in both stock and flow terms. The flow measure is the non-wage share of value added, while the stock measure is defined as the ratio of the physical capital stock to value added. While under certain conditions (perfectly competitive markets, no uncertainty) the two measures will yield identical rankings of the industries, in practice they will not. The flow measure contains a risk premium which varies across industries. In turn, the valuation of capital stocks at historical rather than replacement cost makes this measure susceptible to distortion, especially during periods of prolonged inflation. Since neither approach is clearly superior *a priori*, both have been used.

Research and development intensity has been defined as the share of research and development expenditures in output value. This definition is not exactly comparable to the share of value added definition used for the other factor intensity variables, but data are only available in this form.

One objection to the specification of the explanatory variables is that the components of value added may fluctuate over the business cycle and lead to shifts in the factor intensity rankings. This problem arises, however, only if the cyclical effects have differential impact across industries. If factor shares fluctuate equiproportionately across industries, the parameter estimates will be unaffected. At any rate, in the case of the United States, where some of the variables did exhibit substantial changes from year to year, averages across several periods have been used to eliminate the business cycle effects.[7]

Estimation has been done by regressing net export indices of comparative advantage for the 167 manufactured product categories on the explanatory variables just described. Estimates have been made for the years 1967, 1971, 1975, 1979, and 1983. They are shown in Tables 6.3 and 6.4 for Japan and in Tables 6.5 and 6.6 for the United States.

The regressions have been specified with the research and development variable both included and excluded. The latter is more consistent with the factor based Heckscher-Ohlin theory, and avoids double counting as R&D expenditures are already included in the renumeration of physical and human capital. This may explain the collinearity between the R&D variables, on the one hand, and the physical and human capital variables, on the other, which reduce the statistical significance of the latter variables in several of the regressions. This is particularly true for the correlation between the human capital variable and the R&D variable, which in large part represents investment in human capital in the form of scientists and engineers.

The regressions have been estimated with the explanatory variable expressed in levels and logs, since trade theory does not provide an indication of the functional form of the relationship between factor intensities and net exports. For the specifications in levels, the constant term has been omitted to avoid a linear dependency in the matrix of explanatory variables. The regressions have been estimated using White's heteroscedastic – consistent covariance matrix estimator which yields a consistent estimate of the covariance matrix (permitting proper inferences to be drawn) even in the presence of heteroscedastic disturbances (White, 1980).

Before interpreting the estimates, it should be noted that the coefficients of determination of the regression equations are very low. This may be explained in part by the existence of large variations in the index of revealed comparative advantage, because of the error possibilities noted earlier, and in part by the difficulties involved in relating trade statistics to the industrial classification scheme. The difficulties are especially pronounced in the case of Japan whose industrial data was more highly aggregated than the trade data. This may explain that the results for Japan are generally weaker in a statistical sense than those for the United States. Nevertheless, the estimates offer considerable interest as a substantial number of the regression coefficients are significant statistically and, even when they are not, the pattern of changes over time conforms to changes in relative resource endowments.[8]

The results in Tables 6.3 and 6.4 show that at the beginning of the period Japan had a strong comparative advantage in unskilled labor-intensive manufactured goods, but it had a strong comparative disadvantage in human capital-intensive products. In most specifications, Japan also appears to have had a comparative advantage in physical capital-intensive products.

Regression equations estimated for later years indicate the transformation of the structure of Japan's comparative advantage in manufactured goods from unskilled labour-intensive to human capital-intensive products. At the same time, Japan's position with regard to physical capital-intensive products was approximately maintained over time.[9]

The pattern of the regression coefficients is not affected, but their statistical significance is reduced, by adding the research and development variable, owing to the existence of collinearity among the explanatory variables, as noted above. The R&D variable itself goes from negative to positive and it is highly significant statistically in later years.

In turn, the United States appears to have had a comparative advantage in human capital-intensive and physical capital-intensive manufactured goods in 1967 while it had a strong disadvantage in unskilled labor-intensive products. The situation changed little in subsequent years. The coefficients obtained for unskilled labor and human capital accord with previous results reported by Branson and Monoyios (1977), Stern and Maskus (1981) and Maskus (1983), though these previous studies obtained negative coefficients on physical capital, in contrast to the more plausible positive coefficients reported in Tables 6.5 and 6.6.

Adding the R&D variable does not change these conclusions and, with the partial exception of the results for the last two years, the regression coefficients of the factor intensity variables remain highly significant. The regression coefficient of the R&D variable, too, is highly significant statistically and it shows the continued comparative advantage of the United States in R&D intensive products.

These results are consistent with the calculations presented in Noland (1985) which indicate that, during the period under consideration, both the United States and Japan were relatively abundant in both physical and human capital. Japan increased its endowments of physical and human capital relative to the rest of the world. In contrast, while the US remained a physical and human capital-abundant country, it accumulated these factors more slowly than the rest of the world; consequently its relative abundance in both of these factors declined.

JAPANESE AND US REVEALED COMPARATIVE ADVANTAGES IN HIGH TECHNOLOGY PRODUCTS

The changing pattern of comparative advantage in high technology products has attracted considerable attention in recent years. For purposes of analysis, high technology products have been defined as products where the ratio of research and development expenditures to the value of output exceeded 3.5 percent in the mid-1970s in the United States.

There are altogether 19 such product categories; their export and net export indices of revealed comparative advantage are shown in Tables 6.7 and 6.8 in the order of the share of R&D expenditures. In addition, the overall rankings of the indices among the 1967 manufacturing product categories are also reported.

The results show much variability, due in part to the considerable disaggregation of the data and in part to possible misclassifications. A case in point is computers where the United States ranks low in 1967 and 1971 and high in subsequent years, while the opposite result obtains for calculating and accounting machines, probably due to changes in classification in reporting the data.

Nevertheless, some general conclusions emerge. It appears that, with few exceptions, the United States increased its comparative advantage in high-technology products over time. In fact, in 1983, these products occupied the first four places in terms of the revealed comparative advantage of the United States as defined by export indices (aircraft, aircraft engines, office machinery, steam engines and turbines) while such was the case for only one product group (aircraft) in 1967.[10]

The exceptions are photographic equipment and supplies, scientific instruments, calculating and accounting machines and medical instruments. In all these product categories, the United States lost and Japan gained comparative advantage, suggesting an inverse relationship between the two countries.

At the same time, according to 'the export index, except for seven product categories Japan increased its comparative advantage in high-technology products. The exceptions are aircraft, optical instruments, agricultural chemicals, synthetic fibers, cellulose fibers, and steam engines and turbines, for which the export index of revealed comparative advantage decreased between 1967 and 1983. These declines represent the mirror image of increases observed in the United States. At the same time, only calculating and accounting machines ranked among the first four in terms of export indices in 1983 in Japan.

An overall indicator of the importance of the high-technology area in the two countries is the average rankings of the high-technology products in the comparative advantage indexes for each country. As shown in Tables 6.7 and 6.8 this average rose over the sample period for both countries. In fact, high tech appears to be relatively more important for the US than Japan: the US averages were higher even at the beginning of the period (1967) than they were for Japan at the end (1983).

None the less, perhaps the most striking thing in Tables 6.7 and 6.8 is the apparently complementary pattern of specialization of Japan and the United States within the high-tech area. A crucial question, then, is what determines this pattern? At least two explanations are consistent with the data.

One possibility is that the pattern of specialization reflects the strategic interactions of firms in internationally oligopolistic markets. US revealed comparative advantage grew in categories in which product development and production are characterized by large sunk costs (aircraft, mainframe computers), while Japan made advances in industries with lower entry costs. Given the earlier specialization of the US in high-technology· products, this pattern would be consistent with strategic trade-theoretic models in which existing firms use investment to precommit production and act as a deterrent to potential entrants. The efficacy of this strategy depends in part on the size of the sunk costs of production, with the greater the sunk costs, the greater the deterrent effect.

A complementary explanation of the pattern of specialization can be found by analyzing the type of R&D activities pursued in different industries. The notion here is that, within the high-technology area, different industries exhibit different types of R&D activities, and that Japan and the US have specialized in different industries according to comparative advantage.

Table 6.7 Export index of revealed comparative advantage: high-technology products (rankings are shown in column 2)

Industry	Japan 1967 (1)	(2)	1971 (1)	(2)	1975 (1)	(2)	1979 (1)	(2)	1983 (1)	(2)	United States 1967 (1)	(2)	1971 (1)	(2)	1975 (1)	(2)	1979 (1)	(2)	1983 (1)	(2)
Telephone and telegraphic equipment	101	120	190	71	199	54	249	41	335	37	85	124	61	129	84	118	127	94	147	82
Aircraft engines	10	161	4	163	7	161	9	159	15	155	452	7	559	5	504	6	545	3	597	2
Aircraft	38	155	17	159	4	164	6	162	5	161	648	1	976	1	924	1	724	1	661	1
Computers	84	132	42	149	68	125	96	109	297	41	87	121	126	90	300	14	518	4	433	8
Photographic equipment and supplies	465	33	343	32	403	20	573	11	620	7	284	27	283	23	257	24	257	26	239	33
Drugs	67	140	62	137	43	137	52	130	44	136	175	72	161	70	152	70	189	50	244	31
Electronic components	208	74	168	76	207	50	316	33	345	33	278	29	283	22	244	29	255	28	278	21
Optical instruments	1145	2	882	3	808	3	910	3	700	5	97	116	123	93	114	100	118	100	149	77
Agricultural chemicals	137	98	91	122	82	113	74	125	106	108	202	52	225	37	223	35	360	11	382	11
Scientific instruments	138	96	110	111	119	92	195	60	165	81	373	12	381	9	288	16	203	41	226	35
Calculating and accounting machines	99	123	433	24	718	4	1076	2	1098	2	455	6	424	7	68	178	57	141	86	118
Synthetic fibers	473	31	361	27	517	14	327	32	286	42	138	94	184	59	121	92	284	22	167	59
Cellulosic fibers	550	21	451	20	501	16	420	20	383	28	33	153	58	133	62	135	191	49	385	10
Platework and boilers	206	75	262	49	253	36	233	48	227	57	287	25	203	46	260	22	216	40	244	32
Steam engines and turbines	188	84	212	62	204	51	250	40	132	92	147	87	196	52	264	21	326	14	594	4
Internal combustion engines	102	119	148	87	177	66	248	42	269	45	317	22	322	16	288	15	322	15	304	18
Office machinery	89	127	73	135	75	119	137	88	139	77	420	9	576	4	534	4	497	6	544	3
Typewriters	194	80	211	64	170	69	261	38	558	11	101	108	47	140	54	142	113	105	149	76
Medical instruments	128	104	144	90	142	82	157	76	151	82	365	13	340	10	312	13	286	21	316	17
Average	89		79		69		61		60		54		47		49		39		32	

Source: GATT tapes.
Note: (1) Revealed comparative advantage index; (2) ranking of revealed comparative advantage indices.

Table 6.8 Net export index of revealed comparative advantage: high-technology products (rankings are shown in column 2)

Industry	Japan 1967 (1)	(2)	1971 (1)	(2)	1975 (1)	(2)	1979 (1)	(2)	1983 (1)	(2)	United States 1967 (1)	(2)	1971 (1)	(2)	1975 (1)	(2)	1979 (1)	(2)	1983 (1)	(2)
Telephone and telegraphic equipment	72.4	77	84.9	17	89.8	22	92.4	15	82.9	27	18.3	86	-14.6	100	33.0	73	16.4	82	-19.7	100
Aircraft engines	-80.3	161	-102.4	159	-82.2	155	-74.2	154	-76.5	156	51.2	44	64.7	29	62.4	29	62.0	27	53.3	27
Aircraft	-83.2	144	-91.5	156	-92.0	157	-85.9	158	-100.5	158	82.8	7	95.4	5	86.9	3	92.8	4	88.5	8
Computers	-29.2	149	-47.3	151	-54.8	150	18.6	133	56.3	81	34.0	68	10.0	98	67.8	25	79.9	8	54.6	25
Photographic equipment and supplies	74.8	76	57.4	77	68.0	62	76.4	50	72.9	55	41.2	59	35.5	60	42.4	62	21.3	77	0.1	76
Drugs	-44.4	155	-53.8	154	-56.1	151	-53.9	145	-60.9	150	54.5	41	51.9	41	50.8	50	40.4	55	39.2	35
Electronic components	48.7	107	27.5	117	44.5	89	58.2	79	58.9	78	47.0	51	37.4	57	23.4	86	7.4	90	3.9	82
Optical instruments	97.6	28	80.8	34	85.8	32	87.6	29	75.5	46	-49.2	131	-36.3	121	-31.7	127	-28.3	124	-26.2	108
Agricultural chemicals	36.8	113	9.7	133	23.6	110	25.4	109	51.3	81	73.5	17	71.5	23	52.7	46	71.9	14	71.4	14
Scientific instruments	13.7	128	7.5	136	26.8	107	31.5	104	26.5	117	67.0	29	72.8	20	66.7	26	30.9	68	27.0	47
Calculating and accounting machines	-24.8	148	46.8	89	89.2	24	98.4	7	89.9	6	57.3	38	40.8	54	-58.6	141	-58.1	143	-55.0	138
Synthetic fibers	104.7	7	88.0	8	99.2	5	64.6	70	78.7	39	15.5	89	48.1	49	60.7	31	93.1	3	46.4	31
Cellulosic fibers	105.1	3	90.1	1	101.4	1	102.6	3	91.6	2	-44.9	127	8.1	96	22.1	90	88.9	6	105.7	3
Platework and boilers	51.0	100	31.5	112	71.0	55	87.2	31	66.3	69	87.0	3	75.6	15	80.6	9	91.0	5	97.0	5
Steam engines and turbines	18.3	124	37.4	102	43.0	92	74.8	52	51.4	86	36.9	63	22.8	74	57.1	35	51.2	37	95.1	7
Internal combustion engines	68.8	92	72.9	52	85.6	35	89.1	25	84.5	21	24.5	80	1.4	93	13.7	95	16.1	83	-1.5	78
Office machinery	-57.6	160	-53.6	153	0.2	126	33.0	101	47.3	94	60.5	35	71.7	22	55.7	38	51.1	39	25.7	48
Typewriters	29.4	117	32.8	110	58.2	81	81.7	37	86.8	14	-50.6	133	-68.6	142	-67.1	144	-50.2	138	-39.1	124
Medical instruments	29.8	116	34.4	107	13.5	115	14.1	115	21.7	118	62.1	33	65.6	27	58.0	33	51.2	37	53.5	26
Average		100		94		79		71		70		57		56		54		52		49

Source: GATT tapes.
Note: See Table 6.7.

Kodama and Honda (1986) estimate a cross-section model which' classifies industries according to three patterns of R&D activities. The fundamental insight of the model is that the rapidity of technological innovation in an industry can be characterized by the likelihood of 'survivability' of a given research project as it moves from exploratory research to investment for production. Three typologies are developed. In the 'traditional pattern' the likelihood of project cancellation, once investment for production has begun, goes to zero. In the 'science-based pattern', the likelihood of project cancellation remains constant throughout the life of the project. In between these extremes, is the 'high-tech pattern' in which the likelihood of project cancellation declines as the project progresses, but the probability of termination always remains non-zero. Even at the point of investment, the introduction of competing technologies may lead to the termination of the project.

This perspective has implications for the pattern of specialization within the high-technology area. Science-based industries, such as chemicals, will be dominated by large firms which can finance the basic science research necessary for innovation. This may help explain why Japan still has not developed a strong comparative advantage in chemicals despite her abundant endowments in human and physical capital.[11] Conversely, Japan has fared better in the 'high-tech pattern' industries where research is more product specific and management of research activities is more important. Areas of future Japanese specialization may be drugs, where the rise of biotechnologies may be shifting R&D activities in this industry from a 'science-based' to a 'high-tech' pattern (Kodama, 1986, p. 294), and computer peripheral devices.

CONCLUSION

This chapter has examined changes in the comparative advantage of the United States and Japan as 'revealed' by indices of relative export shares and ratios of net exports. This has been done both by comparing the two sets of indices, and their changes over time, and by relating the structure of comparative advantage to factor intensities and R&D expenditures in an econometric investigation.

Comparisons of export and net export indices show increased specialization in Japan in human capital-intensive products, at the expense of unskilled labor-intensive and natural resource products between 1967 and 1985. In turn, the United States became increasingly specialized in natural resource-intensive products.

The above results have been obtained by calculating indices of 'revealed' comparative advantage for all merchandise trade. In turn, the econometric investigation of the determinants of comparative advantage has been limited to manufactured goods. At the same time, in addition to factor intensity, these estimates consider the research intensity of the individual industries.

The econometric estimates revealed the transformation of Japan's comparative advantage from unskilled labor-intensive to human capital- and R&D-intensive manufactured goods, with its position with regard to physical capital-intensive products being approximately maintained over time. In turn, in the United States the principal change involved increased specialization in R&D-intensive products while the strong US disadvantage in unskilled labor-intensive products and its relative advantages in human capital- and physical capital-intensive products changed little over time.

An inspection of data for high-technology (R&D-intensive) product groups confirms these conclusions as both countries are shown to have increased their comparative advantages in these product groups. At the same time, there is some evidence that the two countries specialized in different industries within high tech. This may have been due to strategic trade considerations, and differences in the kinds of R&D activities pursued in different industries.

To the extent that the pattern of specialization is determined by relative endowments, one would expect both the US and Japan to maintain comparative advantage in human capital-intensive products, since the stock of human capital embodied by the labor force changes gradually and human capital is relatively immobile internationally. Thus, it is likely that endowments change slowly relative to the rest of the world. Likewise, the US could be expected to maintain its specialization in natural resource-intensive products.

A major uncertainty is the future rate of Japanese physical capital accumulation. If Japan maintained its saving rate of the past 30 years, Japan would develop a very high degree of abundance in physical capital relative to the rest of the world, and would specialize in physical capital-intensive products. However, Japan's saving rate has been falling in recent years. Furthermore, as physical capital becomes more mobile internationally it ceases to be a source of comparative advantage. Thus, the future importance of physical capital endowments in determining the international pattern of production is uncertain.

One can imagine a future pattern of specialization in which the US specializes in natural resource-based products and high-technology products, while Japan specializes in a broader range of manufactures. This implies that in the long run the development of the newly industrialized countries of East Asia will pose greater problems of structural adjustment for Japan than for the US.

APPENDIX

The industrial data for Japan have been taken from *1973 Census of Manufactures, Report by Industry*, Research and Statistics Department, Ministry of International Trade and Industry, May 1976. The Japanese unskilled wage has been defined as the average wage of workers 17 years old and under, and those 24 years old and under. As Urata (1983, p. 679) observed 'Japanese workers usually gain their professional skills through on-the-job training so that close relation exists between workers' skill level and their duration of employment at a particular company. While data on duration of employment are not available, the immobility of Japanese labor markets means that the workers' age may be a good proxy for employment and hence skill level.' The data derive from the Ministry of Labor, *1973 Industrial Wage Structure*, 1974. They have been collected by Dr Anne Loup-Richards of the OECD. Data on research and development expenditures have been kindly provided by Mr H. Katayama of the Agency of Industrial Science and Technology, Ministry of International Trade and Industry. Since the R&D data cover the period 1971–82 the 1971 values were used in the 1967 regressions, and 1982 values in the 1983 regressions.

For the United States, data on value added, employment and wages have been obtained from the Census Bureau, *Census of Manufactures*, various issues. The unskilled wage data (annual earnings of full-time workers aged 18–19) originate in the Bureau of Labor Statistics Bulletin 2031, *Annual Earnings and Employment Patterns of Private Non-Agricultural Employees, 1973–1975*, 1979, Tables A-3, B-3, and C-3.

The research and development data have been taken from the Federal Trade Commission, Statistical Report: *Annual Line of Business 1974; 1975; and 1976*, September 1981, September 1981 and May 1982, respectively. This data is preferable to the widely used National Science Foundation data on two counts. It is far more disaggregated (approximately four-digit SIC vs two-digit SIC for the NSF data) and, in contrast to the NSF figures which are calculated using raw data classified by firm, the FTC figures are constructed using raw data classified by plant, hence yield a more accurate indication of research and development expenditures in different product classes for multiproduct firms.

The data for value added, wages and employment have been averaged for the period 1973–5. The data on research and development expenditures have been averaged over the mid-sample period, 1974–6, which were the only years available.

NOTES

1. Under this procedure, it is possible for the normalized net export index (NX'_{ij}) to exceed 1.0 in absolute value if, for instance, the non-normalized index (NX_{ij}) is 1.0 and the country has an aggregate trade deficit. In the tables, each index has been multiplied by 100 for purposes of presentation.
2. The non-normalized indices have been used in estimation. The lack of normalization does not affect the estimated results of these cross-section regressions, as the effects of the overall trade balance are absorbed in the intercept term.

3. Australia, Austria, Belgium, Canada, Denmark, Finland, France, Germany, Ireland, Israel, Italy, Japan, Netherlands, Norway, Sweden, Switzerland, United Kingdom, and the United States.

4. Argentina, Brazil, Egypt, Greece, Hong Kong, Indonesia, Korea, Malaysia, Mexico, Morocco, Philippines, Portugal, Singapore, Spain, Taiwan, Thailand, Tunisia, Turkey, and Yugoslavia (India and Pakistan meet the criteria but have not been included for lack of data while Indonesia has been added, although it meets the second criterion but not the first.)

5. In conformity with the system of international trade classification, the data do not include food, beverages and tobacco; agricultural raw materials; and non-oil mineral products. However, the average includes petroleum and coal products.

6. The results obtained using the unadjusted measure are available from the authors upon request.

7. The data sources are described in the Appendix.

8. Leamer and Bowen (1981), and Aw (1983) have demonstrated that regressions of trade on factor intensity variables may yield misleading inferences in the absence of data on factor endowments in the multifactor model. In this chapter, however, reference will be made to data on factor endowments below.

9. These results are broadly similar to those obtained by Urata for unskilled labor and physical capital. However, Urata was unable to obtain significant coefficient estimates for his human capital-intensity variable in the net export regressions. It may be added that Urata did not have a research and development variable while he included an energy variable that was significant statistically for 1975, although not for 1967, the two years for which estimates were made.

10. There is only one such category (cellulose fibers) if use is made of the net export index of revealed comparative advantage but the results are, nevertheless, broadly similar. The following discussion will be based on the export indices alone.

11. Japan's unexpected weakness in chemicals has also been identified by Dixit (1987, p. 7).

REFERENCES

Aw, Bee-Yan (1983) 'The Interpretation of Cross-Section Regression Tests of the Heckscher-Ohlin Theorem with Many Goods and Factors', *Journal of International Economics*, 14: 163–7.

Balassa, Bela (1965) 'Trade Liberalization and "Revealed" Comparative Advantage', *Manchester School* 33: 99–123. Reprinted as Chapter 4 in this volume.

Balassa, Bela (1977) ' "Revealed" Comparative Advantage Revisited: An Analysis of Relative Export Shares of the Industrial Countries, 1953–1971', *Manchester School* 45: 327–44. Reprinted as Chapter 5 in this volume.

Balassa, Bela (1979) 'The Changing Pattern of Comparative Advantage in Manufactured Goods', *Review of Economics and Statistics*, 61: 259–66. Reprinted as Chapter 2 in this volume.

Balassa, Bela (1986) 'Comparative Advantage in Manufactured Goods: A Reappraisal', *Review of Economics and Statistics*, 68: 315–19. Reprinted as Chapter 3 in this volume.

Branson, William H., and Nicholaos Monoyios (1977) 'Factor Inputs in US Trade', *Journal of International Economics*, 7: 111–31.

Dixit, Avinash (1987) 'Prospects for High-Technology Industries and Trade Between the US and Japan', paper presented at the MITI symposium on 'Cooperative Development of the Japanese and US Economies', Tokyo, 29–30 January 1987.

Kodama, Fumio (1986) 'Technological Diversification in Japanese Industry', *Science*, 233: 291–6.

Kodama, Fumio, and Yukichi Honda (1986) 'Research and Development Dynamics of High-Tech Industry–Toward the Definition of High Technology', *Journal of Science Policy and Research Management*, 1: 65–74.

Leamer, Edward E., and Harry P. Bowen (1981) 'Cross-Section Tests of the Heckscher-Ohlin Theorem: Comment', *American Economic Review*, 71: 1040–3.

Maskus, Keith E. (1983) 'Evidence on Shifts in the Determinants of the Structure of US Manufacturing Foreign Trade, 1958–1976', *Review of Economics and Statistics*, 65: 415–22.

Noland, Marcus (1985) 'The Determinants of Comparative Advantage: Empirical Analysis in a Multicountry Time-Series Cross-Section Framework', The Johns Hopkins University, unpublished dissertation.

Stern, Robert M. and Keith E. Maskus (1981) 'Determinants of the Structure of US Foreign Trade, 1958–1976', *Journal of International Economics*, 11: 207–24.

Urata, Shijiro (1983) 'Factor Inputs and Japanese Manufacturing Trade Structure', *Review of Economics and Statistics*, 65: 678–84.

White, Halbert (1980) 'A Heteroscedastic Consistent Covariance Matrix Estimator and a Direct Test for Heteroscedaticity', *Econometrica* 47: 817–38.

PART II

TARIFFS AND TRADE

7 · TRADE CREATION AND TRADE DIVERSION IN THE EUROPEAN COMMON MARKET

I

Following the lead provided by Jacob Viner, several contributors to the theory of customs unions have suggested that the desirability of a union be evaluated with reference to its trade-creating and trade-diverting effects.[1] At the same time, while a number of criteria have been put forward for appraising the chances of trade creation and trade diversion in a union, it seems to be generally agreed that an *a priori* judgement regarding the *net* effect of customs unions on trade flows cannot be made.[2] This circumstance lends especial interest to empirical studies of trade creation and trade diversion in a customs union. Such investigations can be of an *ex ante* or an *ex post* character; one may attempt to evaluate the possible repercussions in advance or after the union has been established.

Among *ex ante* estimates, those of P. J. Verdoorn, L. H. Janssen and L. B. Krause may be mentioned.[3] Verdoorn and Janssen used a general-equilibrium framework in their investigation and inquired into the effects of changing one variable – eliminating internal tariffs in the union – on trade flows and on the terms of trade. Their work has been subject to criticism on theoretical as well as on empirical grounds, and they have been said to have underestimated prospective trade creation – in part because of their failure to take account of intra-industry specialization following the elimination of tariffs within a union.[4] On the other hand, Krause appears to have over-estimated the trade-diverting effects of the European Common Market for United States exports by assuming a high supply elasticity for the 'dominant suppliers' within the EEC.[5]

In discussions on the actual effects of integration on trade flows, the rise of

At various stages in the preparation of this chapter I have had the able collaboration of M. Alain Camu, Economic Adviser to the Belgian Prime Minister. I am also indebted to Messrs Mesnage of the Commission of the EEC and Nederveen of the OECD for helpful discussions. Much of the research on this chapter was financed by the Economic Growth Center of Yale University. First published in *The Economic Journal*, March 1967.

intra-area trade as a proportion of the total (intra- and extra-area) exports and imports of the EEC countries has often been interpreted as evidence for the trade-creating effects of the Common Market.[6] But these results may conceivably be explained by the increasing importance of the EEC in world markets and by changes in its competitive position. To abstract from the influence of the latter factors, Alexandre Lamfalussy has suggested that we should compare changes in the share of the European Economic Community, as an import market, in the exports of participating and non-participating countries, and should examine the relative performance of the EEC countries in the markets of the Community and elsewhere.

Having considered changes in trade flows between 1958 and 1960, as well as between 1960 and 1962 (first three quarters), Lamfalussy has not found clear evidence for either a positive (trade-creating) or a negative (trade-diverting) effect of the Common Market.[7] Similar conclusions have been reached by R. L. Major of the United Kingdom National Institute of Economic and Social Research, who has examined the share of individual exporters in Common Market imports for 11 commodity groups.[8]

While the method used by Lamfalussy avoids the pitfalls of arguing from a comparison of the relative proportions of intra-area and extra-area trade, it is open to the objection that, by proceeding in a piecemeal fashion, it does not provide fully consistent results. To remedy this deficiency, Jean Waelbroeck has proposed that comparisons be made between actual and hypothetical trade flows, the latter being calculated under the assumption that the structure of world trade indicated by the world trade matrix of an earlier year has remained unchanged.[9] This solution amounts to the application of a procedure suggested by Richard Stone and Alan Brown for examining changes in input–output matrices.

Extrapolating the 1951–2 world trade matrix to 1959–60, and the 1960 matrix to 1962 and first half of 1963, Waelbroeck has concluded that 'the existence of a "Common Market effect" on the composition of world trade can hardly be doubted'.[10] Analogous conclusions have been reached by P. J. Verdoorn and F. J. M. Meyer zu Schlochtern who used a similar method.[11] But, as Waelbroeck notes, results obtained by the use of these procedures do not permit us to judge whether the observed 'deformation' of the world trade matrix has been due to trade creation or to trade diversion. The finding that actual intra-EEC trade exceeds hypothetical trade, calculated under the assumption of an unchanged composition of world trade, is compatible with trade creation as well as trade diversion: the Common Market countries trade more with each other, either because the reduction of intra-area tariffs has created new trade or because trade has been diverted from extra-area to intra-area channels.

To provide an indication of the trade-creating and trade-diverting effects of the EEC, Waelbroeck has suggested the application of a method used by Tinbergen and two Finnish economists, P. Pöyhönen and K. Pullianinen, to the problem at hand.[12] These authors attempted to explain trade flows by regression analysis, with gross national products and geographical distance as the principal determining variables. In the Finnish study the following formula was used to describe the influences affecting the exports of country i to country j:

$$x_{ij} = cc_i c_j \frac{y_i{}^a y_j{}^b}{r^d{}_{ij}} \qquad (1)$$

when y_i and y_j are the gross national products of the two countries, c_i and c_j are their export and import parameters indicating the 'openness' of their economies, r_{ij} is the distance between them and c is a scale factor.

Waelbroeck has assumed that the coefficients c, c_i and c_j would remain unchanged over time, and has utilized the values of coefficients a and b, estimated from a cross-section investigation of world trade in the year 1958, to extrapolate the matrix of world trade from 1958 to 1962. Comparing the hypothetical trade figures derived by the use of this method with actual trade, Waelbroeck has found that intra-EEC trade has increased considerably more than the Finnish model would have led us to expect. At the same time there is no evidence for trade diversion on imports from North America and from the countries of the European Free Trade Association, inasmuch as actual imports exceed hypothetical imports in trade with these areas, too.

But similar developments had taken place between 1954 and 1958, and hence the results do not provide a clear indication of the trade-creating and the trade-diverting effects of the Common Market.[13] At any rate, one may question the validity of a method that applies average income elasticities of export supply and import demand, calculated in a cross-section analysis of *all* trading countries, to the European Economic Community. In fact, these elasticities are generally higher in the industrial economies, and lower in less-developed areas, since increased international specialization within the manufacturing sector tends to raise the share of foreign trade in GNP in the former group of countries, while industrialization cum protectionism have the opposite effect in the latter. Thus, the relatively high income elasticities of export supply and import demand in the Common Market countries will explain, in part, the presumed internal *and* external trade creation.[14] Further, a consideration of total exports and imports has only limited interest, since the aggregate results may conceal changes in opposite directions with respect to individual commodities and commodity groups.

In turn, in a cross-section study of 38 commodities, Verdoorn and Meyer zu Schlochtern have attempted to explain inter-commodity differences in the expansion of imports into the Common Market by utilizing as explanatory variables a weighted average of internal and external tariff reductions and an index representing 'effective import demand'. The latter has been calculated as an unweighted average of the rates of change of imports of the commodities in question into the United Kingdom, Sweden, Denmark and Switzerland, and is taken to reflect the expansion of trade that would have taken place in the absence of the EEC's establishment.[15]

Depending on the form of the regression equation used, the apparent impact of tariff changes on trade corresponds to an elasticity of -2.1 or -3.9 with respect to price, when the latter, but not the former, is significantly different from zero at the 5 percent confidence level. The results thus provide some evidence of the trade-creating *and* trade-diverting effects of the EEC.[16] But the method utilized is open to the usual objections against calculating substitution elasticities from cross-section data. Further, one may question the validity of using the data of four EFTA countries with lower growth rates and rather different economic structure as a yardstick for the expansion of trade that would have taken place in the absence of the Common Market's establishment, especially in view of the fact that by 1962 – the terminal year of the calculations – there might have already been an 'EFTA effect'.

II

This short survey indicates some of the problems encountered in the estimation of trade creation and trade diversion in a customs union. In particular, we note the need for: (a) abstracting from the effects of economic growth on trade flows; (b) ensuring the comparability of the estimates of trade creation and trade diversion; (c) providing for a disaggregation of the results according to the main commodity categories; and (d) indicating the effects on individual supplying areas.

I earlier suggested that a comparison of *ex post* income elasticities of import demand[17] in intra-area and extra-area trade, for periods preceding and following integration, may provide a way of dealing with the first two problems.[18] Under the assumption that income elasticities of import demand would have remained unchanged in the absence of integration, a rise in the income elasticity of demand for intra-area imports would indicate gross trade creation, while an increase in the income elasticity of demand for imports from all sources of supply would give expression to trade creation proper. In turn, a fall in the income elasticity of demand for extra-area imports would provide evidence of the trade-diverting effects of the union.[19]

In other words, it is assumed that the Common Market's establishment has been the single largest influence affecting trade flows in the EEC, and long-run influences or special factors would not have appreciably altered the relationships between imports and GNP – expressed by the income elasticities of import demand for the period preceding integration – during the period that has elapsed since.[20] At the same time, by comparing the relationship of internal and external trade to GNP between the pre-integration and the post-integration periods, the proposed method abstracts from changes in the growth rate of national income, and provides comparable estimates of trade creation and trade diversion.[21]

In applying this method, separate consideration can also be given to individual commodity categories and supplying areas. The commodity categories distinguished in the present study are temperate zone foods, beverages and tobacco (SITC $0+1$ less 07), raw materials $(2+4)$, fuels (3), chemicals (5), machinery $(71+72)$, transport equipment (73) and other manufactured goods $(6+8)$.[22] Estimates relating to these commodity categories have further been utilized to indicate the impact of the Common Market's establishment on imports from various groups of non-member countries.[23]

In the calculations the pre-integration period has been taken to include the years 1953–9, and the post-integration period 1959–65. Thus, 1959, the year when the actual operation of the Common Market began, has been chosen as the 'benchmark' year that separates the two periods. Although tariff reductions were undertaken already on 1 January of that year, these were extended to non-member countries, so that there was no discrimination against outsiders until 1960. At the same time the choice of the year 1959 has appeared preferable to using an average of the years 1958–60. With the exception of trade in ships and acroplanes, 1959 was apparently a 'normal' year as far as the internal and external trade relations of the Common Market are concerned. On the other hand, imports in 1958 declined due to the recession in that year, and trade flows in 1960 were already affected by the EEC's establishment.

By abstracting from the influence of changes in the rate of growth of GNP on trade, this method purports to indicate the static effects of integration, i.e., the impact of the elimination of internal duties on trade under *ceteris paribus* assumptions. But the results are not meant to reflect the full impact of the union's establishment on trade flows, since no account is taken of the possible influence of integration on economic growth. Should the actual growth rate exceed the rate that would have been obtained in the absence of integration, the increase in intra-area trade resulting from the establishment of the union would be understated, and the decrease in extra-area imports generally overestimated.[24]

The influence of non-recurring factors, structural changes and uncertainties relating to the underlying relationships also gives rise to errors. A further consideration is that the statistical reliability of the estimates cannot be tested. Correspondingly, the results shown in the following sections should be considered as being indicative of general tendencies rather than expressing exact magnitudes.

III

A consideration of *ex post* income elasticities of demand for imports of all commodities, taken together, provides evidence of trade creation in the

European Common Market, while there is no indication of trade diversion (Table 7.1). Between the periods 1953–9 and 1959–65 the income elasticity of demand increased from 1.8 to 2.1 with respect to total (intra- and extra-area) imports, it rose from 2.4 to 2.8 for intra-area trade and it hardly changed in regard to extra-area imports (1.6 as against 1.7). But the results vary to a considerable extent between commodity groups, and more useful conclusions can be reached if the data are appropriately disaggregated.

Table 7.1 Ex-post income elasticities of import demand in the European Common Market

| | | Annual rate of growth | | Ex-post income elasticity of import demand | | |
		1953–9	1959–65	1953–9	1959–65	Difference
Total imports (M_t)						
0+1−07	Non-tropical food, beverages, tobacco	9.0	8.3	1.7	1.6	−0.1
2+4	Raw materials	5.9	5.9	1.1	1.1	0
3	Fuels	8.9	12.2	1.6	2.3	+0.7
5	Chemicals	16.1	18.0	3.0	3.3	+0.3
71+72	Machinery	8.0	15.4	1.5	2.8	+1.3
73	Transport equipment	14.2	18.4	2.6	3.4	+0.8
6+8	Other manufactured goods	14.4	13.3	2.6	2.5	−0.1
0 to 8−07	Total of above	9.6	11.2	1.8	2.1	+0.3
Intra-area imports (M_t)						
0+1−07	Non-tropical food, beverages, tobacco	13.8	13.2	2.5	2.4	−0.1
2+4	Raw materials	10.3	10.3	1.9	1.9	0
3	Fuels	5.9	7.0	1.1	1.3	+0.2
5	Chemicals	16.2	21.4	3.0	4.0	+1.0
71+72	Machinery	11.3	16.9	2.1	3.1	+1.0
73	Transport equipment	15.6	20.6	2.9	3.8	+0.9
6+8	Other manufactured goods	15.1	15.8	2.8	2.9	+0.1
0 to 8−07	Total of above	12.8	15.1	2.4	2.8	+0.4
Extra-area imports (M_e)						
0+1−07	Non-tropical food, beverages, tobacco	7.7	6.3	1.4	1.2	−0.2
2+4	Raw materials	5.3	5.0	1.0	0.9	−0.1
3	Fuels	9.9	13.6	1.8	2.5	+0.7
5	Chemicals	16.0	14.8	3.0	2.7	−0.3
71+72	Machinery	5.0	13.6	0.9	2.5	+1.6
73	Transport equipment	12.1	14.1	2.2	2.4	+0.2
6+8	Other manufactured goods	13.7	10.3	2.5	1.9	−0.6
0 to 8−07	Total of above	8.3	9.0	1.6	1.7	+0.1
	Gross national product	5.4	5.4			

Sources: OECD (formerly OEEC), *Foreign Trade, Statistical Bulletins*, 1953–65, Office Statistique des Communautés Européennes, Commerce Extérieur, Tableaux Analytiques, 1958–65.
Note: To express import values in current prices, unit value indices have been derived by utilizing the appropriate indices for individual countries. An exception has been made in the case of tropical products, machinery and transport equipment, where the indices have been calculated from the original data.

To begin with, the data of Table 7.1 do not show trade creation in food, beverages and tobacco. This conclusion is not affected if, instead of the gross national product, food consumption is used as the explanatory variable, since the income elasticity of demand for food failed to decline between the pre-integration and the post-integration period. On the other hand, there is some indication of trade creation in the raw materials category if imports are related to industrial production rather than to GNP.[25]

Further, the data point to the existence of trade diversion in food and raw materials, inasmuch as changes in income elasticities of demand between the two periods show a shift from foreign to partner-country sources of supply. Within the food, beverages and tobacco group, member-country producers have increased their share to a considerable extent in imports of live animals, dairy products, wheat and sugar into the food-deficit countries of the EEC. In the case of these products, the actual – and anticipated – effects of Common Market agricultural policy appear to have been of importance.[26] The reduction in the preferential advantages accorded to Algerian wine in France and the lowering of internal tariffs on tobacco have further contributed to this result.

Tariff preferences have affected the pattern of trade in some raw materials, too. Shifts from foreign producers to partner-country sources of supply have taken place in the case of rubber, where the reduction of internal duties has been accompanied by substitution against natural and synthetic rubber originating in non-member countries. Moreover, subsidies to the production of rapeseed and tariff discrimination against vegetable oils of foreign origin have tended to discourage extra-area imports of oils and oil-seeds.

Different considerations apply to fuels where an acceleration of extra-area imports is shown. Observed changes in trade patterns reflect the policy followed by the EEC countries which aims at reducing reliance on high-cost domestic coal. The chief beneficiaries of this policy have been the less-developed countries that provide over 80 percent of oil consumed in the Common Market. In view of the considerations underlying the energy policy of the Community, recent trends with regard to oil imports are expected to continue.

With the exception of semi-manufactures and non-durable consumer goods, included in the group of other manufactures, the establishment of the Common Market appears to have led to trade creation in manufactured products. At the same time there is evidence of trade diversion in two of these groups of commodities, whereas the increase in the income elasticity of demand for extra-area imports of machinery and transport equipment points to 'external trade creation'. It is the latter result that requires explanation, since tariff discrimination against outsiders would have been expected to lead to a deceleration rather than an acceleration of purchases from non-member countries.

I noted above that the choice of the year 1959 as the benchmark between the pre-integration and the post-integration periods gives rise to distortions in the calculations concerning transport equipment. By reason of a large decline in the imports of ships and aeroplanes occurring in 1959, the extra-area imports of transport equipment of that year were considerably below the level of the preceding and the following years.[27] Thus, if we replace the data for 1959 by an average of the years 1958–60, trade diversion rather than external trade creation is shown.

As regards machinery, one may argue that it is incorrect to relate imports to gross national product in the calculations, since an accelerator-type relationship may exist between investment in machinery and national income. However, the results are hardly affected if, instead of GNP, purchases of machinery and equipment are used as the explanatory variable, inasmuch as the ratio of these purchases to the gross national product hardly changed between the two periods.[28] It would appear, then, that the explanation must lie elsewhere.

It is suggested here that the observed acceleration in Common Market imports of machinery from non-participating countries can, in great part, be explained by reference to the investment boom that accompanied the establishment of the EEC. The investment boom necessitated substantial purchases of machinery and equipment which domestic capacities could not cope with. In turn, the rate of increase of extra-area imports of machinery declined as the investment boom subsided and domestic machine-building capacities caught up with demand.

According to this explanation, an accelerator-type relationship exists between machinery purchases, on the one hand, and the imports of machinery from non-member countries, on the other, so that the share of foreign suppliers in the incremental purchases of machinery will tend to rise with the increase in the rate of growth of these purchases. The data of Table 7.2 provide support to this proposition. With machinery purchases rising at an average annual rate of 16.4 percent during the investment boom of 1959–61, the imports of machinery from non-member countries increased 35.4 percent a year.

In turn, with the slackening of investment activity after 1961, there has been a decline in the annual rate of increase of extra-area machinery imports.[29] A year-to-year comparison of the relevant figures indicates that this decline has led to a continuous fall of the share of imports in the incremental purchases of machinery.[30]

IV

I have shown that while aggregate relationships provide no indication of trade diversion following the establishment of the European Common Market, different conclusions apply if the data are appropriately disaggregated. Thus,

Table 7.2 Common Market machinery purchases and imports (In current prices)

| | Purchases of machinery and equipment | | Extra-area machinery imports | | Ratio of annual rate of change (4):(2) | Relative prices of EEC machinery Index 1959 = 100[a] |
| | Index 1959 = 100 | Annual rate of change | Index 1959 = 100 | Annual rate of change | | |
	(1)	(2)	(3)	(4)	(5)	(6)
1959	100.0	—	100.0	—	—	100.0
1960	118.1	+ 18.1	135.3	+ 35.3	2.0	101.6
1961	135.6	+ 14.8	183.6	+ 35.6	2.4	102.0
1962	150.1	+ 10.7	225.2	+ 18.6	1.7	105.1
1963	160.9	+ 7.2	236.3	+ 8.5	1.2	106.5
1964	169.9	+ 5.6	250.0	+ 5.8	1.0	107.6
1965	n.a.	n.a.	251.0	+ 0.4	n.a.	n.a.

Source: See Appendix Table 7.1 and Organization for Economic Co-operation and Development, *General Statistics*, January 1965.
[a] The index of relative prices has been calculated as a ratio of the implicit deflator for purchases of machinery and equipment in the EEC to the average of the corresponding deflators for the United States and the United Kingdom, weighted by their respective machinery exports to the Common Market in 1959.

for all non-market countries, taken together, trade diversion in several commodity categories has apparently been compensated by changes in the opposite direction in fuels and machinery. But this result conceals substantial inter-regional differences, and the net effect on individual suppliers will depend on the composition of their exports to the Common Market.

In the present section I will examine some of the factors determining the export performance of non-member countries in EEC markets. Non-member countries have been classified in seven groups: (1) the United States; (2) the United Kingdom; (3) the Continental countries of the European Free Trade Association; (4) Other developed countries;[31] (5) Communist economies; (6) Countries and territories associated with the Common Market; and (7) Other less-developed countries. Among the factors determining export performance, I have attempted to separate a 'Common Market effect', a 'competitive effect', and have further calculated differences in the value of exports expressed in current and in constant prices.

For each supplying area the 'Common Market effect' has been taken as the difference between two sets of estimates of hypothetical imports into the EEC, calculated by applying actual growth rates of total extra-area imports in the periods 1959–65 and 1953–9, respectively, to the 1959 imports of the main commodity categories. In turn, the 'competitive effect' gives expression to changes in the shares of the seven supplying areas in the extra-area imports of these groups of commodities into the Common Market; it has been derived by summing up the differences between actual imports, measured in constant prices, and hypothetical imports, calculated by applying growth rates of total extra-area imports in the post-integration period to the 1959 imports of each commodity category.[32]

Price changes between 1959 and 1965 provide the third influence on export values. However, in the absence of reliable information on price elasticities and on changes in relative prices in the appropriate commodity breakdown, the impact of changes in price-relationships on import volume has not been

Table 7.3 Extra-area imports into the European Common Market, 1959 and 1965

	Actual imports 1959	Hypothetical imports in 1965 calculated at growth rates of extra-area imports for the period		Actual imports, 1965	
		1953–9	1959–65	In 1959 prices	In 1965 prices
		(In 1959 prices)			
	(1)	(2)	(3)	(4)	(5)
United States	2,448	4,135	4,354	4,952	5,214
	100.0	168.9	177.9	202.3	213.0
United Kingdom	1,298	2,383	2,482	2,400	2,537
	100.0	183.2	191.2	184.9	195.5
Continental EFTA	2,448	4,215	4,160	3,874	4,160
	100.0	172.2	170.0	158.3	170.0
Other developed countries	1,866	2,896	2,730	2,955	3,194
	100.0	155.2	146.3	158.4	171.2
Communist economies	942	1,594	1,587	1,700	1,751
	100.0	169.2	168.5	180.5	185.9
Associated countries	1,344	2,113	1,980	2,041	2,041
	100.0	157.2	147.3	151.9	151.9
Other less-developed countries	5,770	9,491	9,776	9,147	8,976
	100.0	164.5	169.4	158.6	155.6
All non-member countries	16,116	26,827	27,069	27,069	27,873
	100.0	166.5	167.9	167.9	172.9

	Differences between actual and hypothetical imports, 1965			
	'Common Market effect' (3)–(2) (6)	'Competitive effect' (4)–(3) (7)	'Price effect' (5)–(4) (8)	Together (5)–(2) (9)
United States	+219	+598	+262	+1079
United Kingdom	+ 99	− 82	+137	+ 154
Continental EFTA	− 55	−286	+286	− 55
Other developed countries	−166	+225	+239	+ 298
Communist economies	− 7	+113	+ 51	+ 157
Associated countries	−133	+ 61	0	− 72
Other less-developed countries	+285	−629	−171	− 515
All non-member countries	+242	—	+804	+1046

Source: Appendix Table 7.1.

TRADE CREATION AND TRADE DIVERSION   119

estimated. Thus, the 'price effect' of Table 7.3 refers to the difference between imports expressed in current and in constant prices. In this connection, it should be noted that the use of the same price deflator with regard to the imports of a given commodity category from all suppliers is likely to give rise to errors in estimating the area breakdown of import volumes.

The results of the calculations are shown in Table 7.3 and in Appendix Table 7.1. It appears that a continuation of past trends in the extra-area imports of the eight commodity groups under consideration[33] would have led to relatively small discrepancies in the exports of the seven groups of countries to the Common Market, with deviations from the overall index of 166.5 rarely exceeding ten percentage points. But changes in the commodity composition of imports following the establishment of the European Common Market have widened inter-area differences in export performance: the range of the relevant index numbers is 146.3 to 191.2.

Apparently, the United States, the United Kingdom and the less-developed countries other than those associated with the EEC have, on balance, benefited from the 'Common Market effect' while other country groupings have suffered a loss. The United States and the United Kingdom have derived a gain from the high share of machinery in their exports to the Community; the less-developed countries have profited from the rapid expansion of EEC petroleum imports. In turn, all other areas have been handicapped by their reliance on exports of food, raw materials, semi-manufactured and non-durable consumer goods, for which trade diversion is shown. In 1965 sales of these commodities accounted for 90 percent of the exports of the group of other developed countries to the Common Market; the corresponding proportions were 72 percent for Continental EFTA, 70 percent for Soviet-type economies, 65 percent for the associated countries and territories, 55 percent for other less-developed countries and the United States, and 47 percent for the United Kingdom.

In addition to benefiting from the 'Common Market effect', the United States has also improved her competitive performance in most commodity categories, the major exception being fuels. American producers have increased their share in Common Market imports of cereals, fruit, fruit preparations and animal feed within the food, beverages and tobacco group, while the rapid expansion of soybean exports has given rise to above-average gains in the raw materials category. Further, the availability of new, technologically advanced, products[34] and the existence of excess capacity in American machine-building industries have contributed to the favorable United States performance in machinery exports, and United States producers have also gained in exporting a variety of non-durable consumer goods. On the other hand, the shift from coal to oil in EEC imports, associated with falling prices of petroleum and petroleum products, has adversely affected the United States performance within the fuels group.

Increases in her exports of livestock to the EEC from $4 million to $64 million largely explain the positive competitive effect shown for the United Kingdom in the food, beverages and tobacco group, with rising exports of whisky as a further contributing factor. However, Britain's competitive position has apparently deteriorated in most other commodity groups. These 'competitive' losses have largely wiped out the gain Britain has derived from the 'Common Market effect'.

A negative 'competitive effect' is indicated also in the case of the Continental EFTA countries. Among these countries, Denmark has been the main loser following the reduction of butter imports into the Common Market, and she also experienced a fall in her share of EEC imports of livestock, fresh meat, cereals and cheese. Furthermore, with capacity limitations restricting the expansion of machinery production and a relatively unfavourable product-mix, the Continental EFTA countries have not been able fully to utilize the opportunities offered through the growth of demand for machinery in the Common Market.

With the exception of food and raw materials, other developed countries appear to have improved their competitive position in all commodity categories. The greatest improvements have taken place in semi-manufactures and non-durable consumer goods, where Japanese exports to the Common Market rose from $46 million in 1959 to $239 million in 1965. Increases have been especially pronounced in exports of steel, clothing as well as photographic, medical and scientific instruments. Japan has also gained in the machinery group, with exports rising from $5 million to $65 million in this period. On the other hand, Australian exports of wheat have been a casualty of Common Market agricultural policy and have accounted for much of the 'competitive' losses shown in the food, beverages and tobacco group.

Communist countries have experienced 'competitive' gains in food and raw materials, as against losses in fuels. Within the first group much of the expansion has taken place in live animals, meat preparations and fruits exported chiefly from Hungary and Poland. Among raw materials, the Soviet Union has made considerable gains in wood and lumber, where resource limitations have restricted the expansion of exports from other areas; in turn, the reduced reliance on Soviet sources of supply of petroleum has found its origin in the energy policy followed by the EEC countries.

The performance of the countries and territories associated with the Common Market has largely been determined by changes in the pattern of French trade with Algeria. On the one hand, the decline in French imports of Algerian wine to a great extent explains the loss shown with regard to the food, beverages and tobacco group; on the other, the rise in imports of Algerian oil from $17 million in 1959 to $418 million in 1965 accounts for the spectacular increase in the associated countries' fuel exports.

But while increased Algerian exports of petroleum cut into the share of the Middle East, there is no evidence that the establishment of the Common Market would have led to a shift in the sources of supply of imports from other developing countries to the associated countries and territories. There has been no change in the relative share of competing suppliers in EEC imports of tropical beverages, for example. On the other hand, among non-associated countries, Zambia has benefited from the relatively slow increase in the exports of copper from the former Belgian Congo that accounts for much of the decline in the share of the associated countries in EEC imports of semi-manufactures.

Finally, in the exports of non-member countries to the Common Market improved prices of some foods and metals, machinery and transport equipment, as well as consumer non-durables and semi-manufactures, have not been fully offset by the fall in the prices of petroleum and chemicals. Still, the 'price effect' has been unfavourable for the group of other developing countries, in whose exports fuels play a major part. And, were we to consider the purchasing power of the exports of non-member countries, it would appear that increases in the prices of their imports from the EEC have more than counterbalanced the rise in export prices.

V

The evidence provided in this chapter points to the trade-creative effects of the Common Market. In turn, while trade diversion is indicated with regard to several commodity categories, the 'external trade creation' observed in the case of fuels and machinery has apparently compensated the non-member countries, taken together, for these trade-diverting effects. At the same time the impact of the Common Market on individual suppliers has been shown to vary greatly, depending on the commodity composition of their exports to the EEC.

The reader will recall that the analysis hinges on the assumption that the *ex post* income elasticities of import demand would have remained unchanged in the absence of integration. Structural changes may indeed have affected the measured *ex post* income elasticities, yet one can hardly find an explanation other than the Common Market effect for the systematic differences observed with regard to changes in the rate of expansion of intra-area and extra-area imports between the two periods.[35] With the exception of the fuels and machinery group, *ex post* income elasticities of import demand are higher for intra-area trade than for imports from non-member countries, and the latter have a negative sign. Autonomous price changes cannot account for the results either, since the competitive position of EEC producers has deteriorated in recent years.

Price (unit value) indices in international trade are subject to a considerable margin of error, hence I have compared changes in domestic prices instead. In the Common Market countries the GNP price deflator in manufacturing rose, on the average, 2.6 percent a year between 1959 and 1965, as against an annual increase of 1.0 percent in the United States and 1.6 percent in the United Kingdom.[36] Thus, price changes have benefited foreign suppliers, and disparities in changes of intra-area and extra-area import demand elasticities between pre-integration and post-integration periods would have been larger rather than smaller in the absence of price increases in the Common Market relative to its competitors.

This chapter has presented some tentative conclusions regarding the impact of the European Economic Community on trade flows during the six-year period that has elapsed since the Common Market's establishment. Thus, the results pertain to the short-term effects of the EEC, and cannot be immediately applied in judging the possible long-term repercussions of the EEC on trade flows. Nevertheless, they can be used to speculate on possible future changes.

There is little doubt that the trade creation observed with regard to manufactured goods will continue as internal tariffs and the uncertainty associated with the possibility of the reimposition of tariffs and other trade barriers disappear. Indications point to an increased exchange of consumer goods, specialization in narrower ranges of products in machine building and the subdivision of production processes without regard to national frontiers. At the same time the application of the common agricultural policy and increasing tariff discrimination against outsiders can be expected to augment the trade-diverting effects of the Common Market.

In fact, the rate of discrimination and changes in extra-area imports have been negatively correlated during the period under consideration: the *ex post* income elasticity of demand for extra-area imports of manufactured goods has declined *pari passu* with the increase in tariff discrimination against non-member countries. This elasticity fell from 2.7 in the years 1959–61 to 2.3 in 1961–3 and again to 1.4 in 1963–5, while internal duties were at 70 percent of their pre-Common Market levels in 1961, 60 percent in 1963 and 30 percent in 1965. Similar observations pertain to the individual categories of manufactured goods as well as to raw materials.

In turn, it has been argued that the trade-diverting effects of the Common Market would be offset by an expansion of imports associated with the acceleration of economic growth resulting from the EEC's establishment. But has the rate of growth of national income in the EEC countries exceeded the growth rate that would have been obtained in the absence of integration? While it is difficult to provide an answer to this question, an indication can be provided of the absolute magnitude of trade creation and its possible implications for the rate of growth.

According to the results shown in Table 7.1, a 1 percent increase in the gross national product has been accompanied by a rise of 2.1 percent in the total imports of the EEC countries in the period 1959–65, while the corresponding elasticity was 1.8 in 1953–9. Assuming that this difference has been due to the Common Market effect, the question remains to what extent the increase in trade has contributed to the growth of GNP. Rather than estimating the once-for-all static gains from improved resource allocation, I will consider the dynamic benefits of increased trade that are derived from economies of scale, longer production runs and increased specialization.[37] In this connection, reference can be made to the results obtained by A. A. Walters on the probable extent of large-scale economies in the United States. According to Walters, in the first half of the century a doubling of inputs in the United States non-agricultural sector has been accompanied by an approximately 130 percent increase in output due to the economies of large-scale production.[38]

Assuming that increases in trade in the Common Market entail a corresponding rise in the output of firms producing for export, we may apply Walters' results to indicate the impact of the expansion of trade on productivity, and hence on GNP. It would appear, then, that the 0.3 percentage point rise in the ratio of the annual increment of trade to that of GNP would be accompanied by a one-tenth of one percentage point increase in the growth rate. By 1965 the cumulative effect of the Common Market's establishment on the gross national product of the member countries would thus have reached one-half of 1 percent of GNP.[39]

While the application of Walters' findings to the Common Market is open to criticism, the results may provide a general order of magnitude. Assume, for example, that the complete elimination of tariffs would double the trade creating effects of the EEC estimated for the period 1959–1965. The impact of the corresponding rise in the growth rate of GNP (from, say, 5.3 to 5.5 percent) on extra-area imports would then offset a decrease in the income elasticity of import demand not exceeding one-twentieth of one percentage point (from 1.6 to 1.55). Needless to say, these figures serve for illustrative purposes only, since trade creation and trade diversion for the case of the complete elimination of tariffs have not been estimated.

Appendix Table 7.1 Extra area imports into the European Common Market, 1959 and 1965

	Actual imports 1959	Hypothetical imports in 1965 calculated at growth rates of extra-area imports for the period 1953–9 (In 1959 prices)	1959–65 (In 1959 prices)	Actual imports, 1965 In 1959 prices	Actual imports, 1965 In 1965 prices	Differences between actual and hypothetical imports in 1965 'Common Market effect' (3)–(2)	'Competitive effect' (4)–(3)	'Price effect' (5)–(4)	Together (5)–(2)
	(1)	(2)	(3)	(4)	(5)	(6)	(7)	(8)	(9)
1. United States									
0+1−07 Food, beverages, tobacco	502	782	722	969	1,117	− 60	+247	+148	+335
2+4 Raw materials	591	807	793	890	947	− 14	+ 97	+ 57	+140
3 Fuels	279	492	600	401	343	+108	−199	− 58	−149
5 Chemicals	226	551	517	658	552	− 34	+141	−106	+ 1
71+72 Machinery	375	502	808	928	1,074	+306	+120	+146	+572
73 Transport equipment	142	282	314	303	318	+ 32	− 11	+ 15	+ 36
6+8 Other manufactures	331	716	597	800	860	−119	+203	+ 60	+144
0 to 8−07 All of above	2,446	4,132	4,351	4,949	5,211	+219	+598	+262	+1,079
07 Tropical beverages	2	3	3	3	3	0	0	0	0
0 to 8 All commodities	2,448	4,135	4,354	4,952	5,214	+219	+598	+262	+1,079
2. United Kingdom									
0+1−07 Food, beverages, tobacco	51	79	74	147	170	− 5	+ 73	+ 23	+ 91
2+4 Raw materials	159	217	213	172	183	− 4	− 41	− 11	− 34
3 Fuels	58	102	125	109	93	+ 23	− 16	− 16	− 9
5 Chemicals	120	292	274	292	245	− 18	+ 18	− 47	− 47
71+72 Machinery	308	412	664	572	663	+252	− 92	+ 91	+251
73 Transport equipment	114	227	252	244	256	+ 25	− 8	+ 12	+ 29
6+8 Other manufactures	486	1,051	877	858	922	−174	− 19	+ 64	−129
0 to 8−07 All of above	1,296	2,380	2,479	2,394	2,532	+ 99	− 85	+138	+152
07 Tropical beverages	2	3	3	6	5	0	+ 3	− 1	+ 2
0 to 8 All commodities	1,298	2,383	2,482	2,400	2,537	+ 99	− 82	+137	+154

3. Continental EFTA

		(1)	(2)	(3)	(4)	(5)	(6)	(7)	(8)	(9)
0+1−07	Food, beverages, tobacco	455	708	655	496	572	− 53	− 159	+ 76	− 136
2+4	Raw materials	666	910	893	915	973	− 17	+ 22	+ 58	+ 63
3	Fuels	12	21	26	22	19	+ 5	− 4	− 3	− 2
5	Chemicals	148	360	338	335	281	− 24	− 3	− 54	− 79
71+72	Machinery	359	481	774	648	751	+293	− 126	+103	+270
73	Transport equipment	44	87	98	96	101	+ 11	− 2	+ 5	+ 14
6+8	Other manufactures	758	1,640	1,368	1,356	1,458	−272	− 12	+102	−182
0 to 8−07	All of above	2,442	4,207	4,152	3,868	4,155	− 55	−284	+287	− 52
07	Tropical beverages	6	8	8	6	5	0	− 2	− 1	− 3
0 to 8	All commodities	2,448	4,215	4,160	3,874	4,160	− 55	−286	+286	− 55

4. Other developed countries

		(1)	(2)	(3)	(4)	(5)	(6)	(7)	(8)	(9)
0+1−07	Food, beverages, tobacco	541	843	778	705	813	− 65	− 73	+108	− 30
2+4	Raw materials	1,005	1,373	1,349	1,277	1,359	− 24	− 72	+ 82	− 14
3	Fuels	5	9	10	21	18	+ 1	+ 11	− 3	+ 9
5	Chemicals	33	80	76	112	94	− 4	+ 36	− 18	+ 14
71+72	Machinery	19	25	41	116	134	+ 16	+ 75	+ 18	+109
73	Transport equipment	7	14	15	24	25	+ 1	+ 9	+ 1	+ 11
6+8	Other manufactures	254	549	458	689	741	+ 91	+231	+ 52	+192
0 to 8−07	All of above	1,864	2,893	2,727	2,944	3,184	−166	+217	+240	+291
07	Tropical beverages	2	3	3	11	10	0	+ 8	− 1	+ 7
0 to 8	All commodities	1,866	2,896	2,730	2,955	3,194	−166	+225	+239	+298

5. Communist economies

		(1)	(2)	(3)	(4)	(5)	(6)	(7)	(8)	(9)
0+1−07	Food, beverages, tobacco	248	386	357	379	437	− 29	+ 22	+ 58	+ 51
2+4	Raw materials	265	362	356	517	550	+ 6	+161	+ 33	+188
3	Fuels	195	344	419	353	302	+ 75	− 66	− 51	− 42
5	Chemicals	48	117	110	99	83	− 7	− 11	− 16	− 34
71+72	Machinery	18	24	39	41	47	+ 15	+ 2	+ 6	+ 23
73	Transport equipment	8	16	18	21	22	+ 2	+ 3	+ 1	+ 6
6+8	Other manufactures	158	342	285	282	303	− 57	− 3	+ 21	− 39
0 to 8−07	All of above	940	1,591	1,584	1,692	1,744	− 7	+108	+ 52	+153
07	Tropical beverages	2	3	3	8	7	0	+ 5	− 1	+ 4
0 to 8	All commodities	942	1,594	1,587	1,700	1,751	− 7	+113	+ 51	+157

Appendix Table 7.1 (continued)

	Actual imports 1959	Hypothetical imports in 1965 calculated at growth rates of extra-area imports for the period (In 1959 prices)		Actual imports, 1965		Differences between actual and hypothetical imports in 1965			
		1953–9	1959–65	In 1959 prices	In 1965 prices	'Common Market effect' (3)–(2)	'Competitive effect' (4)–(3)	'Price effect' (5)–(4)	Together (5)–(2)
	(1)	(2)	(3)	(4)	(5)	(6)	(7)	(8)	(9)
6. Associated countries									
0+1−07 Food, beverages, tobacco	469	730	675	412	475	− 55	− 263	+ 63	− 255
2+4 Raw materials	441	602	592	536	570	− 10	− 56	+ 34	− 32
3 Fuels	32	56	69	556	476	+ 13	+487	− 80	+420
5 Chemicals	12	29	27	12	10	− 2	− 15	− 2	− 19
71+72 Machinery	1	1	2	0	0	− 1	− 2	0	− 1
73 Transport equipment	0	0	0	0	0	+ 0	0	0	0
6+8 Other manufactures	193	417	348	265	285	− 69	− 83	+ 20	− 132
0to8−07 All of above	1,148	1,835	1,713	1,781	1,816	−122	+ 68	+ 35	− 19
07 Tropical beverages	196	278	267	260	225	− 11	− 7	− 35	− 53
0 to 8 All commodities	1,344	2,113	1,980	2,041	2,041	−133	+ 61	0	− 72

7. Other less-developed countries

Code	Category									
0+1—07	Food, beverages, tobacco	927	1,443	1,334	1,487	1,716	−109	+153	+229	+273
2+4	Raw materials	1,602	2,189	2,150	2,039	2,203	−39	−111	+164	+14
3	Fuels	1,879	3,313	4,040	3,827	3,259	+727	−213	−568	−54
5	Chemicals	95	232	217	51	84	−15	−166	+33	−148
71+72	Machinery	1	1	2	25	44	+1	+23	+19	+43
73	Transport equipment	4	8	9	18	15	+1	+9	−3	+7
6+8	Other manufactures	693	1,499	1,250	933	989	−249	−317	+56	−510
0to8—07	All of above	5,201	8,685	9,002	8,380	8,310	+317	−622	−70	−375
07	Tropical beverages	559	806	774	767	666	−32	−7	−101	−140
0 to 8	All commodities	5,770	9,491	9,776	9,147	8,976	+285	−629	−171	−515

8. Extra-area imports, total

Code	Category									
0+1—07	Food, beverages, tobacco	3,193	4,971	4,595	4,595	5,300	−376	—	+705	+329
2+4	Raw materials	4,729	6,460	6,346	6,346	6,785	−114	—	+439	+325
3	Fuels	2,460	4,337	5,289	5,289	4,510	+952	—	−779	+173
5	Chemicals	682	1,661	1,559	1,559	1,349	−102	—	−210	−312
71+72	Machinery	1,081	1,446	2,330	2,330	2,713	+884	—	+383	+1267
73	Transport equipment	319	634	706	706	737	+72	—	+31	+103
6+8	Other manufactures	2,873	6,214	5,183	5,183	5,558	−1,031	—	+375	−656
0to8—07	All of above	15,337	25,723	26,008	26,008	26,952	+285	—	+944	+1,229
07	Tropical beverages	779	1,104	1,061	1,061	921	−43	—	−140	−183
0 to 8	All commodities	16,116	26,827	27,069	27,069	27,873	+242	—	+804	+1,046

Sources: Organization for Economic Co-operation and Development (formerly OEEC), *Foreign Trade, Statistical Bulletins,* 1953–1965. Office Statistique des Communautés Européennes, *Commerce Extérieur,* 1958–1965. Table 1.

NOTES

1. Cf. Jacob Viner (1950) *The Customs Union Issue* (London: Carnegie Endowment for International Peace); H. Makower and G. Morton (1953) 'A Contribution Towards a Theory of Customs Unions', *Economic Journal*, March, pp. 33–49; and J. E. Meade (1955) *The Theory of Customs Unions* (Amesterdam, North Holland).
2. On this point, see R. G. Lipsey (1960) 'The Theory of Customs Unions: A General Survey', *Economic Journal*, September, pp. 496–513; and Bela Balassa (1961) *The Theory of Economic Integration* (Homewood, Illinois: Richard D. Irwin), Ch. 2.
3. P. J. Verdoorn (1954) 'A Customs Union for Western Europe – Advantages and Feasibility', *World Politics*, July, pp. 482–500; L. H. Janssen (1961) *Free Trade, Protection and Customs Union* (Leiden: H. E. Stenfert Kroese); and L. B. Krause (1963) 'European Economic Integration and the United States', *American Economic Review*, Papers and Proceedings, May, pp. 185–96, and 'The European Economic Community and the United States Balance of Payments', W. S. Salant, ed. (1963) *The United States Balance of Payments in 1968* (Washington: The Brookings Institution).
4. Cf. B. Balassa, *op. cit.*, pp. 49–51; and H. G. Johnson's review of Janssen's book in the *Journal of Political Economy*, April 1964, pp. 208–9.
5. B. Balassa (1966) 'Tariff Reductions and Trade in Manufactures among the Industrial Countries', *American Economic Review*, June, pp. 466–72.
6. Between 1959 and 1965, the share of intra-area trade in total exports rose from 32.4 to 43.5 percent and in total imports from 33.3 to 41.7 percent.
7. Alexandre Lamfalussy (1963) 'Intra-European Trade, and the Competitive Position of the EEC', paper read at the Manchester Statistical Society, on 13 March.
8. R. L. Major (1962) 'The Common Market: Production and Trade', *National Institute Economic Review*, August, pp. 24–36.
9. J. Waelbroeck (1964) 'Le Commerce de la Communauté Européene avec les Pays Tiers', in *Intégration Européene et Réalité Economique* (Bruges), pp. 139–64.
10. *Ibid.*, p. 157.
11. P. J. Verdoorn and F. J. M. Meyer zu Schlochtern, 'Trade Creation and Trade Diversion in the Common Market', in *Intégration Européene et Réalité Economique*, pp. 95–137. These calculations are also cited in L. Duquesne de la Vinelle (1965) 'La création du commerce attribuable au Marché commun et son incidence sur le valeur du produit national de la Communauté', *Informations Statistiques*, No. 4.
12. Jan Tinbergen (1963) *Shaping the World Economy* (New York: Twentieth Century Fund; P. Pöyhönen (1963) 'Toward a General Theory of International Trade', *Ekonomiska Samfundets Tidskrift*, (2), pp. 69–77; and K. Pulliainen, 'A World Trade Study: An Econometric Study of the Pattern of the Commodity Flows in International Trade, 1948–60', *ibid.*, pp. 78–91.
13. Waelbroeck, 'Le Commerce de la Communauté Européenne avec les Pays Tiers', *op. cit.*, pp. 160–63.
14. The expression 'external trade creation' is used in this chapter to refer to increased imports from third countries, accompanying the establishment of a union, and is therefore the opposite of trade diversion.
15. P. J. Verdoorn and F. J. M. Meyer zu Schlochtern, 'Trade Creation and Trade Diversion in the Common Market', *op. cit.*, pp. 113–14.
16. Verdoorn and Schlochtern use the results as evidence for trade creation only; yet if tariff reductions lead to increased trade, the opposite conclusion also holds: an increase in *relative* tariff levels will lead to a shift in imports from third-country to partner-country suppliers.

17. *Ex post* income elasticities of import demand have been defined as the ratio of the average annual rate of change of imports to that of GNP. In carrying out the present investigation, I have also experimented with regression analysis but, given the shortness of the time series and the variability of data, satisfactory results have not been obtained. The introduction of variables expressing changes in relative prices and tariffs have not improved the results either.

18. Bela Balassa (1963) 'European Integration: Problems and Issues', *American Economic Review*, Papers and Proceedings, May, pp. 175–84. For an application of this method to the 1953–63 period, see Bela Balassa and Alain Camu (1966) 'Les effets du marché commun sur les courants d'échanges internationaux', *Revue d'Economie Politique*, (2), pp. 201–27.

19. Gross trade creation refers to increases in intra-area trade, irrespective of whether this has been due to substitution for domestic or for foreign source of supply. In turn, trade creation in the Vinerian sense relates to newly created trade due to a shift from domestic to partner-country sources of supply, while trade diversion entails a shift from foreign to partner-country producers.

20. The effects of autonomous price changes on trade flows provide a further problem; I will return to this at a later point.

21. The reader will note that, rather than comparing trade shares at the beginning and the end of the period, this method implicitly considers trends in shares over time.

22. It may be suggested that the imports of the various groups of commodities be related to some other variable that would have a more direct influence on imports than GNP does. I have chosen to use GNP in the calculations, in part because of the difficulties encountered in ascertaining the 'proximate' income variable for some of the commodity groups and in part for ensuring the comparability of the results. Nevertheless, calculations have also been carried out with alternative explanatory variables in the case of the imports of food, raw materials and machinery.

23. On the other hand, no account has been taken of differential changes in tariffs within the Common Market.

24. The latter conclusion would not hold, however, if economic growth had a strong anti-trade bias (cf. Bela Balassa (1963) 'The Future of Common Market Imports', *Weltwirtschaftliches Archiv*, Vol. 90, 2, pp. 308–9). Pro- or anti-trade bias in Common Market growth would also affect the results obtained by the use of the proposed method, but these influences cannot be separated from trade creation and trade diversion proper.

25. The total import elasticities for raw materials, calculated with respect to industrial production, are 0.8 in the period 1953–9 and 0.9 in the period 1959–65; the relevant figures for intra-area trade are 1.4 and 1.5 and for extra-area trade 0.7 and 0.7.

26. The common agricultural policy entails the use of variable levies designed to bring the prices of foreign exporters to the domestic level. The variable levy system, in fact, amounts to the application of variable quotas since the purpose of the levy is to ensure that imports from non-member countries are admitted only after all produce of member-country suppliers has been sold.

27. The relevant figures (in 1953 prices) are: 1958, $538 million; 1959, $318 million; and 1960, $564 million.

28. The ratio of the annual rate of change of machinery purchases to that of the gross national product was 1.5 in the period 1953–9 and 1.6 in 1959–64. Data on machinery purchases in 1965 are not available.

29. While data on purchases of machinery and equipment are not available for 1965, indications are that the increase over the previous year was of negligible magnitude.

30. Changes in the prices of Common Market machinery as compared to the prices of her two largest competitors appear also to have contributed to these results, although they cannot provide a full explanation.
31. This group includes, in addition to the Western European countries that are not members of either of the two trade blocs (Finland, Greece, Iceland, Ireland, Spain, Turkey), Canada, Japan, Australia and New Zealand.
32. The 'competitive effect' as defined here reflects the influence of supply as well as demand factors, and it is affected by the commodity composition of exports within each category.
33. To include all commodities in SITC classes 0–8, I have added here tropical beverages (SITC 07).
34. The commodities in question include computer equipment, telecommunication equipment, electronic tubes and measuring devices, special machine tools, etc.
35. In this connection it should be emphasized that the impact of the formation of the EEC on trade flows is hardly confined to the effects of tariff reductions actually undertaken. Rather, in making decisions regarding production, investment and trade, entrepreneurs take account of future reductions – and the prospect of an ultimate and irrevocable elimination – of tariffs. Accordingly, the Common Market effect can be assumed to operate through actual tariff changes, anticipations of future changes in tariffs and the decrease in the risk and uncertainty associated with the possibility of a reimposition of tariffs and other trade barriers.
36. Organization for Economic Co-operation and Development, *General Statistics*, January 1965, and *National Accounts Statistics*, 1955–64 (Paris, 1966). To ensure international comparability, I have adjusted the domestic price indices for changes in the exchange rates. United States data refer to the period 1959–64.
37. On the static gains of tariff reductions, see Bela Balassa and M. E. Kreinen (1967) 'Trade Liberalization and the Kennedy Round: The Static Effects', *Review of Economics and Statistics*, May, pp. 125–37.
38. A. A. Walters (1963) 'A Note on Economies of Scale', *ibid.*, November, pp. 425–7.
39. In the paper cited above, Duquesne de la Vinelle concludes that, by 1964, trade creation has contributed to an increase of the gross national product of the Common Market by 4.5 percent. But this result does not stand up to close scrutiny since it is predicated on the assumption that the statistical relationship between increases in GNP and in trade is bidirectional. With an income elasticity of import demand of 2, this would mean that a 1 percent increase in trade would lead to a $\frac{1}{2}$ percent rise in the gross national product. Since in the Common Market trade accounts for about one-fourth of GNP, and Duquesne de la Vinelle calculated with a 9 percent increase in trade, the absolute increase in the gross national product due to trade creation would be double the increment in EEC trade.

8 · TARIFF REDUCTIONS AND TRADE IN MANUFACTURES AMONG THE INDUSTRIAL COUNTRIES

This chapter uses empirical evidence to examine the proposition advanced by Lawrence B. Krause that the establishment of the Common Market will seriously harm US exports because 'dominant suppliers'[1] in EEC countries receive increased protection from the averaging of national tariffs (Krause, 1963a, 1963b). Subsequently, the results are used to re-interpret the traditional conclusions regarding the effects of tariff reductions on the domestic economy, and additional tests are offered to indicate the predominance of intra-industry – as against inter-industry – specialization in trade in manufactures among the industrial countries.

I

Upon finding that, in the case of dominant suppliers, national duties are generally lower than the common external tariff, Krause claims that 'a comparison of the new EEC tariff for each commodity group with the former national tariff of the leading exporting country in intra-Community trade of each product gives the vivid impression that the new EEC tariff is much more protective than the old national tariff' (1963b, pp. 101–2). Now, under the assumption that 'the expansion of the output of these suppliers will not significantly change their average costs' (1963b, p. 101), Krause reaches the conclusion that the dominant suppliers present a threat to foreign – and particularly to US – exporters in the markets of the partner countries.

I have elsewhere criticized Krause's argument and noted that the effects of the Common Market on imports from third countries should properly be

The author was associate professor of economics at Yale University when this chapter was written. Data collection and calculations were carried out in the framework of the Atlantic Trade Project, directed by the author and sponsored by the Council on Foreign Relations. Comments by Richard Cooper, Donald Hester and Stephen Hymer are gratefully acknowledged. First published in *American Economic Review*, June 1966.

considered in two steps: (a) the implications of the averaging of national tariffs, and (b) the discriminatory effects of eliminating duties on intra-EEC trade. The averaging of tariffs *by itself* is likely to reduce, rather than increase, protection in the European Common Market: low-cost dominant suppliers who compete in the world market will receive greater – but largely unnecessary – protection while the lowering of duties will expose high-cost producers to foreign competition[2]. Further, I have expressed doubts about the possibility of dominant suppliers being able to expand output at constant costs to exploit the possibilities offered by tariff discrimination and to replace third-country exporters in the markets of partner countries (Balassa, 1963).

With data available for several years since the creation of the EEC, it is now possible to test empirically the validity of Krause's hypothesis. Since, after the lowering of tariffs in the partner countries, dominant suppliers would first increase their sales at the expense of partner-country producers, Krause's hypothesis should be accepted or rejected, depending on whether the share of dominant suppliers in intra-EEC trade has increased or declined following the Common Market's establishment.

For purposes of the investigation, I have divided the Common Market manufacturing sector into 91 industries and have considered changes in intra-EEC trade between 1958 and 1963. The general principle of classification has been to group together products that have a high degree of substitutability in production, although the limited availability of data has often constrained our choices. In 56 cases the categories utilized correspond to three-digit SITC items, in 28 instances a four-digit breakdown has been used, and seven categories involve combining two or more three-digit items.[3]

The results shown in Table 8.1 indicate that the share of dominant suppliers in intra-EEC trade declined in the period 1958–63. Thus, while the dominant suppliers in individual industries, taken together, accounted for 51.0 percent of trade among the Common Market countries in 1958, their share in the *increment* of intra-area trade between 1958 and 1963 was only 39.5 percent. It should be emphasized that this decline is not explained by changes in the identity of the dominant suppliers between 1958 and 1963, since the largest exporters in intra-area trade in 1963 provided 45.9 percent of exports in that year, as compared to 43.4 percent furnished by the dominant suppliers of the year 1958.

The conclusions hardly change if industry-by-industry comparisons are made. Dominant suppliers accounted for over one-half of trade among the Common Market countries in 52 out of the 91 industries in 1958, but their share in the increment of trade between 1958 and 1963 exceeded 50 percent in 20 industries only. Moreover, among the 84 industries where intra-EEC trade expanded during this period, an absolute reduction in the exports of any one country is observed in only 12 cases; of these, the decline pertains to more than one country in two instances. Finally, considering the two largest suppliers within each industry, we find that their combined share declined from 72.8

Table 8.1 Market shares of dominant suppliers[a] in intra-EEC exports for 91 manufacturing industries (percent)

Intra-EEC exports in 1958	Common Market	Belgium	France	Germany	Italy	Netherlands
Combined share of dominant suppliers[b]	51.0	46.2	15.5	84.2	18.1	12.6
	(91)[c]	(22)	(8)	(50)	(5)	(6)
Combined share of second largest suppliers	21.8	33.8	36.3	5.3	18.3	40.5
	(91)	(23)	(21)	(17)	(9)	(21)
Combined share of two largest suppliers	72.8	80.0	51.8	89.5	36.4	53.1
	(182)	(45)	(29)	(67)	(14)	(27)
Increment in intra-EEC exports between 1958 and 1963						
Combined share of dominant suppliers	39.5	33.1	6.9	78.6	8.8	13.7
Combined share of second largest suppliers	17.0	31.7	18.9	5.6	13.7	36.7
Combined share of two largest suppliers	56.5	64.8	25.8	84.2	22.5	50.4

Source: Office Statistique des Communautés Européennes, *Commerce Extérieur*, 1958 and 1963.

[a] The largest exporters in intra-EEC trade within each commodity category in the year 1958.

[b] The combined share of the dominant suppliers in the intra-EEC exports of the individual member countries, or the six countries taken together.

[c] Numbers in parentheses refer to the number of suppliers in each category.

percent in 1958 trade to 56.5 percent in the increment of intra-EEC trade during the period under consideration.

Similar results are obtained if we examine the export performance of the dominant suppliers in each of the five member countries. The data of Table 8.1 show a decline in the share of these suppliers within the intra-EEC exports of every country, the only exception being the Netherlands. The Dutch sample is rather small, however, since in 1958 the Netherlands was ahead in only six industries. And Dutch producers, too, follow the general pattern if the two largest exporters are considered in every industry, or if changes in the shares of dominant suppliers in the intra-area exports of individual commodities are calculated.[4]

Thus, dominant suppliers have apparently lost ground since the establishment of the Common Market and we are led to reject Krause's hypothesis. This conclusion is not affected if the data are regrouped according to the industry classification employed by Krause. We find, then, that in the 20 industries he considered (1963b, p. 103)[5] the dominant suppliers accounted for 56.4 percent of intra-area trade in 1958, and their share in the increment of this trade between 1958 and 1963 declined to 40.9 percent. Accordingly, it would appear that Krause has overestimated the ability of dominant suppliers to expand production at constant costs, and hence the chances of trade diversion.

II

Aside from their usefulness in judging the validity of Krause's hypothesis, these results have more general implications both for the theory of international specialization and for commercial policy. According to the familiar textbook exposition, multilateral reductions in duties would lead to a reallocation of resources from import-competing industries to export industries, accompanied by a contraction in the activity of the former and an expansion of the latter. Correspondingly, despite the ensuing improvements in productive efficiency, the welfare consequences of a move towards free trade are not unambiguous since – in the absence of appropriate compensation – the factors used more intensively in the production of importables would experience a decline in their real income.

The losses that import-competing industries might sustain in countries participating in multilateral tariff reductions have also received considerable attention in public discussions. The possible adverse consequences of lowering tariffs for particular industries have been emphasized by the opponents of entry into the European Common Market, especially in France and Italy, and arguments along these lines have recently been invoked in connection with the Kennedy Round of tariff negotiations. It would also appear that such fears have often slowed down the process of negotiations held under the auspices of GATT, and have limited the extent of reductions in duties.

Since, according to the traditional explanation, tariff reductions would be followed by inter-industry specialization, the validity of this hypothesis requires that within each industry the largest supplier, or suppliers, of the pre-integration period have the lion's share in the expansion of intra-area trade. Our results do not reveal such a tendency; instead of concentration, an increasing diversification in export patterns is indicated. Rather than increasingly specializing in industries where they had been leading exporters prior to the establishment of the European Common Market, the member countries have lost ground in these industries and have reduced reliance on them in expanding their exports.

It is suggested here that the failure of the traditional explanation stems from the inadequacies of conventional models that deal exclusively with standardized commodities. In the case of standardized goods, cost differences are the main determinants of trade, and a country cannot protect and export the same commodity. In such instances, the traditional conclusions on the reallocation of resources from import-competing to export industries follow: reductions in tariffs lead to a contraction in the former and an expansion in the latter.

Only a few manufactured goods (e.g. steel ingots, non-ferrous metals, paper) traded among the industrial countries are standardized commodities, however, while the large majority are differentiated products that can be protected *and* exported. In the presence of national product differentiation, multilateral tariff reductions may lead to an increased exchange of clothing articles, automobiles and other consumer goods, for example, without substantial changes in the structure of production. Further, the expansion of trade in machinery and in intermediate products at a higher level of fabrication, following all-round reductions in duties, may entail specialization in narrower ranges of products rather than the demise of national industries. These changes, then, would involve intra-industry rather than inter-industry specialization.

While the results of the calculations constitute a rejection of the traditional explanation, they are consistent with the hypothesis that tariff reductions would result in intra-industry specialization.[6] This hypothesis receives further support from evidence pertaining to the pattern of intra-area exports of the Common Market countries and the relationships between exports and imports in the various industries of these countries.

To begin with, the calculations reported in Table 8.2 show a positive correlation between the structure of intra-area exports of the individual EEC countries. It is also apparent that the export patterns of these countries have become more uniform since the establishment of the Community. Thus, the rank correlation coefficients calculated with regard to 91 industries ranked by the value of intra-EEC exports are larger in 1963 than in 1958 for all pairs of

Table 8.2 Rank correlation coefficients for the structure of intra-EEC exports of manufactured goods[a]

		Belgium	France	Germany	Italy	Netherlands
Belgium	1958	x	0.576	0.433	0.403	0.539
	1963	x	0.791	0.595	0.485	0.682
France	1958	0.576	x	0.643	0.528	0.651
	1963	0.719	x	0.760	0.716	0.782
Germany	1958	0.433	0.643	x	0.416	0.566
	1963	0.595	0.760	x	0.592	0.682
Italy	1958	0.403	0.528	0.416	x	0.549
	1963	0.485	0.716	0.592	x	0.688
Netherlands	1958	0.539	0.651	0.566	0.549	x
	1963	0.682	0.782	0.682	0.688	x

Source: See Table 8.1

[a] Spearman rank correlation coefficients calculated from data for 91 industries ranked by the value of intra-area exports. All coefficients are statistically significant at the 0.01 level.

countries, with the differences amounting to at least one-fifth of the value shown for 1958. A shorthand expression of the results can be given if we consider that the unweighted average of the rank correlation coefficients rose from 0.53 to 0.67 in the period under consideration.

The increasing uniformity of export patterns in the EEC countries provides evidence that the creation of new trade among these countries as a result of the 50 percent reduction in intra-area tariffs accomplished by 1963 has taken the form of intra-industry specialization.[7] Another approach to the problem is to consider the relative magnitudes of the export (import) balances of individual countries for the 91 commodity categories. For this purpose, I have expressed the absolute difference between exports and imports in each category as a ratio of the sum of exports and imports and have calculated, for every country, an unweighted average of these ratios.[8] Should inter-industry specialization predominate, one would expect the resulting 'representative ratios' to approach unity since a country would either export or import a commodity. By contrast, in the case of intra-industry specialization, the ratios would tend towards zero because exports and imports would tend towards equality within each category.

In the countries under consideration the relevant ratios were approximately in the 0.4 to 0.6 range in 1958 and 0.3 to 0.5 in 1963, indicating the relative importance of intra-industry specialization (Table 8.3). And while the figures shown for a given country and a particular year are difficult to interpret, changes in these ratios over time permit us to draw inferences regarding the effects of tariff reductions on specialization. With the 'representative ratios' falling in every country following the Common Market's establishment, one may conclude that reductions in duties have led to increasing intra-industry specialization in the EEC. Further, the higher values

Table 8.3 Representative ratios of trade balances for 91 commodity categories

Representative ratios of trade balances[a]		
	1958	1963
Belgium	0.458	0.401
France	0.394	0.323
Germany	0.531	0.433
Italy	0.582	0.521
Netherlands	0.495	0.431

Source: See Table 8.1.

[a] Calculated as unweighted averages of the ratio of the absolute difference of exports and imports to the sum of exports and imports for 91 industries by the use of the following formula:

$$\frac{1}{n}\sum\frac{|X_i - M_i|}{X_i + M_i}$$

shown for Italy may be taken to indicate that intra-industry specialization increases with the development of manufacturing industry.

The results point to the importance of intra-industry specialization in trade among industrial countries and provide support to the hypothesis that trade liberalization would result in intra-industry rather than inter-industry specialization. It follows that we have to revise the conclusions derived from traditional theory regarding the welfare consequences of tariff reductions.

According to the traditional explanation, the reallocation of resources from import-competing to export industries would improve productive efficiency and result in a redistribution of incomes from the former to the latter. Different conclusions are reached for the case of intra-industry specialization: the welfare effects of an increased exchange of consumer goods may now consist largely of improvements in the efficiency of exchange (the satisfaction of consumer wants) whereas specialization in narrower ranges of machinery and intermediate products will permit the exploitation of economies of scale through the lengthening of production runs. Correspondingly, in the absence of declining industries, the income redistributional effects of trade liberalization are expected to be smaller than in the traditional case.

It would further appear that the difficulties of adjustment to freer trade have been generally overestimated. It is apparent that the increased exchange of consumer goods is compatible with unchanged production in every country while changes in product composition can be accomplished relatively easily in the case of machine building, precision instruments and various intermediate products. These considerations may explain why the fears expressed in various member countries of the Common Market concerning the demise of particular industries have not been realized. There are no examples of declining manufacturing industries in any of the member countries, nor have they experienced a wave of bankruptcies. Indeed, the number of bankruptcies has fallen since the Common Market's establishment, and there is little evidence of frictional unemployment.[9]

III

In the present chapter, I have attempted to derive certain conclusions regarding the effects of tariff reductions on trade among the industrial countries on the basis of information about changes in trade flows since the Common Market's establishment. The experience of the EEC is of particular interest in this regard, in part because – aside from Italy – these countries are on similar levels of industrial development, and in part because the relatively large reductions in duties within a short period of time make it possible to derive conclusions regarding the effects of trade liberalization on specialization. Although further research would be necessary to explore the experience of other countries, the findings of the chapter support the hypothesis that trade among the industrial countries is characterized by intra-industry rather than inter-industry specialization, and the results augur well for the consequences of multilateral tariff reductions in the Kennedy Round negotiations.

NOTES

1. The expression 'dominant supplier' denotes the largest exporter in intra-area trade within each commodity category prior to the formation of the EEC.
2. A similar argument has recently been made in Flanders (1965).
3. A similar classification has been used in Balassa (1965).
4. In the latter case, adjustment has been made for inter-country differences in the expansion of the total exports of manufactured goods.
5. We have excluded miscellaneous chemicals and manufactured goods, n.e.s., because these could not be identified with SITC categories.
6. Similar conclusions have been derived for the Benelux union by P. J. Verdoorn (1960) and for trade in machinery and precision instruments among the major industrial countries by the present author (Balassa, 1965).
7. For an analysis of trade creation and trade diversion in the Common Market, see Balassa (1967).
8. The following formula has been used in the calculations:

$$\frac{1}{n} \Sigma \frac{|X_i - M_i|}{X_i + M_i}$$

where X_i and M_i refer to the intra-EEC exports and imports of commodity category i, and n is the number of the commodity categories considered.

9. According to national statistics on bankruptcies, after a temporary increase to 17,000 in the recession year 1958, the number of business failures in the countries of the EEC declined from slightly over 16,000 in 1956 and 1957 to 14,500 in the early 1960s. At the same time, while data on frictional unemployment are not reported, it is questionable that this could have been substantial in a period when total unemployment in the Common Market fell by two-thirds.

REFERENCES

Balassa, Bela (1963) 'The Future of Common Market Imports', *Weltwirtschaftliches Archiv*, (2), pp. 292–316.

Balassa, Bela (1967) 'Trade Creation and Trade Diversion in the European Common Market', *Econ. J.*, March, pp. 1–21. Reprinted as Chapter 7 in this volume.

Balassa, Bela, (1965) 'Trade Liberalization and "Revealed" Comparative Advantage', *Manchester School*, May, pp. 99–123. Reprinted as Chapter 4 in this volume.

Flanders, June M. (1965) 'Measuring Protectionism and Predicting Trade Diversion', *J. Pol. Econ.*, April, pp. 165–9.

Krause, Lawrence B. (1963a) 'European Economic Integration and the United States', *Am. Econ. Rev. Proc.*, May, pp. 185–96.

Krause, Lawrence B. (1963b) 'The European Economic Community and the United States Balance of Payments', in W. S. Salant, ed., *The United States Balance of Payments in 1968*, Washington, The Brookings Institution, pp. 95–118.

Verdoorn, P. J. (1960) 'The Intra-Bloc Trade of Benelux', in E. A. G. Robinson, ed., *Economic Consequences of the Size of Nations*, Proceedings of Conference held by the International Economic Association, London, pp. 291–318.

9 · INTRA-INDUSTRY SPECIALIZATION IN A MULTI-COUNTRY AND MULTI-INDUSTRY FRAMEWORK

Over the past two decades a vast literature, starting with Balassa (1966a), has developed on the subject of intra-industry – as compared to inter-industry – trade.[1] Early efforts concentrated on the measurement of the extent of intra-industry specialization. Subsequently, several contributions were made to the theory of intra-industry trade and empirical investigations were undertaken to examine the determinants of intra-industry specialization.

This chapter sets out to test alternative hypotheses about the factors influencing the extent of intra-industry trade, defined as the share of this trade in total trade, within a multi-country and multi-industry framework. The investigation is limited to trade in manufactured goods where product differentiation predominates – in contrast to trade in primary commodities which consists largely of standardized products. Seasonal and border trade apart, intra-industry specialization is not expected to occur in standardized commodities, except in a very particular case.[2]

The determinants of intra-industry specialization are analyzed in the trade of every country with every other country in each industry category, in respect to country and industry characteristics. Country characteristics pertain to pairs of countries; they include common (average per capita income, income differences, average country size, size differences, distance, common borders, and average trade orientation) and specific (participation in economic integration schemes and common language) country characteristics.[3] Industry characteristics pertain to individual industries; they include product

Written with Luc Bauwens. This chapter was prepared in the framework of the World Bank's research project, 'Changes in Comparative Advantage in Manufactured Goods' (RPO 672-41). The authors are grateful to Marcus Noland for reviewing alternative explanatory variables and suggesting possible specifications, to Linda Pacheco for data collection, to Jerzy Rozanski for generating the trade data, and to Shigeru Akiyama for running the final set of regressions. However, the authors alone are responsible for the opinions expressed in the chapter, which should not be interpreted to reflect the views of the World Bank. First published in *Economic Journal*, December 1987.

differentiation, marketing costs, variability of profit rates, scale economies, industrial concentration, foreign investment, foreign affiliates, tariff dispersion, and offshore assembly.

The same country characteristics were used in an investigation of intra-industry specialization in a multi-country framework (Balassa, 1986a) while the same country and industry characteristics were used to examine intra-industry specialization in trade between the United States and the rest of the world (Balassa, 1986b). The present investigation represents an extension of the former analysis by including industry characteristics in addition to country characteristics, and an extension of the latter by examining the extent of intra-industry specialization of every country with every other country. Apart from an attempt by Loertscher and Wolter (1980), referred to below, no other author has made estimates that combined the inter-country and the inter-industry determinants of intra-industry trade in a multilateral framework.

The study covers 38 countries whose manufactured exports exceeded $300 million, and accounted for at least 18 percent of their total merchandise exports, in 1979. Apart from trade among all the countries concerned, estimates have been made for trade among developed countries, among developing countries, as well as between developed and developing countries. The developed country group consists of 18 countries with per capita incomes of $2,254 or higher in 1973;[4] 20 countries with per capita incomes of $2,031 or lower in 1973[5] form the developing country group.[6]

The investigation covers 152 industry categories in the manufacturing sector as defined by the United States Standard Industrial Classification (SIC), omitting natural resource products whose manufacture is importantly affected by the availability of natural resources in a particular country.[7] The classification scheme has been established by merging four-digit SIC categories in cases when the economic characteristics of particular products have been deemed to be similar.[8] The use of an economically meaningful classification scheme is of importance, so as to identify 'genuine' as compared to spurious intra-industry trade – the latter being a creation of the classification scheme employed. The individual industry categories have further been matched against the three- and four-digit categories of the United Nations Standard International Trade Classification (SITC).[9]

Section I of the chapter describes the methodology utilized. Section II lists the hypotheses to be tested and the variables used in empirical testing. Section III provides the empirical results obtained for bilateral trade between all the countries concerned, among developed countries, among developing countries, as well as between developed and developing countries, introducing country and industry characteristics simultaneously. Section IV reports on results obtained by introducing these variables separately and adding interaction terms for selected country and industry characteristics.

I

The index of intra-industry trade, IIT_{jki}, has been defined as in (1), where X^e_{jki} and M^e_{jki} stand for the adjusted exports and imports of industry i in trade between countries j and k. The formula makes an adjustment for imbalance in total trade between countries j and k, when X_{jk} and M_{jk} represent the total exports and imports of country j in trade with country k.[10] The index takes values from 0 to 1 as the extent of intra-industry trade increases.

$$IIT_{jki} = 1 - \frac{|X^e_{jki} - M^e_{jki}|}{X^e_{jki} + M^e_{jki}} = 1 - \frac{\left|\dfrac{X_{jki}}{X_{jk}} - \dfrac{M_{jki}}{M_{jk}}\right|}{\dfrac{X_{jki}}{X_{jk}} + \dfrac{M_{jki}}{M_{jk}}} \tag{1}$$

In the regression equations explaining inter-country and inter-industry differences in the extent of intra-industry trade, IIT_{jki} has been used as the dependent variable while the explanatory variables include the country and industry characteristics referred to above. The next few paragraphs discuss some considerations determining the choice of functional form utilized in the estimation.

To begin with, a linear or loglinear equation may give predicted values that lie outside the 0–1 range. While a logistic function does not have this shortcoming, its logit transformation[11] cannot handle values of 0 and 1. Although values of 1 (representing complete intra-industry specialization) do not occur in the sample, values of 0 (representing complete inter-industry specialization) are of importance.

In trade among all countries concerned, there are 106,856 potential observations.[12] IIT_{jki} is, however, not defined in 41 percent of the cases, because $X_{jki} = M_{jki} = 0$, i.e. no trade takes place in a particular industry category between two particular countries. Among the remaining 62,770 observations, 51 percent are equal to 0, because either X_{jki} or M_{jki} is zero, i.e. there is complete inter-industry specialization.

Given the importance of zero observations, we have used the non-linear least squares estimation of the logistic function to handle such observations. We have thus estimated (2), where $\mathbf{b}$ is the vector of the regression coefficients, $\mathbf{z}_{jki}$ is the vector of the explanatory variables, and ε_{jki} is a random disturbance term. The estimation has been done by decomposing $\mathbf{b}'\mathbf{z}_{jki}$ as shown in (3), where $\mathbf{b}^c$ and $\mathbf{b}^I$ are vectors of the regression coefficients of the explanatory variables, $\mathbf{z}^C_{jk}$ is the vector of characteristics of countries j and k[13] and $\mathbf{z}_i$ is the vector of industry characteristics.

$$IIT_{jki} = \frac{1}{1 + \exp(-\mathbf{b}'\mathbf{z}_{jki})} + \varepsilon_{jki} \tag{2}$$

$$\mathbf{b}'\mathbf{z}_{jki} = b_0 + \mathbf{b}^{C'}\mathbf{z}^C_{jk} + \mathbf{b}^{I'}\mathbf{z}_i \tag{3}$$

While none of the individual terms in (3) includes both the country and the industry dimensions of the variation of the dependent variable IIT_{jki}, they are both incorporated in the entire function. This means that the effects of country characteristics on the index of intra-industry specialization are assumed to be invariant across industries and the effects of industry characteristics on the index of intra-industry specialization are assumed to be invariant across country pairs.

It may be asked if it is necessary to include country and industry characteristics in a single equation rather than making separate estimates using only one of the two sets of characteristics. The answer to this question turns on whether the estimated coefficients differ as between the alternative formulations. This issue is considered in Section IV.

A second question is whether there is an interaction between country and industry characteristics. While the introduction of all possible pairs of country and industry characteristics, involving the estimation of a very large number of regression coefficients, would be computationally difficult, an attempt has been made to introduce interaction terms in cases when these can be regarded as economically meaningful.[14]

II

In what follows, we state the hypotheses that have been tested in the present investigation and define the explanatory variables utilized in the estimation. In so doing we refer to the theoretical literature where the hypotheses originate, as well as to the use of the explanatory variables in empirical investigations.

Country characteristics

It is hypothesized that the extent of intra-industry trade between any pair of countries will be:

1. positively correlated with average per capita incomes, representing the extent of demand for differentiated products (Linder, 1961);
2. negatively correlated with differences in per capita incomes, representing differences in demand structures (Linder, 1961) and/or differences in resource endowments (Dixit and Norman, 1980; Helpman, 1981);
3. positively correlated with average country size, indicating the possibilities for increasing the variety of differentiated products manufactured under economies of scale (Lancaster, 1980); and
4. negatively correlated with differences in country size, indicating differences in their ability to manufacture differentiated products (Dixit and Norman, 1980; Helpman, 1981).

In testing hypotheses 1 to 4, per capita income has been represented by GNP per head and country size by GNP.[15] Instead of taking the absolute values of inter-country differences in per capita incomes and size, however, we have used a measure indicating relative differences that takes values between 0 and 1. This measure is superior to utilizing the absolute values of the differences, which are affected by the magnitudes of the particular country characteristics in the different countries. The relative difference measure is shown in (4),

$$INEQ = 1 + [w \ln w + (1 - w)\ln(1 - w)]/\ln 2 \qquad (4)$$

where w refers to the ratio of a particular country characteristic in country j to the sum of this characteristic in country j and partner country k.[16]

It is hypothesized that the extent of intra-industry trade between any pair of countries will be:

5. negatively correlated with the distance between them, representing the availability and the cost of information necessary for trading differentiated products; and
6. positively correlated with the existence of common borders, indicating the possibilities for intra-industry trade in response to locational advantages (Grubel and Lloyd, 1975).

In testing hypothesis 5, distance has been measured in terms of miles between the centres of geographical gravity for each pair of countries. In turn, the existence of common borders (hypothesis 6) has been represented by a dummy variable.

It is hypothesized that the extent of intra-industry trade between any pair of countries will be:

7. negatively correlated with their average level of trade barriers, indicating the possibilities for intra-industry specialization under trade liberalization (Balassa, 1967); and
8. positively correlated with participation in regional integration schemes, including the European Common Market (Balassa, 1966a), the European Free Trade Association (Balassa, 1975) and the Latin American Free Trade Association (Balassa, 1979), indicating the possibilities of intra-industry trade in the framework of regional integration schemes.

Estimates of tariff levels are not available for a number of countries and the tariff equivalent of quantitative import restrictions is not known with any confidence for others. An indicator of trade orientation has therefore been used to represent the extent of trade restrictions for the individual countries. Trade orientation has been defined in terms of percentage deviations of actual from hypothetical values of per capita exports (X/P) with positive (negative) deviations taken to represent a low (high) degree of restrictiveness. Hypothetical values have been derived from a regression equation estimated for

1971 that, in addition to the per capita income (Y/P) and population (P) variables utilized in early work by Chenery (1960), includes variables representing the availability of mineral resources and propinquity to markets.[17]

Mineral resource availability has been represented by the ratio of mineral exports (X^m) to the gross national product, while propinquity has been defined as the weighted average of the inverse of distance between country j and partner country k (D_{jk}), the weights being the gross national product of the partner countries (Y_k): $\Sigma_k(Y_k/D_{jk})/\Sigma_k Y_k$. The results are reported in equation (5), with t values shown in parenthesis; all the regression coefficients are significant at the 1 percent level, using a one-tail test.[18]

$$\ln \frac{X_j}{P_j} = -0.1864 + 0.9212 \ln(Y_j/P_j) - 0.3541 \ln P_j$$
$$\phantom{\ln \frac{X_j}{P_j} =} (0.38) \quad (15.02) (6.83)$$

$$+ 0.0251\, X_j^m/Y_j + 0.0598 \sum_k \frac{Y_k/D_{jk}}{\sum_k Y_k}; \quad \bar{R}^2 = 0.9404 \tag{5}$$
$$ (2.91) (2.06)$$

For any pair of countries, the sum of their trade orientation index has been introduced in the estimating equations to test the hypothesis that the extent of intra-industry trade is positively correlated with trade orientation. In turn, dummy variables have been introduced to represent participation in the European Common Market (EEC), the European Free Trade Association (EFTA), and the Latin American Free Trade Area (LAFTA) by the trading partners.

It is hypothesized that the extent of intra-industry trade between any pair of countries will be:

9. positively correlated with the use of a common language, including English, French, Spanish, German, Portuguese and Scandinavian (Danish, Norwegian and Swedish).

Hypothesis 9. has been tested by introducing dummy variables for each of these languages for any pair of countries where the same language is spoken.

Industry characteristics[19]

It is hypothesized that the extent of intra-industry trade in the products of a particular industry will be:

10. positively correlated with the degree of product differentiation (Krugman, 1979; Lancaster, 1980; Helpman, 1981);
11. negatively correlated with the degree of product standardization (ibid.).

Hypothesis 10. has been tested by defining product differentiation in terms of (a) the coefficient of variation of export unit values (Hufbauer, 1970); (b) marketing expenditures expressed as a percentage of total costs (Caves, 1981); and (c) the standard deviation of profit rates on equity capital (Caves, 1981).

Hypothesis 11. has been tested by defining product standardization in terms of (a) the extent of plant economies of scale, measured by dividing the ratio of the average size of the largest plants in US industry (accounting for approximately one-half of industry shipment) to total industry shipment, by the ratio of value added per worker in smaller plants (again accounting for one-half of industry shipments) to value added per worker in larger plants (Caves, 1981) [20] and (b) the extent of industry concentration, measured by dividing the combined share of the largest four firms in an industry's output, by the share of imports in industry output (Toh, 1982).[21]

It is hypothesized that the extent of intra-industry trade in the products of the particular industry will be:

12. negatively correlated with the extent of foreign direct investment, representing the replacement of the export sales of differentiated products (Balassa, 1966b);
13. negatively or positively correlated with the extent of trade with foreign affiliates, depending on whether the 'replacement effect' dominates the 'input effect' (Caves, 1981);
14. positively correlated with offshore assembly that encourages the international division of labour, involving vertical specialization; and
15. negatively correlated with the dispersion of tariff rates.[22]

Hypothesis 12. has been tested by taking the sum of dividends received from foreign affiliates and foreign tax credits, divided by total business receipts of the industry, as an indicator of the extent of foreign direct investment. Hypothesis 13. has been tested by taking the ratio of trade (exports plus imports) with majority-owned foreign affiliates to the industry's total exports as an indicator of the extent of trade with affiliates (Caves, 1981). Hypothesis 14. has been tested by utilizing data on the relative importance of offshore assembly in individual industries in the United States. Hypothesis 15. has been tested by using industry data on tariff dispersion among the developed countries.

III

The estimates reported in Table 9.1 relate to trade in manufactured goods in 1971[23] among all the countries concerned (column 1), among developed countries (column 2), among developing countries (column 3), and between developed and developing countries (column 4).

Table 9.1 Estimation of intra-industry trade in a multi-country and multi-industry framework (regression co-efficients, with t values in parentheses)

	(1)		(2)		(3)		(4)	
Constant	1.516	(17.01)	1.906	(8.15)	−2.000	(3.35)	1.723	(12.13)
ln AY/P	0.691	(27.10)	0.434	(5.95)	0.788	(7.97)	0.704	(13.67)
$INEQY/P$	−1.038	(20.89)	0.209	(0.74)	−0.362	(1.95)	−0.727	(11.43)
ln AY	−0.348	(36.42)	0.359	(17.10)	−0.425	(4.21)	0.432	(25.26)
$INEQY$	−0.862	(27.02)	−0.827	(14.61)	0.973	(3.02)	−1.145	(18.50)
ATO	0.453	(32.83)	0.365	(5.29)	0.256	(7.90)	0.532	(26.60)
ln D	−0.372	(49.15)	−0.357	(26.06)	−0.392	(10.54)	−0.394	(29.40)
$BORDER$	0.302	(11.94)	0.273	(7.78)	0.606	(4.12)	0.547	(10.48)
EEC	0.163	(5.00)	0.148	(3.54)	—	—	—	—
$EFTA$	0.308	(12.67)	0.294	(9.07)	—	—	0.358	(6.35)
$LAFTA$	0.601	(4.92)	—	—	1.346	(7.69)	—	—
$ENGLISH$	0.085	(2.97)	−0.084	(1.83)	0.600	(8.10)	0.084	(1.84)
$FRENCH$	0.193	(2.67)	0.390	(3.57)	−0.499	(0.58)	0.033	(0.24)
$SPANISH$	0.066	(0.34)	—	—	1.207	(4.63)	—	—
$GERMAN$	0.268	(5.11)	0.309	(4.74)	—	—	—	—
$PORT.$	0.633	(2.07)	—	—	0.986	(3.73)	—	—
$SCAND.$	0.053	(1.25)	0.102	(1.89)	—	—	—	—
PD	0.254	(12.03)	0.338	(11.01)	0.243	(2.85)	0.002	(0.06)
MKT	3.628	(12.08)	2.672	(6.06)	3.373	(3.11)	8.647	(15.81)
$SDPR$	0.371	(2.56)	0.122	(0.59)	0.340	(0.69)	0.556	(2.08)
$ECSC$	−2.248	(8.01)	−3.104	(7.63)	−1.515	(1.36)	0.170	(0.40)
$IACR$	−2.085	(14.71)	−1.444	(8.44)	−0.914	(1.70)	−8.686	(15.92)
FDI	−0.395	(2.67)	−0.046	(0.22)	—	—	−1.601	(5.48)
$AFFL$	−0.121	(2.69)	0.018	(0.29)	—	—	−0.468	(5.64)
OAP	0.406	(10.20)	0.173	(3.02)	—	—	1.043	(14.90)
TSD	−2.753	(6.00)	−3.900	(5.81)	0.637	(0.35)	−1.474	(2.01)
R^2	0.4430		0.5680		0.2249		0.2484	
N	62,770		21,250		6,697		34,823	

Sources: See text.

Notes: (1) Trade among developed and developing countries combined. 2. Trade among developed countries. 3. Trade among developing countries. 4. Trade between developed and developing countries.

The empirical results in column 1 support the hypotheses put forward in Section II of the chapter as far as common country characteristics are concerned. As expected, the extent of intra-industry trade is positively correlated with average per capita incomes (AY/P), average country size (AY), average trade orientation (ATO), and the existence of a common border ($BORDER$), and it is negatively correlated with income differences ($INEQY/P$), difference in country size ($INEQY$) and distance (D). All the variables are highly significant statistically.

Among specific country characteristics, the EEC, EFTA and LAFTA dummy variables have the expected positive sign and are highly significant statistically. In turn, the regression coefficients of the language dummy variables have a positive sign, but their level of statistical significance varies. The English, French and German language variables are significant at the 1 percent level, the Portuguese language variables at the 5 percent level, while the Spanish and Scandinavian language variables are not significant at even the 10 percent level.

Among industry characteristics, the Hufbauer measure of product differentiation (PD) has the expected positive sign and is highly significant statistically. This is also the case for the marketing variable (MKT). As expected, the standard variation of profit rates ($SDPR$) is also positively related to the extent of intra-industry trade and is statistically significant at approximately the 2 percent level.

The economies of scale ($ECSC$) and the industrial concentration ($IACR$) variables are negatively correlated with the extent of intra-industry trade and are highly significant statistically. The results again correspond to expectations, as the variables are considered to be indicators of product standardization.

The foreign direct investment (FDI) and foreign affiliates ($AFFL$) variables have a negative sign and are significant at the 1 percent level. The result for foreign direct investment corresponds to expectations; in turn, the negative coefficient for the foreign affiliates variable points to the conclusion that the 'replacement effect' is more important than the 'input effect'.

The offshore assembly variable (OAP) has the expected positive sign and is highly significant statistically. Finally, the tariff dispersion variable (TSD) is highly significant statistically and has a negative sign, thus conforming to the hypothesis put forward by Pagoulatos and Sorensen.

The results for the developed country group confirm the conclusions obtained for the entire group of countries as regards common country characteristics, the only exception being the income difference variable whose coefficient does not differ significantly from zero.[24] This exception may be explained by the fact that the relatively small differences in per capita incomes among developed countries tend to make their demand structure similar. Correspondingly, one may not expect large variations to occur in the extent of intra-industry trade as a function of income differences.

The stated hypotheses are also confirmed with regard to participation in integration arrangements and the responsiveness of intra-industry trade to having French and German as common languages among the developed countries. However, the English language variable has the incorrect sign, possibly reflecting the effect of long-standing economic separation among the countries concerned. Finally, the level of statistical significance approached 10 percent for the Scandinavian language in the developed country group.

Except for the standard deviation of profit rates, all product differentiation and product standardization variables continue to be highly significant in the developed country group. Also, the offshore procurement and tariff dispersion variables are significant at the 1 percent level while the foreign direct investment and foreign affiliate variables lose their statistical significance.

The results obtained for intra-industry trade among developing countries, reported in column 3 of Table 9.1,[25] also confirm the stated hypotheses about average income levels, income differences, trade orientation, distance and border trade. All the coefficients are highly significant statistically, except for the income difference variable (which is significant only at the 5 percent level). The explanation for this result is similar to that adduced above with regard to trade among developed countries.

The hypotheses are not confirmed, however, for the average size and size difference variables; in fact, the signs are the opposite to those expected. In this connection, it should be noted that only about one-quarter of trade in manufactured goods among these countries is intra-industry trade and a few aberrant data may have influenced the outcome.

Among specific country characteristics, the LAFTA, English, Spanish and Portuguese language variables are significant at the 1 percent level in the developing country group. The French language variable is not significantly different from zero, however, and has the wrong sign.

The foreign direct investment, foreign affiliate and offshore procurement variables are not relevant for trade among developing countries and have thus been excluded from the estimates. Of the remaining industry variables, product differentiation and marketing costs are statistically significant at the 1 percent level, while the industrial concentration variable is significant at the 10 percent level and the economies of scale variable approaches this level. In turn, the coefficients of the standard deviation of profit rates and the tariff dispersion are not significantly different from zero.

Finally, all the variables representing common country characteristics are highly significant in intra-industry trade between developed and developing countries (column 4 of Table 9.1). This conclusion also applies to the EFTA variable, while the English language variable is significant at the 10 percent level. The French language variable, however, is not statistically significant.

Among industry characteristics, the marketing cost, industrial concentration, foreign direct investment, foreign affiliate and offshore procurement variables are all highly significant statistically. In turn, the level of statistical significance is 5 percent for the standard deviation of profit rates and for the tariff dispersion variable. The Hufbauer measure of product differentiation and the economies of scale variables, however, are not statistically significant.

On the whole, then, the various hypotheses introduced in Section II have been successfully tested for intra-industry trade among various groups of countries. At the same time, the explanatory power of the regression is relatively low, with a coefficient of determination of 0.44 in regard to intra-industry trade among all countries that export manufactured goods. This is hardly surprising given the great variability of intra-industry trade in individual industries between pairs of countries. In fact, the R^2 for intra-industry trade among the same group of countries is 0.87 if country averages for all industries are taken (Balassa, 1986a).

The coefficient of determination is 0.57 for trade among developed countries. The observed differences in the explanatory power of the regressions are likely to find their origin in the greater homogeneity of the economic structure of the developed country group.[26]

Estimates made for developed countries by Loertscher and Wolter have a much lower coefficient of determination (0.07). There may be two possible explanations for this result. First, Loertscher and Wolter estimated a logit equation that involves excluding zero observations; second, while these authors adjusted the explanatory variables for heteroscedasticity, they failed to make this adjustment for the dependent variable.[27]

The coefficient of determination is 0.22 for intra-industry trade among developing countries and 0.25 for trade between developed and developing countries. In both cases, the heterogeneity of the sample and the relatively large proportion of zero observations appear to have reduced the explanatory power of the regression equations.[28] As far as trade among the developing countries is concerned, the prevalence of quantitative import restrictions may also reduce the extent of the correlation.

A further question concerns the relative importance of the individual variables in explaining variations in the extent of intra-industry trade. A full treatment of this question would have required examination of all combinations of the explanatory variables, to take account of their joint contribution; this has not been attempted here. In what follows we report the increase of the coefficient of determination resulting from the inclusion of an explanatory variable, given the use of all the other variables, with regard to intra-industry trade among all countries.

The results show that distance and average country size are the country characteristics that contribute the most to the explanatory power of the regression equations, followed by trade orientation, country size differences and income differences. By contrast, introduction of the language variables adds little to the explanatory power of the equations.

Among industry characteristics, the industrial concentration variable has the greatest explanatory power, followed by the variables for marketing costs and offshore assembly. In turn, the variables for standard deviation of the profit rate and foreign affiliates hardly increase the explanatory power of the regression equation.

I V

At this point it is appropriate to ask whether the results might differ if the country and industry variables are introduced separately, rather than simultaneously, into the estimation. This question has been addressed by decomposing equations (1)–(3) into equations containing only country characteristics and only industry characteristics, respectively. Table 9.2 reports the results obtained for intra-industry trade among all countries included in the investigation.

Table 9.2 Estimation of intra-industry trade in a multi-country and multi-industry framework: disaggregation of the variables (regression co-efficients with t values in parentheses)

	Multi-country model		Multi-industry model	
Constant	1.746	(21.49)	−1.805	(38.93)
ln AY/P	0.677	(26.34)	—	—
$INEQ Y/P$	−1.041	(20.52)	—	—
ln AY	0.339	(35.29)	—	—
$INEQ Y$	−0.859	(26.74)	—	—
ATO	0.453	(32.49)	—	—
ln D	−0.366	(48.08)	—	—
$BORDER$	0.301	(11.90)	—	—
EEC	0.150	(4.62)	—	—
$EFTA$	0.303	(12.45)	—	—
$LAFTA$	0.576	(4.13)	—	—
$ENGLISH$	0.073	(2.56)	—	—
$FRENCH$	0.204	(2.83)	—	—
$SPANISH$	0.057	(0.29)	—	—
$GERMAN$	0.264	(5.05)	—	—
$PORT.$	0.541	(1.61)	—	—
$SCAND.$	0.051	(1.20)	—	—
PD	—	—	0.086	(3.59)
MKT	—	—	2.721	(7.93)
$SDPR$	—	—	0.661	(3.88)
$ECSC$	—	—	−1.024	(3.20)
$IACR$	—	—	−1.473	(8.44)
FDI	—	—	−0.844	(4.75)
$AFFL$	—	—	−0.233	(4.39)
OAP	—	—	0.466	(10.21)
TSD	—	—	−1.767	(3.40)
R^2	0.4356		0.2705	
N	62,770		62,770	

Sources: See text.
Note: Trade among developed and developing countries combined.

A comparison of Tables 9.1 and 9.2 shows that differences in the values of the regression coefficients for common country characteristics in no case attain 2 percent. The differences are larger for specific country characteristics, slightly exceeding 10 percent for the English and the Spanish language variables. At the same time, the statistical significance of the regression coefficients is hardly affected by the separate estimation of the two equations.

Different considerations apply to the industry variables. The regression coefficients of these variables show substantial differences, some negative and other positive. Coefficient values are approximately double for the foreign direct investment and foreign affiliate variables and are four-fifths higher for the standard deviation of profit rate variable if industry characteristics are introduced separately rather than simultaneously with country characteristics in the estimation. In turn, the regression coefficient of the Hufbauer product differentiation variable is three times smaller in the first case than in the second, and that of the economies of scale variable is more than one-half smaller. At the same time, the t values of most of the regression coefficients are reduced, although increases are observed for the standard deviation of profit rates, foreign direct investment and foreign affiliates variables.

These results are confirmed by estimates made for the other three country groups. They thus indicate the appropriateness of introducing country and industry characteristics simultaneously in the estimating equation. At the same time, they point to the desirability of examining the interaction between country and industry characteristics. This has been done by testing hypotheses that derive from those introduced earlier.

It is hypothesized that, for any pair of countries:

16. as per capita incomes and average country size rise and differences in incomes and country size fall, product differentiation will increase, and product standardization will reduce, the extent of intra-industry trade; and

17. community and language and participation in economic integration schemes will enhance the negative effects of foreign direct investment on intra-industry trade, by facilitating the replacement of export sales by sales from foreign subsidiaries.

The estimated results are shown in Table 9.3 for intra-industry trade among all the countries covered in the investigation, with the exclusion of those coefficients of the interaction terms that are not significant at the 10 percent level. While the number of significant coefficients is relatively small, they support the above hypotheses with two exceptions.

It is observed that higher average per capita incomes and smaller differences in incomes enhance the contribution of product differentiation (measured by the Hufbauer variable) to intra-industry trade. Also, the negative effects of product standardization, measured by the industrial concentration variable, on intra-industry trade are enhanced by increases in

Table 9.3 Estimation of intra-industry trade in a multi-country and multi-industry framework, with interaction terms (regression co-efficients, with t values in parentheses)

Constant	0.042	(0.18)
ln AY/P	0.537	(8.54)
$INEQY/P$	−0.244	(1.74)
ln AY	0.354	(35.09)
$INEQY$	−0.601	(6.92)
ATO	0.451	(32.70)
ln D	−0.372	(49.22)
$BORDER$	0.305	(12.04)
EEC	0.052	(1.28)
$EFTA$	0.307	(12.61)
$LAFTA$	0.584	(4.28)
$ENGLISH$	0.119	(3.27)
$FRENCH$	0.300	(3.27)
$SPANISH$	0.067	(0.35)
$GERMAN$	0.364	(5.52)
$PORT.$	0.613	(1.98)
$SCAND.$	0.221	(4.28)
PD	−0.133	(0.65)
MKT	3.579	(12.03)
$SDPR$	0.394	(2.72)
$ECSC$	−0.920	(2.33)
$IACR$	−2.595	(7.77)
FDI	−0.319	(2.00)
$AFFL$	−0.129	(2.85)
CAP	0.410	(10.31)
TSD	−2.758	(6.03)
ln $AY/P \times PD$	0.155	(2.63)
$INEQY/P \times PD$	−0.790	(5.72)
$INEQY \times IACR$	−0.234	(1.77)
ln $AY \times IACR$	−0.131	(1.80)
$INEQY \times ECSC$	−3.981	(4.37)
$EEC \times FDI$	2.253	(4.70)
$ENGLISH \times FDI$	−0.755	(1.60)
$FRENCH \times FDI$	−1.990	(1.61)
$GERMAN \times FDI$	−1.812	(2.34)
$SCAND. \times FDI$	−3.353	(5.19)
R^2	0.4445	
N	62,770	

Sources: See text.
Notes: Trade among developed and developing countries combined.

average country size. Contrary to expectations, however, large country size differences appear to augment the negative effects of product standardization, measured by the industrial concentration and the economies of scale variables, on intra-industry trade.

It is further apparent that the negative effects of foreign direct investment on intra-industry trade are enhanced by most common languages (English,

French, German and Scandinavian). The opposite conclusion applies to participation in the European Common Market, apparently reflecting the importance of the international subdivision of the production process, in e.g. automobiles, among EEC member countries – a factor that tends to increase the extent of intra-industry specialization *pari passu* with foreign direct investment.

While the results obtained by introducing interaction terms have an economic interpretation, their introduction affects the coefficient values of some of the country characteristics. However, the level of statistical significance declines for only two variables, per capita income differences and the EEC dummy. In turn, the Scandinavian language variable becomes significant at the 1 percent level – having not reached even a 10 percent level of significance without the introduction of interaction terms.

Among industry characteristics, the Hufbauer product differentiation variable loses its statistical significance when interaction terms are introduced in the estimating equation. The remaining variables, however, retain their sign and statistical significance and, except for the economies of scale variable, their coefficient values are little affected by the introduction of interaction terms.

CONCLUSIONS

This chapter has tested various hypotheses about the determinants of intra-industry specialization in manufactured goods, including common and specific country characteristics as well as industry characteristics. The study covers 38 countries exporting manufactured goods; calculations have been made for bilateral trade flows among all the 38 countries, among 18 developed countries, among 20 developing countries, as well as between the 18 developed and the 20 developing countries.

The hypotheses put forward in the theoretical literature with regard to common country characteristics are generally confirmed by the empirical results. Thus, the extent of intra-industry trade is positively correlated with average income levels, average country size, trade orientation and the existence of common borders and it is negatively correlated with income inequality, inequality in country size and distance.[29] All the variables are highly significant statistically in the four calculations, except for the income inequality variable in trade among developed countries and among developing countries; in both cases income differences are smaller than in the entire country sample.

We also found that the extent of intra-industry trade and participation in the European Common Market, the European Free Trade Association and the Latin American Free Trade Association are positively correlated, with all the coefficients being highly significant in the relevant equations. Also, the language variables have the expected positive sign whenever they are statistically significant, which is the case in most instances.

The extent of intra-industry trade is expected to be positively correlated with product differentiation, represented by the Hufbauer measure of product differentiation, marketing costs and the variability of profit rates, and negatively correlated with product standardization, represented by economies of scale and industrial concentration. All the regression coefficients have the expected sign and are generally significant statistically, the exceptions being the standard deviation of profit rates in the case of trade among developed and among developing countries; the economies of scale variable in the case of trade among developing countries and between developed and developing countries; and the product differentiation variable in the case of trade between developed and developing countries.

The variables associated with foreign investment (foreign direct investment and foreign affiliates) have a negative sign and are statistically significant, except for trade among developed countries. The offshore procurement variable also has the expected positive sign and it is highly statistically significant in all cases. Finally, the tariff dispersion variable is statistically significant, except for trade among developing countries.

The estimates presented in this chapter combine the inter-country and the inter-industry determinants of the extent of intra-industry trade. The explanatory power of the regression equation is greatest for trade among developed countries, which have a relatively homogeneous economic structure and for which intra-industry trade represents an important proportion of total trade. However, the heterogeneity of the sample and the relatively large proportion of zero observations appear to have reduced the explanatory power of the regressions for intra-industry trade among developing countries, and between developed and developing countries.

It has further been shown that the simultaneous introduction of country and industry characteristics offers advantages over decomposition of the estimating equation into equations containing only country or industry characteristics. Finally, interaction terms between country and industry characteristics have an economic interpretation whenever they are significant statistically, but their introduction modifies the results obtained with regard to several industry variables.

NOTES

1. The expressions 'intra-industry specialization' and 'intra-industry trade' will be used interchangeably in the chapter.
2. This is the case of intra-industry trade in standardized commodities under conditions of Cournot-type duopoly (Brander, 1981).
3. Common characteristics pertain to all countries in the sample; specific characteristics apply to only some of them.

4. In order of per capita GNP, these countries are Switzerland, United States, Sweden, Denmark, Germany, Australia, Canada, Norway, France, Belgium, Netherlands, Japan, Finland, Austria, United Kingdom, Israel, Italy and Ireland.
5. In order of per capita GNP, they are Spain, Singapore, Greece, Argentina, Hong Kong, Portugal, Yugoslavia, Mexico, Brazil, Taiwan, Malaysia, Tunisia, Korea, Morocco, Turkey, Egypt, Thailand, Philippines, India and Pakistan.
6. Among empirical studies of the inter-country determinants of intra-industry trade, Havrylyshyn and Civan (1983) included countries such as Algeria, the Central African Republic, Nigeria and Sudan, where manufactured goods accounted for less than 1 percent of total exports, while Bergstrand (1983), Clair et al. (1984), and Loertscher and Wolter (1980) limited their investigations to trade among developed countries. All the other empirical studies of intra-industry trade referred to in note 9 below examined the inter-industry determinants of this trade.
7. The investigation excludes foods and beverages (SIC 20), tobacco (SIC 21), non-ferrous metals (SIC 333), as well as several four-digit categories covering textile waste, preserved wood, saw mill products, prefabricated wood, veneer and plywood, woodpulp, dyeing and tanning extracts, fertilizers, adhesives and gelatin, carbon black, petroleum refining and products, asbestos and asphalt products, cement and concrete, lime, gypsum products, cut stone products and lapidary work. It also excludes ordnance (SIC 19), for which comparable trade data are not available.
8. The principal criteria have been high substitution elasticities in production and consumption. Needless to say, even the best of efforts could not overcome the deficiencies of the underlying four-digit industrial classification scheme.
9. Among other empirical studies of intra-industry trade, Havrylyshyn and Civan (1983) and Pagoulatos and Sorensen (1975) used 102 three-digit SITC categories; Loertscher and Wolter selected 59 such categories because of a lack of sufficient reliable export data for others (1980, p. 285n); Caves chose 84 three-digit SITC categories which could be matched with four-digit SIC categories (1981, p. 206); Toh utilized 112 four-digit SIC categories for which comparable trade data could be 'derived from aggregating comparable and not too many SITC numbers in order to keep the extent of statistical aggregation bias to the minimum' (1982, p. 288); Lundberg (1982) made calculations for the 77 manufacturing sectors of the International Standard Industrial Classification; Bergstrand (1983) used three digit categories within SITC class 7, and Clair et al. (1984) utilized five-digit categories in SITC classes 5 and 7. None of these authors attempted to replace the statistical categories by more appropriate industry categories or to exclude natural-resource products. Several of them introduced variables to evaluate the implications for the index of intra-industry trade of the heterogeneity of the statistical categories, which is not necessary if an economically meaningful system of classification is used.
10. While Aquino (1978) made an adjustment for the imbalance in trade in manufactured goods, the present study follows Balassa (1979) in adjusting for the imbalance in total trade, so as to allow for inter-industry specialization between primary and manufactured goods that is of particular importance in trade between developed and developing countries.
11. $\ln[IIT_{jki}/(1 - IIT_{jki})] = \mathbf{b}'\mathbf{z}_{jki} + u_{jki}$.
12. There are 38 countries trading with 37 countries in 152 commodity categories, but one-half of the observations are eliminated since $IIT_{jki} = IIT_{kji}$.
13. On the definition of country characteristics, for pairs of countries, see Section II.
14. No attempt has been made, however, to examine interactions between pairs of country characteristics or pairs of industry characteristics.
15. While the domestic consumption of manufactured goods would have been a more

appropriate measure of the size of the domestic market for these products, the necessary data are not available for some countries and are subject to considerable error with regard to others. At the same time, from available information it appears that the consumption of manufactured goods and the gross national product are highly correlated.

16. This measure is symmetrical with respect to country characteristics; it is not affected by a change in the unit of measurement; and it is a convex function of w.

17. Although the chapter deals with trade in manufactured goods, the extent of trade orientation with regard to all products is the appropriate variable. This is because protection is a relative concept and trade barriers on primary products affect trade in manufactured goods as well.

18. While population appears on both sides of the equation, as in Chenery's original formulation, and mineral exports are part of total exports, this should not affect the appropriateness of using deviations from hypothetical values as an indicator of trade orientation.

19. This section is based on Balassa (1986b), where the author acknowledges the receipt of data provided by Professor Caves, excluding several variables that have not proven to be statistically significant in the estimates. With the exception of the tariff variables, all data derive from US statistics; their use in regard to other countries is predicted on the assumption that the inter-industry pattern of the individual variables is invariant among countries. This has been done as comparable data for other countries are not available.

20. Caves expects a negative sign for this variable on the grounds that extensive scale economies would confine production to a few locations. An appropriate measure could not be devised for the length of the production run that represents economies of scale in differentiated products, which is considered to contribute to intra-industry trade in the theoretical literature.

21. While Toh considers this measure to reflect the oligopolistic interdependence of industries, it can be assumed to be positively correlated with the degree of product standardization.

22. Pagoulatos and Sorensen (1975) further suggest that intra-industry trade is negatively correlated with the height of tariffs. Caves (1981) notes, however, that theoretical considerations do not lead to a definite hypothesis as far as this relationship is concerned. In the present investigation, a statistically significant relationship between the two variables has not been obtained and the variable has been excluded from further analysis.

23. While the calculations refer to 1971, data for manufactured exports in the year 1979 have been used as a benchmark for the choice of the countries for the present investigation, so as to include countries that have shown a potential to export manufactured goods.

24. The estimated results are shown in column 2 of Table 9.1, omitting the dummy variables for LAFTA and for the Spanish and Portuguese languages, which are not relevant for trade among developed countries.

25. The EEC, EFTA, German and Scandinavian language variables are irrelevant in this context, and have been excluded from the estimation.

26. The proportion of observations for which intra-industry trade is equal to 0 is 22 percent in trade among developed countries, while it is 51 percent in trade among all countries. In the former case, the potential number of observations is 23,256, but there are 2,006 cases where no trade takes place.

27. At the same time, as shown in Balassa (1986a), the values of the regression coefficients and their statistical significance are significantly affected by the use of the incorrect weighting procedure. Hence, little purpose would be served by comparing the results of this study with those of Loertscher and Wolter.

28. The index of intra-industry specialization takes the value of 0 in 75 percent of the cases in trade among developing countries, and in 64 percent of the cases in trade between developed and developing countries.
29. This conclusion, however, does not apply to the size variables as far as trade among developing countries is concerned.

REFERENCES

Aquino, A. (1978) 'Intra-industry Trade and Inter-industry Specialization as Concurrent Sources of International Trade in Manufactures', *Weltwirtschaftliches Archiv*, Vol. 114, No. 2, pp. 175–96.
Balassa, B. (1966a) 'Tariff Reductions and Trade in Manufactures among Industrial Countries', *American Economic Review*, Vol. 56 (June), pp. 466–73. Reprinted as Chapter 8 in this volume.
Balassa, B. (1966b) 'American Direct Investments in the Common Market', *Banca Nazionale del Lavoro Quarterly Review*, No. 77 (June), pp. 121–46.
Balassa, B. (1967) *Trade Liberalization among Industrial Countries: Objectives and Alternatives*. New York, McGraw-Hill for the Council on Foreign Relations, Chapter 5.
Balassa, B. (1975) *European Economic Integration*. Amsterdam, North-Holland, Chapter 2.
Balassa, B. (1979) 'Intra-industry Trade and the Integration of Developing Countries in the World Economy', in *On the Economics of Intra-Industry Trade* (ed. H. Giersch), pp. 245–70. Tubingen, J. C. B. Mohr.
Balassa, B. (1986a) 'Intra-industry Trade among Exporters of Manufactured Goods', in *Imperfect Competition and International Trade: Policy Implications of Intra-Industry Trade* (ed. D. Greenway and P. Tharakan), pp. 108–28, Brighton, Wheatsheaf Books.
Balassa, B. (1986b) 'The Determinants of Intra-industry Specialization in United States Trade', *Oxford Economic Papers*, Vol. 38 (July), pp. 220–33.
Bergstrand, J. (1983) 'Measurement and Determinants of Intra-industry International Trade', in *Intra-Industry Trade* (ed. P. Tharakan), pp. 201–41. Amsterdam, North-Holland.
Brander, J. (1981) 'Intra-industry Trade in Identical Commodities', *Journal of International Economics*, Vol. 11 (February), pp. 1–14.
Caves, R. (1981) 'Intra-industry Trade and Market Structure in the Industrial Countries', *Oxford Economic Papers*, Vol. 33 (July), pp. 203–23.
Chenery, H. (1960) 'Patterns of Industrial Growth', *American Economic Review*, Vol. 50 (September), pp. 624–54.
Clair, C., Gaussens, O., and Phan, D. (1984) 'Le commerce international intra-branche et ses déterminants d'après le schéma de concurrence monopolistique: une vérification empirique', *Revue Economique*, Vol. 35 (March), pp. 347–78.
Dixit, A., and Norman, V. (1980) *Theory of International Trade*. Welwyn, J. Nisbet.
Grubel, H., and Lloyd, P. (1975) *Intra-industry Trade*. London, Macmillan.
Havrylyshyn, O., and Civan, E. (1983) 'Intra-industry Trade and the Stage of Development: A Regression Analysis of Industrial and Developing Countries', *Intra-industry Trade* (ed. P. Tharakan), pp. 111–40. Amsterdam, North-Holland.
Helpman, E. (1981) 'International Trade in the Presence of Product Differentiation, Economies of Scale and Monopolistic Competition: A Chamberlain–Heckscher–Ohlin Approach', *Journal of International Economics*, Vol. 11 (August), pp. 305–40.

Hufbauer, G. (1970) 'The Impact of National Characteristics and Technology on the Commodity Composition of Trade in Manufactured Goods', in *The Technology Factor in International Trade* (ed. R. Vernon), pp. 145–231. New York, National Bureau of Economic Research.

Krugman, P. (1979) 'Scale Economies, Product Differentiation, and the Pattern of Trade', *American Economic Review*, Vol. 70 (December), pp. 950–9.

Lancaster, K. 1980) 'Intra-Industry Trade under Perfect Monopolistic Competition', *Journal of International Economics*, Vol. 10 (May), pp. 151–75.

Linder, B. (1961) *An Essay on Trade and Transportation*. New York, John Wiley.

Loertscher, R., and Wolter, F. (1980) 'Determinants of Intra-Industry Trade: Among Countries and Across Industries', *Weltwirtschaftliches Archiv*, Vol. 116, No. 2, pp. 280–92.

Lundberg, L. (1982) 'Intra-Industry Trade: The Case of Sweden', *Weltwirtschaftliches Archiv*, Vol. 118, No. 2, pp. 303–16.

Pagoulatos, E., and Sorensen, R. (1975) 'Two-Way International Trade: An Econometric Analysis', *Welwirtschaftliches Archiv*, Vol. III, No. 3, pp. 454–65.

Toh, K. (1982) 'A Cross-Section Analysis of Intra-Industry Trade in US Manufacturing Industries', *Welwirtschaftliches Archiv*, Vol. 118, No. 2, pp. 282–301.

10 · TARIFF PROTECTION IN INDUSTRIAL COUNTRIES: AN EVALUATION

I

Viner expressed the opinion in 1950 that 'there is no way in which the "height" of a tariff as an index of its restrictive effect can be even approximately measured, or, for that matter, even defined with any degree of significant precision'.[1] Undaunted by Viner's and others' critical remarks, a long line of investigators, using more or less ingenious methods, have made attempts to compare the height of tariff levels in industrial countries.[2] More recently, these inquiries have been given added impetus by the establishment of the European Common Market[3] and tariff negotiations undertaken in the framework of the Kennedy Round.[4]

Estimates of the height of national tariff levels are designed to give expression to the restrictive effect of duties on trade flows.[5] In a general equilibrium framework, the restrictive effect of a country's tariff can be indicated by the difference between potential and actual trade, when the former refers to trade flows that would take place under *ceteris paribus* assumptions if the country in question eliminated all its duties. Tariffs affect the pattern of production and consumption and generally reduce imports *and* exports under full employment conditions as changes in relative prices associated with the imposition of tariffs lead to resource shifts from export industries to import-competing industries. In empirical investigations, however, attention is focused on imports, so that the difference between potential and actual imports is presumed to express the restrictive effect of duties.[6]

Among the *ceteris paribus* assumptions, two are of special interest: the assumption of given exchange rates and of given tariffs in other countries. For

Data collection and calculations have been carried out within the framework of the Atlantic Trade Project, sponsored by the Council on Foreign Relations and directed by the author. He is indebted to G. Basevi, R. N. Cooper, and W. M. Corden for comments on an earlier draft. Special thanks are due to Harry G. Johnson, whose advice and suggestions have been of great help in improving the argument of the chapter. First published in *Journal of Political Economy*, December 1965.

one thing, the maintenance of balance-of-payments equilibrium would prob-ably necessitate a devaluation in the country that unilaterally reduced its tariffs;[7] for another, actual changes in trade flows would depend on the changes that occurred in all the national tariffs. To avoid the complications associated with changing more than one variable, in the following discussion we will consider the restrictive effects of national tariffs under the assumption that exchange rates (and domestic prices) remain unchanged, and we will disregard at the earlier stages of the argument the interaction of tariffs imposed in individual countries.

II

In international comparisons of the height of tariff levels, two procedures have been generally employed: the calculation of weighted and unweighted aver-ages of duties. Under the first alternative, duties on individual commodities are often weighted by the imports of the country in question, which is equivalent to expressing the amount of duty paid in a given year as a percentage of the value of total imports. In turn, the second procedure entails calculating a simple average of all duties from national tariff schedules.

Although there are several recent examples of weighting with own imports,[8] this approach should not claim our attention since it has been repeatedly shown to provide distorted results: low duties associated with high levels of imports are given large weights, whereas high duties that restrict imports have small weight and prohibitive duties zero weight. Thus, while on the basis of a comparison of tariff averages weighted by own imports France would have been classified among low-tariff countries in 1955, this result appears to have been due to the restrictive effect of high duties on the imports of various categories of products.[9]

To remedy these deficiencies, it has been suggested that domestic pro-duction or consumption should be used as weights.[10] But these choices, too, are open to several objections. The composition of imports under free trade will differ from the composition of consumption under protection, in part because of the distorting effects of duties on consumer's choice, and in part because of inter-commodity differences in 'tradeability', when the latter depends, among other things, on the relative importance of specific inputs and the ratio of transportation costs to the value of output. Thus, over nine-tenths of the world production of coffee and tin enters international trade, but only a small fraction of the output of construction materials is traded.[11]

In turn, following the suggestions made in a League of Nations report (see note 2), Raymond Bertrand has calculated an unweighted average of duties for the approximately 1,100 four-digit headings of the Brussels Tariff No-menclature (BTN). This method has also been applied by the Commission of the European Economic Community (EEC) in comparing tariff levels in the

United States, the United Kingdom and the Common Market.[12] Actually, the calculation of unweighted averages involves giving equal weights to all BTN headings under the assumption that the 'law of large numbers' will lend meaning to the results. But the relative importance of the individual BTN headings differs considerably. In the Common Market countries, for example, imports of automobiles (BTN 87.02) amounted to $667.6 million in 1962 as against imports of zinc articles for construction (BTN 79.05) of $14 thousand.[13]

To give expression to the relative importance of individual products in international exchange, one may instead weight tariffs by the value of world trade. We will thereby escape, in a large part, the distorting effects of the idiosyncrasies of national tariffs on imports, although inter-country similarities in the structure of tariffs will still affect the commodity composition of international exchange. At the same time, weighting by the value of world trade will offer further advantages over the use of unweighted averages if we consider groups of commodities rather than all goods taken together.

This last observation brings us to the question whether one should calculate an average of tariffs on *all* commodities entering international trade. Calculations of this type have a long history, and an overall average has recently been used in evaluating the protectiveness of the US and Common Market tariffs by the Committee for Economic Development.[14] In turn, the EEC Commission has suggested restricting the investigation to non-agricultural products.

There are good reasons for excluding food, beverages and tobacco, since the tariff is only one of the protective measures employed in the case of these commodities. A comparison of tariffs on agricultural commodities in the Common Market and the United Kingdom would make little sense, for example, since the former employs duties and the latter subsidies to protect domestic agriculture. Neither would comparisons with the United States be meaningful, given that the latter's system of agricultural protection involves the use of price-support measures and quotas.[15] Finally, revenue duties on coffee, tea, alcoholic beverages and tobacco further complicate the picture.

These considerations suggest that the usefulness of tariff comparisons will be enhanced if we excluded from the scope of the investigation agricultural products that are subject to non-tariff measures. Adjustments would also have to be made for non-agricultural commodities that are protected by quotas or receive domestic subsidies.[16] But aside from the effects of non-tariff measures, we face a further problem that has been largely disregarded in making international tariff comparisons: the implications of duties on raw materials and intermediate products for the protection of goods at a higher level of fabrication.[17] It is easy to see that high duties on materials and intermediate products will raise the average level of tariffs on non-agricultural commodities but will reduce the degree of protection accorded to final goods by increasing the cost of inputs.

We have to distinguish, therefore, between nominal and effective rates of tariffs when the latter will take account of duties levied on material inputs.[18] Under the usual assumptions of the international immobility of labor and capital, the effective rate of duty will indicate the degree of protection of value added in the manufacturing process.[19] If input coefficients are constant in the relevant range, the effective rate of duty (z) for any commodity can be expressed in the framework of an input–output system. Let t denote the nominal rate of tariffs, a the material input coefficients, and v the proportion of value added to output, all measured at world-market prices. For commodity i we have, then, equation (1):

$$z_i = \frac{(1+t_i) - \sum_j a_{ji}(1+t_j) - \left(1 - \sum_j a_{ji}\right)}{1 - \sum_j a_{ji}} = \frac{t_i - \sum_j a_{ji} t_j}{v_i} \tag{1}$$

For given world-market prices, this formula will indicate the excess in domestic value added, obtainable by reason of the imposition of tariffs, as a percentage of value added in a free-trade situation. It is easy to see that the effective and the nominal rates of duty will be identical if the weighted average of duties on material inputs is the same as the tariff on the final product; the effective tariff will be higher than the nominal rate of duty if the product bears a higher tariff than its inputs, and vice versa.

These relationships can also find application in international comparisons. Assume, for example, that material inputs account for 60 percent of the value of output of a given commodity in a free-trade situation, and country A levies a 10 percent duty on the materials and 20 percent on the product itself, while B admits the materials duty free and applies a 16 percent tariff to the final product. Now, according to the conventional analysis, the higher rate of duty in country A would provide a greater degree of protection to the final product than B's lower tariff does, and the average of nominal rates of tariffs will also be higher in country A, regardless of the system of weighting. On the other hand, the effective tariff on the final product will be 40 percent in country B as against 35 per cent in country A. It appears, then, that the protectiveness of national tariffs cannot be indicated by comparing nominal rates of duties and averages of these duties – weighted or unweighted.[20]

III

We have concluded that, in international comparisons of the protective effect of national tariffs, one should use effective rather than nominal rates of duties. In the present chapter, effective tariffs have been calculated for the United States, the European Common Market, the United Kingdom, Sweden and Japan. These countries are the main participants in the Kennedy Round of tariff negotiations and account for about 80 percent of world exports and over 40 percent of world imports of manufactured goods. The investigation has been limited to manufactured products, and raw materials have been considered only as inputs. This solution has been chosen in part because the countries in question compete largely in the field of manufactures and in part because tariffs provide the principal means of protection in the case of manufactured goods, while quotas and subsidies predominate in agriculture.

In order to calculate the effective rates of tariffs, we need comparable data on nominal tariff rates and input–output coefficients *net* of duties. Input–output tables, using a common system of classification that also insures comparability with trade statistics, have been published for the five Common Market countries (Belgium, France, Germany, Italy, Netherlands), pertaining generally to the year 1959.[21] Comparable tables for the other countries under consideration are not available, however, and we have chosen to use 'standardized' input–output coefficients in all cases. In deriving these coefficients, we have relied largely on the input–output tables for Belgium and the Netherlands.[22] The choice has been made for these countries because they had nil or low duties on most commodities in 1959, and hence the distortion in input–output relationships, due to the existence of duties, is relatively small.

The application of identical input–output coefficients for all countries is justified if the countries in question have identical production functions with unitary substitution elasticity in all industries, or if inter-country differences in efficiency are neutral in the sense that production functions differ only by a multiplicative constant. Under these assumptions, differences in the relative prices of inputs would not affect the coefficients.[23]

While the above assumptions have often been made in empirical research,[24] they may not be fulfilled in the real world. One may argue, however, that we can abstract from non-neutral differences in production functions, since firms in the industrial countries under consideration presumably have the same 'technological horizon'. At the same time, the use of standardized coefficients has the important advantage that the results will not be affected by international differences in the composition of output in individual industries.

Standardized input–output coefficients have been derived for 36 industries, including all manufacturing except for food processing. In the system of classification applied we have been constrained by the breakdown used in the input–output tables of the Common Market countries which provide a rather narrow definition of some industries (e.g. cleansing agents and perfumes), while a number of diverse commodities are included in others (e.g. miscellaneous chemical products). A more detailed breakdown has been employed with regard to inputs, however, whenever the use of a specific input could be ascertained. For example, from the category 'synthetic materials' we have selected synthetic rubber as an input for rubber goods.

For each industry, separate consideration has been given to all inputs that contribute at least 4 percent of the value of output. The number of inputs distinguished in the case of individual industries has been between one and six, with automobiles at the upper end of the range. Other material inputs and non-material inputs (transportation, trade, etc.) have been included in separate categories. Within the group of other material inputs, fuels, paper, non-metallic minerals and metal manufactures predominate; hence we have used a weighted average of tariffs on these products in the calculations. There are no duties on non-material inputs.

With regard to tariffs, we have used the BTN which is employed by the EEC, the United Kingdom, Sweden and Japan. For the United States, tariff categories have been reclassified according to the BTN in *Comparative Tariffs and Trade*;[25] we have relied on this compilation while adjusting the results for reductions in duties accomplished in the Dillon Round of tariff negotiations. Further, the specific duties applied chiefly in Britain have been expressed in *ad valorem* equivalents, whereas the common external tariff has been used in the case of the EEC.

Tariffs shown for the four-digit BTN headings have been expressed in terms of the four-digit items of the Standard International Trade Classification (SITC) that is employed in reporting trade statistics by all the countries under consideration.[26] Since the industrial classification applied is less detailed than the four-digit SITC, it has been necessary to average the tariff figures relating to the latter.[27] In averaging tariffs, we have used the combined imports of the five industrial areas as weights.[28] Subsequently, effective rates of duties have been calculated by utilizing the formula given in the previous section.

IV

Nominal and effective rates of duties for the 36 industries of the five countries (country groupings) under consideration are shown in Table 10.1. In turn, Table 10.2 provides the country ranking of tariffs for each industry, the industry ranking of tariffs for each country, and unweighted averages of the latter rankings for the five countries (country groupings) under consideration. In the same table, the 36 industries are also ranked according to the labor intensiveness of the manufacturing process, expressed in terms of labor–input coefficients.[29]

With few exceptions, we find effective duties to be higher than nominal rates. This result is explained, in part, by the relatively low duties on materials as compared to semi-manufactures and finished goods and, in part, by the absence of tariffs on non-material inputs that do not enter international trade. The differences are especially pronounced – and effective rates are more than double nominal rates – in the case of textile fabrics and hosiery, leather, chemical materials, steel ingots and non-ferrous metals. Being semi-finished products that require little technological sophistication for their manufacture, these commodities are actual or potential exports of the less-developed

Table 10.1 Nominal and effective tariff rates, 1962

	United States N	E	United Kingdom N	E	Common Market N	E	Sweden N	E	Japan N	E
21. Thread and yarn	11.7	31.8	10.5	27.9	2.9	3.6	2.2	4.3	2.7	1.4
22. Textile fabrics	24.1	50.6	20.7	42.2	17.6	44.4	12.7	33.4	19.7	48.8
23. Hosiery	25.6	48.7	25.4	49.7	18.6	41.3	17.6	42.4	26.0	60.8
24. Clothing	25.1	35.9	25.5	40.5	18.5	25.1	14.0	21.1	25.2	42.4
25. Other textile articles	19.0	22.7	24.5	42.4	22.0	38.8	13.0	21.2	14.8	13.0
26. Shoes	16.6	25.3	24.0	36.2	19.9	33.0	14.0	22.8	29.5	45.1
29. Wood products including furniture	12.8	26.4	14.8	25.5	15.1	28.6	6.8	14.5	19.5	33.9
32. Paper and paper products	3.1	0.7	6.6	8.1	10.3	13.3	2.0	-0.7	10.5	12.9
33. Printed matter	2.5	2.2	2.7	0.2	3.3	-0.7	0.7	0.0	1.6	-4.2
35. Leather	9.6	25.7	14.9	34.3	7.3	18.3	7.0	21.7	19.9	59.0
36. Leather goods other than shoes	15.5	24.5	18.7	26.4	14.7	24.3	12.2	20.7	23.6	33.6
37. Rubber goods	9.3	16.1	20.2	43.9	15.1	33.6	10.8	26.1	12.9	23.6
38. Plastic articles	21.0	27.0	17.9	30.1	20.6	30.0	15.0	25.5	24.9	35.5
39. Synthetic materials	18.6	33.5	12.7	17.1	12.0	17.6	7.2	12.9	19.1	32.1
40. Other chemical material	12.3	26.6	19.4	39.2	11.3	20.5	4.5	9.7	12.2	22.6
42. Cleaning agents and perfumes	11.2	18.8	11.1	11.2	13.8	26.7	10.9	27.9	26.2	61.5
43. Miscellaneous chemical products	12.6	15.6	15.4	16.7	11.6	13.1	2.5	0.0	16.8	22.9
45. Non-metallic mineral products	18.2	30.4	13.6	20.9	13.3	19.8	6.0	10.0	13.5	20.8

46. Glass and glass products	18.8	29.3	18.5	26.2	14.4	20.0	13.8	22.6	19.5	27.4
48. Pig iron and ferromanganese	1.8	9.3	3.3	17.9	4.0	−13.8	0.0	−0.7	10.0	54.3
49. Ingots and other primary steel forms	10.6	106.7	11.1	98.9	6.4	28.9	3.8	40.0	13.0	58.9
50. Rolling-mill products	7.1	−2.2	9.5	7.4	7.2	10.5	5.2	13.2	15.4	29.5
51. Other steel products	5.1	0.5	17.0	46.8	9.9	20.9	5.4	9.5	13.4	14.1
54. Non-ferrous metals	5.0	10.6	6.6	19.4	2.4	5.0	0.4	0.6	9.3	27.5
55. Metal castings	6.6	10.0	16.0	26.9	12.4	21.0	8.0	34.7	20.0	32.5
56. Metal manufactures	14.4	28.5	19.0	35.9	14.0	25.6	8.4	16.2	18.1	27.7
57. Agricultural machinery	0.4	−6.9	15.4	21.3	13.4	19.6	10.0	16.0	20.0	29.2
58. Non-electrical machinery	11.0	16.1	16.1	21.2	10.3	12.2	8.8	11.6	16.8	21.4
59. Electrical machinery	12.2	18.1	19.7	30.0	14.5	21.5	10.7	17.7	18.1	25.3
60. Ships	5.5	2.1	2.9	−10.2	0.4	−13.2	0.9	−5.8	13.1	12.1
61. Railway vehicles	7.0	7.3	21.1	33.3	11.1	−0.2	8.7	13.8	15.0	18.5
62. Automobiles	6.8	5.1	23.1	41.4	19.5	36.8	14.7	30.5	35.9	75.7
64. Bicycles and motorcycles	14.4	26.1	22.4	39.2	20.9	39.7	17.1	35.8	25.0	45.0
65. Airplanes	9.2	8.8	15.6	16.7	10.5	10.8	3.7	3.0	15.0	15.9
66. Precision instruments	21.4	32.2	25.7	44.2	13.5	24.2	6.6	14.9	23.2	38.5
67. Sport goods, toys, jewelry, etc.	25.0	41.8	22.3	35.6	17.9	26.6	10.6	16.6	21.6	31.2

Source: Tariffs: National tariff schedules. Trade: National and international trade statistics. Input–output coefficients: Office Statistique des Communautés Européennes, *Tableaux 'Entrées–Sorties' pour les pays de la Communauté Européenne Économique*, October, 1964.

Note: N = nominal, E = effective.

Table 10.2 Rankings of labor–input coefficients, nominal and effective tariff rates, 1962

	Standardized labor–input coefficients[a]	United States N		United States E		United Kingdom N		United Kingdom E		Common Market N		Common Market E		Sweden N		Sweden E		Japan N		Japan E		Five areas together N	Five areas together E
		A[b]	B[c]	A	B	A	B	A	B	A	B	A	B	A	B	A	B	A	B	A	B	C[d]	C
21. Thread and yarn	29	1	19	1	8	2	30	2	19	3	34	4	32	5	31	3	29	4	35	5	35	32	27
22. Textile fabrics	27	1	4	1	2	2	10	4	7	4	9	3	1	5	9	5	5	3	14	2	7	9	3
23. Hosiery	17	2	1	3	3	2	3	2	7	4	6	5	2	5	1	4	1	1	4	1	3	1	1
24. Clothing	26	3	2	3	5	1	2	2	9	4	7	2	14	5	5	5	14	2	5	1	10	2	7
25. Other textile articles	24	3	7	3	19	1	4	1	6	2	1	2	4	5	8	4	13	4	25	5	32	8	14
26. Shoes	22	4	11	4	17	2	5	2	12	3	4	3	7	5	6	5	10	1	2	1	8	4	8
29. Wood products and furniture	23	4	15	3	14	3	25	4	23	2	10	2	10	5	22	5	21	1	16	1	13	17	16
32. Paper and paper products	18	4	33	4	33	3	32	3	33	2	27	1	26	5	32	5	35	1	32	2	33	33	34
33. Printed matter	7	3	34	1	31	2	36	2	35	1	33	4	34	5	34	3	32	4	36	5	36	36	35
35. Leather	32	3	23	3	16	2	24	2	15	4	29	5	24	5	21	4	12	1	13	1	4	24	12
36. Leather goods other than shoes	13	3	12	3	18	2	15	2	21	4	12	4	15	5	12	5	15	1	8	1	14	11	17
37. Rubber goods	16	5	24	5	22	1	11	1	5	1	11	2	6	4	12	3	8	3	30	4	24	16	11
38. Plastic articles	21	2	6	4	12	4	17	2	17	3	3	3	8	5	3	5	9	1	7	1	12	3	4
39. Synthetic materials	28	2	9	1	6	3	27	4	29	4	21	3	25	5	20	5	24	1	17	2	16	18	22
40. Other chemical materials	25	2	17	2	13	1	13	1	10	4	23	4	20	5	27	5	27	3	31	3	26	25	21
42. Cleaning agents and perfumes	30	3	20	4	20	4	29	5	32	2	16	3	11	5	11	2	7	1	3	1	2	15	13
43. Miscellaneous chemical products	12	3	16	3	24	2	23	2	31	4	22	4	27	5	30	5	33	1	21	1	25	26	25

Industry	a	b	c	b	c	b	c	b	c	b	c	b	c	b	c	b	c	b	c	b	c	d	d
45. Non-metallic mineral products	11	1	10	1	9	2	26	2	26	4	19	4	22	5	24	5	26	3	26	3	28	23	23
46. Glass and glass products	5	2	8	1	10	3	16	3	22	5	14	5	21	5	7	4	11	1	15	2	22	12	19
48. Pig iron and ferromanganese	35	4	35	3	27	3	34	2	28	2	32	5	36	5	36	4	34	1	33	1	6	35	30
49. Ingots and other primary steel	−36	3	22	2	1	2	28	2	1	4	31	5	9	5	28	4	2	1	29	3	5	30	2
50. Rolling-mill products	33	4	26	5	35	2	31	4	34	3	30	3	30	5	26	2	23	1	22	1	18	29	32
51. Other steel products	31	5	31	5	34	4	18	1	3	3	28	3	19	4	25	4	28	2	27	3	31	28	24
54. Non-ferrous metals	34	3	32	3	25	2	33	3	27	4	35	4	31	5	35	5	31	1	34	1	21	34	31
55. Metal castings	3	5	29	3	26	2	20	3	20	3	20	4	18	4	19	5	4	1	12	3	15	19	18
56. Metal manufactures	10	3	13	2	11	1	14	1	13	3	15	4	18	4	19	5	18	5	19	3	20	14	15
57. Agricultural machinery	15	5	36	5	36	2	22	2	24	3	18	3	23	5	15	4	15	1	1	1	19	22	26
58. Non-electrical machinery	8	3	21	3	23	2	19	2	25	4	26	4	28	5	16	5	25	1	20	1	27	21	28
59. Electrical machinery	4	4	18	4	21	1	12	1	18	3	13	3	17	5	13	5	16	2	18	2	23	13	20
60. Ships	9	2	30	2	32	3	35	4	36	5	36	5	35	4	33	3	36	1	28	1	34	31	36
61. Railway vehicles	6	5	27	4	29	1	9	1	16	3	24	5	33	4	17	3	22	2	24	2	29	20	29
62. Automobiles	19	5	28	5	30	2	6	2	8	3	5	3	5	4	4	3	6	1	1	1	1	7	6
64. Bicycles and motorcycles	20	5	14	5	15	2	7	3	11	3	5	2	3	2	2	3	3	1	5	1	5	5	5
65. Airplanes	1	4	25	4	28	1	21	1	30	3	25	3	29	5	29	5	30	2	23	2	30	27	33
66. Precision instruments	2	3	5	3	7	1	1	1	4	4	17	4	16	5	23	5	20	2	9	2	11	10	9
67. Sport goods, toys, jewelry, etc.	14	1	3	1	4	2	8	2	14	4	8	4	12	5	14	5	17	3	10	3	17	6	10

Note: N = nominal, E = effective.

a Ranking of industries according to the share of wages plus employer-financed social security payments in the value of output, derived from the input–output tables previously cited.

b Ranking of countries (country groupings) according to the rate of duty for individual industries.

c Ranking of industries according to the rate of duty for individual countries (country groupings).

d Unweighted average of the ranking of industries according to the rate of duty in the five areas.

countries; hence, the results provide evidence for the validity of complaints recently voiced by these countries regarding the protective effect of 'graduated' tariffs in industrial areas.[30]

In turn, effective duties are lower than nominal tariffs in the case of printed matter and ships, and, in some of the countries, the protective effect of the low duties levied on these goods is more than offset by duties on their inputs, so that the effective rate of tariff is negative.[31] Further instances of negative effective duty are agricultural machinery in the United States, pig iron in the EEC and Sweden, and paper in Sweden. Finally, a comparison of the ranking of individual commodity categories according to nominal and effective rates of duties indicates that high tariffs on semi-manufactures reduce the *relative* degree of protection in the case of most consumer goods (clothing and textile articles, shoes and other leather goods, sports goods, toys and jewelry) and investment goods (electrical and non-electrical machinery, railway vehicles and airplanes).

The calculation of effective duties also influences the country ranking of tariffs with regard to individual industries. In terms of effective tariffs, the United States and Sweden appear to be more protective than nominal duties would indicate, while the opposite conclusion holds for the United Kingdom, the EEC and especially Japan. Thus, if comparisons are made by using effective rather than nominal rates of tariffs, the United States has a higher 'rank' with regard to eight commodities and a lower rank with respect to three products, and Sweden has a higher rank in thirteen cases and a lower rank in none. In turn, in the case of the United Kingdom, upward adjustments are made in three instances, and downward adjustments in nine, while the relevant figures for the Common Market are five and ten, and for Japan two and eleven. These changes in rankings find their origin in the relatively low duties on materials in the United States and Sweden that raise the protective effect of a given nominal duty in these countries.

V

So far the discussion has proceeded in terms of changes in the relative position of countries and commodities as we calculate effective instead of nominal rates of duties. To make inter-commodity comparisons of effective tariff *levels*, some further clarification of the assumptions underlying the analysis is called for. In this connection, separate consideration should be given to homogeneous (standardized) and heterogeneous (differentiated) products.

In theoretical models of international trade, it is generally assumed that traded goods are homogeneous, and a distinction is made between export- and import-competing industries. The same commodity may be imported and produced domestically in this case, and tariffs will have no protective effect on a commodity exported by the tariff-imposing country.[32] Only a few manufactures (gray cloth, paper, steel ingots, unwrought metals) qualify as standardized products, however, while product differentiation characterizes consumer goods, machinery and transport equipment, as well as intermediate products at a higher level of fabrication (e.g. rolled-steel products, worked metal and textile fabrics). At the same time, heterogeneous commodities can be exported *and* protected, and hence the distinction between export- and import-competing industries becomes blurred.

Correspondingly, tariffs levied on differentiated products can have a protective effect in every country and lead to the substitution of domestic for foreign merchandise in everyone's consumption. A multilateral reduction of duties will, then, give rise to an increased exchange of consumer goods without necessarily affecting produced quantities in the participating countries. In turn, tariff reductions on investment goods and intermediate products at higher levels of fabrication may result in intensified intra-industry specialization and longer production runs through a decrease of product variety in the individual firms.

Among the developed countries under consideration, a broad similarity exists with respect to the ranking of industries according to their effective duties. Effective tariff rates are generally high on textile fabrics and hosiery, clothing and shoes, steel ingots and, with a few exceptions, on other textile articles (chiefly sacks, bags and linen goods), sports goods, toys and jewelry, as well as on automobiles, motorcycles and bicycles. In turn, relatively low effective duties are shown for paper and printed matter, ships and airplanes, pig iron, rolling-mill products and non-ferrous metals, and also for machinery and railway equipment.

The observed similarities in the ranking of commodities by effective tariffs provide an indication of the possibilities for increased intra-industry exchange among the countries in question. In order to derive more definite conclusions with regard to individual industries, however, account should be taken of substitution elasticities between domestic and foreign products, and one should also consider the implications of tariffs for trade with outsiders – most of which are developing countries.

The general tendency among developed countries is to protect the domestic production of textile fabrics. The textile industry has long been the 'sick man' of the manufacturing sector in many of these countries, and it has often been compared to agriculture by the proponents and the opponents of its protection alike. At the same time, its 'footloose' character, the relative simplicity of the technological process, and the labor intensiveness of its manufacture make the textile industry a candidate for becoming the first manufacturing export industry in many developing countries. Correspondingly, the main effect of the all-round protection of textile fabrics in developed economies is likely to be a retardation of the expansion of exports from less-developed areas. Similar considerations apply to sacks and bags, toys and sports goods and, among mechanical goods, to bicycles.

In most of the developed countries, effective duties are also high on consumer goods, including clothing and shoes, as well as automobiles. As a possible explanation, it may be suggested that in the case of these commodities cost differences are relatively small among the industrial countries, while the possibilities of substituting foreign commodities for domestic merchandise are considerable and protectionist pressures are also strong. The strength of protectionist pressures is partly explained by the fact that, whereas the opposing economic interest will influence – and moderate – tariffs on intermediate products and investment goods, the consumers rarely have a say in tariff setting.

Effective duties are low on intermediate products that utilize specific – and bulky – inputs in their manufacture, such as paper, non-ferrous metals and, with the exception of Japan, pig iron.[33] Moderate levels of protection are shown in the case of machinery and railway equipment, too. These products are generally highly differentiated and their international exchange contributes to lower manufacturing costs in all industrial countries. On the other hand, the low degree of protection of ships is largely illusory, since industrial countries generally provide subsidies to domestic shipbuilding, whereas 'buy-national' provisions assist the domestic airplane manufacturers in some of the producing countries.

But can these admittedly 'partial' explanations of the structure of tariffs in the industrial countries be replaced or supplemented by the application of some general principle? One such classifying principle is the labor intensiveness of the manufacturing process in individual industries. It has often been suggested that industrial countries, and especially the United States, tend to protect labor-intensive manufactures.[34] Our results do not reveal such a tendency, however, and no definite relationship is shown between labor intensiveness and effective rates of duties. Thus, the rank correlation coefficient between labor–input coefficients and effective duties is between -0.08 and -0.14 in European countries and the United States, and -0.41 in Japan. With the exception of the Japanese case, these estimates are not significantly different from zero at the 5 percent level of confidence, and the results are little affected if – following Basevi – we calculate effective rates of protection for labor under the assumption that capital is freely mobile between countries.[35]

It is suggested here that the explanation lies in the inadequacy of Heckscher–Ohlin-type theories that rely on a single classifying principle – factor proportions – in attempting to explain international specialization and consider protection in its effect on the income of the scarce factor. In appraising the structure of protection in the industrial countries, however, we can hardly neglect technological factors. It would appear that these countries find it expedient to protect heavily industries where developing economies can easily compete because labor-intensive production methods can be used and the technological process is rather simple. In turn, relatively low tariffs are levied on machinery whose manufacture is relatively labor intensive but requires advanced technology and organizational know-how that are not available in less-developed countries.

Interest attaches also to inter-country differences in the protection of individual industries. Rank correlation coefficients calculated with regard to effective tariffs for pairs of countries indicate considerable similarities within western Europe. On the other hand – aside from the United Kingdom–Japanese comparison – the discrepancies in the structure of tariffs are the most pronounced between the United States and Japan, which are at the opposite end of the spectrum in terms of industrial development. Thus, while in intra-European comparisons the rank correlation coefficients are in the 0.65–0.85 range, in the US–Japan comparison the relevant coefficient is 0.395 (Table 10.3).

It stands to reason, then, that the United States and Japan show the largest deviations from the ranking of duties in the five importing areas, taken together. Among the European countries, discrepancies are the most pronounced in the case of the United Kingdom, where selected industries are heavily protected. In turn – possibly as a result of the averaging of national tariffs undertaken in connection with the EEC's establishment – the European Common Market fits the general pattern rather well, and neither do we observe large deviations in the case of Sweden. Thus, the rank correlation coefficient between effective tariffs in the various countries and country groupings, on the one hand, and an unweighted average of these rankings, on the other, is 0.732 in the case of Japan, 0.737 for the United States, 0.770 for the United Kingdom, 0.867 for Sweden and 0.907 for the EEC.

Among individual commodities and commodity groups, synthetic and other chemical materials, as well as glass and non-metallic mineral products, are high on the US list. In the case of synthetic and chemical materials, the effective rate of duty is raised by reason of the use of the American selling price as a basis for determining duties on several of these products,[36] while US tariffs are notoriously high on glass and its manufactures. In turn, in the case of agricultural machinery, airplanes and automobiles, the degree of protection

Table 10.3 Rank correlation coefficients for effective tariffs in 36 industries, 1962[a]

	United States	United Kingdom	Common Market	Sweden	Japan	Five areas together
United States	—	0.481	0.512	0.506	0.395	0.737
United Kingdom	0.481	—	0.746	0.650	0.362	0.770
Common Market	0.512	0.746	—	0.827	0.565	0.907
Sweden	0.506	0.650	0.827	—	0.689	0.867
Japan	0.395	0.362	0.565	0.689	—	0.732
Five areas together	0.737	0.770	0.907	0.867	0.732	—

[a] Spearman rank correlation coefficient. All coefficients except those relating the United States and Japan, and the United Kingdom and Japan, are statistically significant at the 1 percent level; the latter are significant at the 5 percent level.

appears to be substantially lower in the United States than in the other countries under consideration. Agricultural machinery and airplanes are leading US exports, whereas the observed disparities in tariffs on automobiles may be related to differences in the degree of substitutability between domestic and foreign cars in the United States as against European countries and Japan. Despite the inroads made by European producers in the American market, the possibilities for substitution between the large American and the small European cars appear to be rather limited. On the other hand, car manufacturers in European countries and Japan have to contend with the competing products of each other's industries, and governments use high tariffs to insure safe outlets for domestic production in the home market. The consequences of a reduction in the degree of protection are evident in France and Italy, where the decrease in tariffs following the establishment of the Common Market has led to an influx of foreign cars.

Mention can be made of the relatively high degree of protection of steel products and railway vehicles in Britain, miscellaneous textile articles (chiefly sacks and bags) and paper in the Common Market, metal castings in Sweden, and pig iron and rolling-mill products in Japan. Finally, in terms of effective tariffs, the ranking of plastic and synthetic materials is lower than the average in the United Kingdom; the same conclusion pertains to precision instruments in the Common Market and in Sweden, and to sacks and bags, as well as to rubber products, in Japan.

VI

We come now to the question raised in the introductory sections of this chapter regarding the 'height' of national tariffs levels.[37] The reader will recall that estimates of the height of tariff levels are designed to indicate the restrictive effect of duties on trade flows, defined as the difference between potential and actual imports. To insure international comparability, the decrease in imports due to the imposition of tariffs (dM) may, in turn, be expressed as a proportion of potential imports (M).

Under the assumption that cross-elasticities of demand and supply can be neglected and that the primary resources used in industries producing import substitutes are available at constant costs, the restrictive effects of tariffs on the imports of a given commodity will consist of three components:

1. the restriction of domestic consumption;
2. the increase in domestic production; and
3. the increase in the demand for this commodity as an input in the production of other protected goods.

Let C_i denote the domestic consumption, P_i the domestic production, and M_i the imports of commodity i in a free-trade situation, while η_i stands for the elasticity of domestic demand and ε_i for the elasticity of supply of value added.[38] The effect of duties on the imports of commodity i can now be written as

$$dM_i = -\eta_i C_i t_i - \varepsilon_i P_i z_i + \sum_j a_{ij} \varepsilon_j P_j z_j \tag{2}$$

And, for all importables, taken together, we have

$$dM = -\sum_i \eta_i C_i t_i - \sum_i \varepsilon_i P_i z_i + \sum_i \sum_j a_{ij} \varepsilon_j P_j z_j$$

$$= -\sum_i \left[\eta_i C_i t_i + \varepsilon_i P_i z_i \left(1 - \sum_j a_{ji}\right) \right]$$

$$= -\sum_i (\eta_i C_i t_i + \varepsilon_i v_i P_i z_i) \tag{3}$$

and

$$\frac{dM}{M} = -\sum_i \left(\eta_i \frac{C_i}{M_i} t_i + \varepsilon_i v_i \frac{P_i}{M_i} z_i \right) \frac{M_i}{M} \tag{4}$$

Let us first assume that identical nominal tariffs (t_o) are levied on every commodity. By transforming equation (4) into (4a), the restrictive effects of tariffs

$$\frac{dM}{M} = -\sum_i \left[\eta_i \frac{C_i}{M_i} t_o + \varepsilon_i \frac{P_i}{M_i} \left(t_o - \sum_j a_{ji} t_o \right) \right] \frac{M_i}{M}$$

$$= -t_o \sum_i \left(\eta_i \frac{C_i}{M_i} + \varepsilon_i \frac{P_i}{M_i} v_i \right) \frac{M_i}{M} \tag{4a}$$

on imports can be shown to vary in proportion with the common tariff, t_o. Further, under the assumption that for individual commodities the share of imports in domestic production and consumption, the proportion of value added to output, as well as domestic demand and supply elasticities and the structure of imports, are identical internationally, the restrictive effect of tariffs would be proportional to the values taken by t_o in the particular countries.

Assume, instead, that C_i/M_i, P_i/M_i, v_i, η_i and ε_i are identical for every commodity in all the countries but allow tariff rates to vary. Utilizing the relationships indicated in equation (5) to transform equation (4) into (4b), it will be apparent that the restrictiveness of national tariffs will depend on inter-country differences with regard to the averages of nominal *and* effective duties, calculated by weighting with potential imports.

$$\frac{dM}{M} = -\left(\eta_i \frac{C_i}{M_i} \bar{t} + \varepsilon_i v_i \frac{P_i}{M_i} \bar{z} \right) \tag{4b}$$

$$\bar{t} = \frac{\sum_i t_i M_i}{\sum_i M_i}; \qquad \bar{z} = \frac{\sum_i z_i M_i}{\sum_i M_i} \tag{5}$$

Correspondingly, under these assumptions, an unambiguous conclusion regarding the restrictiveness of national tariffs could be given as long as both nominal and effective tariff averages pointed in the same direction.

A comparison of tariff averages indicates that, among the countries under consideration, the overall average of nominal as well as that of effective duties is the highest in Japan, with the United Kingdom as a close second and Sweden at the opposite end of the scale. The United States and the EEC occupy the middle ground: the overall average of nominal duties is slightly higher in the Common Market than in the United States, while the opposite conclusion holds with regard to averages of effective tariffs (Table 10.4).[39]

Aside from comparisons of tariff averages, much attention has been given to the dispersion of tariffs, and it has been alleged that a greater dispersion of the tariff distribution in the United States, as compared to the Common Market, increases the restrictiveness of US duties.[40] The data of Table 10.4, indeed, show greater tariff dispersion for the United States than for the Common Market, although the differences are reduced if the dispersion of effective, rather than nominal, duties is calculated. But, a perusal of equation (4b) suggests that the restrictive effect of duties is unrelated to their dispersion. This result can be understood if we consider that, in the absence of 'excess protection', there is no presumption that a 20 percent duty on refrigerators and a 10 percent tariff on washing machines would restrict imports more than a 15 percent tariff on both.[41] At the same time, it may be argued that, after the successive tariff reductions undertaken over the past 15 years, much of the 'fat' of protection has been sliced off.

Next, we remove the assumption that the ratios of imports to consumption and to production are identical in the countries under consideration. In fact, these shares differ considerably from country to country, thereby affecting the restrictiveness of tariffs in the individual areas. The proportion of the imports of industrial goods to value added in manufacturing is the lowest in the

Table 10.4 Overall tariff averages and standard deviations, 1962[a]

	Nominal tariffs			Effective tariffs			Uniform tariff equiva- lents
	Weighted average	Standard deviation	Coefficient of variation	Weighted average	Standard deviation	Coefficient of variation	
United States	11.6	6.9	0.59	20.0	16.6	0.83	16.7
United Kingdom	15.5	6.2	0.40	27.8	12.1	0.44	23.8
Common Market	11.9	3.6	0.30	18.6	11.5	0.62	17.3
Sweden	6.8	4.6	0.67	12.5	10.6	0.85	12.2
Japan	16.2	7.6	0.47	29.5	15.6	0.53	26.4

Source: Table 10.1 and United Nations (1964) *Commodity Trade Statistics, 1962* (New York).
[a] Tariff averages calculated by weighting with the combined imports of the five areas.

United States (4.7 percent in 1961) and the highest in Sweden (44.9 percent). In turn, the relevant ratio is 16.4 percent for the United Kingdom, 12.1 percent for Japan and, if trade among the member countries is excluded, it is 10.5 percent in the European Common Market.[42] Thus, it would appear that the tariff figures overestimate the relative degree of protection in Sweden and, to a lesser extent, in the United Kingdom, and underestimate it in the case of the United States, while the EEC and Japan occupy a middle position.

The restrictiveness of tariffs is further affected by inter-country differences in domestic demand and supply elasticities. The paucity of comparable estimates does not permit us to derive definite conclusions with regard to the former, but we may assume that, among the industrial countries, differences are relatively small. On the other hand, information on the rate of unemployment and capacity utilization indicates that domestic supply elasticities may be higher in the United States than elsewhere. High supply elasticities, then, would increase the restrictive effect of a given tariff on US imports.

Nothing has been said so far of inter-commodity differences with regard to the variables determining the effects of tariffs on imports. It will be apparent that, in the presence of such differences, overall tariff averages will not appropriately indicate the restrictiveness of duties. Nevertheless, if information on all the relevant variables is available, we can calculate a 'uniform-tariff equivalent' – defined as the common rate of duty levied on all imported commodities that has the same restrictive effect on imports as the actual tariffs.[43] The formula for the uniform-tariff equivalent is

$$\bar{t}_o = \frac{\sum_i \left[\eta_i C_i t_i + \varepsilon_i P_i \left(t_i - \sum_j a_{ji} t_j \right) \right]}{\sum_i \left[\eta_i C_i + \varepsilon_i P_i \left(1 - \sum_j a_{ji} \right) \right]}$$

$$= \frac{\sum_i (\eta_i C_i t_i + \varepsilon_i v_i P_i z_i)}{\sum_i (\eta_i C_i + \varepsilon_i v_i P_i)} \tag{6}$$

VII

In the previous section, we have assumed that the primary resources utilized in producing import substitutes are available at constant costs. This assumption is indeed appropriate if unemployment prevails in the tariff-imposing country, since, in this case, an expansion in the output of import-competing industries does not necessitate drawing resources from other sectors of the economy. But, under full-employment conditions, resources will move into the import-competing sector from other industries and, if all countries impose tariffs, production for export will decline. The shift in primary resources will, then, be accompanied by a fall in demand for material inputs in the export sector, and equation (2) has to be amended by adding a term for the reduction in the demand for imported inputs used in the contracting industries.

Let us now consider the effects of multilateral tariff reductions on trade in manufactured products among the industrial countries. Correspondingly, in equation (2), C_i', P_i', and M_i' will replace C_i, P_i, and M_i, when the former refer to actual ('tariff-ridden') rather than potential consumption, production and imports, while $t_i' = t_i/1 + t_i$ will replace t_i. Tariff reductions will be associated with an expansion of exports and imports in every country, and the demand for imported inputs used in producing exports and import-competing goods will change in opposite directions.

But, as we have noted in Section V, with respect to differentiated commodities produced in industrial countries of similar economic structure, a clear distinction between exports and import-competing products cannot be made. Thus, following a reduction of tariffs, the British will buy more Italian cars and vice versa, and similar developments are expected with regard to other consumer goods. In turn, in the case of machinery and intermediate products at higher levels of fabrication, increased intra-industry specialization is foreseen. The import content of exports and of import-competing goods may, then, differ little; and if – as a first approximation – we assume that every country will experience a balanced expansion of its exports and imports, the effects of tariff reductions on imported inputs can be neglected. Accordingly, equation (2) would take the form[44]

$$dM_i' = \eta_i C_i' t_i' + \varepsilon_i P_i' z_i'$$

Assume further that, while the variables determining the restrictiveness of tariffs may differ from commodity to commodity, these are identical for commodities at the same level of fabrication that serve similar needs. Under this assumption, we can use averages of nominal and effective tariffs calculated for individual commodity categories to provide an indication of the expansion of imports following the elimination of tariffs. Such a calculation will have added interest, since inter-country differences in the tariff averages pertaining to individual commodity categories will also indicate the relative advantages and disadvantages bestowed on large sectors of the economy through tariff protection.

Averages of nominal and effective duties have been estimated for consumer goods,[45] investment goods,[46] and two categories of intermediate products. Semi-manufactures whose main inputs are natural raw materials have been classified as intermediate products I,[47] while all intermediate goods at higher levels of fabrication have been included in intermediate products II.[48] Finally, industries that produce intermediate as well as final goods have been classified according to the main uses of their products as determined from the input–output tables.[49]

Table 10.5 Average of nominal and effective rates of duties for four commodity categories, 1962[a]

	United States		United Kingdom		Common Market		Sweden		Japan	
	N	E	N	E	N	E	N	E	N	E
Intermediate products I	8.8	17.6	11.1	23.1	7.6	12.0	3.0	5.3	11.4	23.8
Intermediate products II	15.2	28.6	17.2	34.3	13.3	28.3	8.5	20.8	16.6	34.5
Consumer goods	17.5	25.9	23.8	40.4	17.8	30.9	12.4	23.9	27.5	50.5
Investment goods	10.3	13.9	17.0	23.0	11.7	15.0	8.5	12.1	17.1	22.0
All commodities	11.6	20.0	15.5	27.8	11.9	18.6	6.8	12.5	16.2	29.5

Source: Table 10.1 and United Nations, *op. cit.*
Note: N = nominal, E = effective.
[a] Tariff averages have been obtained by weighting with the combined imports of the five areas.

The results of the calculations shown in Table 10.5 support our previous conclusions regarding the disparities between nominal and effective duties and the general similarity of tariff structures in the main industrial countries.[50] As regards effective duties, we find that the large share of products requiring specific and bulky resource inputs for their manufacture tends to reduce the average of duties for the first group, while tariff averages are uniformly higher for intermediate products at higher levels of fabrication, and generally increase again in the case of consumer goods. Still, an inter-country comparison of tariff averages indicates a higher-than-average degree of discrimination in favor of consumer goods in Japan, and a lower-than-average one in the United States, whereas the Common Market and the Swedish tariff structures appear to favor intermediate products at the lowest levels of fabrication. Finally, with the exception of the latter two countries, the lowest duties are levied on investment goods.

We have also utilized the information provided in Table 10.5 to prepare illustrative estimates of the probable effects of the elimination of duties on imports into the individual countries for assumed values of the relevant variables. In the first place, we have assumed that, in the countries under consideration, the following demand and supply elasticities apply to the four commodity categories: intermediate products I, −0.2 and 0.1; intermediate products II, −0.3 and 0.2; consumer goods, −1.0 and 0.8; and investment goods, −0.3 and 0.3.[51]

The next question concerns the ratio of domestic production and consumption to imports in the various countries. For several reasons, information on the proportion of imports to value added cannot be directly utilized for this purpose. To begin with, while the latter involves calculating the ratio of the value of trade to value added in manufacturing, the relevant comparison is between the value of trade and the value of industrial output – or apparent consumption – that also includes non-industrial inputs as well as imports used as inputs. Accordingly, the figures previously cited should be adjusted downward. At the same time, as I have elsewhere shown, the required adjustment will depend on the size of the country, because the proportion of imported inputs to the value of output (consumption) tends to decline as the size of the country increases.[52] Thus, while in the case of Belgium and the Netherlands the adjustment factor is 2.5, it is 2.1 for Italy, 1.8 for France and Germany, and approximately 1.6 for the United States.[53]

Allowance should further be made for product differentiation, transportation costs and inter-country differences in tastes. All these factors tend to reduce the amount of domestic output that is competing with imports, thereby necessitating an upward adjustment in the calculated shares of imports and a further narrowing in inter-country differences in these shares. This conclusion can be readily understood if we consider that in larger countries a wider assortment of domestic goods is available that are designed to serve particular needs, and transportation costs from the frontier to the place of consumption are also generally higher.

The latter factors are of special importance in the United States, and we have followed J. E. Floyd in assuming a ratio of consumption to imports of 4 in this country.[54] In turn, we have assigned a value of 2 to Sweden, under the assumption that the factors necessitating downward and upward adjustments with regard to the share of imports in value added approximately balance in this case. Finally, we have calculated with consumption–import ratios of 3 for the European Common Market and Japan and 2.5 for the United Kingdom. In all instances, we have taken consumption–import and production–import ratios to be identical, given the fact that the countries in question export *and* import the commodities included in our four commodity categories.[55]

Substituting the assumed values into equation (7),[56]

$$\frac{dM}{M} = \sum_k \left(\eta_k \frac{C'_k}{M_k} \bar{t}'_k + \varepsilon_k \frac{P'_k}{M'_k} \bar{z}'_k \right) \frac{M'_k}{M'} \tag{7}$$

we find that the elimination of duties on manufactured goods would lead to the largest relative increases in imports in Japan (39.9 percent), followed by the United States (38.2 percent), the United Kingdom (30.9 percent), the European Common Market (28.2 percent) and Sweden (14.0 percent). At the same time, we can indicate the influence of assumed differences in consumption–import ratios on the results by comparing the latter with estimates of uniform-tariff equivalents; under the assumption of identical consumption–import and production–import ratios for all countries, increases in imports would conform to inter-country differences with regard to $\bar{t}_o$. The estimated uniform-tariff equivalents are 26.4 for Japan, 23.8 for the United Kingdom, 17.3 for the Common Market, 16.7 for the United States and 12.2 for Sweden.

It appears, then, that the relatively small share of imports in domestic consumption (production) increases the restrictiveness of the American tariff to a considerable extent, while the opposite conclusion applies to Britain and Sweden. Should we also consider that domestic-supply elasticities may possibly be higher in the United States than elsewhere – or assume larger differences in consumption–import ratios – the US tariff may appear to be the most restrictive among the countries in question. Thus, if supply elasticities in the United States were one-half higher than in other industrial countries, American imports of manufactured products would rise by 54.1 percent following the elimination of duties. On the other hand, the increase in imports would be 67.8 percent if consumption–import and production–import ratios were assumed to be 5 rather than 4 in this country.

These conclusions provide some indication of the possibilities of increases in imports of manufactures in the countries under consideration following an all-around reduction of duties, and they can be useful in evaluating the possible consequences of the Kennedy Round of tariff negotiations on trade flows. With regard to the latter, however, consideration should also be given to export-supply elasticities, since the expansion of exports associated with tariff reductions will be attenuated if exported commodities are supplied at increasing costs.

Inter-country differences in export-supply elasticities are determined, to a considerable extent, by the share of exports in manufacturing production and the availability of excess capacity. Both these factors point to higher export-supply elasticities in the United States than elsewhere. Thus, the degree of capacity utilization is generally lower in the United States than abroad, and the proportion of industrial exports to value added in manufacturing is also the lowest in the United States.[57] Relatively high export-supply elasticities in the United States, as compared to the other main industrial countries, would, then, contribute to the expansion of US exports following an all-around reduction of tariffs.[58]

Finally, in attempting to use these results in appraising the possible consequences of the Kennedy Round, it would be necessary to take account of the fact that our conclusions pertain to relative changes in exports and imports rather than to absolute increments; the latter will also depend on the balance of trade of these countries and the share of manufactured goods in their exports and imports.[59] At the same time, notwithstanding the export orientation of the industrial countries, the expansion of exports does not provide a measure of welfare gains. The relative magnitudes of welfare gains will be determined by the reduction in the cost of protection and changes in the terms of trade, when the need for a realignment of exchange rates in case of an unbalanced expansion of trade further complicates the picture.

NOTES

1. Jacob Viner (1950) *The Customs Union Issue* (New York, Carnegie Endowment for International Peace), pp. 66–7.

2. The earliest efforts were: United Kingdom Board of Trade (1905) *Publications* (2nd ser., Cd. 2.337); League of Nations (1927) *Tariff Level Indices, 1927* (Geneva); and J. G. Crawford (1934) 'Tariff Level Indices', *Economic Record* (December), pp. 213–21.
3. Raymond Bertrand (1958) 'Comparaison du niveau des tarifs douaniers des pays du Marché Commun', *Cahiers de l'Institut de Science Économique Appliquée*, Series R, No. 2 (February); and H. C. Binswanger (1958) 'Der Zollschutz in den Ländern der Europäischen Wirtschaftsgemeinschaft und in der Schweiz', *Aussenwirtschaft* (March–June), pp. 119–46.
4. See, e.g., M. Mesnage (1963) 'Comparaison statistique du tarif douanier commun de la CEE, du tarif des Etats-Unis d'Amerique et du tarif du Royaume-Uni de Grande-Bretagne de l'Irlande du Nord', *Informations Statistiques* (Office Statistique des Communautés Européennes), No. 3, pp. 101–23, and Research and Policy Committee of the Committee for Economic Development (1964) 'The Height of United States and EEC Tariffs', *Trade Negotiations for a Better Free World Economy: A Statement on National Policy* (Washington).
5. While the terms-of-trade effects of tariffs occupy a central place in the theory of tariffs, these are largely disregarded in empirical investigations that have used a partial-equilibrium framework and have, explicitly or implicitly, assumed infinite export-supply elasticities. Cf., e.g., R. N. Cooper (1964) 'Tariff Dispersion and Trade Negotiations', *Journal of Political Economy* (December), pp. 597–606. See, however, M. E. Kreinen (1961) 'Effect of Tariff Changes on the Prices and Volume of Imports', *American Economic Review* (June), pp. 310–24.
6. The decline in imports following the imposition of duties will generally be associated with a fall in the consumption and an increase in the domestic production of the protected commodities; the latter is customarily referred to as the protective effect of the tariff.
7. Correspondingly, if exchange rates vary over time, an international comparison of national tariff levels will have little meaning. For a recent attempt, see E. Lerdau (1957) 'On the Measurement of Tariffs: The US over Forty Years', *Economia Internazionale*, pp. 232–47.
8. See, e.g., European Economic Community, Commission (1960) *Third General Report on the Activities of the Community* (Brussels); and Joint Economic Committee, US Congress (1961) *Trade Restrictions in the Western Community* (Washington).
9. See my *The Theory of Economic Integration* (Homewood, Ill., Richard D. Irwin, Inc., 1961), pp. 45–6; see also K. Bieda (1963) 'Trade Restrictions in the Western Community', *American Economic Review* (March), pp. 130–2.
10. Swedish Customs Tariff Commission (1957) *Revision of the Swedish Customs Tariff* (Stockholm), pp. 33–6.
11. Production (consumption) weights would be of use, however, in measuring the production (consumption) cost of protection.
12. See notes 2, 3, and 4.
13. A further difficulty with the commission's study is that in cases when a range rather than a single figure is indicated for a BTN heading in the US or United Kingdom tariff classification, the lower and upper limits have been taken separately, and the BTN heading in question has been assigned double weight. Since in these two countries duties are generally given in terms of a range for commodities that are protected by relatively high tariffs, the tariff averages calculated by the use of this method are subject to an upward bias.
14. *Trade Negotiations for a Better Free World Economy* (cited in note 4); see also R. N. Cooper, *op. cit.*
15. The difficulties associated with the international comparison of duties on

agricultural commodities are exemplified by a calculation made in the Committee for Economic Development study. According to the latter, using US imports as weights, the EEC tariff averages at 12.1 percent if sugar is included and 9.6 percent without sugar (*Trade Negotiations for a Better Free World Economy*, p. 72). And, whatever the weights, the tariff average of the Common Market will be affected by its high duty on sugar imports, while US sugar production is protected by quotas. Thus, using combined US-EEC imports as weights, the average of EEC tariffs is 8.6 excluding sugar and 10.2 including sugar.

16. Petroleum, petroleum products, lead and zinc, and steel flatware are subject to import quotas in the United States, while the United States as well as the Common Market relies on formal and informal agreements to limit imports of some manufactures from Japan, Hong Kong and India. Finally, subsidies are given to shipbuilding in most industrial countries.

17. Several writers have considered this problem in a national context in regard to Canada and Australia. The most important contributions are: Clarence L. Barber (1955) 'Canadian Tariff Policy', *Canadian Journal of Economics and Political Science* (November), pp. 513–30, and W. M. Corden (1963) 'The Tariff', in Alex Hunter (ed.), *The Economics of Australian Industry* (Melbourne, Melbourne University Press).

   More recently, the effects of protection in the presence of intermediate goods have attracted the attention of several economists. After the first version of this chapter had been completed, I had the occasion to see Harry G. Johnson's 'The Theory of Tariff Structure, with Special Reference to World Trade and Development', *Trade and Development* ('Études et Travaux de l'Institut Universitaire de Hautes Études Internationales' [Geneva: Librairie Droz, 1965]); and G. Basevi (1966) 'The US Tariff Structure: Estimates of Effective Rates of Protection of US Industries and Industrial Labor', *Review of Economics and Statistics* (May), pp. 147–60. Also, W. M. Corden is engaged in research on the theoretical aspects of tariff structures.

18. At the same time, there is no need to take account of tariffs paid at earlier stages of production, since material inputs are available to the domestic producer at the world-market price, inclusive of transportation costs, plus the duty.

19. Similar calculations should be made for estimating the effective duty on the exports of manufactures from less-developed areas. I have noted elsewhere that, from the point of view of the entrepreneur's decision to transform a raw material into semi-finished or finished products for exportation to developed countries, the tariff burden on value added in the production process rather than the nominal rate of duty is relevant (*Trade Prospects for Developing Countries* [Homewood, Ill., Richard D. Irwin, Inc., 1964], p. 116). See also Harry G. Johnson (1964) 'Tariffs and Economic Development: Some Theoretical Issues', *Journal of Development Studies*, October.

20. Nominal tariffs, however, will continue to have relevance for the consumer's choice between domestic goods and imports. The effects of nominal duties on the domestic consumption of protected commodities will be considered in Section VI below.

21. Office Statistique des Communautés Européennes (1964) *Tableaux 'Entrées–Sorties' pour les pays de la Communauté Européenne Économique*, October.

22. The input–output tables of the other three countries have served as a basis, however, with regard to automobiles, aircraft and precision instruments that are not produced in substantial quantities in Belgium and the Netherlands.

23. The reader will note that the coefficients derived from input–output tables are expressed in value rather than in quantity terms and hence indicate relative shares.

24. Cf., e.g., Kenneth Arrow, H. B. Chenery, B. Minhas, and R. M. Solow (1960) 'Capital-Labor Substitution and Economic Efficiency', *Review of Economics and Statistics* (August), pp. 225–50.
25. Committee for Economic Development (1964) *Comparative Tariffs and Trade* (Washington). US tariffs have further been adjusted to express them on a cif basis.
26. The BTN headings by and large correspond to the four- and five-digit items of the SITC. Whenever necessary, averages have been calculated by using import values for individual countries as weights. This solution has been chosen by reason of the incomparability of the national classifications and the small number of observations within each four-digit item.
27. The correspondence has been established by the use of the *Classification Statistique et Tarifaire* (Luxembourg, Office Statistique des Communautés Européennes, April, 1963).
28. In view of our previous discussion, this solution appears to be superior to weighting with own imports, or using unweighted tariff averages, while data on world trade are not available in the appropriate breakdown. At the same time, it has been judged permissible to average nominal rates of duties pertaining to individual commodities, since the commodity categories of the industrial classification employed generally include goods on the same level of fabrication.
29. The share of wages plus employer-financed social security payments in the value of output, derived from the input–output tables cited above.
30. See my *Trade Prospects for Developing Countries*, p. 116; and United Nations (1963) *World Economic Survey, 1962, Part I* (New York), p. 79.
31. As noted below, however, the case of ships is hardly more than a *curiosum*, since most industrial countries subsidize their shipbuilding industries in one form or another.
32. Product differentiation is implicitly assumed, however, when calculating substitution elasticities between commodities sold on the world market. Cf., e.g., G. D. A. MacDougall (1951; 1952) 'British and American Exports: A Study Suggested by the Theory of Comparative Costs', *Economic Journal* (December; September), pp. 697–726 and pp. 487–521, respectively.
33. Still, as we have noted above, duties on non-ferrous metals provide a disincentive to the transformation of ores into metals in the less-developed countries. In turn, considerations of fuel economy may limit trade in the case of pig iron.
34. Cf., e.g., Beatrice N. Vaccara (1960) *Employment and Output in Protected Industries* (Washington, Brookings Institution); and William P. Travis (1964) *The Theory of Trade and Protection* (Cambridge, Mass., Harvard University Press), pp. 191–3.
35. For the United States, similar conclusions have been reached by Basevi, who compared various measures of labor intensiveness, on the one hand, and effective duties on value added and on labor costs, on the other (*op. cit.*).
36. To achieve international comparability, we have estimated the rates of duties with respect to import values in cases where the American selling price is used as a basis for the determination of tariffs. The commodities in question include coaltar-based chemical materials and products and rubber footwear.
37. I am indebted to Harry G. Johnson for improvements in the mathematical formulation of the argument.
38. Under the assumption of constant input–output coefficients, ε_i is also the elasticity of domestic supply.
39. Tariff averages have been calculated by using the combined imports of the countries in question as weights. For reasons mentioned above, the combined imports of these countries have been taken as a 'proxy' for the structure of their potential imports.
40. The existence of a positive correlation between tariff dispersion and the

restrictiveness of duties has been claimed by R. Bertrand and M. Mesnage (for reference see notes 3 and 4), while their argument has been criticized by R. N. Cooper, *op. cit.* Note, however, that Cooper considers nominal tariffs only.

41. However, if equation (2) is transformed so as to indicate the expansion of imports following the elimination of duties, changes in import prices will be denoted by $t_i/1+t_i$ rather than $t_i/1$, and, under *ceteris paribus* assumptions, the country with the greater dispersion of tariffs will experience a smaller increase in imports (for proof, see Harry G. Johnson (1965) *The World Economy at the Crossroads* [Oxford, Clarendon Press]). This result follows from the properties of the harmonic mean but, under present day conditions, its practical significance is negligible. Thus, in the example cited above, the elimination of tariffs would lead to an increase of imports by 39.7 percent in the former case, and 39.1 percent in the latter if imports of refrigerators and washing machinery were of equal value and had an import demand elasticity of -3.0.

42. Organization for Economic Cooperation and Development (1964) *Statistics of National Accounts, 1955–1962* (suppl.; Paris); and United Nations (1964) *Commodity Trade Statistics, 1962* (New York).

43. This concept is due to W. M. Corden; its application has been suggested to me by Professor Johnson. For simplicity's sake, I have assumed that no inputs are exported.

44. We have assumed that the values of the domestic demand and supply elasticities are not affected by the move from C to C' and from P to P'.

45. Hosiery, clothing, other textile articles, shoes, other leather goods, cleansing agents and perfumes, automobiles, bicycles and motorcycles, precision instruments, toys, sport goods and jewelry.

46. Agricultural machinery, electrical and non-electrical machinery, railway vehicles and airplanes.

47. Thread and yarn, wood products, paper and paper products, leather, synthetics, other chemical materials, non-metallic mineral products, glass, pig iron and non-ferrous metals.

48. Textile fabrics, rubber goods, plastic articles, miscellaneous chemical products, ingots and other primary forms of steel, rolling-mill products, other steel products, metal castings, metal manufactures.

49. We have not included printed matter and ships in any of these categories; the former has been omitted because of the special character of its trade, the latter because of the prevalence of subsidies.

50. To ensure comparability with the preceding tables, the averages of t_i rather than $t_i/1+t_i$ have been calculated.

51. By comparison, Robert M. Stern assumed demand and supply elasticities of -0.25 and zero for crude materials, -0.4 and 0.2 for semi-manufactures, -0.5 and 0.25 for non-durable finished manufactures, and -1.0 and 0.5 for durable finished manufactures ('The U.S. Tariff and the Efficiency of the US Economy', *American Economic Review*, Papers and Proceedings [May, 1964], pp. 459–79), while J. E. Floyd calculated with a demand elasticity of -0.3 and a supply elasticity of 0.5 for all commodities, taken together ('The Overvaluation of the Dollar: A Note on the International Price Mechanism', *American Economic Review* [March, 1965]). In contrast with these authors, we have assumed that the relationship between demand and supply elasticities differs as between commodity categories.

52. For the Common Market countries I have calculated the proportion of industrial imports to value added in manufacturing and to apparent consumption from the input–output tables. The relevant magnitudes are 90.2 and 36.4 for Belgium, 35.6 and 19.9 for France, 48.1 and 27.4 for Germany, 31.2 and 14.5 for Italy, and 82.9 and 34.3 for the Netherlands ('Planning in an Open Economy', 1984).

53. US Bureau of the Census (1965) *US Commodity Exports and Imports as Related to Output* (Washington), and note 52.
54. The same ratio has been applied to every commodity category.
55. The relationship utilized by Floyd, $P/M = C/M - 1$, would apply only if we dealt with standardized commodities.
56. Subscript k refers to the individual commodity categories.
57. The relevant figures are 9.0 percent for the United States, 20.0 percent for the European Common Market, 33.3 percent for Japan, 36.3 percent for the United Kingdom, and 45.1 percent for Sweden.
58. These essentially short-run considerations assume relevance in the long run if wage and price adjustments are not fully reversible.
59. In turn, an improvement (deterioration) in the trade balance will be mitigated through an increase (decline) in imports of material inputs.

11 · INDUSTRIAL PROTECTION IN THE DEVELOPED COUNTRIES

Much has been said in recent years about growing industrial protectionism in the developed countries, but little effort has been made to assess quantitatively the increases in protection that have actually occurred. This chapter will provide estimates for the major developed countries (the United States, the European Community and Japan) on changes in their tariffs and non-tariff measures affecting manufactured imports in general and imports from the developing countries in particular. The protection of agricultural products, however, will not be considered.[1]

TARIFF REDUCTIONS IN THE TOKYO ROUND NEGOTIATIONS

In the framework of the Kennedy Round of multilateral trade negotiations, conducted under the auspices of the General Agreement on Tariffs and Trade (GATT) in 1964–7, tariff rates were lowered by 50 percent across the board, with exceptions made for so-called sensitive items – such as steel, textiles, clothing and footwear. As a result of these changes, average tariffs on the total imports of manufactured products declined by 41 percent in the United States, 40 percent in the European Community and 42 percent in Japan. Since reductions were smaller on several products of export interest to the developing countries, the average tariff on manufactured products imported from these countries decreased to a lesser extent, by 31 percent in the United States, 36 percent in the Community and 35 percent in Japan.[2]

Following these reductions, average tariffs on manufactured products, weighted by total imports, were 7.0 percent in the United States, 8.3 percent in the European Community and 10.0 percent in Japan.[3] Tariff averages, however, were generally higher on industrial products imported from the

Written with Carol Balassa. First published in *The World Economy*, June 1984.

developing countries, on which smaller reductions were agreed in the Kennedy Round negotiations as well as in the course of the earlier tariff negotiations (Table 11.1).

In the Tokyo Round negotiations of 1973–9, the United States proposed an across the board tariff cut of 60 percent, whereas the European Community put forward a 'harmonization' formula aimed at reducing high tariffs to a greater extent than low tariffs. The position taken by the Community reflected the desire for an evening-out of the tariff structure in the United States which earlier occurred in the Community where the common external tariff was set as the average of tariffs in the individual member countries.

In the event, a compromise Swiss formula was adopted, involving tariff reductions calculated as the ratio of the pre-Tokyo Round tariff to itself plus 14 percent. Under the formula, a 20 percent duty was to be reduced by 59 percent; a 10 percent duty, by 42 percent; and a 5 percent duty, by 26 percent. But exceptions were again made for sensitive items such as textiles, clothing and footwear.

The tariff reductions which were agreed in the Tokyo Round negotiations will be fully implemented in the second half of the 1980s, although advance reductions have been made by the European Community and Japan. Once the reductions are completed, tariff averages weighted by the total imports of manufactured products will decline by 30 percent in the United States, 28 percent in the Community and 46 percent in Japan (see Table 11.1). In the case of Japan, additional tariff reductions on machinery and transport equipment will have contributed to the results, but the extent of the decrease in tariffs is considerably smaller if comparisons are made with the duties actually applied rather than with legal tariffs.[4]

As in the Kennedy Round negotiations, tariff reductions have been smaller than the average on imports from the developing countries, which supply a high proportion of sensitive items. Reductions in most-favored-nation (MFN) tariffs weighted by the imports of manufactured products from developing countries will be 24 percent in the case of the United States, 25 percent in the European Community and 32 percent in Japan.[5]

Following these reductions, tariffs on manufactured products, weighted by total imports, will average 4.9 percent in the United States, 6.0 percent in the European Community and 5.4 percent in Japan.[6] The corresponding averages, weighted by imports from the developing countries, will be higher: 8.7 percent in the United States, 6.7 percent in the Community and 6.8 percent in Japan.

Jeffrey Nugent, of the University of Southern California, has shown that for a given tariff average the protective effect of tariffs is the higher, the greater is their dispersion.[7] The dispersion of tariffs will be reduced to a considerable extent once the Tokyo Round agreement has been fully implemented, especially in Japan, but in the latter case the change will again be much smaller if comparisons are made with the tariffs actually applied before the

Table 11.1 Tariff averages before and after the implementation of the Tokyo Round agreement and percentage changes in tariffs in the major developed countries

| | Tariffs on total imports | | | | | | | | | | | | Tariffs on imports from developing countries | | |
| | Raw materials | | | Semi-manufactures | | | Finished manufactures | | | Semi- and finished manufactures | | | Semi- and finished manufactures | | |
	Pre-	Post-	% change	Pre-	Post-	% change	Pre-	Post-	% change	Pre-	Post-	% change	Pre-	Post-	% change
United States															
Weighted	0.9	0.2	77	4.5	3.0	33	8.0	5.7	29	7.0	4.9	30	11.4	8.7	24
Simple	3.3	1.8	45	10.0	6.1	39	13.0	7.0	46	11.6	6.6	43	12.0	6.7	44
European Community															
Weighted	0.2	0.2	15	5.8	4.2	27	9.7	6.9	29	8.3	6.0	28	8.9	6.7	25
Simple	1.9	1.6	16	8.9	6.2	30	9.9	7.0	29	9.4	6.6	30	8.5	5.8	32
Japan															
Weighted	1.5	0.5	67	6.6	4.6	30	12.5	6.0	52	10.0	5.4	46	10.0	6.8	32
Simple	2.5	1.4	45	9.8	6.3	36	11.6	6.4	45	10.8	6.4	41	11.0	6.7	39

Source: The Tokyo Round of Multilateral Trade Negotiations, Supplementary Report by the Director-General of the GATT (Geneva, GATT Secretariat, 1980) pp. 33–7.

Tokyo Round negotiations (Table 11.2). The dispersion of post-Tokyo Round tariffs remains the most pronounced in the United States, thereby increasing the protective effect of the American tariff compared with that of the other major developed countries.

As is well known, averaging tariffs by import value introduces a downward bias in the calculations, for high tariffs are given a small weight and low tariffs are given a large weight. An alternative is to calculate a simple average of tariffs. These averages show larger tariff reductions for the United States and the European Community, and smaller reductions for Japan, than the weighted averages. At the same time, the unweighted averages are uniformly higher than the weighted averages (Table 11.1). While the unweighted averages do not involve a downward bias, they are subject to the shortcoming of giving equal weight to all tariff items (irrespective of their relative importance), when the number of items varies to a considerable extent among product categories, with textiles and clothing accounting for nearly one-third of the total. Also, comparisons of unweighted tariff averages for total imports and for imports from the developing countries, as published by the GATT Secretariat, have little economic meaning.[8]

Irrespective of the averaging procedure employed, it is apparent that tariffs have a tendency to escalate from lower to higher degrees of fabrication, thereby raising the effective rate of protection (protection of value added). In the major developed countries, post-Tokyo Round weighted averages of tariff rates are 0.5 percent or less on raw materials, 3–5 percent for semi-manufactures and 5–7 percent for finished manufactures (Table 11.1). Tariff escalation does not continue, however, to machinery and transport equipment. Tariffs on these products, exported chiefly by developed countries, are lower than tariff averages for all finished manufactures and, to an even greater extent, tariffs on products of interest to the developing countries, such as clothing, footwear and travel goods.

Thus, as shown in Table 11.3, there is a considerable degree of tariff escalation for individual product categories. And while quantitative limitations in the framework of the Multi-Fiber Arrangement (MFA) represent the binding constraint in the case of textiles and clothing, tariff escalation tends to discriminate against finished goods within this category. More generally, the escalation of tariffs discriminates against the imports of processed goods from the developing countries.

At the same time the finished manufactures of interest to the developing countries are subject to higher tariffs than other finished products. And although these countries receive preferential treatment under the Generalized System of Preferences (GSP), the imports of textiles, clothing and shoes are not covered by the system and products which came to be imported in larger quantities are also excluded.[9] The developing countries, however, have benefited from MFN-type tariff reductions that have been unilaterally extended to them.

Table 11.2 Percentage distribution of tariffs for industrial products, including raw materials, in the major developed countries before and after the implementation of the Tokyo Round agreement

Tariff	Pre-Tokyo Round				Post-Tokyo Round		
			Japan				
	United States	European Community	Legal	Applied	United States	European Community	Japan
Free	26.1	35.4	53.1	59.4	31.0	37.9	56.3
0.1–5	32.2	7.4	8.4	7.8	44.1	19.0	25.2
5.1–10	26.7	31.2	22.1	23.5	17.8	32.5	14.6
10.1–15	6.1	17.2	9.0	7.1	1.9	9.1	2.9
15.1–20	3.5	8.6	5.1	1.6	2.2	1.3	0.8
20.1–25	1.9	0.2	1.5	0.5	0.8	0.2	0.1
25.1–30	0.8	—	0.7	0.1	1.2	—	0.1
30.1–35	1.2	—	—	—	0.9	—	—
35.1–40	1.1	—	0.1	—	0.0	—	—
40.1–45	0.4	—	—	—	0.1	—	—
45.1–50	0.0	—	—	—	—	—	—
Over 50	—	—	—	—	—	—	—
Total	100.0	100.0	100.0	100.0	100.0	100.0	100.0

Source: 'Reports on Results of MTN', Office of the United States Trade Representative, Executive Office of the President, Washington, mimeograph, June 1979.

All in all, following the implementation of the Tokyo Round agreement, tariffs on manufactured goods will be lowered to a considerable extent, thereby extending the tariff reductions that had begun on an item-by-item basis in the period following the Second World War and continued with across the board reductions (with some exceptions) following the Dillon Round negotiations (1960–61) and the Kennedy Round negotiations. In fact, while tariff reductions in the post-war period were originally aimed at reversing increases in protection during the depression of the 1930s, tariffs fell below these levels at the end of the 1950s and declined to a considerable extent afterwards.[10]

But from the mid-1960s the United States and the European Community imposed quantitative limits on imports of textiles and clothing, first from Japan and subsequently from the developing countries. Furthermore, non-tariff measures were applied to the imports of certain manufactured goods from Japan in the second half of the 1960s and such restrictions came into greater use after 1973.

In the next section non-tariff restrictions on manufactured products which were in effect at the end of 1980 and the barriers imposed (or removed) in 1981, 1982 and 1983 will be briefly described. In addition, alternative ratios will be used to indicate the scope of these restrictions in the United States, the European Community and Japan. Then, in the final section, an attempt will

Table 11.3 Sectoral tariff averages for the development countries combined, before and after the implementation of the Tokyo Round agreement

	Import-weighted averages			Simple averages		
	Before	After	% change	Before	After	% change
Textiles and clothing						
Raw materials	1.1	0.8	25	3.7	2.9	21
Semi-manufactures	14.7	11.5	22	13.7	9.6	30
Finished manufactures	20.6	16.7	19	17.6	11.8	33
Leather, footwear, rubber and travel goods						
Raw materials	0.2	0.0	80	2.0	1.0	50
Semi-manufactures	6.8	4.4	35	6.9	4.5	35
Finished manufactures	11.5	10.2	11	14.4	10.2	29
Wood, pulp, paper and furniture						
Raw materials	0.4	0.2	54	1.3	0.7	46
Semi-manufactures	3.1	1.9	38	6.3	3.7	41
Finished manufactures	7.1	4.2	41	8.6	5.1	41
Base metals						
Raw materials	0.3	0.0	82	0.5	0.2	61
Semi-manufactures	4.3	3.2	26	7.0	4.6	34
Finished manufactures	9.4	5.9	37	10.2	6.1	40
Chemicals						
Semi-manufactures	7.8	5.0	36	10.2	6.2	39
Finished manufactures	10.5	6.0	43	11.1	6.2	44
Non-electrical machinery						
Finished manufactures	7.7	4.1	47	8.1	4.4	46
Electrical machinery						
Finished manufactures	9.2	6.1	34	13.2	5.0	42
Transport equipment						
Finished manufactures	7.8	5.0	36	10.0	6.5	35

Source: *The Tokyo Round of Multilateral Trade Negotiations*, Supplementary Report by the Director-General of the GATT (Geneva, GATT Secretariat, 1980) pp. 33–7.

be made to evaluate the restrictive effects of non-tariff measures in these countries.

NON-TARIFF MEASURES AFFECTING TRADE

The non-tariff measures considered here include global and bilateral import quotas, import licensing, orderly marketing arrangements (OMAs), 'voluntary' export-restraint agreements (VERs), safeguard measures and the restrictive application of standards. The discussion will not cover production and export subsidies or anti-dumping and countervailing measures. The trade implications of subsidies are difficult to gauge, while anti-dumping and countervailing actions have been assumed to offset distortions introduced by exporters.

Non-tariff restrictions may pertain to all imports or to imports from particular sources. The United States and the European Community limit the imports of textiles and clothing originating in developing countries in the framework of the MFA; in several other cases, restrictions are targeted against particular suppliers.

Apart from the MFA, non-tariff restrictions in effect at the end of 1980 in the United States included an OMA with South Korea and Taiwan on imports of non-rubber footwear, safeguard measures limiting the imports of color television sets from these two countries and safeguard measures on citizen band radios, porcelain-on-steel cookware, high carbon ferro-chromium, industrial fasteners (nuts, bolts and screws) and spin dryers applying to all sources of supply.[11]

In the European Community, non-tariff barriers employed at Community level in 1980 included those under the MFA as well as OMAs on jute products and iron and steel applying to major suppliers. There were also a number of non-tariff measures imposed by Community countries, usually pertaining to suppliers that made inroads in the domestic markets of the individual countries. Restrictions were imposed by France, Italy and the United Kingdom on imports of passenger automobiles from Japan as well as on imports of radios, televisions and communication equipment from Japan, South Korea and Taiwan, by the Federal Republic of Germany and the United Kingdom on imports of flatware from Japan and by France and Italy on imports of various consumer goods, mainly from South Korea and Taiwan.

Japan in turn made use of discretionary licensing to limit her imports of leather footwear, telecommunication equipment and pharmaceuticals and applied standards to protective effect on automobiles. Japan also employs informal restrictions on imports, but for reasons noted below these are not considered in the chapter.

The United States negotiated in 1981 a VER with Japan limiting her exports of passenger automobiles. In the following year, VERs were negotiated on carbon steel products with the European Community and, in 1983, the United States implemented safeguard measures in the form of tariff increases on motorcycles and tariff increases as well as a quota on specialty steels. But restrictions on imports of non-rubber footwear from South Korea and Taiwan were eliminated in 1981 and restrictions on imports of color television sets from the same countries were lifted in 1982.

In 1981, the European Community extended import restrictions on steel to South Korea; Belgium and West Germany introduced limits on the imports of automobiles from Japan; and the United Kingdom imposed import restrictions on video-tape recorders from Japan. In the following year, France introduced restrictions on motorcycles and video-tape recorders from Japan. Finally, in March 1983, the Community reached an agreement with Japan on export restraints for video-tape recorders and large color television tubes as well as on the 'surveillance' of imports of hi-fi equipment, quartz watches, forklift trucks, light vans and motorcycles. In the same year France and Britain imposed restrictions on imports of tableware from South Korea.

In renegotiating the MFA in 1981, the United States and the European Community limited the possibilities of transferring quotas from one category to another as well as from one year to the next. Additional limitations were imposed on the growth of imports of particular items in the United States in December 1983.

Japan did not introduce new restrictive measures between 1980 and 1983 and liberalized her administrative system on imports. At the same time, it is difficult to evaluate the 'informal' barriers to imports that remain in effect in Japan.

In this connection, it should be emphasized that the non-tariff measures considered here are of the 'visible' kind; for lack of information, no attempt has been made to identify administrative measures that may impinge on imports. Such measures are of particular importance in Japan, followed by France, while the United States relies on visible forms of import restraint. Since the following calculations refer only to visible measures, a bias is introduced in the comparisons.

The GATT Secretariat has used the ratio of restricted imports to total imports (the 'import ratio') to indicate the extent of the application of restrictive measures. The same ratio has been employed for this purpose by William Cline, of the Institute for International Economics in Washington,[12] and, in the framework of a programming model, by Alan Deardorff and Robert Stern, of the University of Michigan.[13] In all these cases, the import ratio has been calculated as an *ex post* measure; that is, the import figures used in the calculations already reflect the restrictive effects of non-tariff measures which have been introduced over the years.

At the same time, the extent to which imports are affected by non-tariff measures varies from country to country. A country whose restrictive actions are more stringent will import less of the restricted commodities than a country whose actions are more liberal. Such is the situation, for instance, with regard to automobiles. France limits imports from Japan to 3 percent of domestic sales while Japanese exports of automobiles are limited to about 25 percent of sales in the American market. A more liberal policy towards automobile imports, then, involves a higher ratio of restricted imports to total imports in the United States than in France.

The import ratio has been calculated for the non-tariff measures in effect at the end of 1980, as well as for the measures introduced in the years 1981, 1982 and 1983 (Table 11.4). In all cases, the estimates refer to the 1980 dollar values of imports, exclusive of trade among the member countries of the European Community. The above objections thus apply to the 1980 estimates reported here, but not to the estimates for subsequent years. The latter provide an *ex ante* measure of import restrictions, since the restrictions introduced subsequently could not have influenced trade flows in 1980.

Table 11.4 Measures of import restrictions for manufactured goods in developed countries

	United States	European Community	Japan
Import ratio[a]			
1980	6.20	10.80	7.20
1981	5.53	1.38	—
1982	0.69	0.18	—
1983	0.30	2.50	—
1981–3	6.52	4.08	—
Import consumption ratio[b]			
1980	0.56	1.30	0.33
1981	0.49	0.16	—
1982	0.06	0.02	—
1983	0.03	0.25	—
1981–3	0.58	0.43	—
Consumption ratio[c]			
1980	20.3	23.7	15.7
1981	12.4	2.3	—
1982	2.1	0.3	—
1983	0.2	2.1	—
1981–3	14.7	4.7	—

Source: Data files of the Office of the United States Trade Representative, Executive Office of the President, Washington, and of the World Bank.
[a] Restricted imports as a share of total manufactured imports.
[b] Restricted imports as a share of total consumption of manufactured goods.
[c] Consumption of restricted manufactured goods as a share of total consumption of manufactured goods.

But both the *ex ante* and the *ex post* measures are affected by the availability of natural resources. Thus, in a country poor in natural resources, such as Japan, simple intermediate products (paper, chemicals, etc.) that are rarely subject to non-tariff measures will account for a large share of imports, thereby reducing the share of restricted imports.

To escape this shortcoming, the ratio of the imports of restricted items to the total consumption of manufactured products (the 'import consumption ratio') has also been calculated. It should be recognized, however, that in its *ex post* form this ratio is subject to the same objections as the commonly used import ratio.

A third measure relates the consumption of restricted items to the total consumption of manufactured products (the 'consumption ratio').[14] This measure is not subject to the bias introduced in the *ex post* case and it is not influenced by inter-country differences in the availability of natural resources. Nevertheless, consumption may have been affected by the imposition of import restrictions. Also, the use of the consumption ratio does not permit the separation of restricted from unrestricted imports within a particular commodity group and, in making calculations, the entire group has been included in the restricted category whenever some of the products are subject to non-tariff restrictions.

The latter considerations explain why in 1980 the ratio of the consumption of restricted products to the total consumption of manufactured goods was relatively high, between 15 and 25 percent, in the major developed countries. The European Community's ratio was at the upper end of the scale, followed by the United States and Japan. The United States improves its position if the other two ratios are considered; its import ratio was in fact lower than that of Japan in 1980. By comparison, Dr Cline found both the ratios which he calculated to be higher in the United States than in the Community countries, with Japan at the end of the line. There are several major differences in the procedures applied which appear to account for the differences in the results.

First, Dr Cline includes processed food in his calculations without, however, allowing for the effects of the European Community's common agricultural policy. This has led to an overestimation of the share of restricted imports in the United States, where Dr Cline lists meat, dairy products, sugar and confectionery among restricted items, while in the Community he includes only meat and canned fish in France and canned fish in Italy.

The inclusion of processed food also raises the share of restricted imports in Japan where the items in question comprise meat, dairy products, canned fruit and vegetables, canned fish and cereals. Dr Cline, however, does not include in his calculations Japanese restrictions on automobiles, telecommunication equipment and pharmaceuticals, thereby lowering the reported Japanese share.

A further difference in the estimates pertains to the treatment of restricted imports. While in the present chapter only imports from countries subject to restrictions have been included in calculating the import ratio, Dr Cline's figures comprise imports from all sources, even if only some of the suppliers are subject to restrictions.

Finally, Dr Cline's calculations include restrictions on imports of color televisions from Japan and footwear from South Korea and Taiwan that were abolished in 1980 and 1981, respectively, as well as American restrictions on automobile imports from Japan that were introduced in 1981. At the same time, Dr Cline has considered the trigger-price mechanism on steel used in lieu of anti-dumping action as a restriction, while in the present chapter steel is included for 1982 when the arrangement with the European Community came into effect.

As shown in Table 11.4, restrictions on automobiles imported from Japan entailed substantial increases in all three ratios in the United States between 1980 and 1983. Increases were smaller in the European Community, although a number of restrictions were introduced on imports from Japan in 1983. Finally, Japan did not add new restrictions in the period 1981–3.

A different picture emerges if restrictions applied to imports from developing countries are considered. Putting aside the stricter implementation of the MFA, the United States actually liberalized imports from these countries between 1980 and 1983 by lifting restrictions on footwear and on color televisions imported from South Korea and Taiwan. There were few instances where member countries of the European Community introduced import restrictions on products originating in developing countries and no such case has been reported in Japan. It appears, then, that the protectionist measures applied by the major developed countries after 1980 were chiefly oriented against each others' exports, with imports from developing countries largely escaping the effects of the new measures.

RESTRICTIVE EFFECTS OF TRADE BARRIERS

In the previous section, alternative ratios were employed to gauge the scope of non-tariff restrictions in the major developed countries. It should be emphasized that none of the three ratios can be used to assess the restrictive effects of such measures. While they show the proportion of imports or consumption subject to non-tariff barriers, they do not provide an indication of the extent to which imports have been reduced as a result of their imposition. Moreover, none of the three ratios indicates changes in the restrictiveness of import barriers over time which has occurred, for example, in the application of the MFA.

Two attempts have recently been made to measure the effects of quantitative restrictions in the United States, leading to very different conclusions. According to a study by Peter Morici and Laura Megna, for the National Planning Association in Washington, these restrictions provided average protection to manufacturing industries in the United States equivalent to a 0.57 percent tariff in 1982.[15] Under the assumptions made by the authors concerning import demand elasticities, the cost of protection can be estimated at $5 billion.[16] In an article in the January–February 1984 number of *Challenge*, Michael Munger, of Washington University in Missouri, estimates the cost of quantitative import restrictions to American consumers to be $11.5 billion in 1980.[17] The reasons for these differences can be found in the methodologies of the two studies, both of which are open to criticism.

The Morici–Megna study underestimates the effects of the two most important restrictions imposed on manufactured goods in the United States, namely the MFA and the limits on Japanese exports of automobiles. As to the first, 'it is assumed that if the MFA were removed, foreign suppliers would only be able to recapture three years of lost import growth in any single typical year.'[18] But the losses have been calculated by taking 1973 as the base year, disregarding the fact that the imports of cotton textiles had been restricted for some years beforehand. Furthermore, the protective effects of quantitative restrictions should be calculated by relating actual imports to imports without restrictions in long-term equilibrium rather than to imports that may be attained one year after the removal of the restrictions. Moreover, the protective effects of limitations on automobile imports from Japan cannot be estimated by reference to 'the depressed state of the automobile market during the first year of the agreement.'[19]

The estimates reported by Dr Munger include coffee, meat and sugar, accounting for one-third of the total,[20] while they exclude automobiles that became subject to restrictions in 1981. At the same time, Dr Munger equates the cost to consumers to the cost of protectionism, although one has to deduct increases in producer surplus and in government revenues in estimating the latter.[21] In fact, considering that imports accounted for only about one-tenth of the consumption of manufactured goods, estimated at $1.4 trillion in 1980, the cost of protection will be a small fraction of the cost to consumers estimated by Dr Munger. To improve on these estimates, information would be needed on the tariff equivalents of quantitative restrictions and on the underlying domestic demand and supply elasticities. Reliable data are not available for the United States and even less are available for the European Community and Japan. Accordingly, in the present chapter the restrictive effects of imports have been indicated in an indirect way.[22]

Two measures will be used to gauge the impact of non-tariff restrictions on imports. The 'import penetration ratio', defined as the percentage share of imports in domestic consumption, will be employed to indicate the restrictive effects of non-tariff measures at a particular time. In turn, for lack of production figures on a disaggregated basis, changes in the ratio of imports to gross domestic product (GDP) will be used to show changes in the restrictiveness of these barriers over time.

The two sets of ratios have been calculated for the total imports from the developing countries of (i) iron and steel, (ii) passenger automobiles and (iii) telecommunication equipment, as well as for imports of (iv) textiles, (v) clothing and (vi) other consumer goods, including footwear, travel goods, sports goods and toys. The results are shown in Table 11.5. In the case of the European Community, the data refer to the four largest countries, namely France, West Germany, Italy and the United Kingdom, which account for 85 percent of the GDP of the Community countries.

A high (low) import penetration ratio has been interpreted to indicate the ease (restrictiveness) of non-tariff measures. It has further been assumed that changes in the ratio of imports to GDP for products subject to non-tariff barriers will provide an indication of changes in the restrictiveness of the measures applied over time.

The obvious drawback of these ratios is that they cannot distinguish between the impacts of restrictive measures and the effects of other factors which may bear on the importation of a particular product or product group. Thus, the import penetration ratio for a particular commodity group will also reflect the country's comparative advantage and the extent of the over-valuation or under-valuation of its currency in a particular year, while changes in the real rate of exchange (the nominal rate, adjusted for changes in relative prices) will affect changes in the ratio of imports to GDP over time.

Table 11.5 Import penetration ratios for 1978 and increase in the ratio of imports to GDP in 1978–81

	United States		European Community		Japan	
	Import penetration ratio, 1978	% change in import–GDP ratio 1978–81	Import penetration ratio, 1978	% change in import–GDP ratio 1978–81	Import penetration ratio, 1978	% change in import–GDP ratio 1978–81
Total imports						
Iron and steel	8.7	25	6.0	−16	0.9	94
Passenger vehicles	8.8	19	7.4	23	1.1	−33
Telecommunication equipment	14.7	31	13.6	32	3.5	23
Imports from developing countries						
Textiles	1.6	13	3.7	−10	2.3	−32
Clothing	11.3	17	11.4	23	7.4	−4
Other consumer products	3.7	40	1.6	36	1.1	3

Sources: International Trade 1981–82 (Geneva, GATT Secretariat, 1982); *Yearbook of Industrial Statistics*, United Nations, New York, various issues; and *Monthly Bulletin of Statistics*, United Nations, New York, various issues.

The first-mentioned factor is of relevance for Japanese imports of passenger automobiles from other developed countries, for Japan is said to possess a comparative advantage with regard to automobiles that will reduce the amount imported, even though imports would be higher in the absence of the discriminatory application of standards. (Note, further, that Japan does not restrict the importation of steel which is included for completeness in Table 11.5.)

Such considerations will not, however, affect imports by the United States and the European Community of the commodities in question. Also, all developed countries are at a comparative disadvantage *vis-à-vis* developing countries as far as textiles, clothing and other consumer goods are concerned, so that import penetration ratios for these product groups can appropriately indicate the restrictiveness of the measures applied against imports from the developing countries.[23]

The American dollar appreciated in real terms *vis-à-vis* other major currencies between 1978 and 1981. The extent of the appreciation, however, was small and the changes took place towards the end of the period, so that trade flows might not have been much affected until 1982. A much larger appreciation occurred in the years 1982 and 1983 which have been excluded from the analysis.

At the same time, it should be emphasized that considerations of comparative advantage and currency over-valuation (or under-valuation) will not be relevant in cases when import restrictions are binding. This is because the binding restrictions limit the amount imported in absolute terms and thus determine the import penetration ratio. Such will generally be the case whenever import quotas, OMAs or VERs are utilized. In turn, import licensing may or may not be binding, depending on the circumstances of the case.[24]

These considerations indicate the usefulness of the import penetration ratio in indicating the restrictiveness of non-tariff barriers, the exception being Japanese imports of automobiles. It should be added that this ratio has the advantage of capturing the effects of not only visible but also invisible barriers to imports. At the same time, import penetration ratios are usefully complemented by data on increases in the ratio of imports to GDP.

The data in Table 11.5 exclude both trade among the countries of the European Community and trade between the United States and Canada which are regarded as internal trade. This adjustment gives rise to a downward bias in the figures for the United States since only about one-third of American trade in manufactured goods with Canada is exempted from tariffs in the framework of the automotive agreement between Canada and the United States.

Nevertheless, in all three industries for which import penetration ratios for total imports have been calculated, these ratios were higher in 1978 in the United States than in the European Community. The differences increased further between 1978 and 1981 as far as iron and steel are concerned while the ratio of imports to GDP increased slightly more in the Community than in the United States in automobiles and equi-proportionate changes occurred in telecommunication equipment.

The import penetration ratio for telecommunication equipment in 1978 was much lower in Japan than in the United States and the European Community. Restrictions on imports, in particular of telephone equipment, appear to have kept this ratio low and subsequent increases fell short of those in the other major developed countries. And while Japan's comparative advantage in automobiles contributed to the low import penetration ratio in 1978, the subsequent decline may be interpreted as reflecting the continuation of regulations with a protective effect.

As far as imports from the developing countries are concerned, the United States had a relatively low import penetration ratio for textiles in 1978, followed by Japan and the European Community. American imports of textiles from the developing countries, however, rose to a considerable extent after 1978 while imports declined in absolute terms in the Community and, in particular, in Japan. As a result, by 1981, the United States reached the Japanese import penetration ratio while differences remained *vis-à-vis* the Community.

Import penetration ratios for clothing in 1978 were approximately equal in the United States and the European Community, with a slightly smaller increase occurring in the latter than in the former between 1978 and 1981. In turn, Japan had much lower import penetration ratios in 1978 and a decline took place over the next three years.

Import penetration ratios in 1978 for other consumer goods, too, were the lowest in Japan which also occupies last place as far as increases in these imports are concerned. At the same time, the import penetration ratio for these products in 1978 was much higher in the United States than in the European Community and the changes that occurred between 1978 and 1981 did not modify this relationship.

With other consumer goods being the mirror image of textiles as far as import penetration ratios in the United States and the European Community are concerned, and the two economies having similar import penetration ratios in clothing, the restrictiveness of their barriers to imports from developing countries appears to have been similar in 1978. Between 1978 and 1981, however, textile imports increased rapidly in the United States, while declining in the Community, and differences in other product groups were small.

Finally, import penetration ratios in 1978 were generally the lowest in Japan, as were increases in imports from developing countries between 1978 and 1981. Yet, with Japan moving up the scale of development, one would have expected her imports from the developing countries to increase rapidly over time.

SUMMARY AND CONCLUSION

This chapter has reviewed recent changes in trade restrictions in the major developed countries: the United States, the European Community and Japan. The investigation has covered tariffs and non-tariff measures affecting the imports of manufactured products from all sources of supply and from the developing countries.

Tariff reductions undertaken during the period since the Second World War have been continued in the framework of the Tokyo Round negotiations, lowering tariffs to levels not seen during this century. While the reductions have been extended to the developing countries under the MFN clause, tariffs have been lowered less than the average on products of interest to these countries. Moreover, notwithstanding the changes that have occurred, the escalation of tariffs continues to discriminate against the imports of processed goods from the developing countries.

Tariff reductions under the Tokyo Round agreement, to be completed in the second half of the 1980s, contrast with the increased use made of non-tariff measures. At the same time, in recent years, the imposition of new barriers has been directed largely against imports from other developed countries rather than against the products of developing countries.

The ratio of restricted imports to total imports and to total consumption and the ratio of the consumption of restricted items to total consumption have been used to gauge the scope of import restrictions. But these measures cannot provide an indication of the extent to which imports have been reduced as a result of (i) the imposition of non-tariff barriers or (ii) changes in the restrictiveness of such barriers over time.

For these purposes, use has been made of the import penetration ratio and changes in the ratio of imports to GDP. While in the absence of binding restrictions these ratios are affected by the structure of comparative advantage, the over-valuation or under-valuation of national currencies and changes thereof, they will indicate appropriately the impact of restrictions which effectively limit imports.

The measures applied show the United States to be somewhat less restrictive than the European Community, although this may have changed with the subsequent imposition of restrictions on automobiles and steel. Given her smaller domestic market, one would have expected import penetration ratios to be higher in Japan than in the United States or the European Community, but the opposite is the case. The results point to the effects of informal barriers that are of particular importance for Japan, but could not be included in the survey of restrictive measures because of lack of information.

The restrictive effects of the measures taken are even more pronounced as far as Japan's imports from the developing countries are concerned. And while, with Japan moving up the scale of development, one would have expected her manufactured imports from the developing countries to have increased rapidly, this has not been the case.

At the same time, the United States and the European Community share the responsibility for having rendered the MFA more stringent and having created new restrictions on the imports of several commodities from Japan. It is in the self-interest of the developed countries to eliminate these barriers, so as to benefit from the reallocation of resources in accordance with their comparative advantage. More generally, it would be desirable to limit reliance on quantitative import restrictions, while ensuring multilateral surveillance in the form of a safeguards code. Finally, there is a need to reduce tariffs on products of interest to the developing countries that are subject to escalation of tariffs and above-average tariffs.

The proposed liberalization of international trade could not be accomplished without a new round of multilateral trade negotiations. In fact, in the absence of such negotiations, there is a danger of backsliding towards protectionism. At the same time, involving the developing countries in the negotiations would not only allow the more industrialized of these countries to adopt more rational trade policies but would also strengthen the argument for trade liberalization in the developed countries and permit attention being given to products of interest to developing countries in the course of the negotiations.

NOTES

1. The authors are indebted to Geza Feketekuty for useful suggestions and for comments on an earlier draft of the chapter. Helpful comments were also received from Costas Michalopoulos and from Martin Wolf. Barry Goldberg provided access to the data files of the Office of the United States Trade Representative on non-tariff measures and Ed Stuart and Jim Lee prepared the material underlying the calculations on the scope of non-tariff measures in the major developed countries. The authors alone are responsible for the opinions expressed in the chapter which should not be interpreted as reflecting the views of the World Bank or the United States Administration.
2. Bela Balassa (1968) 'The Structure of Protection in Industrial Countries and its Effects on the Exports of Processed Goods from Developing Countries', in *The Kennedy Round: Estimated Effects on Tariff Barriers*. New York, United Nations.
3. The data refer to MFN tariffs and do not take account of tariff preferences under the Generalized System of Preferences (GSP). They differ somewhat from the results reported in *ibid*. because of differences in coverage. While the earlier study defined manufactured products as SITC classes 5 to 8 less 68 (non-ferrous metals), the cited figures pertain to semi-manufactures and finished manufactures as defined by the General Agreement on Tariffs and Trade (GATT).
4. For raw materials, semi-manufacturers and finished manufacturers taken together,. actual tariff reductions were estimated to have been only slightly more than one

half, on the average, than reductions in legal tariffs in Japan. See *Twenty-Fourth Annual Report of the President of the United States on the Trade Agreements Program.* Washington, US Government Printing Office, 1979, p. 59.

5. Estimates of the effects of Tokyo Round tariff reductions on trade and employment are provided in Alan V. Deardorff and Robert M. Stern (1981) 'A Disaggregated Model of World Production and Trade: an Estimate of the Impact of the Tokyo Round', *Journal of Policy Modelling*, May, pp. 127–52. For a critique of the methodology used, see Balassa, 'Comment' on Deardorff and Stern, 'The Economic Effects of Complete Elimination of Post-Tokyo Round Tariffs', in William R. Cline (1983) (ed.) *Trade Policy in the 1980s.* Washington, Institute for International Economics.

6. Alternative estimates for industrial products, inclusive of raw materials, are reported in *Twenty-Fourth Annual Report of the President of the United States on the Trade Agreements Program, op. cit.,* pp. 53–62, and, inclusive of processed food, in Cline (1984) *Exports of Manufactures from Developing Countries: Performance and Market Access.* Washington, Brookings Institution.

7. Jeffrey Nugent (1974) *Economic Integration in Central America: Empirical Investigations.* Baltimore, Johns Hopkins Press, Chapter 2.

8. A more appropriate weighting scheme involving the use of production values has not been used here because of the lack of comparable data.

9. Excluding duty-free items, two-thirds of industrial imports from the developing countries, inclusive of raw materials, were classified as GSP items and one-third of the total was not subject to ceilings or other limitations, although ceilings will be imposed if certain limits are exceeded. See *The Tokyo Round of Multilateral Trade Negotiations*, Supplementary Report by the Director-General of the GATT (Geneva, GATT Secretariat, 1980) p. 40.

10. See Balassa (1978) 'The "New Protectionism" and the International Economy', *Journal of World Trade Law*, September–October, pp. 409–36, republished in Balassa (1981) *Tne Newly Industrializing Countries in the World Economy.* New York, Pergamon Press, pp. 109–26.

11. Restrictions applied earlier to specialty steels and to color television sets imported from Japan were lifted in 1980.

12. Cline, *op. cit.*

13. Deardorff and Stern, 'A Disaggregated Model of World Production and Trade: An Estimate of the Impact of the Tokyo Round', *loc. cit.*

14. This measure has also been used by Cline, *op. cit.*

15. Peter Morici and Laura L. Megna (1983) *US Economic Policies Affecting Industrial Trade: A Quantitative Assessment* (Washington, National Planning Association), p.47.

16. Manufactured imports of the United States in 1982 were $146 billion. Under the assumption of an average import demand elasticity of 2.14 (*ibid.*, p. 106), quantitative import restrictions with a tariff equivalent of 0.57 percent would have reduced imports by $1.8 billion. Assuming linear demand and supply curves, the cost of protection approximately equals one half of the tariff equivalent of quantitative restrictions (0.29 percent) times the change in imports resulting from the imposition of these restrictions ($1.8 billion), or $5 million.

17. Michael C. Munger (1984) 'The Costs of Protectionism', *Challenge*, January–February, p. 56.

18. Morichi and Megna, *op. cit.*, p. 23.

19. *Ibid.*, p. 27.

20. Munger, *loc. cit.*, p. 56.

21. Harry G. Johnson (1970) 'The Cost of Protection and the Scientific Tariff', *Journal of Political Economy*, August.

22. The procedures applied do not, however, permit estimating the welfare costs of the restrictions applied.
23. It should be added, however, that technological changes have improved the competitive position, in particular in the United States, in recent years.
24. If non-tariff measures are not binding, imports will also be affected by tariffs.

12 · THE EXTENT AND THE COST OF PROTECTION IN DEVELOPED–DEVELOPING COUNTRY TRADE

INTRODUCTION

The focus of this chapter is the measures of protection applied to trade between developed and developing countries. This choice reflects concern with the adverse repercussions of recently imposed protectionist measures in the two groups of countries as well as the increasing importance of mutual trade for their national economies.

The chapter analyzes the extent and the cost of protection in developed and in developing countries, with special attention to measures affecting trade between the two groups of countries. The first section reviews the tariff and non-tariff measures applied by the developed countries and provides empirical evidence on the cost of protection in these countries. We then examine the use of protective measures in the developing countries and indicate the resulting cost to their national economies. In conclusion we briefly indicate the policy implications of the findings.

PROTECTION IN THE DEVELOPED COUNTRIES

Tariff protection

The successes of the post-war period with tariff disarmament in the developed countries are well known and do not require detailed discussion. While the original purpose had been to undo the damage resulting from the competitive imposition of import duties during the 1930s, tariffs in the major developed countries were reduced below pre-depression levels by the end of the 1950s. These reductions, undertaken on an item-by-item basis, were followed by across the board tariff reductions in the framework of the Dillon Round

Written with Constantine Michalopoulos. The authors alone are responsible for the contents of this chapter, which should not be interpreted to reflect the views of the World Bank. First published in *New Protectionist Threat to World Welfare*, ed. Dominick Salvatore, North-Holland, Amsterdam, 1987.

(1960–1), the Kennedy Round (1964–7), and the Tokyo Round (1974–7) of trade negotiations.

Taken together, in the course of the Dillon, Kennedy, and Tokyo Round negotiations, tariffs on manufactured goods imported by the developed countries were lowered, on the average, by nearly two-thirds. Table 12.1 shows that post-Tokyo Round tariff levels in major developed countries averaged 6–7 percent for finished manufactures and were even lower for semi-manufactures and raw materials. Apart from overall reductions, the procedure applied in the Tokyo Round also lessened the dispersion of tariffs as higher tariff rates were cut proportionately more than lower rates.

The question arises, however, if the remaining tariffs bear disproportionately on products imported from the developing countries. There are two aspects to this question. First, whether tariffs on products of interest to developing countries are higher (or lower) at each level of processing; second, whether there is tariff escalation that affects developing-country exports of manufactures.

Table 12.1 shows that manufactured products of interest to the developing countries are in general subject to higher tariffs than products on the same level of fabrication originating in the developed countries. Thus, post-Tokyo Round tariffs on all imports of semi-manufactures and finished manufactures, and on such imports from developing countries, respectively, average 4.9 and 8.7 percent in the United States, 6.0 and 6.7 in the European Common Market, and 5.4 and 6.8 percent in Japan (Table 12.1).

Furthermore, there is evidence of tariff escalation. Thus, post-Tokyo Round average tariffs on raw materials, semi-manufactures and finished manufactures are 0.2, 3.0 and 5.7 percent for the United States; 0.2, 4.2 and 6.9 percent for the European Common Market; and 0.5, 4.6 and 6.0 percent for Japan (Table 12.1).[1]

The cited averages pertain to all processing chains, several of which have little relevance for most developing countries. Such is the case in particular for petroleum-based products and for metal products, where processing is highly capital intensive and requires a considerable degree of technological sophistication that is found only in developing countries at higher levels of industrialization. Excluding these products would raise the extent of tariff escalation even further.

Table 12.2 provides data on average tariffs in the developed countries for products in 12 processing chains that are of interest to developing countries and, among them, to countries at lower levels of industrial development. The raw materials in question weigh heavily in the exports of the countries concerned, and the processing of these materials is frequently within their technical competence. Also, with the major exception of paper, processing is not a highly capital-intensive activity.

It is apparent that, except for wood, tariffs escalate in all cases. But this exception is more apparent than real, since the major input into furniture is

Table 12.1 Post-Tokyo Round tariff averages in the major developed countries

	Tariffs on total imports				Tariffs on imports from LDCs
	Raw materials	Semi-manufac-tures	Finished manufac-tures	Semi- and finished manufac-tures	Semi- and finished manufac-tures
United States	0.2	3.0	5.7	4.9	8.7
European Common Market	0.2	4.2	6.9	6.0	6.7
Japan	0.5	4.6	6.0	5.4	6.8

Source: General Agreement on Tariffs and Trade. *The Tokyo Round of Multilateral Trade Negotiations*, II–Supplementary Report (January 1980): 33–7.

Table 12.2 Pre- and post-Tokyo Round tariffs for 12 processing chains

Stage of processing	Product description	Tariff rate[a]		1981 developing countries exports to industrial countries[b] (US $ millions)
		Pre-Tokyo	Post-Tokyo	
1	Fish, crustaceans and molluscs	4.3	3.5	1,145
2	Fish, crustaceans and molluscs, prepared	6.1	5.5	580
1	Vegetables, fresh or dried	13.3	8.9	1,291
2	Vegetables, prepared	18.8	12.4	20
1	Fruit, fresh, dried	6.0	4.8	2,409
2	Fruit, provisionally preserved	14.5	12.2	2,474
3	Fruit, prepared	19.5	16.6	1,321
1	Coffee	10.0	6.8	4,385
2	Processed coffee	13.3	9.4	288
1	Cocoa beans	4.2	2.6	994
2	Processed cocoa	6.7	4.3	433
3	Chocolate products	15.0	11.8	43
1	Oil seeds and flour	2.7	2.7	579
2	Fixed vegetable oils	8.5	8.1	1,374
1	Unmanufactured tobacco	56.1	55.8	1,117
2	Manufactured tobacco	82.2	81.8	39
1	Natural rubber	2.8	2.3	2,045
2	Semi-manufactured rubber (unvulcanized)	4.6	2.9	3
3	Rubber articles	7.9	6.7	390
1	Raw hides and skins	1.4	0.0	144
2	Semi-manufactured leather	4.2	4.2	437
3	Travel goods, handbags, etc.	8.5	8.5	1,082
4	Manufactured articles of leather	9.3	8.2	748

Table 12.2 (*continued*)

Stage of processing	Product description	Tariff rate[a] Pre-Tokyo	Tariff rate[a] Post-Tokyo	1981 developing countries exports to industrial countries[b] (US $ millions)
1	Vegetable textiles yarns (excluding hemp)	4.0	2.9	150
2	Twine, rope and articles; sacks and bags	5.6	4.7	203
3	Jute fabrics	9.1	8.3	73
1	Silk yarn, not for retail sale	2.6	2.6	38
2	Silk fabric	5.6	5.3	176
1	Semi-manufactured wood	2.6	1.8	1,241
2	Wood panels	10.8	9.2	744
3	Wood articles	6.9	4.1	524
4	Furniture	8.1	6.6	681
1	Total			27,171

Memorandum items

Total manufactures	57,910
Textiles, footwear, iron and steel	23,373
Manufactured exports subject to tariff escalation (except textiles, footwear, iron and steel)	6,490
Total Non-fuel primary	43,792
Non-fuel primary subject to tariff escalation	20,681

Source: Alexander J. Yeats (1981) 'The Influence of Trade and Commercial Barriers on the Industrial Processing of Natural Resources,' *World Development* 9(5)(May): 485–94 and World Bank Trade Data System.
[a] Unweighted average of the tariffs actually facing developing-country exports (i.e. Generalized System of Preference, most-favored nation, other special preferential rates, etc.) in market of EEC, Japan, Australia, New Zealand, Canada, Austria, Switzerland, Finland, Norway and Sweden.
[b] includes exports to the United States, Japan and the EEC.

semi-manufactured wood that has lower tariffs. And the overall importance of tariff escalation is indicated by the fact that the products in question account for 47 percent of the exports of non-fuel primary and semi-processed products from the developing to the developed countries but for only 11 percent of manufactured exports. At the same time, the data reported in Table 12.2 exclude textiles and clothing, iron and steel, and footwear, where there is also tariff escalation but where quantitative import restrictions tend to be the effective barrier to developed-country markets.

Escalation of tariffs can cause effective rates of protection to exceed nominal rates by a substantial margin. At the same time, for developing-country producers, the relevant consideration is the protection of the processing margin (value added), or effective protection, rather than the nominal tariffs levied on individual products.

Data provided in an earlier paper by Yeats (1974) permit estimating effective rates in the post-Tokyo Round situation for three semi-manufactured products: processed cocoa (15.8 percent), leather (13.5 percent) and vegetable oil (70.2 percent). In the cases considered, the ratio of effective to nominal tariffs ranges from 3.2 (leather) to 8.7 (vegetable oil); the differences in the ratios are explained largely by inter-industry differences in the share of value added in output.[2]

Such protection tends to discriminate against industrial processing in these countries and, in particular, in countries at lower levels of industrial development. Other things being equal, a 20 percent effective rate of protection in developed countries means that firms engaged in processing in a developing country would have to compress their processing margin (value added) by 25 percent in order to compete with processing activities in the developed countries. With some of the costs of processing, including the cost of capital, not being compressible, tariff escalation in the developed countries thus puts industrial processing in the developing countries at a considerable disadvantage.

Non-tariff barriers

Parallel with reductions in tariffs, quantitative import restrictions were liberalized during the 1950s in Western Europe, where these restrictions had been applied largely for balance-of-payments purposes after the Second World War. Import liberalization also proceeded, albeit at a slower rate, in Japan – where restrictions had been employed on balance-of-payments as well as on infant-industry grounds, although a number of products remained subject to quantitative import restrictions until the early 1970s. Finally, the United States continued with its broadly liberal trade policy and abandoned the American selling-price provisions on coal-tar-based chemicals but imposed limitations on the imports of Japanese cotton textiles.

Agriculture was an exception to the process of import liberalization during the post-war period. In fact, apart from the United States (a large net exporter of food and feeding stuffs), agricultural protection in the developed countries was reinforced after 1960. The European Community has encouraged high-cost production by setting high domestic prices in the framework of the Common Agricultural Policy, thereby turning an import surplus in major foods into an export surplus. Also, with higher wages raising domestic production costs, agricultural protection has intensified in Japan.

Increased use has been made of non-tariff protection in manufacturing industries as well. The developed countries have generally refrained from applying the GATT safeguard clause; they have relied instead on so-called voluntary export restraints and orderly marketing arrangements to limit imports.

Measures of non-tariff protection on textiles and clothing apply exclusively to developing-country exporters. Thus, while the Long-term Arrangement

Regarding Cotton Textiles (1962) was originally aimed largely at Japan, its successor, the Multi-Fiber Arrangement (MFA) (1979), limits the imports of textiles and clothing from the developing countries. And whereas the MFA earlier permitted annual import growth of 6 percent in volume, in the course of its subsequent renewals and re-interpretations it has become increasingly restrictive. While Japan is not party to the MFA, there is evidence of informal limitations on the imports of textiles and clothing from the developing countries.

Japan severely limits the importation of footwear from all sources, whereas several of the larger European countries restrict footwear imports from the developing countries alone. Finally, during the 1970s, the United States limited the imports of non-rubber footwear from Korea and Taiwan (China) and the International Trade Commission has again recommended the imposition of restrictions on the importation of footwear.

Since the early 1970s, non-tariff measures have also assumed increased importance for steel. In the United States there are formal and informal limitations on the importation of carbon and specialty steel from Japan, from the European Community, and from several developing countries; the Community restricts imports from Japan and from developing countries; and informal measures limit steel imports from Korea into Japan.

France and Italy have long restricted automobile imports from Japan. In recent years they have been joined by Belgium, Germany and the United Kingdom. In turn, the United States negotiated limitations on the imports of automobiles from Japan in 1981 but let the agreement expire in early 1985.

In the electronics industry, the European Community has imposed limitations on the imports of several products from Japan and, to a lesser extent, Korea and Taiwan. In turn, the United States has eliminated earlier restrictions on the importation of color television sets. Finally, informal barriers limit the importation of telecommunication equipment into Japan.

Table 12.3 shows the extent of non-tariff barriers applied by the major developed countries following recent increases in these barriers. The table provides information on the use of non-tariff measures affecting imports from the other developed countries, from the developing countries and from all countries taken together, in the United States, the European Common Market and Japan, based on a joint World Bank–UNCTAD research effort.

Non-tariff barriers have been defined to include all transparent border measures that directly or indirectly limit imports. Quantitative import restrictions and so-called voluntary export restraints limit imports directly. In turn, variable import levies that equalize domestic and import prices, minimum price requirements for imports, voluntary export price agreements, as well as tariff quotas involving the imposition of higher duties above a predetermined import quantity, have an indirect effect on imports.

Table 12.3 shows the share of imports subject to non-tariff measures, calculated by using world trade weights. The use of world trade weights allows

Table 12.3 Relative shares of imports subject to non-tariff measures, May 1985 (world trade weighted)[a]

	Non-fuel products	Agriculture	Manufac- turing	Textiles and clothing	Footwear	Iron and steel	Electrical machinery	Transport equipment	Rest of manufac- turing
United States									
Imports from									
all countries[b]	6.4	11.5	5.6	47.8	0.1	21.8	0.0	0.0	0.4
industrial countries	3.4	11.7	2.7	25.5	0.0	24.6	0.0	0.0	0.0
developing countries	12.9	11.8	14.4	65.3	0.1	4.5	0.0	0.0	1.9
European Community									
Imports from									
all countries[b]	13.9	37.8	10.1	42.4	10.2	37.9	4.2	3.9	3.8
industrial countries	10.5	46.7	5.7	13.6	0.3	33.7	3.1	3.8	2.6
developing countries	21.8	27.5	21.4	65.2	12.5	28.9	4.7	4.6	5.3
Japan									
Imports from									
all countries[b]	9.6	33.8	5.4	14.0	39.6	0.0	0.0	0.0	6.0
industrial countries	9.5	35.7	5.5	14.0	34.3	0.0	0.0	0.0	7.1
developing countries	10.5	30.2	5.4	14.2	42.2	0.0	0.0	0.0	1.9

Source: Julio J. Nogues, Andrzej Olechowski, and L. Alan Winters (1985) 'The Establishment of Non-tariff Barriers to Industrial Countries' Imports', World Bank Development Research Department Discussion Paper No. 115 (January) and the sources cited therein.

[a] The data collected by Nogues, Olechowski and Winters for 1983 have been adjusted for the termination of the US–Japanese automotive agreement. Other changes in protection occurring between 1983 and 1985 have been relatively minor.

[b] All countries include the socialist countries of Eastern Europe, hence the overall average does not necessarily lie between average for imports from the industrial and from the developing countries.

for differences in the relative importance of individual tariff items in international trade while abstracting from the idiosyncrasies of national protection. In contrast, calculating for a particular country the percentage share of own imports subject to restrictions is equivalent to using own imports as weights, which means that the more restrictive the measure the lower its weight in the calculations; in the extreme, prohibitive tariffs have zero weight.[3] Also, calculating the percentage share of tariff items has the disadvantage that it gives equal weight to all items, even though they may vary in importance to a considerable extent.[4]

Table 12.3 reports non-tariff barriers for non-fuel imports and, within this total, for agricultural and for manufactured imports; it further disaggregates manufactured goods into textiles and clothing, footwear, iron and steel, electrical machinery, transport equipment and other manufactures. Fuels have not been included because the non-tariff measures applied do not appear to aim at protecting the domestic production of competing fuels.

The results are indicative of the high protection of EEC and Japanese agriculture, where most commodities competing with domestic production encounter non-tariff barriers. With protection applying chiefly to temperate-zone products, these barriers affect a somewhat higher proportion of agricultural imports from developed than developing-country suppliers. The proportions are about the same in the case of the United States, where the extent of non-tariff barriers of agricultural products is relatively low.

In the United States and the European Community, non-tariff barriers on manufactured imports discriminate to a considerable extent against developing-country exporters. This discrimination is largely due to the restrictions imposed on developing-country exports of textiles and clothing in the framework of the Multi-Fiber Arrangement (MFA). As noted above, Japan is not party to the MFA but is said to use informal measures to limit its imports of textiles and clothing from the developing countries; in fact, as shown below, its imports have been growing at a lower rate and account for a smaller proportion of domestic consumption than in the United States and the European Common Market.

The data reported in Table 12.3 do not include other border measures that could, but may not, be used with protective effect, such as anti-dumping and countervailing duties, price monitoring and investigations of alleged practices that may give rise to the imposition of such duties and automatic import authorizations. There is some evidence that these practices have been applied in certain circumstances in lieu of safeguards and with both the intent and effect of protecting domestic industry rather than simply offsetting distortions introduced by the exporter (Finger, Hall, and Nelson, 1982). Their use has also increased since the late 1970s (Nogues, Olechowski, and Winters, 1985).

Nevertheless, given the legitimate role that such practices can play in trade, they have to be treated differently from other non-tariff measures. Thus, rather than eliminating the measures themselves, one should assure that they are not used for protective purposes.

As an illustration, the non-tariff measures reported in Table 12.3, as well as the other border measures just described, are reported in Table 12.4. It should be noted, however, that for lack of information, the data on other border measures do not include Japan.

The data reported in Tables 12.3 and 12.4 do not include health and safety measures and technical standards that may be used with a protective intent.[5] Nor do the data comprise various informal measures that are prevalent in countries which rely to a considerable extent on administrative discretion rather than on codified rules to limit imports. Finally, the data are limited to trade-related measures with the exclusion of domestic measures (e.g. producer subsidies and regional development measures) that bear on trade indirectly through their effect on domestic production.

Despite increasing barriers to trade, the share of imports from the developing countries in the consumption of manufactured goods by the major developed countries continued to rise during the last decade. Table 12.5 shows the relationship between manufactured imports from the developing countries and the consumption of manufactured products, defined as production plus imports less exports, in the United States, the European Community and Japan. Information is provided on the developing countries' market shares in the years 1973, 1978, 1981 and 1983.

There are no signs of a slowdown in the growth of the developing countries' share in industrial countries' markets except for the group of other semi-manufactures, which are heavily weighted by natural-resource products, and for the category of textiles and clothing, where the MFA has become increasingly restrictive. At the same time, until recently, the import shares of textiles and clothing continued to rise, reflecting the upgrading of products exported by the developing countries in the face of limitations imposed on increases in volume. Furthermore, developing-country exporters increasingly shifted to the exportation of products that did not encounter barriers, such as engineering goods and iron and steel, which later has subsequently become subject to restrictions.

The data further show that differences between the United States and the European Community, on the one hand, and Japan, on the other, were increasing over time as far as the share of imports from developing countries in their domestic consumption is concerned. Thus, while this share was 1.1 percent in the United States, 0.9 percent in the Common Market and 0.7 percent in Japan in 1973, the corresponding shares were 3.0, 2.1 and 1.0 percent in 1983.

It appears, then, that although Japan is not a party to the MFA and has few formal barriers to imports from the developing countries (the major exception being footwear), it has increasingly lagged behind the other major developed countries in importing manufactured goods from the developing countries.

Table 12.4 Relative shares of non-tariff measures and other border measures (all products less fuels; all countries; world trade weighted)

	Non-tariff measures[a] (1)	Other border measures[b] (2)	Sum of columns (1) and (2) (3)[c]
European Community	13.9	11.6	21.0
United States	6.4	3.4	9.5
Japan	9.6	0.0	9.6

Source: See Table 12.3.

[a] See Table 12.3.

[b] Countervailing and anti-dumping duties, price surveillance, price investigation, quantity surveillance and automatic licensing.

[c] The figures in this column are less than the sum of those in the columns reported because some trade flows face several barriers.

Table 12.5 Relative importance of manufactured imports from developing countries

	Import–consumption ratio (in current prices)			
	1973	1978	1981	1983
United States				
Iron and steel	0.6	0.9	1.4	2.3
Chemicals	0.4	0.5	0.6	0.9
Other semi-manufactures	0.9	1.5	1.7	1.9
Engineering products	0.7	1.3	2.0	2.6
Textiles	1.8	1.6	2.3	2.2
Clothing	5.6	11.3	14.0	15.1
Other consumer goods	1.9	3.7	4.8	5.2
All manufactures	1.1	1.8	2.4	3.0
European Community				
Iron and steel	0.4	0.4	0.6	0.7
Chemicals	0.5	0.6	0.8	1.1
Other semi-manufactures	1.3	2.5	1.9	2.3
Engineering products	0.3	0.9	1.3	1.4
Textiles	2.6	3.7	4.1	4.4
Clothing	5.7	11.4	16.4	16.0
Other consumer goods	1.1	1.6	2.9	3.1
All manufactures	0.9	1.6	2.0	2.1
Japan				
Iron and steel	0.2	0.3	1.0	1.6
Chemicals	0.3	0.5	0.8	0.9
Other semi-manufactures	1.0	0.9	0.9	0.9
Engineering products	0.2	0.3	0.5	0.4
Textiles	2.2	2.3	2.1	1.9
Clothing	7.6	7.4	8.9	8.2
Other consumer goods	0.8	1.1	1.3	1.5
All manufactures	0.7	0.8	0.9	1.0

Source: GATT, *International Trade*; United Nations, *Yearbook of Industrial Statistics*; and OECD, *Indicators of Industrial Activity*, various years.

Yet, with its rapid economic growth and the accumulation of physical and human capital, Japan has approached the other developed countries in terms of factor endowments and thus one would have expected it to resemble their import pattern more closely. The fact that the opposite has happened may be taken as an indication of the use of informal measures of protection against developing-country exports in Japan.

Note finally that, while increased protection through non-tariff measures in developed-country markets has been accompanied by increased penetration of developing-country exports in these markets, this should not be interpreted to mean that such protection would not have involved an economic cost in the developed countries or would not have adversely affected developing countries. It rather means that protection has been concentrated in particular sectors and that developing countries have been able to alleviate its impact on their foreign-exchange earnings through export diversification and product upgrading.

The cost of protection

Apart from its adverse effects on foreign exporters, import protection imposes a cost on the domestic economy. Earlier estimates of the cost of protection in the developed countries were generally low, rarely attaining 1 percent of the gross national product. These estimates, however, failed to consider the losses involved in forgoing the exploitation of economies of scale in protected markets. Taking account of economies of scale, it has recently been estimated that protection has reduced potential output by about 10 percent in Canada (Harris, 1983, p. 115). Further losses are incurred in the event of the use of voluntary export restraints, which involve an income transfer to foreign exporters.

Table 12.6 reports available estimates on the welfare cost of voluntary export restraints, which have come into increased use in recent years. This cost consists of the loss of consumer surplus, the resource cost of producing the additional quantity domestically, and increased payments on imported goods as exporters charge higher prices for the limited quantity they sell. It has been calculated for clothing in the United States and the European Community and for automobiles and steel in the United States.

Rows (1) to (4) of Table 12.6 show the components of the cost of protection, as well as its total, for the industries in question. Row (5) further indicates the number of jobs saved in the protected industries on the assumption that labor productivity is not affected thereby. In turn, row (6) shows the welfare cost per job saved in the industries in question.

While the data refer to different years, this will hardly affect the results since prices changed little during the period. Thus, it is apparent that the welfare cost of saving a job is considerably higher in the clothing industry than in the case of automobiles and steel.

Table 12.6 Effects of some major VERs in developed countries[a]

	Clothing		Auto-mobiles	Steel
	USA 1980	EC 1980	USA 1984	USA 1985
1. Increased payments on imported goods ($ million)	988	1,050	1,778	1,530
2. Loss of consumer surplus ($ million)	408	289[b]	229	455
3. Resource cost of producing the additional quantity domestically ($ million)	113	70	185	7
4. Cost to the national economy in the protecting country (welfare cost) ($ million), (1)+(2)+(3)	1,509	1,409	2,192	1,992
5. Jobs saved through protection (thousands)	8.9	11.3	45.0	28.0
6. Welfare cost per job saved ($ thousand) (4)/(5)	169.6	124.7	48.7	71.1
7. Average labor compensation ($ thousand), (annual)	12.6	13.5	38.1	42.4
8. Ratio of welfare cost to average compensation, (6)/(7)	13.5	9.2	1.3	1.7
9. Lost revenues for exporters ($ million)	9,328	7,460	6,050	1,508
10. Ratio of increased payments on imported goods to lost revenues for exports, (1)/(9)	0.11	0.14	0.29	1.01

Source: Orsalia K. Kalantzopoulos, 'The Cost of Voluntary Export Restraints for Selected Industries in the US and the EC.' Washington, DC, World Bank.
[a] US dollar estimates are evaluated at current prices for the year indicated.
[b] Foregone tariff revenues, due to the quota introduction, are not included.

Data on the ratio of the welfare cost to average labor compensation, reported in row (8), are directly comparable across industries, since the numerator as well as the denominator of the ratio are expressed in the prices of the same year. The results show that this ratio was 13.5 in the United States and 9.2 in the EEC clothing industry while it was 11.3 in the US automobile industry and 1.7 in the US steel industry.

The welfare cost of saving a job in the protected industries thus exceeds the wages paid in these industries by a considerable margin, with the differences being by far the highest in the case of clothing, where the import limitations pertain to products originating in developing countries. The cost to the consumer, including higher prices for domestic products resulting from protection, exceeds even this figure. Nor do the estimates take account of job losses in other industries that are discriminated against by protection.

At the same time, while higher prices paid on imports represent a transfer to foreign suppliers, the volume of their exports is adversely affected by the protectionist measures applied. As shown in row (10) of Table 12.6, the transfer implicit in the higher prices paid to exporters compensated for hardly more than one-tenth of the loss in revenues owing to the reduced volume of exports. The corresponding ratio was 0.14 for automobiles; it was 1 for steel, where higher prices apparently offset for the loss in export volume.

Although similar calculations have not been made for agricultural products, comparisons of domestic and world market prices provide an indication of the relative costs of protection in various markets, although world market prices would rise if protection measures were dismantled. The calculations reported in Table 12.7 pertain to the 1978–80 average, that is, before the rise in the value of the US dollar had distorted international price relationships.

The cost of protecting domestic agriculture is indicated by the high ratio of domestic to world market prices in the European Community and Japan. In both cases, domestic prices exceeded world market prices by approximately one-half for wheat. In the Community the price differential exceeded 100 percent for maize; comparable data for Japan are not available. By contrast, domestic prices were slightly below world market prices for both wheat and maize in the United States.

The domestic prices of beef and veal were especially high in Japan, exceeding the international price two to three times. In the EEC, the price differential surpassed one-third for beef and veal and approached one-half in the case of lamb and sheep. In the United States, domestic prices were slightly below world market prices for beef and veal and slightly above the prices for lamb and sheep.

While the United States protects the domestic production of sugar, the excess of domestic over world market prices for this commodity was greater in the EEC and Japan than in the United States. This situation has continued despite the overvaluation of the dollar. Also, the EEC countries have subsidized their sugar exports, with the subsidy reaching 1.2 billion in 1984. Over the last eight years, the Common Market exported 38 million tons of sugar as domestic output rose from 10.8 to 13.3 million tons and consumption declined. During the same period, US sugar imports declined from 6 to 3 million tons (*The Economist*, 10 August 1985).

In conclusion, it should be emphasized that, apart from the measured cost imposed on the national economy, the protection of non-competitive, low-productivity sectors has unfavorable long-term effects on the developed countries by postponing adjustment as well as the upgrading of labor. Non-tariff barriers have particularly adverse effects by reducing competition, introducing discriminatory practices, and keeping out new entrants which frequently are developing countries. In particular, the Multi-Fiber Arrangement has perverse effects in encouraging the upgrading of products in the developing countries while considerations of comparative advantage would call for such upgrading to occur in the developed countries.

Finally, high protection involves the misallocation of new additions to the capital stock. This is because, apart from safeguarding existing firms, protection provides an inducement for new investments in sectors where the developed countries have a comparative disadvantage. Correspondingly, less capital is available to high-skill, high-technology industries where these

Table 12.7 Nominal protection coefficients for agricultural products, 1978–80[a]

	US	EEC	Japan
Wheat	0.90	1.52	1.49
Maize	0.85	2.10	n.a.
Beef and veal	0.81	1.36	2.41[b]
Lamb and sheep	1.10	1.48	n.a.
Sugar	1.48	1.76	1.59

Source: US Department of Agriculture.
[a] The nominal protection coefficient is the ratio of domestic to world market prices.
[b] Data provided by the Australia–Japan Research Center, Australia National University, Canberra, Australia.

countries possess important advantages. Ultimately, then, protection unfavorably affects economic growth in the developed countries as well as in their trading partners among developing countries.

PROTECTION IN THE DEVELOPING COUNTRIES

The extent of import protection

Comparable estimates on the level of protection and the share of imports subject to quantitative import restrictions are available for relatively few developing countries. At the same time, available information indicates that the scope of non-tariff measures is much greater, and levels of protection are both higher and show greater variation, in these countries than in the developed countries.

Studies by Balassa and Associates (1971), Bhagwati (1978), Krueger (1978) and Balassa and Associates (1982) showed considerable differences in the trade regimes of the developing countries during the 1960s. These differences pertained to the protection of the manufacturing sector and the consequent bias against primary activities (in particular, agriculture) as well as to the extent of the bias against exports. The countries in question may be divided into three groups on the basis of the policies applied during this period.

The first group included Argentina, Brazil, Chile, Pakistan and the Philippines, all of which highly protected their manufacturing industries, discriminated against primary production and biased the system of incentives against exports. In these countries, the average net effective protection of the manufacturing sector, reflecting adjustment for the overvaluation of the exchange rate associated with protection, ranged between 40 and 150 percent.

The countries of the second group, including Colombia, Israel and Mexico, had considerably lower levels of industrial protection. Also, the extent of discrimination against primary activities was less than in the countries of the first group. None the less, there was substantial bias against manufactured exports, with value added obtainable in domestic markets exceeding that obtainable in exporting by 40 to 90 percent compared with 120 to 320 percent in the first group.

Finally, in Korea, Singapore and Malaysia, there was little discrimination against manufactured exports, with the excess of value added obtainable in domestic markets over that obtainable in export markets ranging from 6 to 26 percent. The same conclusion applies to the primary exports of the countries of this group that did not discriminate against primary activities.

More recent estimates are available for several of these countries. They show little change in relative incentives to manufacturing and to primary production in the case of Korea. At the same time, reforms undertaken in the second half of the 1960s reduced, to a lesser or greater extent, the protection of manufacturing activities and discrimination against the primary sector in Brazil, Colombia, Mexico and the Philippines. In turn, changes in the opposite direction occurred in Malaysia (Roger, 1985).

On the whole, however, while several developing countries had liberalized their trade regimes in the late 1960s, trade policies in most of these countries discriminate in favor of import substitution and against exports, and there is considerable dispersion in the effective protection provided to various economic activities. Also, in several large Latin American countries protection was increased again in response to the external shocks of the post-1973 period.

The cost of protection

The cost of protection in developing countries can be rather high. Estimates for several of the countries cited above showed this cost to equal 9.5 percent of GNP in Brazil, 6.2 percent in Chile, 6.2 percent in Pakistan, 3.7 percent in the Philippines and 2.5 percent in Mexico during the 1960s (Balassa and Associates, 1971).

These results were obtained in a partial equilibrium framework and do not allow for the losses of economies of scale in protected domestic markets. Subsequently, De Melo estimated the cost of protection for Colombia in a general equilibrium framework, incorporating intermediate products, non-traded goods, as well as substitution among products and among primary factors (De Melo, 1978). Excluding land reallocation within agriculture and postulating an optimal export tax for coffee, the cost of protection was estimated at 11.0 percent of GNP, assuming labor to be fully employed, and 15.8 percent, assuming that additional supplies of labor are available at a constant real wage.

De Melo's results are considerably higher than the estimates made in a partial equilibrium framework, even though Colombia was in the middle range among developing countries in terms of levels of protection. Thus, De Melo estimated effective protection to average 25 percent in the Colombian manufacturing sector, without an exchange-rate adjustment, while the comparable result in the Balassa study was 35 percent.

It would appear, then, that the estimates obtained in a partial equilibrium framework understate the cost of protection. Part of the reason is that estimates made in this framework do not allow for the fact that the cost of protection rises with the dispersion of inter-industry rates of protection (Nugent, 1974, pp. 62–3). Yet the dispersion of protection rates is much greater in developing than in developed countries and, within the former group, in highly protected rather than less protected economies.

Protection and economic growth

Protection has traditionally been justified on the grounds that it will enable industries to grow up and eventually to confront foreign competition. The assumptions underlying this infant-industry argument is that protection is required on a temporary basis to offset the costs firms incur upon undertaking a new productive activity that will not be fully recouped by the firm itself but by the industry as a whole. This is because the firms initially entering upon a new activity will generate so-called externalities through labor training and technological improvements.

While these changes are supposed to permit productivity to increase more rapidly in protected infant industries of the developing countries than in the developed countries, the evidence suggests that protection has rather retarded productivity growth. Thus, in the early post-war period, the protected Latin American countries experienced virtually no increase in productivity (Bruton, 1967).

Also, in the 1960–73 period, incremental capital–output ratios were the highest in Chile (5.5) and India (5.7), which had by far the highest protection levels. In turn, these ratios were the lowest in Singapore (1.8) and Korea (2.1), which had the lowest levels of protection. Finally, incremental capital–output ratios declined in countries such as Brazil (from 3.8 in 1960–6 to 2.1 in 1966–73) which reduced their levels of protection during the latter part of the period (Balassa and Associates, 1982, p. 3).

High incremental capital–output ratios reflect slow productivity growth under protection, which tends to discourage exports, as production in the confines of domestic markets limits the exploitation of economies of scale, capacity utilization and technological improvements, thereby aggravating the adverse effects of inefficient resource allocation. By contrast, in national economies where protection levels are low, exports are encouraged, permitting the exploitation of economies of scale and higher-capacity utilization, with the carrot and the stick of competition in foreign markets providing inducements for technological change.

The above considerations may explain the observed positive correlation between exports and economic growth. This was first shown by Michalopoulos and Jay (1973) in a cross-section production-function type relationship, with exports added to the conventional explanatory variables of capital and labor. Subsequently, Feder (1983) found that the use of primary factors in export production, rather than in producing non-export products, entailed a 1.8 percentage-point difference in economic growth rates during the 1964–73 period in a group of 31 semi-industrial countries.

These results relate to a period of rapid expansion in the world economy. The question was raised if they would also apply following the deterioration of world market conditions as a result of increases in petroleum prices and the slowdown of economic growth in the developed countries after 1973. This question has been answered in the affirmative in studies by Krueger and Michalopoulos (1985) and by Balassa (1984).

Krueger and Michalopoulos (1985) showed that the average rate of growth of both exports and GNP was higher for outward-oriented developing economies with relatively balanced trade incentives than for inward-oriented developing countries characterized by high protection during the 1960–73 period of high world economic growth as well as during the 1973–81 period of external shocks. Balassa further showed that while the external shocks of the latter period entailed a greater economic cost for outward-oriented countries, which had a larger trade share relative to GNP, the excess cost was offset several-fold through more rapid economic growth in these countries than in inward-oriented economies (Balassa, 1984). Differences in growth performance, in turn, were attributed to differences in the adjustment policies applied in response to external shocks.

In subsequent research the trade policies applied at the beginning of this period of external shocks and policy responses to external shocks was introduced simultaneously in a cross-section investigation of 43 developing countries in the 1973–9 period (Balassa, 1985). The trade policies applied at the beginning of the period have been represented by an index of trade orientation estimated as deviations of actual from hypothetical values of per capita exports, the latter having been derived in a regression equation that includes per capita incomes, population and the ratio of mineral exports to the gross national product as explanatory variables. In turn, alternative policy responses to external shocks have been represented by relating the balance-of-payments effects of export promotion, import substitution and additional net external financing to the balance-of-payment effects of external shocks.

The results show that initial trade orientation as well as the character of policy responses to external shocks affected rates of economic growth in the 1973–9 period in an important way. Thus, GNP growth rates differed by 1.0 percentage point between countries in the upper and in the lower quartiles of the distribution in terms of their trade orientation in 1973. There was further a

1.2 percentage-point difference in GNP growth rates between countries in the upper and the lower quartiles of the distribution in terms of reliance on export promotion, as against import substitution and additional net external financing, in response to the external shocks of the 1973–8 period.

The results are cumulative, indicating that both the initial trade orientation and the choice of adjustment policies in response to external shocks contributed to economic growth during the period under review in a crucial way. In fact, these two factors explain a large proportion of inter-country differences in GNP growth rates, which averaged 5.0 percent in the 43 developing countries under consideration during the 1973–9 period, with an upper quartile of 6.5 percent and a lower quartile of 3.3 percent.

CONCLUSION AND POLICY IMPLICATIONS

The review of protection in developed countries showed that, on average, trade barriers tend to be higher on agricultural products than on manufactures and within manufacturing tend to be concentrated in a few sectors. By contrast, developing countries protect manufacturing industries more than agriculture, and their barriers are both more widespread and more variable.

Non-tariff barriers are more important than tariffs in inhibiting trade between developed and developing countries; nevertheless, because of their escalation, tariffs continue to restrain access to developed-country markets in certain manufactured products. At the same time, with some important exceptions such as high-technology products, the developed countries' non-tariff barriers tend to be more prevalent, and their tariffs tend to be higher, on products of interest to developing countries than on their trade with each other.

It was further shown that the developed countries pay a large cost for maintaining employment in a few manufacturing sectors through protection. At the same time, such calculations underestimate the long-term costs of protection. This is because protection tends to slow down technological progress and leads to the misallocation of new investment.

The analysis of the cost of protection in developing countries focused primarily on the fact that countries with liberal trade regimes tend to grow faster and withstand better adverse developments in the international economy. The reason for their superior performance lies primarily in the lower degree of economic distortions and the greater flexibility associated with their trade regimes, which provide similar incentives to production for domestic and for foreign markets as well as to industry and agriculture.

Despite increasing protection in recent years, the extent of market penetration by developing countries in developed-country markets has risen, as has overall trade interdependence between the two groups of countries. This increased interdependence, in turn, raises the opportunity for mutually advantageous trade liberalization that can promote structural adjustment and stimulate long-term growth in both developed and developing countries.

Multilateral trade negotiations in the framework of the GATT provide an appropriate – indeed, the only – avenue for significant trade liberalization. Such negotiations would need to encompass all items of importance to trade between developed and developing countries in manufactures, agriculture and services, and include both tariff and non-tariff barriers. All developing countries and (especially) the Newly Industrialized Countries (NICs) need to be active participants in such negotiations and be prepared to offer a certain degree of reciprocity consistent with their level of development.[6]

NOTES

1. Table 12.1 reports import-weighted tariff averages that are relevant for comparisons of overall tariff averages and tariffs on products exported by the developing countries. As noted in Balassa and Balassa (1984), unweighted tariff averages show a similar pattern of escalation. At the same time, unweighted averages are higher than the weighted averages as the latter are reduced by reason of the fact that high (low) tariffs that discourage (encourage) imports are given low (high) weights.
2. The Tokyo Round did little to reduce the extent of tariff escalation; the ratios of effective to nominal protection are similar to those calculated by Yeats (1974) for the post-Kennedy Round situation.
3. For example, France limits the imports of automobiles from Japan to 3 percent of domestic sales while, for several years, the United States restricted imports from Japan to about 20 percent of domestic sales. Correspondingly, the own-import ratio was substantially lower in France than in the United States, even though non-tariff measures were much more restrictive in the first case than in the second.
4. At the same time, to the extent that all, or most, countries apply quantitative import restrictions to the same commodities, e.g., textiles, their share in world trade will be lowered, thereby affecting the world trade-weighted average of non-tariff measures.
5. The only country covered in the chapter for which such information is available is Japan. According to UNCTAD, health and safety measures and technical standards pertain to 48 percent of Japan's imports from industrial countries and to 17 percent of its imports from developing countries. See UNCTAD, *Problems of Protectionism and Structural Adjustment*, Report by the Secretariat, Part I: Restrictions to Trade and Structural Adjustment TD/B/1039, 28 January, 1985, Table 2.
6. A companion paper by the authors, 'Liberalizing Trade between Developed and Developing Countries', examines the objectives, scope and modalities of multilateral trade liberalization between developed and developing countries.

REFERENCES

Balassa, Bela (1984) 'Adjustment Policies in Developing Countries: A Reassessment', *World Development* 12(9): 955–72.
Balassa, Bela (1985) 'Exports, Policy Choices, and Economic Growth in Developing

Countries After the 1973 Oil Shock', *Journal of Development Economics* 18(1): 23–36. Reprinted as Chapter 18 in this volume.

Balassa, Bela, and Associates (1971) *The Structure of Protection in Developing Countries*. Baltimore, Johns Hopkins University Press.

Balassa, Bela, and Associates (1982) *Development Strategies in Semi-Industrial Economies*. A World Bank Research Publication. Baltimore, Johns Hopkins University Press.

Balassa, Bela, and Balassa, Carol (1984) 'Industrial Protection in the Developed Countries', *The World Economy* 7(2): 179–86. Reprinted as Chapter 11 in this volume.

Bhagwati, Jagdish N. (1978) *Anatomy and Consequences of Exchange Control Regimes*. Cambridge, Mass., Ballinger, pp. 19–78.

Bruton, H. J. (1967) 'Productivity Growth in Latin America', *American Economic Review* 57: 1099–116.

De Melo, Jaime (1978) 'Estimating the Costs of Protection: A General Equilibrium Approach ', *Quarterly Journal of Economics* 92(2): 209–26.

Feder, Gershon (1983) 'On Exports and Economic Growth', *Journal of Development Economics* 12(1): 59–73.

Finger, J. M., Hall, H. K. and Nelson, D. R. (1982) 'The Political Economy of Administered Protection', *American Economic Review* 72(3): 452–66.

Harris, R. G., with Cox, D. (1983) *Trade, Industrial Policy and Canadian Manufacturing*. Toronto, Ontario Economic Council.

Krueger, Anne O. (1978) *Liberalization Attempts and Consequences*. Cambridge, Mass., Ballinger.

Krueger, Anne O., and Michalopoulos, C (1985) 'Developing-Country Trade Policies and the International Economic System', in Ernest M. Preeg, ed., *Hard Bargaining Ahead: US Trade Policy and Developing Countries*. Overseas Development Council, US–Third World Policy Perspectives No. 4. New Brunswick, NJ, Transaction Books, pp. 39–57.

Michalopoulos, Constantine, and Jay, Keith (1973) 'Growth of Exports and Income in the Developing World: A Neoclassical View', AID Discussion Paper No. 28. Washington, DC, Agency for International Development.

Nogues, Julio J., Olechowski, Andrzej, and Winters, L. Alan (1985) 'The Establishment of Non-tariff Barriers to Industrial Countries' Imports'. World Bank Development Research Department Discussion Paper No.115. January.

Nugent, Jeffrey B. (1974) *Economic Integration in Central America: Empirical Investigations*. Baltimore, Johns Hopkins University Press.

Roger, Neil (1985) 'Trade Policy Regimes in Developing Countries'. Washington, DC, World Bank. Mimeographed.

Yeats, Alexander J. (1974) 'Effective Tariff Protection in the United States, the European Economic Community, and Japan', *The Quarterly Review of Economics and Business* 14(2): 41–50.

PART III

DEVELOPMENT STRATEGIES, EXPORTS AND GROWTH

13 · GROWTH STRATEGIES IN SEMI-INDUSTRIAL COUNTRIES

I

It has become fashionable to classify countries into three groups: developed, developing and Soviet-type economies.[1] This scheme of classification may have its usefulness from the point of view of international economic policy but its value for economic investigations is open to doubt. The separation of market economies into developed and developing divides a continuum into two segments and disregards the diversity found within each. Thus, although Argentina and Bolivia are both classified as developing countries and Italy as developed, the economy of Argentina offers greater similarities to that of Italy than to that of Bolivia.[2] There are considerable differences among the socialist countries too and – the special characteristics of their socio-economic system notwithstanding – they may be ranked along with market economies according to the level of their economic development. For example, Czechoslovakia has more in common with Austria than with North Vietnam, while the latter can be usefully compared to South Vietnam or Cambodia.

Despite its shortcomings, this threefold compartmentalization has carried over into economic work. Among economists, there are specialists of socialist countries and developing-area specialists, while integration in Western Europe has attracted people to the study of developed economies. Specialization along these lines has often led to oversimplification in studies dealing with any one of the three groups, and it accounts for the virtual absence of comparative investigations of countries that belong to different groups.

Research on this chapter was carried out as part of a consultant arrangement with the World Bank; it should not, however, be taken to represent the Bank's views. The author is indebted to Helen Hughes, Donald Keesing, Boris Pesek, Daniel Schydlowsky and Paul Streeten for helpful suggestions on an earlier draft. Comments received on the occasion of lectures on the topic at the Karl Marx University of Economic Science in Budapest and at Columbia and Stanford Universities are also gratefully acknowledged. First published in *Quarterly Journal of Economics*, February 1970.

This chapter takes a different approach; its aim is to evaluate the economic policies followed by semi-industrial countries in the post-war period, irrespective of their place in the conventional classification scheme. Rather than contrasting the experience of market economies and socialist economies, or that of developed and developing countries, the emphasis will be on similarities and dissimilarities in the attitudes taken towards participation in the international division of labor. The benefits of this participation depend chiefly on factors such as the level of industrial development and the size of the domestic market, which are independent of socio-economic systems.

An inward-looking strategy tends to minimize these benefits by fostering the expansion of production to serve domestic needs and favoring it over exports *and* imports. In so doing, discrimination is introduced among domestic activities since import-competing industries are benefited at the expense of export sectors. There is also discrimination in favor of domestic production as against imports, and, in individual industries, production for domestic needs is encouraged as compared to exports. These three forms of discrimination are negligible or non-existent under an outward-looking strategy. Such a strategy provides essentially the same opportunities for individual industries; it does not create a bias against imports; and it does not discriminate between the domestic and the foreign sales of a given industry.[3]

In market economies, the extent of the discrimination among domestic activities can be indicated by the effective rates of protection, defined as the percentage excess of domestic value added over free trade value added, obtainable by reason of the imposition of tariffs, subsidies and other measures which affect relative prices in the domestic economy.[4] In turn, the degree of discrimination against imports in import-competing industries, and that against exports in traditional export industries, is shown by adjusting the effective rates calculated at actual exchange rates by the extent of overvaluation as compared to the free trade situation.[5] Finally, we can estimate the extent of discrimination against exports and in favor of production for domestic use in protected industries; such discrimination exists because protection permits firms to charge higher prices in domestic markets, whereas they have to sell abroad at the going world market price.[6]

Estimates on the extent of the three forms of discrimination can be made for market economies where the allocation of resources responds to price signals. This is not the case in socialist countries where firms act on the basis of central directives pertaining to output targets and input allocations. Although prices play a role in influencing the product composition of output in industrial firms, and especially in agricultural establishments, they do not express relative scarcities and have no market-clearing function. In socialist countries we have to rely, therefore, on actual allocations to evaluate the economic policies followed. The same conclusion applies to imports which are subject to licensing in centrally planned economies. Licensing or quantitative restrictions are, however, used in some market economies too.

The described characteristics represent inward-looking and outward-looking strategies in ideal or pure form. There are, however, a variety of intermediate solutions between these extremes under which the three forms of discrimination may appear in varying degrees, and such solutions are also observed in practice. But to analyze the major characteristics of inward-looking and outward-looking strategies, and the results they lead to, one should select relatively 'pure' cases of each. This purpose is served in the chapter by taking Argentina and Chile among market economies, as well as Czechoslovakia and Hungary among centrally planned economies, as examples of countries applying inward-looking policies and by selecting Denmark and Norway as representatives of an outward-looking strategy. I will examine the post-war experience of these countries until the mid-1960s, when various reforms were proposed or partially introduced in countries following inward-looking policies. These reforms will be noted in the concluding section of the chapter.

Since the purview of the chapter extends over the post-war period, I have relied on data for 1953, the first 'normal' year after the Korean War ended, in classifying countries according to the level of their industrial development. For this purpose, I have used data on the share of manufacturing in commodity production[7] rather than in the gross national product since the latter comparison is affected to a considerable extent by the rising share of services at higher income levels.

Among larger countries, the United States, with manufacturing accounting for 70 percent of value added in commodity production, and the United Kingdom, France and Germany, with ratios of approximately 65 percent, belong to the industrial group. In turn, the semi-industrial category has been defined to include countries where the share of manufacturing is in the 40–50 percent range. Among the six countries selected for this study, in 1957 the share of manufacturing in commodity production was 50 percent in Argentina, 44 percent in Chile, 47 percent in Denmark, and 51 percent in Norway. By adjusting market prices to reflect factor costs, the relevant figure is estimated at about 40 percent in Hungary in 1955,[8] whereas Czechoslovakia was at the upper end of the range.[9]

The countries in question all have relatively small domestic markets. Their 1955 gross national products, expressed in purchasing power parities, ranged from $4 billion in Chile and Norway to $14–15 billion in Argentina and Czechoslovakia; by comparison, the GNP of the three large European countries (France, Germany and the United Kingdom) was in the range of $50–70 billion.[10] This choice has been made because the effects of economic policies, as well as the recommendations made for their improvement, depend on the size of national markets.

II

An inward-looking strategy may conceivably aim at the expansion of industry, mining or agriculture; in practice, countries following such a strategy have favored manufacturing industries at the expense of primary producing sectors. This purpose has been served by turning the terms of trade against primary activities and by using direct and indirect measures to ensure the flow of investment funds to the manufacturing sector.[11] At the same time, the protection of industry has entailed discrimination against imports and against export activities.

In Argentina and Chile quantitative restrictions or high tariffs – averaging over 150 percent in 1960[12] – on imports of manufactured goods have protected this sector from foreign competition, favored production for domestic use over exports and discriminated against primary activities. Exports have been further penalized by tariffs on their inputs and by the overvaluation of the exchange rate. In turn, in Czechoslovakia and Hungary, the movement of resources from primary activities into manufacturing has been accomplished by keeping the prices of agricultural products at low levels and channeling investment funds into manufacturing industries by administrative fiat. Protection against imports has taken the form of licensing, while the system of incentives applied on the firm level has generally discriminated against exports.

By contrast, in Denmark and Norway tariffs are not only substantially lower than in Latin America but are also below the level of duties in the major industrial nations. In 1958, tariffs on manufactured goods averaged 6.5 percent in Denmark and 11.7 percent in Norway, while the corresponding figures were 18.8 percent in the United Kingdom, 16.8 percent in the United States, and 14.5 percent in the European Common Market.[13] Thus, there is little discrimination against imports and against production for exports. The dispersion of duties being low,[14] the system of incentives in effect hardly creates discrimination between manufactured and primary goods, or among individual industries in the manufacturing sector.

Relative prices in Denmark and Norway thus roughly correspond to world market price relations and, in the absence of government intervention, the allocation of investments responds to the incentives provided by these prices. By eschewing discrimination among domestic industries, between domestic and foreign goods in home markets, and between production for home and foreign markets, these policies have encouraged specialization within the manufacturing sector according to comparative advantage. Apart from the electro-metallurgical and electro-chemical industries based on the availability of hydro-electricity, Norway has specialized in products with a strong home market base (e.g., shipbuilding and water-power machinery), as well as in industries requiring skilled labor. Skilled labor-intensive industries also contribute in an important way to Denmark's exports while the availability of domestic raw materials has given an impetus to the development of the Danish food-processing and construction machinery industries. In turn, industries relying to a large extent on unskilled and semi-skilled labor (leather, textiles, footwear and clothing) have grown at a slower rate and imports provide an increasing proportion of domestic consumption in the two countries.

Conversely, inward orientation is characterized by the parallel development of a wide range of industries. In disregard of comparative advantage, countries applying this strategy generally aimed at limiting imports to goods which are not produced at home or are not available in sufficient quantities. Import licensing and quantitative restrictions serve this purpose in Czechoslovakia and Hungary. These measures were also used by Argentina and Chile in the post-war period, although in Argentina they have been replaced by tariffs which are often prohibitive.

Differences in the system of incentives between the two groups of countries further affect the pattern of intra-industry specialization and the extent of participation in the international division of the production process. Low tariffs and realistic exchange rates in Denmark and Norway provide inducement to firms to specialize in narrow ranges of products within a given commodity category while other varieties are imported. Firms in these countries also participate in the international division of the production process by manufacturing parts, components and accessories for assembly abroad. On the other hand, in countries pursuing inward-looking policies, the protection of domestic manufacturing activities and discrimination against exports of manufactured goods limit the scope of intra-industry specialization and the countries' participation in the international division of the production process.

The effects of these policies are exemplified in consumer goods industries. Imports of non-durable consumer goods in countries applying an inward-looking strategy are non-existent or negligible. In 1965, the share of imports in the domestic consumption of textiles, clothing and footwear did not exceed 1–2 percent in Argentina, Chile, Czechoslovakia and Hungary, while the corresponding import proportions were 62, 19 and 20 percent in Denmark, and 51, 23 and 29 percent in Norway.[15] Also, Argentina and Czechoslovakia import few passenger automobiles,[16] and all four countries applying an inward-looking strategy have made a start in the import substitution of durable consumer goods. In turn, Denmark and Norway continue to rely chiefly on imports of consumer durables.

The lack of an adequate consideration of the economic cost of policy alternatives is also characteristic of countries applying an inward-looking strategy. Raul Prebisch notes with regard to the Latin American countries that 'the criterion by which the choice was determined was based not on considerations of economic expediency but on immediate feasibility, whatever the cost of production'.[17] The governments of these countries granted requests for protection by individual entrepreneurs more or less auto-matically, without paying attention to the cost of protection for the national economy. Decisions to this effect originally responded to balance-of-pay-ments difficulties and subsequently reflected a policy of 'import substitution at any cost'.[18]

But the economic evaluation of alternative policies would encounter difficulties in these countries even if this were the policy makers' intentions since, due to the haphazard application of protective measures, prices do not express relative costs on the national economy level. Variations in the rate of protection of value added in processing – the effective rate of protection – are even larger,[19] yet it is the latter that is relevant in judging the effects of trade policies on the allocation of resources.

Similar considerations apply to Czechoslovakia and Hungary. Throughout much of the post-war period there was little concern with the economic costs of policy alternatives, and, at any rate, the lack of scarcity prices would have hardly permitted such an appraisal.[20] Correspondingly, plans often became a matter of bargaining between the industrial ministry and the individual firms, as well as between the planning board and the industrial ministries. The bargaining power of the ministries also influenced the allocation of invest-ment funds, and contributed to the continuation of the policy of simulta-neously expanding all industries.

The interrelationships of individual industries are also often neglected in countries following an inward-looking strategy. In Argentina and Chile, at the request of their would-be producers, high tariffs were imposed on inter-mediate goods without much consideration given to the impact on the cost of final products. An example is the case of caustic soda, where the imposition of tariffs made Argentine soap exports unprofitable. In turn, in Hungary the high cost of domestic coal and steel raised the cost of the coal- and steel-using industries, and large investments in steel delayed the substitution of alumi-num for steel in Hungarian industries.

The neglect of the time factor in making investment decisions in countries engaged in inward-looking policies is a further consideration. Because of inflation, real rates of interest in Argentina and Chile were negative during much of the post-war period, necessitating a rationing of investment funds by the banks. In an inflationary situation, the method of valuing capital at historical costs further entails an underestimation of depreciation allowances for fixed capital. The low cost of capital, in turn, may have contributed to the application of capital-intensive methods and to the expansion of capital-intensive industries.[21]

For ideological reasons, interest on capital was not included in cost calculations in Czechoslovakia and Hungary, and depreciation charges were set overly low by excluding "moral" depreciation due to technological change. Correspondingly, government decisions on choice among investment projects took no account of the time factor, and favored relatively capital-intensive methods. At the same time, in the absence of interest charges, firms often regarded capital practically as a free good.

III

The inefficiencies in resource allocation resulting from discrimination among and within sectors, and from distortions in the relative prices of outputs and inputs, entail a static cost for the national economies of the countries following an inward-looking strategy. This cost has been estimated by A. C. Harberger as 2.5 percent of national income in Chile;[22] in a criticism of this estimate I have suggested that it may actually surpass one-tenth of Chile's national income.[23] Rough calculations based on data on nominal and effective tariffs shown in the same paper give similar results for Argentina. Comparable estimates have not been made for Czechoslovakia and Hungary, but available information on the allocation process under centralized planning points to substantial inefficiencies in the two countries.[24]

The infant industry argument of international trade theory suggests that an industry should be protected if the cost of protection is recouped as the industry becomes competitive in the world market.[25] In a more general form, the infant industry argument can be re-interpreted by considering as acceptable a reallocation of resources that raises the discounted value of future national income without additional sacrifices in terms of work or saving. Such an allocation would lead to increases in productivity on the national economy level which offset the initial loss due to protection.

Whichever formulation is chosen, the gist of the matter is that the present (static) cost of protection is accepted for the sake of future (dynamic) benefits, when it is assumed that infant industries will 'grow up' and become competitive in the world market. The emphasis is on the temporary nature of protection, which is needed to shelter the fledgling industry and will be removed after maturity is reached.

In countries following an inward-looking policy, however, there are generally no expectations for the removal of protection, and governments as well as firms act on the assumption that protection will be maintained *ad infinitum.* Inward-looking policies, then, bear only a superficial resemblance to the infant industry argument; the former envisages continuing protection of manufacturing industry, while the latter considers protection as a temporary deviation from the free trade norm.[26] The continued sheltering of domestic industry from foreign competition, in turn, involves a dynamic cost to the national economy in the form of opportunities forgone for improvements in productivity.

Various factors hinder increases in productivity in countries that follow an inward-looking strategy. For one thing, the countries in question are characterized by sellers' markets; producers have a dominant position and users have practically no choice between domestic and foreign products nor often among domestic products. For another, the limitations imposed by the size of domestic markets provide a constraint to the application of large-scale production methods.

In Argentina and Chile, the limited size of the home markets has led to monopoly positions in some industries, while in others there is rarely effective competition because the high profits ensured by protection are conducive to a 'live and let live' attitude on the part of the entrepreneur. Domestic firms, as well as the subsidiaries of foreign companies, generally follow a policy of low turnover and high profits. This is exemplified by the case of the Argentine automobile industry, where in 1965 12 firms had a combined turnover one-sixth that of Fiat in Italy.

In centrally planned economies, the system of material allocation in effect does not allow the buyer to choose among suppliers. At the same time, the suppliers have little inducement to cater to the users' wishes since the incentive system generally rewards the fulfillment of the production plan that is accomplished on the completion of the product rather than on its sale. The users, then, may not get the products they want or may have to accept products which do not correspond to their needs.[27]

Inflationary pressures due to excessive aggregate demand further contribute to the existence of sellers' markets. While this is not a necessary concomitant of an inward-looking strategy, it has been observed in semi-industrial countries following such a strategy. In Argentina and Chile, public policies created disproportions between aggregate demand and supply which led to rapid inflation. In turn, in centrally planned economies, 'taut planning' which aimed at the mobilization of all available resources gave rise to shortages and queuing in commodities at various levels of fabrication.[28]

The lack of incentives to cater to the users' needs has often led to deterioration of product quality in countries pursuing inward-looking policies,[29] and the existence of sellers' markets has failed to provide adequate inducements for technical progress. As long as firms have assured outlets for their products, they will not concern themselves with product quality and will tend to avoid the risk associated with the introduction of new products and innovating activity in general. In market economies, the easy profits ensured by protection, and in centrally planned economies, the objective of fulfilling the production plan, explain the tendency for risk aversion on the part of the firm. On the other hand, the carrot and the stick of competition keep firms on their toes in open economies, where success depends on the firm's ability to satisfy the buyers' needs, to improve product quality and technology, and to introduce new products.

The inward-looking strategy also restricts the application of large-scale production methods which can be employed in open economies that in part rely on foreign outlets. Economies of scale depend on the size of the market and can be obtained through the construction of larger plants to produce a single product (economies of scale in the traditional sense), through reducing product variety in individual plants (horizontal specialization), and through the manufacturing of various parts, components and accessories of a given product or products in separate establishments (vertical specialization).[30]

Available evidence suggests that an outward-looking policy may lead to considerable gains in countries of the size considered in this chapter. Among individual industries, aluminum and automobiles provide examples of economies of scale in one-product industries. In the case of aluminum, the cost of production has been estimated to decline from $1250 to $600 per ton as plant output rises from 10 to 180 thousand tons a year. Norway produces aluminum in efficient-sized plants, with an annual output totalling 330 thousand tons, while Czechoslovakian and Hungarian plants are relatively small and the two countries have an annual output of only 60 thousand tons each. In turn, efficient scale exceeds 250 thousand cars a year in the production, and 60 thousand in the assembly, of automobiles. Yet the annual production of the Czech Skoda factory hardly reaches 100 thousand; in Argentina 12 factories share an annual output of 140 thousand cars, while in Chile 20 firms assemble some 10 thousand automobiles a year.[31] Furthermore, a study of six Latin American industries shows potential savings of 15–20 percent for methanol and formaldehyde, pulp and paper, and lathes, and savings of 10–15 percent for nitrogenous fertilizers, tractors, and powdered milk and cheese, in the event that production were to be undertaken in an integrated Latin America rather than in the individual countries.[32]

Comparisons of unit costs in domestic and foreign plants of American firms, reported in a National Industrial Conference Board study covering a wide range of industries, also provide evidence of scale economies. According to the study, costs in foreign operations are on the average 29 percent higher than in the United States whenever the foreign plant's output is less than 5 percent of that of the US plant; the percentage ratio of foreign to domestic costs falls to 106 in the case of output ratios of 5 to 10 percent, it is 98 in the case of output ratios of 10 to 50 percent, and 85 if the foreign plant produces more than one-half of the US factory's output.[33] Finally, an investigation of 221 US firms, mainly in the chemical industry, petroleum refining and electric power, showed investment costs as well as operating costs per unit to decline by 0.2–0.3 percent for a 1 percent increase in output.[34]

Horizontal specialization through reducing product variety in individual plants results in further scale economies. In large countries multiproduct plants can specialize in a narrower range of commodities and hence have longer production runs. The lengthening of production runs, in turn, permits improvements in manufacturing efficiency through 'learning by doing', reduces the expenses associated with resetting machines and reorganizing work, and allows for the use of specialized machinery. As I have elsewhere shown, horizontal specialization may bring considerable gains even in the large European industrial countries;[35] the benefits are correspondingly higher in the smaller countries under consideration. Textiles, machine tools and shipbuilding are frequently mentioned examples.

Finally, gains derived from vertical specialization through the separation in individual plants of various activities leading to the production of a given commodity should be noted. While in some instances the final product may be produced on an efficient scale in a small country, this will rarely be the case with regard to the manufacturing of parts, components and accessories, so that the 'backward integration' of production involves considerable costs.[36] The benefits of vertical specialization are of especial importance in the case of machinery and transport equipment, and have contributed to the international division of the production process in countries following an outward-looking strategy. By contrast, countries engaged in inward-looking policies aim at the national production of parts, components and accessories for domestic use although not for exports.[37]

It may be objected that while the conclusions on scale economies apply to Argentina and Chile, where exports of manufactured goods are negligible, this is not the case in Czechoslovakia and Hungary, which export manufactures to other Comecon member countries. But although specialization agreements on trucks, tractors and some machine tools have permitted large-scale production in the framework of Comecon, such agreements have been restricted to a relatively small group of products.[38] Also, there are few instances of the division of the production process within Comecon, and intra-area trade in non-durable consumer goods is at low levels.

IV

As regards the economic effects of alternative development strategies, their influence on foreign trade should first be noted. To begin with, the inward-looking strategy has detrimental effects on traditional primary exports. In market economies, the high degree of protection of manufactured goods discriminates against primary products, which are also put in an unfavorable position in the world market due to overvalued exchange rates and high input prices. Low prices paid for farm products provide disincentives for the agricultural exports of centrally planned economies, too.

In Argentina, the situation was aggravated by reason of the fact that low prices on beef, the major Argentine export product, led to increased consumption and thus further reduced the export surplus. These measures contributed to the decline in Argentina's share in world markets; between 1934-8 and 1964-6, major Argentine primary exports on the average remained unchanged while world exports of the same commodities doubled.[39] In turn, despite excellent market possibilities, Hungarian exports of several agricultural commodities (e.g. cattle, goose liver, fodder seeds and beans) decreased in absolute terms from levels reached during the inter-war period, and the slow growth of productivity necessitated imports of cereals and meat, which were formerly major export products.[40] Finally, Chile's share fell from 28 percent in 1938 to 22 percent in 1964–6 in world exports of copper, which accounts for three-fifths of the country's export earnings.[41] The economic policies followed also hindered the development of Chilean agriculture, thereby impeding the expansion of exports and contributing to increased food imports.

There is practically no discrimination against primary exports in countries following an outward-looking strategy. Among these countries, Denmark competes with Argentina in beef and canned meat and has greatly increased its share in the world exports of both these products. All in all, the major Danish primary exports rose by three-fourths between 1934–8 and 1964–6 although the increase in the world exports of the same commodities hardly exceeded 40 percent.[42] Comparable data are not available for Norway.

Of even greater interest is the success of semi-industrial countries in transforming their export pattern in the face of unfavorable trends in the demand for their traditional exports. In the post-war period, world demand increased at a lower rate for primary products than for manufactures, and a shift towards the latter could have contributed to a rapid growth of exports. Such was the case in Denmark and Norway, where the adoption of realistic exchange rates and low tariffs on inputs and outputs favored the export orientation of manufacturing industries. Firms had to compete with foreign producers in home markets, and they could reduce costs by selling abroad since higher output levels and greater specialization have made it possible to use large-scale production methods.

These considerations largely explain the increase in the ratio of exports to value added in manufacturing from 14 percent in 1950 to 33 percent in 1965 in Denmark, and from 26 percent to 44 percent in Norway. In the same period, the share of manufactured goods in total exports increased from 19 to 42 percent and from 36 to 52 percent in the two countries respectively, while their total exports rose at an annual rate of 7 percent.[43] It should be added that, in the case of Norway, a large proportion of exports were relatively simple intermediate products (fertilizer, paper, aluminum and ferro-alloys) in the early post-war period. Excluding these products, the shift appears to be considerably larger, with the share of manufactured exports rising from 9 to 42 percent as a proportion of value added in manufacturing, and from 10 to 32 percent as a proportion of total exports.[44]

By contrast, the inward-looking strategy discriminates against the exports of manufactured goods. Overvalued exchange rates and high material costs often make exports unprofitable, and, at any rate, there is little incentive to export as long as safe domestic outlets are provided through protection against foreign competition. This may explain why in Argentina and Chile exports of manufactures actually declined from 1952–3 to 1962–3, amounting to less than 3 percent of value added in manufacturing in the two countries.[45]

Only after the establishment of the Latin American Free Trade Area did exports in these countries approach the earlier figure.

The inward-looking strategy aims to substitute domestic for foreign goods and thus to reduce reliance on imports. If, following Chenery, import substitution is defined by reference to changes in imports as a percentage of domestic consumption, this policy does not appear to have been successful in Argentina and Chile during the post-war period.[46] While these countries have reduced the share of imports in the domestic consumption of manufactured consumer goods, this decline has been more than offset by the rise in foreign purchases of food, raw materials, fuels, intermediate products and machinery, due in part to the needs of domestic manufacturing industries for imported inputs and in part to the adverse repercussions of inward-looking policies on primary production.

These – in part unforeseen – effects of the inward-looking strategy contributed to the rise in the ratio of imports to GNP from 4.9 percent in 1953 to 7.1 percent in 1965 in Argentina, and from 9.9 to 12.4 percent in Chile.[47] Along with the slow expansion of exports, increases in the share of imports thus imposed a limitation on the rate of economic growth in these countries. At the same time, the rising importance of input-imports increased their vulnerability to foreign exchange crises.

In the early post-war period the declared aim of both Czechoslovakia and Hungary was to follow the Soviet example in proceeding on a broad front of industrial expansion and limiting imports to a necessary minimum. Thus, it was held that 'the primary task of socialist foreign trade is to procure, through import, those producer goods and consumer goods which are not produced and not available in necessary quantity at home'.[48] However, just as in the case of Latin American countries, the results did not correspond to expectations. For one thing, the concentration of the expansion in the material-intensive branches of manufacturing, such as metals, non-electrical machinery and transport equipment, required increasing imports of raw materials as well as machine tools. For another, discrimination against agriculture led to rising food imports. Greater import needs, in turn, necessitated higher exports.[49]

The growth of exports from Czechoslovakia and Hungary was concentrated in the Comecon countries, where 'taut planning' brought with it an increased need for imports. Nevertheless, there is evidence that the countries of Eastern Europe have not fully utilized their trade potential. Thus, while in 1928 there was no significant difference in the volume of trade of countries in Eastern and Western Europe which had about the same per capita incomes and population, in 1956 and 1962 the volume of trade in East European countries was only 50–60 percent of that in comparable West European nations.[50]

An important factor hindering the expansion of trade has been risk aversion on the part of the planners, who aimed at reducing the uncertainties associated with foreign trade and, in the absence of scarcity prices, had no reliable guide as to what to export or import.[51] And while political considerations limited trade with market economies, the practice of bilateralism, the lack of success of planning on the Comecon level, as well as problems pertaining to pricing,[52] have been restrictive influences on trade among socialist countries. Finally, on the firm level, the preponderance of sellers' markets and overcentralization in the organization of trade have provided disincentives to export.[53]

As regards the composition of trade, we find that Czech and Hungarian exports to Comecon countries consist largely of manufactured goods, with machinery and transport equipment accounting for nearly one-half of the total. These countries have been less successful in selling manufactured goods in the West; the share of machinery and equipment in Hungarian exports to Western developed countries was only 4.5 percent in 1965, somewhat lower than during the 1930s.[54]

The explanation lies in differences in technical requirements between the two markets; Czech and Hungarian producers could meet the higher technological standards of the West only in relatively few commodities. At the same time, with firms having assured outlets for their products at home and in the sheltered markets of the socialist countries, there was little incentive for technological improvements that would make possible increasing exports to the West. A Hungarian observer speaks of 'conservative anti-innovation tendencies at home, while abroad a marathon race of innovations was taking place'.[55] In general, in both Hungary and Czechoslovakia, considerable attention is now given to the existence of a double technological gap, between the United States and Western Europe, as well as between Western Europe and Eastern Europe.[56]

V

The policies followed in Czechoslovakia and Hungary, as well as in Argentina and Chile, have led to the isolation of the manufacturing industries of these countries from the world market. At the same time, the limitations of their domestic markets impose a constraint on the possibilities of internal expansion. Thus, the growth of production necessarily slows down after the import substitution process has been completed in industries where this has been relatively easy. In turn, the cost of import substitution tends to rise as production is undertaken in industries where large-scale economies are of greater importance.

An inward-looking policy may make possible a period of rapid growth – as it actually did, especially in Czechoslovakia and Hungary – but these factors eventually necessitate increasing efforts for an additional increment in output, so that a deceleration in the rate of economic growth will take place unless there is a compensating rise in the share of investments in GNP. In the four inward-looking economies under consideration this stage was reached around 1960. While comparisons for relatively short periods have obvious limitations and there are difficulties in interpreting incremental capital–output ratios, changes in these ratios may be used as a rough indication of the rise in effort per unit increase of output.

Between 1955–60 and 1960–5, the incremental capital–output ratio quadrupled in Czechoslovakia and doubled in Hungary,[57] and, despite the increased share of resources devoted to investment, the rate of growth of the net material product declined from 5.4 to 2.0 percent in the former and from 6.6 to 4.5 percent in the latter. Incremental capital–output ratios rose between the two periods from 5.3 to 6.3 in Argentinà and from 2.4 to 2.9 in Chile so that an increase in the share of investment was necessary to maintain the rate of growth of GNP at the level reached in the first period. By contrast, Denmark and Norway showed an acceleration in the growth rate (from 4.6 to 4.9 percent and from 3.5 to 5.5), and Norway, although not Denmark, also experienced a decline in the incremental capital–output ratio.

It should be added that the rate of growth of national income is generally overestimated in countries following an inward-looking strategy. This is the case because distortions of relative prices in these countries entail the overvaluation of manufacturing output, which grew relatively rapidly, and the undervaluation of primary production, which increased at a slower rate. In the case of Argentina, I have estimated that valuing output at world market prices would reduce the annual rate of growth of GDP from 2.6 to 2.2 percent in the period 1953–63. In turn, the adjustment of prices to reflect production costs, including an allowance for capital, would reduce the growth rate in the period 1960–5 from 4.5 to 3.5 percent in Hungary.[58]

VI

This chapter has examined the economic policies followed by selected semi-industrial countries in the post-war period. It has contrasted the inward-looking strategies applied by Argentina and Chile, as well as by Czechoslovakia and Hungary, with the outward-looking strategies of Denmark and Norway. Countries applying inward-looking strategies tend to minimize the gains from international specialization by favoring production for domestic use over exports and imports and by benefiting manufacturing activities at the expense of primary production. Firms in these countries do not have to meet the test of the world market, whereas the outward-looking strategy exposes domestic producers to world competition by providing essentially the same opportunities for domestic and foreign producers in home markets and for domestic producers in home and in foreign markets.

The outward-looking strategy thus encourages specialization according to comparative advantage, and also provides incentives for intra-industry specialization and for participation in the international division of the production process. By contrast, inward orientation is characterized by the parallel development of a wide range of industries, and it aims to limit imports to goods which are not available at home or are not available in sufficient quantities. This objective, along with the discrimination against export activities, leaves little scope for intra-industry specialization or for participation in the international division of the production process.

Nor is there evidence that the static cost of protection would be outweighed by the dynamic benefits of the inward-looking strategy. Rather, the continued sheltering of domestic industry from foreign competition and disincentives to exporting involve a dynamic cost to the national economy in the form of opportunities forgone for improvements in productivity. On the one hand, there is little incentive to improve production methods and product quality; on the other, discrimination against exports and the objective of industrial expansion on a broad fron limit the scope of exploiting large-scale economies.

Thus, we cannot accept as a criterion of success the fact that the structure of manufacturing industry in countries following an inward-looking strategy approaches that of the industrial nations.[59] While the former group of countries has established a wide range of industries, the industries in question generally use backward technical methods, manufacture products of low quality, and have not achieved the extent of intra-industry specialization that is desirable under modern conditions. Using an apt expression introduced by Béla Kádár in his book cited earlier, one may say that countries pursuing inward-looking policies have built up an industrial structure which is 'prematurely old' in the sense that it is based on small-scale production with inadequate specialization and outdated machinery. Moreover, the countries in question have had little success in expanding the most modern branches within individual industries and they have also fallen behind Denmark and Norway in some technologically advanced industries, such as chemicals and plastics.

The adverse consequences of inward-looking policies have become especially pronounced after the import substitution process has been completed in industries where the replacement of imports by domestic products has been relatively easy. The result has been increasing efforts per the unit increment of output, accompanied by a deceleration in the rate of growth of output and/or an increase in the share of investments in GNP. During the period under review, to a varying extent, both these results are observable in the countries in question.

The increasing difficulties experienced by countries following an inward-looking strategy have led governments to introduce changes in their economic policies. In Argentina, the extent of discrimination against primary production and exports has been reduced and the protection of manufacturing industries moderated through a simultaneous devaluation and a lowering of tariffs. In Chile an effort has been made to reduce the degree of overvaluation while subsidies are used to promote non-traditional exports.

In Czechoslovakia and in Hungary, too, the economic reforms are intimately linked up with the desire for greater participation in the international division of labor and for increasing the benefits of such participation.[60] The deficiencies of the system of centralized planning are especially pronounced in the foreign sector, yet international trade is of great importance for countries of this size. At the same time, it is understood that the proposed decentralization of decision making and the application of profit incentives cannot be successful without the establishment of a more rational price structure linked to world market prices, and without competition from imports. It has also been proposed that these countries participate in the international division of the production process by manufacturing parts and components for assembly abroad.

The principal questions seem to be how far-reaching the new policies will be and whether they will be carried out consistently. The answers to these questions will greatly depend on political considerations. Changes in the present system of protection and resource allocation are bound to give rise to unemployment in adversely affected industries and also encounter opposition on the part of vested interests. In Argentina and Chile, most firms appear to be opposed to changes in the status quo, which ensures comfortable profits, and their opposition largely explains the lack of success of the Latin American Free Trade Association (LAFTA). In Czechoslovakia and Hungary, the international political situation, opposition from high-cost industries, and fear of loss of positions on the part of officials of a conservative bent will influence the outcome.

It follows that in countries which have thus far applied inward-looking policies, a 'strategy' would need to be devised for the transition to a more outward-looking stance. Apart from the political constraints, such a strategy would have to take account of the country's existing industrial structure and its special characteristics, such as market size, resource endowment, geographical location and market access. The enumerated characteristics are also pertinent for the choice of development strategies in countries at a lower level of industrialization. At the same time, these countries can learn from the successes and the failures of the semi-industrial countries whose policies were examined in this chapter.

NOTES

1. This is not to say that there would be unanimity as to the composition of these groups. Thus, the countries of Southern Europe are considered developed by the United Nations and less developed by the International Bank for Reconstruction and Development and the Organization for European Cooperation and

Development. Moreover, at one time or another, Yugoslavia has been classified in each of the three groups.

2. Needless to say, the differences are magnified if comparison is made with backward economies in Africa and Asia.

3. A similar distinction is made by D. B. Keesing in his 'Outward-looking Policies and Economic Development', *Economic Journal*, June 1967, pp. 303–20, but Keesing groups together all developing countries regardless of the stage of their economic development, and restricts his attention to policies applied within the manufacturing sector.

4. On the concept and measurement of effective rates, see Bela Balassa (1965) 'Tariff Protection in Industrial Countries: An Evaluation', *Journal of Political Economy*, Dec., pp. 573–94. Reprinted as Chapter 10 in this volume; and W. M. Corden (1966) 'The Structure of the Tariff System and the Effective Protection Rate', *idem*, June, pp. 221–37.

5. This adjustment is necessary because of the interdependence of protective measures and the exchange rate. For a detailed argument, see Bela Balassa (1971) *The Structure of Protection in Developing Countries*. (Baltimore, The Johns Hopkins University Press).

6. This would not be the case if export subsidies were applied at the same rate as tariffs. But the application of such subsidies is the exception rather than the rule in semi-industrial countries.

7. Commodity production has been defined to include agriculture, forestry, hunting and fishing; mining and quarrying; manufacturing; construction; electricity, gas and water.

8. Thad Paul Alton (1963) *Hungarian National Income and Product in 1955* (New York, Columbia University Press), p. 76; and United Nations (1963) *The Growth of World Industry, 1938–1961* (New York), p. 372.

9. While there are no data on manufacturing taken by itself, in 1955 the combined share of manufacturing, mining, electricity, gas and water in commodity production, estimated at factor costs, was 58 percent in Czechoslovakia if returns to labor in agriculture are taken to equal total net income at the realized prices (Thad Paul Alton and Associates (1962) *Czechoslovak National Income and Product, 1947–1948 and 1955–1956*, New York, Columbia University Press, p. 61). The corresponding figure for Hungary was 47 percent (*Hungarian National Income and Product in 1955*, p. 76).

10. The relevant figures (in 1955 US dollars) are Argentina, $14.0 billion; Chile, $3.8 billion; Denmark, $5.6 billion; Norway, $4.4 billion; Czechoslovakia, $15.3 billion; and Hungary, $8.2 billion. Sources: Bela Balassa (1964) *Trade Prospects for Developing Countries* (Homewood, Ill., R. D. Irwin), pp. 370, 384–5; S. N. Braithwaite (1968) 'Real Income Levels in Latin America', *Income and Wealth*, June, pp. 113–82; F. L. Pryor and G. F. Staller (1966) 'The Dollar Values of the Gross National Products in Eastern Europe 1955', *The Economics of Planning*, (1), pp. 1–26.

11. On the basis of data on the share of industry in the allocation of capital and labor in the Argentine economy, Diaz-Alejandro argues, however, that 'it seems hardly justified to say that the problem in Argentina during the last 35 years has been one of "too much industry".' Nevertheless, among the commodity-producing sectors, the share of manufacturing industry in the allocation of capital and labor increased to a considerable extent. These proportions rose from one-fourth for 1925–9 to three-fourths for the increment between 1925–9 and 1957–61 in the case of capital, and from one-third to two-thirds in the case of labor. Thus, if we adjust for the growth of the service sector which, apart from policies favoring housing

and the public sector, was caused by the secular rise in the demand for services, the data show the preponderant role assigned to the industrial sector. See Carlos F. Diaz-Alejandro (1966) 'An Economic Interpretation of Argentine Growth since 1930', Part I, *Journal of Development Studies*, Oct., pp. 19–20.

12. Unweighted averages of tariffs, special charges, and the tariff equivalent of prepayment requirements on durable and non-durable consumer goods and capital goods were 159 percent in Argentina and 177 percent in Chile. See Santiago Macario (1964) 'Protectionism and Industrialization in Latin America', *United Nations Economic Bulletin for Latin America*, March, p. 75.

13. Weighted averages of tariffs for 91 three- and four-digit Standard International Trade Classification categories are shown in Political and Economic Planning, *Atlantic Tariffs and Trade* (London, Allen & Unwin, 1962) pp. 3–62. The combined imports of the OECD countries have been used as weights in averaging the Political and Economic Planning tariff data for the individual categories, which themselves are unweighted averages.

14. In 1958, tariffs exceeded 20 percent in only 1 out of 91 industrial categories in Denmark and in 11 categories in Norway, while this was the case for 37 categories in the United States and 35 categories in the United Kingdom (*ibid.*). This comparison does not hold for the European Economic Community, where the averaging of the tariffs of the member countries reduced the dispersion of duties.

15. National production and import statistics.

16. It should be noted that while Czechoslovakia exported automobiles before the Second World War, imports then exceeded exports by a considerable margin.

17. Raul Prebisch (1964) *Towards a Dynamic Development Policy for Latin America* (New York, United Nations), p. 71.

18. Santiago Macario, 'Protectionism and Industrialization in Latin America', *op. cit.* p. 61.

19. For example, in 1958, nominal and effective tariffs in Argentina were estimated at 235 and 1024 percent for textiles, and 388 and 806 percent for clothing and shoes (Bela Balassa (1966) 'Integration and Resource Allocation in Latin America', mimeo).

20. Professor Bergson notes: 'Imaginably, domestic production could have been fostered and imports limited in such a way that different industries would have been affected in a more or less uniform way, and with little effect on the structure of trade. But the system's directors in Communist countries have sought rather to favor some industries over others, and apparently with little regard to costs : . . even where costs have been a concern, the system's directors in undertaking any meaningful appraisal have been handicapped again and again by their imperfect understanding of costs and by distortions in their own prices'. (Abram Bergson (1968) 'On Prospects for Communist Foreign Trade', in *International Trade and Central Planning*, A. A. Brown and Egon Neuberger, eds, Berkeley, University of California Press, p. 387.)

21. Empirical evidence on the latter point is provided with respect to Chile in R. F. Mikesell (1966) 'Foreign Trade Import Substitution and Aid Strategy: The Case of Chile' (Washington, DC, US Department of State, Agency for International Development, mimeo).

22. A. C. Harberger (1958) 'Using the Resources at Hand More Effectively', *American Economic Review*, Papers and Proceedings, May, pp. 134–55.

23. Bela Balassa, 'Integration and Resource Allocation in Latin America', *op. cit.*

24. See on Czechoslovakia Ota Sik (1967) *Plan and Market under Socialism* (Prague), Chapter 1. 2; on Hungary, my *The Hungarian Experience in Economic Planning*

(New Haven, Yale University Press, 1959), Chapter 3 and 'The Economic Reform in Hungary', Economica, Feb. 1970.

25. This is the Mill-Bastable test of infant industry protection. See M. C. Kemp (1960) 'The Mill-Bastable Infant Industry Dogma', Journal of Political Economy, Feb., pp. 65–7. A further condition is that some of the gain accrues to other firms or that the entrepreneur attaches a lower value to this gain than the community.

26. For an argument along these lines, see Hla Myint (1972) 'International Trade and the Developing Countries', in The Future of International Relations, Proceedings of the September 1968 Congress of the International Economic Association, London, Macmillan.

27. See B. P. Pesek (1965) Gross National Product of Czechoslovakia in Monetary and Real Terms, 1946–58 (Chicago, University of Chicago Press), Chapter 7 and my The Hungarian Experience in Economic Planning, Chapter 5.

28. See Holland Hunter (1961) 'Optimal Tautness in Development Planning', Economic Development and Cultural Change, July, pp. 561–72; and H. S. Levine, 'Pressure and Planning in the Soviet Economy', in H. Rosovsky, ed., (1966) Industrialization in Two Systems: Essays in Honor of Alexander Gerschenkron (New York, Wiley).

29. A description by a Hungarian observer of quality deterioration in developing countries engaged in an inward-looking strategy applies equally well to centrally planned economies: 'The atmosphere of protectionism and the priority of quantitative goals do not provide sufficient inducement for quality improvements. The quality of products in enterprises that had earlier been competitive internationally has declined, and in general with the emphasis on increases in the quantity of output it was not possible to keep up with the quality requirements of development. As industrialization proceeded in the consumer goods sector, the deterioration of quality did not create economic problems (although it hindered exports). However, with the production of investment goods and especially the development of machine building industries based on complex sectoral interrelationships, the deterioration of quality became cumulative and, through the chain of users, it led to the decline of quality in various branches of the national economy, as well as to losses due to rejects'. Béla Kádár (1967) Gazdaságfejlesztés és nemzetközi munkamegosztás a fejlodo országokban (Economic Progress and the International Division of Labor in Developing Countries), Budapest, pp. 112–13.

It should be added that, according to a publication of the Hungarian Statistical Bureau, the quality of consumer goods deteriorated by about 15 percent between 1938 and 1955. See Aralakulás Magyarországon 1938-ban és 1945–1955-ben (Prices in Hungary in 1938 and 1949–55), Budapest, 1957, p. 70.

30. For a discussion of these scale economies, see my Economic Development and Integration (Mexico DF, Centro de Estudios Monetarios Latinoamericanos, 1965), Chapter IV.

31. Cost estimates are from studies by the Economic Commission for Latin America; and data on production volume, from United Nations, Statistical Yearbook, 1967. An exception is automobile assembly in Chile, where the source is Leland L. Johnson (1967) 'Problems of Import Substitution: The Chilean Automobile Industry', Economic Development and Cultural Change, Jan.

32. Martin Carnoy (1969) 'Industrialization in a Latin American Common Market' (Washington, DC, The Brookings Institution, mimeo).

33. T. R. Gates and F. Linden (1961) Costs and Competition: American Experience Abroad (New York, National Industrial Conference Board), p. 129.

34. John Haldi and David Whitcomb (1967) 'Economies of Scale in Industrial Plants', Journal of Political Economy, Aug., Part I, pp. 373–85.

35. Bela Balassa (1967) *Trade Liberalization among Industrial Countries* (New York, McGraw-Hill), Chapter 5.

36. According to Baranson, the excess cost of domestic car production in Argentina, Brazil and Mexico rises from 1–6 percent to 36–105 percent as we move from assembly to 60 percent domestic content of the automobile. (Jack Baranson (1969) 'Automotive Industries in Developing Countries', *World Bank Occasional Papers*, Washington, DC.

37. In Czechoslovakia and Hungary, this objective is achieved by the outright prohibition of imports; in Argentina and Chile, the high tariffs on these products are reinforced by legal requirements on the minimum proportion of nationally fabricated components. In the case of the Chilean automobile industry, this requirement rose from 27 percent in 1964 to 32 percent in 1965 and again to 45 percent in 1966. (See L. L. Johnson, *op. cit.*)

38. A Soviet author notes that 'in the field of specialization and cooperation of production only a little has been done so far, since "specialized" production covers, for instance, only 2–6 percent of the number of types of machinery and equipment produced in various member countries [of Comecon]'. (V. Morozov (1968) *Voprosy Ekonomiki*, (5), p. 76. Cited in A. Nove, 'East-West Trade', in *The Future of International Trade Relations, op. cit.*)

39. 1960–1 prices and weights have been used in the calculations. The commodities in question include beef, mutton, canned meat, wheat, maize, linseed oil, oilseed cake and wool, which accounted for two-thirds of Argentine exports in 1960–1; at the same time, Argentina provided 5 (wheat) to 28 (beef) percent of the world exports of these commodities (Food and Agricultural Organization, *Trade Yearbook*, various issues).

40. I. Deák and K. Urbán (1966) 'Mezogazdasági és élelmiszerexportunk néhány jellemvonása' (Some Characteristics of Our Agricultural and Food Exports), *Közgazdasági Szemle* (Economic Review), (2), pp. 141–55.

41. Metallgesellschaft, *Metal Statistics*, various issues.

42. The commodities in question include cattle, beef, bacon and ham, canned meat, butter, cheese and eggs, which accounted for three-fifths of primary exports and two-fifths of total exports from Denmark in 1960–1. The share of Denmark in the world exports of these commodities ranged from 6 percent in the case of beef to 69 percent in the case of bacon and ham. (FAO, *Trade Yearbook*, various issues.)

43. United Nations, *Yearbook of International Trade Statistics* and *Yearbook of National Accounts Statistics*, various issues.

44. Norwegian input–output statistics. See Bela Balassa (1969) 'Industrial Development in an Open Economy: The Case of Norway', *Oxford Economic Papers*, Nov.

45. The relevant figures are $89 and $63 thousand in Argentina and $78 and $21 thousand in Chile (Barend A. de Vries (1967) 'The Export Experience of Developing Countries', *World Bank Staff Occasional Papers No. 3*, Washington, DC, p. 6).

46. However, the share of imports in GNP in the two countries had declined between the inter-war and the early post-war period, reflecting the relative ease of early import substitution.

47. *Yearbook of National Accounts Statistics*, various issues. Data are expressed in current prices but similar trends are shown by the constant price figures also. The relevant figures are 8.6 and 10.0 percent in Argentina (in 1960 prices) and 8.9 and 13.3 percent in Chile (in 1961 prices).

48. E. Illyés (1954) 'A külkereskedelem szerepe és tervezésünk jelenlegi feladatai' (The Role of Foreign Trade and the Present Tasks of its Planning), *Társadalmi Szemle* (Social Review), (5), p. 96.

49. The average share of exports and imports in Hungarian national income rose from 13 percent in 1950 to 21 percent in 1955 and to 29 percent in 1965. *Közgazadasagi Szemle* (Economic Review), 1957 (6), p. 645, and *Statisztikai Szemle* (Statistical Review), 1967 (11), p. 1086.

50. F. L. Pryor, 'Discussion of J. M. Montias'. Trade in Machinery Products', in Brown and Neuberger, eds, *International Trade and Central Planning*, pp. 163–4.

51. According to a student of the problem: 'Given the irrationality of internal prices, resident convertibility (free imports) cannot be allowed because it will lead to large-scale importation of commodities which have relatively high prices but which, in fact, may be more cheaply produced at home (for example, many consumers' goods). On the other hand, strict controls over exports, discouraging potential ruble holdings by foreigners, must be maintained lest non-residents compete in domestic markets for goods which, owing to subsidies or some other costing quirk, have a low price but, in fact, are expensive to produce'. (Franklyn D. Holzman, 'Foreign Trade Behavior of Centrally Planned Economies', in Rosovsky, ed., *Industrialization in Two Systems*, p. 246.)

52. While world market prices served as a point of reference, contract prices in Comecon trade were the subject of bargaining between the trading partners. This explains the large differences in the export prices of indentical commodities, depending on the importer. It has been shown that 'price differences for identical products are much larger in bilateral accounting among Comecon countries than in such arrangements anywhere and anytime in the past'. Around 1960, the price differences exceeded one-half in 17 percent of Hungarian exports and one-fourth in 29 percent of Hungarian exports, while such differences did not surpass 5–15 percent in Hungary in 1936. S. Ausch and F. Bartha (1967) 'Az árak elméleti problémái a KGST-országok közötti kereskedelemben' (The Theoretical Problems of Prices in Trade among the Comecon Countries), *Közgazdasagi Szemle*, (3), p. 281. See also S. Jiranek (1965) 'The Position of the Czechoslovak Crown in International Relations', *Planovane hospodarstvi*, (5), cited in F. D. Holzman, 'Soviet Central Planning and Its Impact on Foreign Trade Behavior and Adjustment Mechanisms', in Brown and Neuberger, eds, *International Trade and Central Planning*, p. 297.

53. For a detailed – albeit sometimes conflicting – discussion of the factors affecting the trade of centrally planned economies, see the various contributions in *International Trade and Central Planning*.

54. Imre Vajda (1966) 'Müszaki fejlodés és külkereskedelem' (Technological Development and Foreign Trade), *Külkereskedelem* (Foreign Trade), (1), p. 13, and *Statistical Yearbook, 1966*.

55. Imre Vajda (1967) 'External Equilibrium, Neo-techniques and Economic Reform', *Acta Oeconomica*, (4), p. 299. According to Vajda, 'those familiar with the problems of Hungarian industry are all aware of its autarkic features and of the consequent inevitable technical backwardness. It is also known that the present organization of CMEA [The Council of Mutual Economic Assistance – Comecon] with its bureaucratic features, as well as the tendencies inherent in centralized planning, which would hinder even a bilateral negotiation, have – within the quantitative progress – been partly responsible for this situation'. (*Ibid.* p. 304.)

56. Thus Sik repeatedly speaks of the 'tremendous backwardness of the technical level' of Czech industry, which increasingly fell behind the West. See, e.g., his speech of 2 May, 1968, published by the Czechoslovak Union of Women in June 1968.

57. United Nations, *Yearbook of National Accounts Statistics*, various issues. Relative changes rather than absolute values (2.2 and 8.8 in Czechoslovakia as compared to 2.0 and 4.0 in Hungary) are relevant here, in part because of inter-country differences in relative prices, and in part because of problems of valuing

investment activity. For Czechoslovakia and Hungary, data refer to net fixed investment and net material product, while for the other countries they pertain to gross investment and gross national product. In all cases, calculations are made for five-year periods, assuming a one-year lag between investment and output.

58. The adjustment has been made on the basis of information provided in Sándor Ganczer (1966) 'Népgazdaságunk fo arányainak elemzése' (Analysis of the Principal Relationships of our National Economy), in *Vita a magyar gazdasági mechanizmus reformjáról* (Discussion on the Reform of the Hungarian Economic Mechanism), Budapest, pp. 127–44.

59. A statement to this effect has been made with regard to Hungary in F. Nyitrai (1967) 'Az ipari struktura változása és a jövedelmezoség' (Changes in the Structure of Industry and Profitability), *Pénzügyi Szemle* (Financial Review), Oct., p. 838. See also the comparison between Argentina and Italy in my 'Integration and Resource Allocation in Latin America', *op. cit.*

60. As an authority on the question notes, 'to a significant extent *all* of the economic reforms or proposed reforms in Eastern Europe – though not in the Soviet Union – have as a main purpose making the given socialist economy more effective as an earner of foreign exchange and as a gainer from the international division of labor' (Gregory Grossman, 'Foreign Trade of the USSR: A Summary Appraisal', in *International Trade and Central Planning*, p. 341). The same point is made in Egon Neuberger, 'Central Planning and Its Legacies: Implications for Foreign Trade', *ibid.*, p. 355.

14 · THE ADJUSTMENT EXPERIENCE OF DEVELOPING ECONOMIES AFTER 1973

This chapter summarizes the results of the Organization for Economic Cooperation and Development (OECD) and the World Bank studies of external shocks and policy responses to these shocks in developing economies during the 1973–8 period.[1] External shocks, in the form of the deterioration of the terms of trade and the slowdown of foreign demand for the exports of developing economies, reflected largely the effects of the quadrupling of oil prices and the 1974–5 world recession. Policy responses, in turn, may have involved additional net external financing and domestic adjustment policies, including export promotion, import substitution and macroeconomic policies affecting the rate of economic growth.

The OECD and the World Bank studies have employed a common analytical framework to estimate the balance-of-payments effects of external shocks and of policy responses to these shocks. In the OECD study, estimates have been made for seven groups of non-Organization of Petroleum Exporting Countries (OPEC) developing economies, classified according to their level of industrialization and resource base, as well as for nine developing economies. The World Bank studies provide estimates for 24 developing economies that were adversely affected by external shocks and four developing economies that experienced favorable external shocks.

The balance-of-payments effects of external shocks have been estimated by postulating a situation that would have existed in the absence of these shocks. Terms-of-trade effects have been calculated as the difference between the current price values of exports and imports and their constant price values, estimated in the prices of the 1971–3 ('1972') base period.[2] This procedure reflects the assumption that price increases after '1972' were due to external shocks, in particular the direct and indirect effects of the quadrupling of oil prices.[3]

First published in *IMF Conditionality*, ed. John Williamson, Institute for International Economics, Washington DC, 1983.

The effects of the slowdown of foreign demand on developing country exports have been calculated as the difference between the trend value of exports and hypothetical exports. The trend value of exports has been derived on the assumptions that the growth rate of foreign demand for particular export products and product groups remained the same as in the 1963–73 period and that the particular economy maintained its '1972' share in these exports. In turn, hypothetical exports have been estimated on the assumption that the economy in question maintained its '1972' market share in the actual exports of individual products and product groups during the period under consideration.

The balance-of-payments effects of adjustment policies undertaken by individual developing economies have also been estimated by hypothesizing a situation that would have existed in the absence of external shocks. Additional net external financing has been derived as the difference between the actual merchandise trade balance and the trade balance that would have been obtained if trends in imports and exports observed in the 1963–73 period had continued and import and export prices had remained at their '1972' level. Non-factor services and private transfers do not enter into the calculation of additional net external financing because they are assumed to be unaffected by external shocks.

The effects of export promotion have been calculated as changes in exports that resulted from changes in the '1972' export market shares of the particular national economy. In turn, import substitution has been defined as savings in imports associated with a decrease in the income elasticity of import demand compared with the 1963–73 period. Finally, the effects on imports of changes in GNP growth rates in response to the macroeconomic policies followed have been estimated on the assumption of unchanged income elasticities of import demand. This pertains to the impact of short-term policies, whereas long-term growth performance is affected by the allocation of existing and incremental resources and the rate of savings.

Particular policy measures may also have been taken independently of external shocks, or may themselves constitute an 'internal shock'. An excessively expansionary fiscal policy or a major transformation of political institutions comes under this heading. The methodology applied does not, however, permit separating the balance-of-payments effects of policy changes taken in response to external shocks from the effects of autonomous policy changes, including internal shocks. Such a distinction necessarily becomes a matter of interpretation; it has been made in the studies of the individual developing economies.

EXTERNAL SHOCKS AND POLICY RESPONSES IN SEVEN GROUPS OF NON-OPEC DEVELOPING ECONOMIES

The classification scheme

Non-OPEC developing economies have been classified according to their level of industrialization and resource base. The groups are: newly industrializing economies (NICs); agriculture-based, relatively industrialized developing economies; mineral-based, relatively industrialized developing economies; agriculture-based, less industrialized developing economies; mineral-based, less industrialized developing economies; and least developed economies. In view of their large size, and the impossibility of separating data for Pakistan and Bangladesh for the 1963–73 base period, these countries, as well as India, have been included in a seventh group.

Table 14.1 provides estimates of the balance-of-payments effects of external shocks and of policy responses to these shocks for the seven groups of developing economies. Estimates for individual years between 1974 and 1978 and averages for the entire period are shown. The following discussion will concentrate on average results for the 1974–8 period.

External shocks

The three more industrialized groups of developing economies suffered the greatest terms-of-trade loss in the 1974–8 period, reflecting largely the effects of oil price increases for these relatively energy-intensive economies. By contrast, increases in export prices, primarily coffee and cocoa, largely offset the adverse effects of higher oil prices in the case of the agriculture-based, less industrialized economies.

The mineral-based, less industrialized economies and the least developed economies occupy a middle position as far as terms-of-trade effects are concerned, while the low share of trade in GNP reduced the relative importance of terms of trade shocks in South Asia. The latter observation also applies to export volume effects. These effects were the largest in the mineral-based, less industrialized economies, with the other groups occupying positions between the two extremes.

All in all, the balance-of-payments effects of external shocks averaged 2.5 percent of the GNP in the agriculture-based, less industrialized economies and in South Asia during the 1974–8 period. These effects slightly exceeded 5 percent in the least developed economies and 6 percent in the remaining four groups.

With the exception of the agriculture-based, less industrialized economies, terms-of-trade effects exceeded export volume effects sevenfold in all the groups. Although export shortfalls acquired increased importance over time, terms-of-trade effects were still two to three times exports volume effects in these groups at the end of the period.

Table 14.1 Balance-of-payments effects of external shocks and of policy responses to these shocks: ratios (percentage)

Balance of payments effects	Newly industrializing countries						Relatively industrialized countries with economies based predominantly on agriculture					
	1974	1975	1976	1977	1978	1974–8	1974	1975	1976	1977	1978	1974–8
External shocks												
Terms of trade effects/average trade	43.0	59.8	43.8	29.5	32.9	41.2	10.7	48.8	33.7	33.1	40.4	33.8
Terms of trade effects/GNP	5.5	7.1	5.4	3.6	4.2	5.1	1.6	6.9	4.8	4.7	5.7	4.8
Export volume effects/exports	1.6	12.3	6.5	14.5	16.2	10.7	5.3	12.9	7.9	14.0	16.2	11.5
Export volume effects/GNP	0.2	1.2	0.7	1.6	1.9	1.1	0.6	1.5	1.0	1.6	1.8	1.3
External shocks/GNP	5.6	8.3	6.1	5.2	6.1	6.2	2.2	8.4	5.8	6.2	7.5	6.1
Policy responses												
Additional net external financing/average trade	50.0	48.1	21.4	-4.2	-8.6	19.9	36.6	76.4	54.1	68.5	72.8	62.4
Additional net external financing/GNP	6.4	5.7	2.6	-0.5	-1.1	2.5	5.4	10.8	7.7	9.7	10.3	8.9
Increase in export shares/exports	-4.9	-1.7	-2.7	0.5	5.1	-0.3	-4.9	-1.7	3.3	0.3	5.6	0.8
Import substitution/imports	-1.2	13.2	17.4	22.4	25.0	15.3	-13.4	-11.6	-10.5	-16.3	-15.6	-13.6
Import effects of lower GNP growth rate/imports	0.6	6.3	9.5	19.7	23.6	11.7	-1.4	-1.6	-3.7	-4.0	-4.4	-3.1

Balance of payments effects	Less industrialized countries with economies based predominantly on mineral production						Least developed countries					
	1974	1975	1976	1977	1978	1974–8	1974	1975	1976	1977	1978	1974–8
External shocks												
Terms of trade effects/average trade	-22.8	44.7	13.4	6.7	n.a.	10.1	29.9	55.6	20.6	-11.4	60.2	31.3
Terms of trade effects/GNP	-7.0	13.1	3.7	1.8	n.a.	2.9	3.5	7.2	2.6	-1.3	7.3	3.8
Export volume effects/exports	0.6	12.1	10.9	17.1	n.a.	9.8	10.2	10.8	9.1	24.9	22.3	15.0
Export volume effects/GNP	0.2	3.9	3.5	5.1	n.a.	3.2	1.0	1.1	1.0	2.2	1.7	1.4
External shocks/GNP	-6.8	17.0	7.2	6.9	n.a.	6.1	4.3	8.3	3.5	0.9	9.0	5.2
Policy responses												
Additional net external financing/average trade	-32.4	39.5	-6.5	-1.7	n.a.	-0.6	49.4	75.8	26.4	14.5	107.3	55.2
Additional net external financing/GNP	-10.0	11.6	-1.8	-0.5	n.a.	-0.2	5.9	9.8	3.3	1.7	13.0	6.7
Increase in export shares/exports	-3.8	-5.1	-11.2	-22.5	n.a.	-10.3	-35.2	-26.9	-24.3	-37.5	-67.5	-37.0
Import substitution/imports	12.2	14.2	33.9	30.3	n.a.	21.9	15.8	6.8	16.3	13.6	-0.6	9.9
Import effects of lower GNP growth rate/imports	4.4	13.1	22.8	29.7	n.a.	16.9	-1.2	1.7	4.3	3.7	8.6	3.6

	Relatively industrialized countries with economies based predominantly on mineral production						Less industrialized countries with economies based predominantly on agriculture					
External shocks												
Terms of trade effects/average trade	-1.7	47.9	41.7	41.9	47.4	35.9	14.5	28.1	-3.6	-34.5	6.4	1.5
Terms of trade effects/GNP	-0.2	6.7	5.5	5.8	6.6	4.9	2.8	5.3	-0.7	-6.7	1.2	0.3
Export volume effects/exports	0.9	11.3	9.1	12.9	15.2	10.0	6.2	11.2	8.4	19.8	20.3	13.0
Export volume effects/GNP	0.1	1.5	1.2	1.8	2.1	1.3	1.2	2.1	1.5	3.2	3.1	2.3
External shocks/GNP	-0.1	8.2	6.7	7.5	8.7	6.2	4.0	7.5	0.9	-3.5	4.3	2.5
Policy responses												
Additional net external financing/average trade	-10.4	54.1	41.2	39.9	46.5	34.8	20.8	31.5	5.7	8.8	60.0	26.0
Additional net external financing/GNP	-1.4	7.6	5.4	5.5	6.5	4.7	4.0	6.0	1.1	1.7	11.6	5.0
Increase in export shares/exports	10.2	12.3	5.4	12.2	14.6	11.1	-2.3	1.5	-5.5	-11.5	-17.5	-6.9
Import substitution/imports	-0.8	-10.8	-2.4	-5.4	-9.0	-5.8	0.8	3.7	0.9	-17.7	-21.9	-8.4
Import effects of lower GNP growth rate/imports	0.2	3.9	6.5	8.1	10.4	5.9	1.2	2.6	3.2	2.8	2.2	2.4

South Asian countries

External shocks						
Terms of trade effects/average trade	47.0	68.5	35.6	29.5	52.4	46.5
Terms of trade effects/GNP	1.9	2.9	1.5	1.2	2.2	1.9
Export volume effects/exports	2.1	13.2	8.5	16.1	22.3	12.7
Export volume effects/GNP	0.1	0.5	0.4	0.6	0.8	0.5
External shocks/GNP	2.0	3.4	1.8	1.8	3.0	2.4
Policy responses						
Additional net external financing/average trade	75.7	114.2	69.2	92.0	135.8	98.7
Additional net external financing/GNP	3.1	4.8	2.9	3.8	5.6	4.1
Increase in export shares/exports	-11.7	-2.7	-2.6	-13.7	-20.5	-10.3
Import substitution/imports	-14.5	-30.1	-23.8	-34.6	-43.0	-30.1
Import effects of lower GNP growth rate/imports	-0.2	1.9	1.4	2.1	2.1	1.5

Source: Bela Balassa, André Barsony, and Anne Richards (1981). *The Balance of Payments Effects of External Shocks and of Policy Responses to These Shocks in Non-OPEC Developing Countries,* OECD.
n.a. = Not available.

Policy responses

There were considerable differences among the seven groups as regards the policies followed in response to external shocks. The NICs offset three-fourths of the adverse balance-of-payments effects of external shocks through domestic adjustment policies of export promotion, import substitution and deflationary measures, with additional net external financing accounting for the remainder. They were followed by the mineral-based, relatively industrialized economies, where additional net external financing exceeded in importance domestic adjustment policies three times.

In turn, in agriculture-based economies, including the least developed economies and South Asia, additional net external financing was one and a half to two times as large as the balance-of-payments effects of external shocks, indicating that domestic policies aggravated the adverse effects of these shocks. However, limitations of external financing imposed wholly domestic adjustment on the mineral-based, less industrialized economies.

There are also substantial differences in the use of domestic policy measures among the individual groups. Only the relatively industrialized mineral producers increased their export market shares; the NICs and the relatively industrialized agricultural economies experienced little change; whereas the four less industrialized groups incurred substantial losses in market shares. In turn, there was import substitution in the NICs; the mineral-based, less industrialized; and the least developed economies. The first two of these groups also relied on deflationary policies to a considerable extent. The remaining groups experienced negative import substitution and made little use of deflationary policies in response to external shocks.

Comparing the four-year pattern of policy responses reveals important differences between the NICs and the rest. The NICs increasingly supplemented external financing by domestic adjustment while, apart from the mineral-based, less industrialized economies that were unable to obtain further financing, the remaining groups remained dependent on external financing to meeet the combined adverse balance-of-payments effects of external shocks, losses in export market shares and increased import shares. At the same time, the adverse balance-of-payments effects of domestic policies declined over time in the relatively industrialized and increased in the less industrialized groups.

EXTERNAL SHOCKS AND POLICY RESPONSES IN INDIVIDUAL DEVELOPING ECONOMIES

The classification scheme

The differential pattern of policy responses to external shocks in national economies at different levels of development is also apparent in the sample of

24 developing economies that experienced adverse external shocks. Of this total, 12 are NICs and 12 less developed economies (LDCs).[4]

The analysis of the individual countries allows a further distinction to be made between outward-oriented and inward-oriented economies. The former group provided, on the whole, similar incentives to domestic and export sales and to primary and manufacturing activities, while the latter biased the system of incentives against exports and discriminated in favor of manufacturing activities. Several inward-oriented economies also experienced internal shocks.

Among the NICs, the three Far Eastern economies – Korea, Singapore and Taiwan – adopted an outward-oriented development strategy in the early 1960s and continued with this strategy after 1973. They were joined by Chile and Uruguay, which had earlier applied an inward-oriented strategy but turned outward following the external shocks of 1974–5. These countries devalued their exchange rate to a considerable extent, eliminated quantitative import restrictions, lowered industrial tariffs and abolished price control.

After earlier efforts to lessen the bias of the incentive system against export, Brazil, Portugal, Turkey and Yugoslavia again increased the extent of inward orientation of their economies by raising levels of industrial protection during the period under consideration. Argentina, Israel and Mexico maintained their relatively inward-looking policy stance, with little change in incentives to exports and to import substitution, and followed excessively expansionary policies that may be qualified as internal shocks. In Portugal, the 1974 revolution and the policies subsequently applied represented an internal shock.

Among LDCs, Kenya, Mauritius, Thailand and Tunisia may be categorized as having followed outward-oriented policies. These economies have relatively low levels of industrial protection compared with the other eight LDCs that can be characterized as inward-oriented. Within the latter group, Jamaica, Peru and Tanzania experienced internal shocks in the form of economic disruptions resulting from policy changes; such was not the case in the other five members of the group, including Egypt, India, Morocco, the Philippines and Zambia.

Table 14.2 provides estimates of the balance-of-payments effects of external shocks and of policy responses to these shocks for the described groupings of developing economies. It should be noted that, whereas the NIC group includes practically all economies that belong to this category, the coverage of the LDCs is necessarily limited. Also, while the distinction between outward- and inward-oriented economies was made on the basis of information derived from research studies and country reports, a binary classification scheme cannot reproduce the richness of country experiences.

Table 14.2 further includes the results for four developing economies that experienced favorable external shocks. Indonesia and Nigeria benefited from the rise in oil prices; in the Ivory Coast increases in the price of cocoa and

Table 14.2 Balance-of-payments effects of external shocks and of policy responses to these shocks percentage

	Newly industrializing economies						Less developed economies						NICs and LDCs					
	1974	1975	1976	1977	1978	Average 1974–8	1974	1975	1976	1977	1978	Average 1974–8	1974	1975	1976	1977	1978	Average 1974–8
External shocks																		
Terms of trade effects/average trade	35.8	47.5	31.5	26.1	26.7	32.9	11.3	50.1	38.8	39.4	57.4	40.3	29.5	48.2	33.4	29.6	34.5	34.9
Terms of trade effects/GNP	3.7	4.6	3.1	2.6	2.8	3.3	1.1	4.9	3.7	3.8	3.5	3.9	3.0	4.7	3.3	2.9	3.6	3.5
Export volume effects/exports	1.8	12.6	6.7	14.1	15.8	10.7	2.8	14.4	11.7	17.2	24.5	14.5	2.0	13.2	8.0	14.9	17.8	11.7
Export volume effects/GNP	0.1	1.0	0.6	1.3	1.5	1.0	0.2	1.1	1.0	1.4	1.9	1.2	0.2	1.1	0.7	1.3	1.6	1.0
External shocks/GNP	3.8	5.6	3.8	3.9	4.4	4.3	1.3	6.0	4.7	5.1	7.3	5.0	3.1	5.7	4.0	4.3	5.2	4.5
Policy responses																		
Additional net external financing/average trade	45.2	43.6	6.8	-2.1	-7.0	15.9	31.9	85.7	58.2	71.4	100.7	71.0	41.5	55.2	21.9	17.3	20.4	30.4
Additional net external financing/GNP	4.6	4.2	0.9	-0.2	-0.7	1.6	3.1	8.4	5.6	6.8	9.6	6.8	4.2	5.4	2.2	1.7	2.1	3.0
Increase in export market shares/exports	-2.9	-0.3	1.9	5.4	8.8	3.2	-10.5	-6.2	-1.9	-4.7	-7.0	-5.9	-5.0	-1.9	0.9	2.9	5.2	0.8
Imports substitution effects/imports	-6.0	3.7	14.6	21.8	25.5	12.3	-0.1	-15.9	-6.9	-11.6	-15.6	-11.9	-6.5	-1.8	8.9	12.6	14.3	5.8
Effects of lower GNP growth rates/imports	1.3	8.9	10.1	11.5	11.8	8.6	0.0	-0.1	0.4	0.0	0.5	0.2	1.0	6.4	7.3	8.3	8.7	6.5

	Outward-oriented NICs						Outward-oriented LDCs						Outward-oriented NICs and LDCs					
	1974	1975	1976	1977	1978	Average 1974–8	1974	1975	1976	1977	1978	Average 1974–8	1974	1975	1976	1977	1978	Average 1974–8
External shocks																		
Terms of trade effects/average trade	28.8	35.7	16.3	11.8	15.4	20.3	9.5	32.8	26.1	35.6	55.0	33.1	25.4	35.2	18.1	13.0	21.4	22.5
Terms of trade effects/GNP	7.4	8.9	4.6	3.3	4.3	5.6	1.5	4.7	3.9	5.6	8.3	5.0	5.9	7.8	4.4	3.9	5.5	5.4
Export volume effects/exports	0.1	12.9	4.8	12.2	13.3	9.2	2.5	13.8	6.3	9.4	12.6	9.0	0.5	13.0	5.1	11.8	13.2	9.2
Export volume effects/GNP	0.0	3.0	1.4	3.3	3.8	2.4	0.3	1.5	0.8	1.2	1.5	1.1	0.1	2.6	1.2	2.8	3.2	2.1
External shocks/GNP	7.5	12.0	6.0	6.6	8.3	8.0	1.8	0.2	4.7	6.8	9.8	6.1	6.0	10.4	5.6	5.6	8.7	7.5
Policy responses																		
Additional net external financing/average trade	20.8	13.6	-19.0	-26.7	-23.5	-10.0	10.0	32.2	8.8	20.7	47.4	26.6	19.0	16.9	-14.5	-17.4	-12.7	-3.9

External shocks

	Inward-oriented NICs						Inward-oriented LDCs						Inward-oriented NICs and LDCs					
Additional net external financing/GNP	5.4	3.4	−5.3	−7.4	−6.9	−2.7	1.7	4.6	1.3	4.5	7.1	4.0	4.4	3.7	−3.5	−4.3	−3.2	−1.0
Increase in export market shares/exports	4.1	7.7	15.5	10.9	23.0	15.2	1.8	1.3	11.9	15.2	15.5	10.0	3.7	6.7	15.0	18.4	22.0	14.4
Import substitution effects/imports	−1.7	10.1	13.6	22.8	25.2	13.3	−1.0	8.4	12.2	3.3	9.3	6.5	−1.6	9.7	13.4	19.1	22.5	13.7
Effects of lower GNP growth rates/imports	5.8	15.3	11.2	8.5	3.4	8.4	0.4	−0.1	−1.2	−1.4	−4.9	−1.6	4.7	12.2	9.0	6.6	2.0	6.5

External shocks

	Inward-oriented NICs						Inward-oriented LDCs						Inward-oriented NICs and LDCs					
Terms of trade effects/average trade	40.0	54.7	42.8	37.5	36.8	42.2	11.9	54.7	42.6	40.7	58.1	42.5	31.6	54.7	42.8	38.6	43.8	42.3
Terms of trade effects/GNP	3.0	3.9	2.9	2.5	2.5	2.9	1.0	4.9	3.7	3.4	4.9	3.7	2.5	4.2	3.1	2.8	3.2	3.1
Export volume effects/exports	3.0	12.7	8.4	15.9	18.2	12.0	2.8	14.6	13.2	19.7	28.4	16.0	2.9	13.3	10.0	17.2	21.3	13.4
Export volume effects/GNP	0.2	0.7	0.5	0.9	1.1	0.7	0.2	1.1	1.0	1.4	2.0	1.2	0.2	0.8	0.6	1.1	1.3	0.8
External shocks/GNP	3.2	4.5	3.4	3.4	3.6	3.6	1.3	6.0	4.7	4.8	6.9	4.9	2.7	4.9	3.7	3.8	4.5	3.9

Policy responses

	Inward-oriented NICs						Inward-oriented LDCs						Inward-oriented NICs and LDCs					
Additional net external financing/average trade	59.8	62.0	30.0	17.6	7.7	35.0	38.4	100.0	73.3	85.6	118.3	84.7	53.5	74.4	44.1	39.8	43.8	50.9
Additional net external financing/GNP	4.5	4.4	2.0	1.2	0.5	2.4	3.3	9.0	6.3	7.2	10.0	7.3	4.2	5.7	3.2	2.8	3.2	3.8
Increase in export market shares/exports	−8.1	−6.4	−10.4	−7.1	−4.9	−7.3	−13.9	−8.1	−5.9	−10.8	−14.3	−10.6	−10.1	−7.0	−8.9	−8.3	−7.8	−8.4
Import substitution effects/imports	−8.2	0.3	15.3	21.0	25.8	10.4	−10.4	−22.6	−13.0	−16.8	−23.9	−17.8	−8.8	−7.0	6.4	8.7	8.9	1.6
Effects of lower GNP growth rates/imports	−1.0	5.5	9.3	13.7	18.8	9.0	−0.1	−0.1	0.9	0.5	2.4	0.8·	−0.8	3.7	6.7	9.4	13.2	6.4

External shocks

	NICs with internal shocks						LDCs with internal shocks						Economies with favorable shocks					
Terms of trade effects/average trade	19.4	41.6	30.9	21.0	11.5	24.2	9.9	50.8	36.1	20.7	37.0	31.5	−142.0	−82.9	−99.6	−114.0	−77.2	−101.2
Terms of trade effects/GNP	1.3	2.5	1.8	1.3	0.8	1.3	1.4	8.1	4.9	2.7	3.2	4.5	−14.4	−9.2	−11.8	−14.3	−9.5	−11.0
Export volume effects/exports	2.2	12.8	4.6	11.4	12.1	8.8	5.8	18.5	23.0	28.8	34.0	22.3	4.4	19.0	15.2	24.2	30.1	18.8
Export volume effects/GNP	0.1	0.6	0.2	0.6	0.7	0.5	0.7	2.2	2.6	3.6	4.6	2.7	0.5	1.8	1.5	2.3	2.8	1.8
External shocks/GNP	1.4	3.0	2.0	2.0	1.5	2.8	2.1	10.3	7.5	6.3	9.9	7.2	−13.9	−7.3	−10.4	−12.0	−6.7	−10.0

Table 14.2 (continued)

	1974	1975	1976	1977	1978	Average 1974–8	1974	1975	1976	1977	1978	Average 1974–8	1974	1975	1976	1977	1978	Average 1974–8
Policy responses																		
Additional net external financing/average trade	42.7	67.7	33.7	10.4	−0.1	29.6	22.2	90.5	54.2	17.8	33.3	45.1	−133.4	−40.6	−49.8	−52.8	−14.8	−53.5
Additional net external financing/GNP	2.8	4.0	2.0	0.7	0.0	1.9	3.2	14.5	7.4	2.3	4.7	6.4	−13.5	−4.5	−5.9	−6.6	−1.8	−6.2
Increase in export market shares/exports	−10.4	−29.1	−34.3	−11.6	−10.1	−17.9	−17.4	−16.3	−25.7	−16.2	−11.3	−17.2	5.3	5.9	5.1	10.1	12.2	7.8
Import substitution effects/imports	−11.0	−6.6	7.6	7.9	3.2	−0.2	3.6	−17.4	4.5	27.2	17.8	5.2	−7.1	−27.9	−33.8	−35.3	−37.9	−31.8
Effects of lower GNP growth rates/imports	0.0	9.9	17.4	20.9	26.3	14.7	3.2	6.3	14.9	15.8	27.6	12.8	−3.1	0.4	−1.6	−1.5	−1.4	−1.4

Source: Bela Balassa (1981) 'Adjustment to External Shocks in Developing Economies', *World Bank Staff Working Paper* No. 472.

coffee more than offset the adverse effects of higher oil prices; and Colombia enjoyed the rise in coffee prices without being burdened by the higher price of petroleum. The experience of countries with favorable external shocks is not considered in this section of the chapter.

External shocks

The LDCs covered by the investigation experienced somewhat larger adverse terms-of-trade and export volume effects than the NICs, irrespective of whether these effects are expressed as a proportion of trade or of GNP. Different considerations apply, however, if outward- and inward-oriented economies are compared.

Among the LDCs and, in particular, among the NICs, outward-oriented economies suffered substantially smaller terms-of-trade losses in relation to the average value of their exports and imports than inward-oriented economies. The opposite result is obtained in relating terms-of-trade losses to GNP; the differences are explained by the higher share of foreign trade in GNP under outward orientation.

Furthermore, outward-oriented economies experienced a smaller export shortfall, expressed as a percentage of export value, than did inward-oriented economies, largely because of relatively favorable changes in demand for manufactured goods, which account for a higher share in the exports of the former group. Thus, the *ex-post* income elasticity of demand in the developed countries for the manufactured goods originating in the developing economies (defined as the ratio of the rate of growth of imports to that of GNP) increased over time and offset one-fourth of the export shortfall due to the deceleration of economic growth in the developed countries. Also, increases in the income elasticity of demand enhanced the favorable effects of the acceleration of economic growth in the developing economies, although this was in part offset by the adverse effects of decreases in GNP growth rates and in the income elasticity of demand in centrally planned economies.

Within the NIC group, however, the ratio of the export shortfall to GNP was higher in outward-oriented than in inward-oriented economies, because the share of exports in GNP was substantially larger in the former than in the latter. The difference between the results was reduced, but a reversal did not occur, in the LDC group.

Taken together, the balance-of-payments effects of external shocks represented a proportion of GNP more than twice as high in the outward-oriented than in the inward-oriented NICs. Among the LDCs, too, outward-oriented economies suffered larger external shocks than inward-oriented economies, although the difference did not exceed one-fourth in this case.

For the period as a whole, terms-of-trade effects exceeded export volume effects more than three times, with little difference shown between NICs and LDCs. And while the ratio of terms of trade effects to export volume effects showed a declining tendency over time, the average terms of trade loss was still about twice the amount of the export shortfall in the NICs and three times as high in the LDCs at the end of the period.

Policy responses

Additional net external financing surpassed the adverse balance-of-payments effects of external shocks in the NICs in 1974. But this proportion declined over time and, towards the end of the period, additional net external financing turned negative as improvements in the balance of payments due to domestic policies came to exceed the adverse balance-of-payments effects of external shocks. This outcome reflects increased export promotion and import substitution as well as import savings at lower GNP growth rates.

After 1973 additional net external financing declined in importance in the LDCs as well. It continued to exceed, however, the balance-of-payments effects of external shocks, indicating that the adverse balance-of-payments impact of domestic policies aggravated the effects of external shocks. The LDCs lost export market shares, experienced negative import substitution, and their GNP growth rates changed little, on the average.

Within both groups, outward-oriented economies relied to a much greater extent on domestic adjustment than inward-oriented economies. The difference is particularly marked among the NICs. With greater reliance on external financing, debt-service ratios – defined as the ratio of interest payments and amortization to merchandise exports – rose on the average by two-thirds in inward-oriented NICs, while no change occurred in outward-oriented NICs.

Similarly, as outward-oriented LDCs relied to a large extent on domestic policies to adjust to external shocks, they experienced little change in debt-service ratios, while this ratio increased by one-half in inward-oriented LDCs. Nothwithstanding reliance on external financing by the LDCs, however, their average debt-service ratios rose only slightly more than in the NICs as several LDCs received foreign grants and concessional loans.

Among the NICS as well as among the LDCs, by far the highest debt-service ratios were observed in economies that experienced internal shocks. This result occurred even though, due to liquidity problems, several of these economies had to cut back foreign borrowing to a considerable extent towards the end of the period.

Further interest attaches to differences in the pattern of domestic adjustment in the individual groups. The results indicate that, among the NICs as well as among the LDCs, outward-oriented economies not only gained export market shares but also did better in import substitution than inward-oriented economies. This result, at first sight surprising, may be explained by reference to the effects of the policies applied. On the one hand, the low extent of discrimination against primary activities, the relatively small degree of variation in incentive rates, and cost reductions through the exploitation of economies of scale in exporting contributed to efficient import substitution in outward-oriented economies. On the other hand, continued import substitution behind high protection brought diminishing returns in terms of net foreign exchange savings and entailed considerable costs under inward orientation.

Finally, import savings associated with the slowdown of economic growth declined after 1975 in economies pursuing an outward-oriented development strategy, whereas the opposite result obtained in economies characterized by inward orientation. The contrast is particularly marked in the case of the NICs, but it is observed in the LDCs as well.

Although outward-oriented NICs accepted a temporary decline in the rate of economic growth, their successful efforts in export promotion and in import substitution led to an acceleration of economic growth in subsequent years. In turn, inward-oriented NICs attempted to avoid a slowdown in economic growth through increased import substitution, but the rate of economic growth fell as import substitution proved to be increasingly costly. Growth rates declined even more in NICs experiencing internal shocks; these economies also incurred considerable losses in export market shares, whereas import substitution was nil.

Import savings associated with the slowdown of economic growth were nil in both outward-oriented and inward-oriented LDCs at the beginning of the period, but growth rates subsequently accelerated in LDCs characterized by outward orientation, whereas the opposite result obtained in inward-oriented LDCs. Within the latter group, the slowdown of economic growth was especially pronounced in countries experiencing internal shocks, reflecting economic dislocation that also led to substantial losses in export market shares. At the same time, increased protection and foreign exchange stringency gave rise to some import substitution in these economies.

DEVELOPMENT STRATEGIES AND GROWTH PERFORMANCE

Outward orientation and economic growth

Table 14.2 indicates the effects of an acceleration or deceleration of economic growth on imports. Further interest attaches to the actual rates of economic growth. These are shown in Table 14.3 for the 1963–73, 1970–73, 1973–6, 1976–9, and 1973–9 periods. The separation of the 1973–6 and 1976–9 periods permits indicating the immediate and the longer-run effects of the policies applied in outward-oriented and in inward-oriented developing countries.

Among the NICs, the average annual rate of growth of GNP in economies pursuing an outward-oriented development strategy declined from 7.4 percent in 1963–73 to 5.9 percent in 1973–6 as several of them adopted deflationary policies, but it rose again to 9.7 percent in 1976–9. In turn, in

Table 14.3 Expenditure shares, incremental capital–output ratios and growth rates

	1963–73	1970–3	1973–6	1976–9	1973–9
	Newly industrializing economies				
Savings ratios					
Domestic savings ratio	19.9	19.8	20.3	22.1	21.2
Foreign savings ratio	1.7	2.3	4.7	2.9	3.8
Incremental capital output ratios[a]	3.0	2.9	4.5	4.3	4.4
Growth rates (constant prices)					
Gross national product	7.1	8.4	5.1	5.8	5.4
Population	2.4	2.4	2.4	2.4	2.4
Per capita GNP	4.7	6.0	2.7	3.8	3.0
	Outward-oriented NICs				
Savings ratios					
Domestic savings ratio	16.9	19.0	21.2	25.8	23.5
Foreign savings ratio	3.2	2.6	4.6	1.5	3.0
Incremental capital output ratios[a]	3.0	3.3	4.9	2.7	3.4
Growth rates (constant prices)					
Gross national product	7.4	7.9	5.9	9.7	8.4
Population	2.1	1.9	1.9	1.7	1.8
Per capita GNP	5.3	6.0	4.1	8.0	6.6

	1963–73	1970–3	1973–6	1976–9	1973–9
	Less developed economies				
Savings ratios					
Domestic savings ratio	17.0	17.5	18.8	19.9	19.4
Foreign savings ratio	1.5	1.1	3.7	4.0	3.9
Incremental capital output ratios[a]	4.7	5.7	4.5	5.1	4.8
Growth rates (constant prices)					
Gross national product	4.3	3.2	5.4	4.7	5.3
Population	2.4	2.3	2.2	2.2	2.2
Per capita GNP	1.9	0.9	3.2	2.5	3.1
	Outward-oriented LDCs				
Savings ratios					
Domestic savings ratio	20.3	21.4	23.3	21.5	22.4
Foreign savings ratio	2.4	1.0	2.2	5.7	4.0
Incremental capital output ratios[a]	3.2	3.1	3.4	2.9	3.1
Growth rates (constant prices)					
Gross national product	7.3	6.6	7.1	7.9	7.6
Population	3.0	2.9	2.9	2.6	2.7
Per capita GNP	4.3	3.7	4.2	5.3	4.9

	1963–73	1970–3	1973–6	1976–9	1973–9
	NICs and LDCs				
Savings ratios					
Domestic savings ratio	18.8	19.0	19.8	21.4	20.7
Foreign savings ratio	1.7	1.9	4.4	3.3	3.8
Incremental capital output ratios[a]	3.4	3.4	4.5	4.5	4.5
Growth rates (constant prices)					
Gross national product	6.2	6.8	5.2	5.5	5.4
Population	2.4	2.3	2.3	2.2	2.3
Per capita GNP	3.8	4.5	2.9	3.3	3.1
	Outward-oriented NICs and LDCs				
Savings ratios					
Domestic savings ratio	18.2	19.6	21.8	24.7	23.3
Foreign savings ratio	2.9	2.2	3.9	2.6	3.2
Incremental capital output ratios[a]	3.0	3.3	4.4	2.7	3.3
Growth rates (constant prices)					
Gross national product	7.3	8.2	5.5	9.3	7.9
Population	2.5	2.4	2.3	2.1	2.3
Per capita GNP	4.8	5.8	2.3	7.2	5.7

Inward-oriented NICs

						Inward-oriented LDCs					Inward-oriented NICs and LDC's				
Savings ratios															
Domestic savings ratio	20.3	20.0	20.1	21.3	20.7	16.6	17.0	18.1	19.7	18.9	18.9	19.0	19.5	20.8	20.2
Foreign savings ratio	1.5	2.2	4.7	3.2	4.0	1.5	1.1	4.0	3.7	3.9	1.4	1.8	4.5	3.4	3.9
Incremental capital output ratios[a]	3.1	2.8	4.4	4.9	4.4	5.1	6.5	4.7	5.8	5.2	3.5	3.4	4.5	5.2	4.8
Growth rates (constant prices)															
Gross national product	6.9	8.5	5.0	5.0	4.9	3.9	2.7	5.1	4.4	4.9	5.9	8.3	4.9	4.7	4.8
Population	2.5	2.6	2.6	2.6	2.6	2.4	2.2	2.2	2.1	2.1	2.4	2.3	2.3	2.2	2.2
Per capita GNP	4.4	5.9	2.4	2.4	2.3	1.5	0.5	2.8	2.3	2.8	3.5	6.0	2.6	2.5	2.6

NICs with internal shocks

						LDCs with internal shocks					Economies with favorable shocks				
Savings ratios															
Domestic savings ratio	19.5	19.4	21.2	24.7	22.9	18.3	16.6	12.4	14.8	13.7	13.8	19.8	25.5	26.5	26.0
Foreign savings ratio	0.6	0.8	2.4	-0.9	0.8	0.6	1.9	7.3	0.5	3.7	1.2	-0.6	-4.5	-0.6	-2.7
Incremental capital output ratios[a]	3.4	3.0	9.5	4.5	6.1	3.8	3.7	6.6	28.6	10.1	2.1	2.1	3.0	4.4	3.7
Growth rates (constant prices)															
Gross national product	5.5	5.7	1.9	4.4	2.9	4.6	4.5	3.0	0.8	1.6	6.2	7.0	8.0	6.1	7.1
Population	2.6	2.6	2.6	2.6	2.6	2.9	3.0	3.0	3.0	3.0	2.3	2.2	2.2	2.2	2.2
Per capita GNP	2.9	3.1	-0.7	1.4	0.3	1.7	1.5	0.0	-2.2	-1.4	3.8	4.8	5.7	5.7	4.8

Source: Bela Balassa (1981) 'Adjustment to External Shocks in Developing Economies', *World Bank Staff Working Paper* No. 472.

[a] Incremental capital–output ratios have been calculated assuming one year lag between investment and output. For example, the 1970–3 ratio has been derived by dividing the sum of gross domestic investment in 1970, 1971 and 1972 by the increment in GNP between 1970 and 1978, both in constant prices.

inward-oriented NICs, rates of economic growth fell from 6.9 percent in 1963–73 to 5.0 percent in 1973–6 and remained at this level in 1976–9. At the same time, in NICs experiencing internal shocks GNP growth rates declined from 5.5 percent in 1963–73 to 1.9 percent in 1973–6, followed by an increase to 4.4 percent in 1976–9 as the internal shocks were increasingly overcome.

Among the LDCs, outward-oriented economies experienced a decline in their average GNP growth rate from 7.3 percent in 1963–73 to 7.1 percent in 1973–6, followed by an increase to 7.9 percent in 1976–9. By contrast, inward-oriented LDCs increased their rates of economic growth from 3.9 percent in 1963–73 to 5.1 percent in 1973–6, but experienced a decline to 4.4 percent in 1976–9. Within the inward-oriented group, an uninterrupted decline is shown for LDCs experiencing internal shocks, from 4.6 percent in 1963–73 to 3.0 percent in 1973–6 and, again, to 0.8 percent in 1976–9.

The favorable effects of an outward-oriented development strategy on economic growth are also indicated by a cross-section investigation of the 24 developing economies experiencing adverse external shocks. For the 1973–9 period taken as a whole, the Spearman rank correlation coefficient between the extent of reliance on export promotion in response to external shocks (defined as the ratio of export expansion associated with increases in export market shares to the balance-of-payments effects of external shocks) and the rate of growth of GNP was 0.60, statistically significant at the 1 percent level.[5]

A positive correlation between the extent of reliance of export promotion and the rate of growth of GNP was also observed for the NICs and for the LDCs, taken separately.[6] The Spearman rank correlation coefficients were 0.59 and 0.66, respectively, in the two cases, statistically significant at the 5 percent level. In turn, reliance on import substitution and rates of economic growth were negatively correlated in the case of the LDCs with a Spearman rank correlation coefficient of −0.54 (statistically significant at the 5 percent level), while no correlation was shown for the NICs.

Outward-oriented developing economies thus had a more favorable growth performance after 1973, even though they experienced substantially larger external shocks than developing economies characterized by inward orientation. In the 1974–8 period, the balance-of-payments effects of these shocks averaged 7.5 percent of GNP in the first case and 3.9 percent in the second. Yet, between 1973 and 1979, cumulative GNP growth was 20 percentage points greater in outward-oriented than in inward-oriented developing economies. And, while the former group succeeded in increasing its average annual GNP growth rate by 0.6 percentage points compared with the 1963–73 period, the latter group experienced a decline of 0.8 percentage points.

The determinants of economic growth

Inter-country differences in GNP growth rates may be decomposed into differences in incremental capital–output ratios and in domestic and foreign savings ratios. In the absence of data that would permit estimating production-function type relationships, inter-country differences in incremental capital–output ratios may be taken as an indication of the efficiency of using existing and incremental resources. The relationship is not entirely unidirectional, inasmuch as variations in the rate of economic growth due to external causes will affect incremental capital–output ratios. Nevertheless, available information indicates that differences in these ratios largely reflect differences in policy performance in the developing economies under study.

Thus, outward-oriented economies that experienced greater than average external shocks had more favorable performance in terms of incremental capital–output ratios than inward-oriented economies. Between 1963–73 and 1973–9, incremental capital–output ratios rose from 3.0 to 3.4 in outward-oriented NICs and from 3.1 to 4.6 in inward-oriented NICs; they declined from 3.2 to 3.1 in outward-oriented LDCs and increased from 5.1 and 5.2 in inward-oriented LDCs.

Savings performance was also more favorable under outward than under inward orientation. Among the NICs, average domestic savings ratios increased from 16.9 percent in 1963–73 to 23.5 percent in 1973–9 in outward-oriented economies, whereas practically no change (from 20.3 percent to 20.7 percent) occurred in inward-oriented economies. And although outward- and inward-oriented LDCs experienced changes of a similar magnitude – from 20.3 percent to 22.4 percent in the first case and from 16.6 percent to 18.9 percent in the second – domestic savings ratios remained higher in economies characterized by outward orientation.

Among inward-oriented economies experiencing internal shocks, incremental capital–output ratios rose from 3.4 to 6.1 in the NICs and from 3.7 to 10.1 in the LDCs between 1963–73 and 1973–9. At the same time, domestic savings ratios rose from 19.5 percent to 22.9 percent in the first group and declined from 18.3 percent to 13.7 percent in the second.

In turn, economies experiencing favorable external shocks were not able to translate these gains into higher rates of economic growth in a sustained fashion. Although their average GNP growth rate increased from 6.2 percent in 1963–73 to 8.0 percent in 1973–6, it declined again to 6.1 percent in 1976–9. The results reflect offsetting changes in incremental capital–output ratios and savings ratios. Domestic savings ratios rose from 13.8 percent in 1963–73 to 26.0 percent in 1973–9, while incremental capital–output ratios increased from 2.1 to 3.7.

Finally, the net inflow of foreign capital averaged slightly below 4 percent of GDP in NICs as well as in LDCs in the 1974–8 period, with the averages being half a percentage point lower in economies characterized by outward orientation within both groups. In turn, developing economies experiencing favorable external shocks had, on balance, a net outflow of capital.

At the same time, there are differences among developing economies in the use to which the inflow of foreign capital has been put. This question will be taken up in conjunction with an examination of policies affecting the efficiency of resource allocation, savings and foreign borrowing in the 28 developing economies.

POLICY RESPONSE TO EXTERNAL SHOCKS: AN EVALUATION

The efficiency of resource use

The efficiency of using existing and incremental resources is affected by relative incentives to exports and import substitution, to manufacturing and primary activities, to traded and non-traded goods, and to capital-intensive and labor-intensive activities, as well as by credit rationing, investment incentives and the choice of investment projects in the public sector.

As noted in the first section of this chapter, outward-oriented economies tended to provide similar incentives to sales in domestic and in export markets as well as to manufacturing and primary activities, while inward-oriented economies discriminated against exports and favored manufacturing over primary activities. Such discrimination lowers the efficiency of resource allocation because activities with higher domestic resource costs of foreign exchange are favored over activities where this cost is lower. Also, in the confines of small domestic markets, economies of scale are forgone, the extent of capacity utilization is limited, and there is little inducement for technological change.

By contrast, outward-oriented economies can ensure resource allocation according to comparative advantage, use large-scale production methods, and attain greater capacity utilization through exporting. Their exposure to foreign markets also provides incentives for technological change, and the experience acquired in changing product composition in response to shifts in foreign demand imparts a certain flexibility to their economies, enabling them to respond better to external shocks than is the case under inward orientation.

Policies favoring import substitution generally take the form of industrial protection that discriminates against primary activities. Price controls on primary products, applied to a much greater extent in inward-oriented than in outward-oriented economies, have a similar effect. In Tanzania, for example, fixing agricultural prices at low levels adversely affected production and exports. Also, failure to raise domestic energy prices *pari passu* with increases in world market prices discouraged energy savings, as well as the replacement of imported energy sources, in a number of inward-oriented economies.

Export promotion and import substitution are further affected by the exchange rate that governs the allocation of resources between traded and non-traded goods. In outward-oriented economies, the real exchange rate (the official exchange rate adjusted for changes in relative prices at home and abroad) depreciated or, in the event of an appreciation, its effects on exports were offset by promotional measures during the period under consideration.[7]

In turn, among inward-oriented economies, the appreciation of the real exchange rate led to losses in export market shares and to increases in import shares[8] in Colombia, Mexico, Egypt, Morocco and Turkey. In the same group, the effects of currency overvaluation on exports were largely offset by measures of export promotion in Indonesia and the Ivory Coast, while measures of import protection led to reductions in import shares in Israel, Portugal, Yugoslavia, Jamaica, Tanzania and Zambia.

Relative incentives to capital-intensive and labor-intensive activities are affected by the rate of interest. Among inward-oriented economies, only India had positive real interest rates. With the exception of Kenya, this was the case in all outward-oriented economies once the immediate effects of the quadrupling of oil prices had been absorbed.

On the whole, therefore, inward-oriented economies biased the system of incentives against labor-intensive activities; such a bias did not exist, or it was less pronounced, under outward orientation.[9] With negative real interest rates, credit rationing, too, was more prevalent under inward orientation than under outward orientation, and it tended to favor import-substituting activities, irrespective of whether rationing was done by the banks or by the government. In the first case, the lower risk of protected activities provided an inducement for lending; in the second case, credit rationing became part of the arsenal of protective measures.

Apart from credit rationing, governments may intervene in the choice of private investment projects through investment incentives in the form of credit and tax preferences. Inward-oriented economies generally used these measures to favor investments in import-substituting industries, while this was not the case in outward-oriented economies.[10]

Incremental capital–output ratios are further affected by the choice of public projects. The share of public investment was generally higher in inward-oriented than in outward-oriented economies, and there was a tendency to give less attention to efficiency considerations in the choice of public projects. The resulting deterioration in the efficiency of investment, with incremental capital–output ratios approximately doubling between 1963–73 and 1976–9, was particularly pronounced in countries that experienced rapid increases in investable funds. This was the case in Indonesia and in Nigeria, where the rise in oil prices, and in Morocco, where the (temporary) rise in phosphate prices, added to foreign exchange earnings. High-cost, capital-intensive investments in the public sector were undertaken, albeit to a lesser extent, also in the Ivory Coast, Portugal, Tanzania and Turkey.

The generation of domestic savings

Domestic savings consist of private (personal and business) savings and public savings. Personal savings are affected by the real interest rate and business savings by investment incentives, while the deficit in the budget of current revenues and expenditures indicates the extent of public savings or dissavings.

There is evidence that real interest rates and domestic savings tend to be positively correlated in developing economies. Various factors may explain the existence of this relationship. Negative real interest rates encourage the (often clandestine) outflow of capital, induce workers to keep their earnings abroad, provide incentives to holding gold, contribute to the accumulation of consumers' durables, and induce the use of borrowed funds to increase consumption.

Among individual economies, the effects of positive real interest rates are apparent in the high and rising domestic savings ratios in outward-oriented economies, the only exception being Uruguay. In turn, apart from countries experiencing favorable external shocks, domestic savings ratios were lower and showed a tendency to decline in inward-oriented economies, the exception being India, which had positive real interest rates after 1974.

Among the economies under study, Korea and Singapore experienced the largest increases in domestic savings ratios, with a rise by two-thirds between 1963–73 and 1976–9. They were followed by Taiwan, where domestic savings ratios increased by one-third during this period. In these instances, the effects of positive real interest rates on personal savings were reinforced by the impact of investment incentives on business savings, and the surplus in the government budget further raised the domestic savings ratio.

In turn, the adverse effects of negative real interest rates on savings were aggravated by government budget deficits in inward-oriented economies experiencing adverse external shocks. Thus, Jamaica, Israel, Egypt and Tanzania, which experienced by far the largest budget deficits among the developing economies under study, had the smallest domestic savings ratios. In the 1977–9 period, average ratios of government budget deficits to GNP were 20, 18, 16 and 9 percent in the four countries respectively, while their domestic savings ratios averaged 12, 12, 12 and 9 percent.

Compared with the 1964–73 period, the domestic savings ratio declined by one-half in Jamaica and Tanzania, where budget deficits increased the most; the ratio fell by one-fourth in Israel, where these deficits rose to a lesser extent; and showed no change in Egypt, whose budget deficits changed little. By contrast, their improved budget position led to a near doubling of average domestic savings ratios in developing economies experiencing favorable external shocks.

The inflow of foreign capital

All developing economies suffering external shocks increased their foreign borrowing in response to the deterioration of their balance of payments that resulted from the quadrupling of oil prices and the world recession. There were differences, however, as regards the extent of foreign borrowing and the uses to which it was put.

Among outward-oriented NICs, Singapore and Taiwan accepted a temporary decline in the rate of economic growth in order to limit reliance on foreign loans and used the proceeds of these loans in productive investments. They were thus able to maintain debt-service ratios at low levels throughout the period. Debt-service ratios stabilized at a higher level in Korea, which relied to a greater extent on foreign borrowing at the outset but was able to subsequently reduce external financing as the amounts borrowed were productively used. Finally, given the large external shocks they suffered, Chile and Uruguay could not forgo continued foreign borrowing but limited increases in debt-service ratios through the productive use of the amounts borrowed.

Among inward-oriented NICs, Brazil, Israel, Portugal and Turkey utilized the proceeds of foreign loans in part to maintain the rate of growth of domestic consumption and channeled a substantial share of new investments into high-cost, import-substituting activities. The latter conclusion also applies to Mexico and Yugoslavia, where the rate of investment increased during the period under consideration. In the absence of rapid increases in exports, debt-service ratios rose to a considerable extent, the exception being Israel, which had a high ratio already at the beginning of the period and benefited from large unilateral transfers. Finally, Argentina, with negligible external shocks, experienced an increase in its debt-service ratio only towards the end of the period.

The inflow of foreign capital was used largely to avoid (Tanzania) or to minimize (Jamaica and Peru) decreases in consumption per head in LDCs experiencing internal shocks. In turn, with the exception of Zambia, foreign borrowing contributed to increases in investment shares in the other LDCs studied. However, with losses in export market shares, debt-service ratios increased in most cases. This ratio declined, or changed little, in outward-oriented LDCs that placed reliance largely on measures of domestic adjustment.

At the same time, in the 1973–9 period, there was a negative correlation between the debt-service ratio and the GNP growth rate, with the Spearman correlation coefficient of -0.35 (statistically significant at the 5 percent level). This result reflects the fact that increases in debt-service ratios eventually constrained economic growth in cases where the proceeds of foreign borrowing were not productively used.

CONCLUSION AND POLICY IMPLICATIONS

The estimates of the OECD study point to the conclusion that developing economies at higher levels of industrialization were more successful in overcoming external shocks through domestic adjustment than their less industrialized counterparts. This result appears to support the proposition that the objective conditions for adjustment were better for the more industrialized than for the less industrialized developing economies. An alternative hypothesis is that policy performance was superior in the first group than in the second.

The size of external shocks provides an indication of objective conditions, inasmuch as the magnitude of the task to be performed will affect the possibilities for successful domestic adjustment. According to the results of the OECD study, the balance-of-payments effects of external shocks represent a higher proportion of GNP in the three more industrialized groups, with the less industrialized, agriculture-based economies and South Asian countries experiencing the smallest external shocks. And, although in the World Bank sample external shocks appeared to get somewhat larger for the LDCs than for the NICs, there was no correlation between the extent of external shocks and economic performance.

Furthermore, the World Bank study indicates the differential performance of developing economies that followed different policies. On the average, outward-oriented NICs fully offset – while outward-oriented LDCs offset two-fifths – the balance-of-payments effects of external shocks through export expansion and import substitution. This ratio was only one-eigth in inward-oriented NICs, and reductions in export shares and the rise in import shares augmented the adverse balance-of-payments effects of external shocks by more than one-half in inward-oriented LDCs.

The differences in the performance of outward-oriented and inward-oriented economies are even greater if one considers export promotion alone, while the differences between the NICs and the LDCs are reduced as a result. Thus, increases in export shares raised export values by 15 percent in outward-oriented NICs and by 10 percent in outward-oriented LDCs, while declines of 7 percent and 11 percent, respectively, occurred in inward-oriented NICs and LDCs, reaching 17 percent in both the NICs and the LDCs experiencing internal shocks.

At the same time, the findings of the World Bank study indicate that export performance is closely linked to economic growth. This result was obtained both in a cross-section investigation and in a comparison of the results for the individual groups. Correspondingly, after a temporary decline, GNP growth rates accelerated in the two outward-oriented groups, whereas the decline in growth rates was maintained in inward-oriented NICs, and the increases experienced in the early part of the period were reversed in inward-oriented LDCs.

It appears, then, that domestic adjustment increasingly involved a rise in output through export expansion and import substitution in outward-oriented economies, boosting the rate of economic growth and providing the foreign exchange necessary to finance the imports associated with higher GNP growth rates. Such was not the case in inward-oriented economies, where the adjustment increasingly took the form of import savings associated with lower rates of economic growth.

The latter conclusion applies with particular force to economies characterized by internal shocks that experienced the largest decline in GNP growth rates, with the resulting import savings offsetting, on the average, 54 percent of the balance-of-payments effects of external shocks in the NICs and 29 percent in the LDCs during the 1974–8 period. The comparable figures for domestic adjustment through export expansion and import substitution were − 48 percent and − 18 percent in the two groups, thus reinforcing the adverse balance-of-payments effects of external shocks.

It should be emphasized that internal shocks reflected policy decisions in each particular case, including that of Portugal, where the policies adopted after the 1974 revolution had adverse effects on the national economy. In these economies, and in all the developing economies studied, the policies applied affected the allocation of existing and incremental resources, the amount of domestic savings, as well as foreign borrowing and its uses.

Outward-oriented economies provided, on the average, similar incentives to exports and imports substitution and to primary production and manufacturing, while inward-oriented economies discriminated against exports and favored manufacturing over primary activities. Outward-oriented economies also placed less reliance on price controls and on interest rate ceilings than did inward-oriented economies. More generally, they gave greater scope to the market mechanism and tended to avoid 'white elephants' in public sector investment that were often observed in inward-oriented economies.

Apart from affecting the efficiency of resource allocation, interest rates also influenced the amount saved. A further determining factor of domestic savings was the balance in the government budget. Except for developing economies benefiting from favorable external shocks, budget deficits tended to be high and rising over time in inward-oriented economies. In turn, outward-oriented economies reduced or eliminated their budget deficits, and several of them provided increased incentives to private investment.

Government budget deficits further contributed to inflation. Throughout the period under consideration, inflation rates were particularly high in Argentina and Israel. High inflation rates, in turn, gave rise to uncertainty, as exchange rates and interest rates fluctuated to a considerable extent in real terms for lack of simultaneous adjustments in these rates, and led to economic disruptions in general. By contrast, reductions in the budget deficit contributed to lower inflation and improved economic performance in Chile and in Uruguay.

By and large, outward-oriented economies were willing to accept lower rates of economic growth in the wake of the quadrupling of oil prices and the world recession in order to stabilize their economies and to avoid large foreign indebtedness. In turn, in inward-oriented economies, except for those experiencing internal shocks, foreign borrowing was used to accelerate economic growth. This proved temporary, however, as the proceeds of foreign borrowing were in part used to increase consumption and the efficiency of investment deteriorated under the policies followed.

These conclusions point to the importance of policies in effecting domestic adjustment in response to external shocks. While temporary retrenchment may be desirable to avoid the creation of economic imbalances and excessive reliance on foreign borrowing, the key to successful adjustment is to increase output through export expansion and efficient import substitution. This, in turn, requires taking measures that contribute to the efficient allocation of existing and incremental resources and to increased savings.

NOTES

1. The references to the chapter list the author's publications which provide detailed estimates for the period under consideration as well as the findings of his earlier research for the 1960–73 period, when world market conditions were favorable. The figures presented in Chapter 6 of the *World Development Report 1981* (New York; Oxford University Press, August 1981) are based on these estimates, with modifications made with regard to the measurement of terms of trade effects as noted below.
2. They have further been decomposed into a 'pure terms of trade effect', calculated on the assumption that the balance of trade expressed in '1972' prices was in equilibrium, and an 'unbalanced trade', indicating the impact of the rise of import prices on the deficit (surplus) in the balance of trade expressed in '1972' prices.
3. The estimates presented in the *World Development Report 1981* took the rise of the price of manufactured goods exported by the developed countries as the benchmark, thereby largely excluding the unbalanced trade effect, with corresponding adjustments in the amount of additional net external financing.
4. The NICs have been defined as developing economies with per capita incomes between $1,100 and $3,500 in 1978 and a share of manufacturing in GDP of at least 20 percent or higher in 1977. The investigation includes every NIC other than Greece, Hong Kong and Singapore. In turn, the LDCs cover the spectrum between the NICs and the least developed economies.
5. This result cannot be explained by differences in the extent of external shocks, market size, incomes per head, or the composition of exports (the share of manufactured goods in merchandise exports and the commodity concentration of exports). Thus, in a cross-section analysis, none of these variables has been found to be significantly correlated with reliance on export promotion in response to external shocks.
6. The findings complement the author's earlier results for NICs concerning the favorable effects of outward orientation on economic growth in the 1960–73 period, when world market conditions were favorable.
7. Towards the end of the period, Korea provides an exception inasmuch as the continued appreciation of its currency led to losses in export market shares in 1978.
8. More accurately, increases in the income elasticity of import demand.

9. Excessively high real interest rates would, however, adversely affect the private sector. This was not the case in any of the developing economies during the period under consideration, as real interest rates in no case exceeded 8 percent.
10. Again, Korea provides an exception towards the end of the period.

REFERENCES

Balassa, Bela (1978) 'Export Incentives and Export Performance in Developing Countries: A Comparative Analysis', *Weltwirtschaftliches Archiv*, (1), pp. 24–61. Spanish translation in *Politicas de Promocion de Exportaciones*, proceedings of seminar on Policies of Export Promotion sponsored by ECLA, the World Bank and the United Nations Development Program (UNDP), Santiago, Chile, November 1976. Santiago, United Nations Economic Commission for Latin America. Vol. III pp. 3–54. World Bank Reprint Series No. 59.

Balassa, Bela (1978) 'Exports and Economic Growth: Further Evidence', *Journal of Development Economics* (June), pp. 181–9. World Bank Reprint Series No. 68.

Balassa, Bela (1981) 'The Newly Industrializing Developing Countries after the Oil Crisis', *Weltwirtschaftliches Archiv*, Band 117, Heft 1, pp. 142–94. Portuguese translation in *Pesquisa e Planejamento Economico* (April 1981), pp. 1–77; Spanish translation in *Integracion Latinoamericana* (September 1981), pp. 3–46. Republished as Essay 2 in Bela Balassa, *The Newly Industrializing Countries in the World Economy*. New York, Pergamon Press, pp. 29–81. World Bank Reprint Series No. 190.

Balassa, Bela (1981) 'Policy Responses to External Shocks in Selected Latin American Countries', *Quarterly Review of Economics and Business* (Summer), pp. 131–64. Also in *Export Diversification and the New Protectionism: The Experience of Latin America*, Werner Baer and Malcolm Gillis, eds. Proceedings of a Conference co-sponsored by the National Bureau of Economic Research, the Bureau of Economic and Business Research, University of Illinois, and the Fundacao Instituto de Pesquisas Economicas of the University of Sao Paulo, Sao Paulo, Brazil, March 1980. Champaign, Ill., National Bureau of Economic Research and the Bureau of Economic and Business Research, University of Illinois, pp. 131–64. Portuguese translation in *Estudos Economicos* (April-June), pp. 11–50. Republished as Essay 3 in Balassa (1981) *The Newly Industrializing Countries in the World Economy*, pp. 83–108.

Balassa, Bela (1981) *The Balance of Payments Effects of External Shocks and of Policy Responses to These Shocks in Non-OPEC Developing Countries* (with André Barsony and Anne Richards). Paris, OECD Development Centre.

Balassa, Bela (1982) 'Structural Adjustment Policies in Developing Countries', *World Development* (January), pp. 23–38. Reprinted as Chapter 4 in Bela Balassa (1983) *Change and Challenge in the World Economy*. London, Macmillan, pp. 63–87.

Balassa, Bela (1982) 'Disequilibrium Analysis in Developing Countries', *World Development* (December) pp. 1027–38.

Balassa, Bela (1984) 'The Policy Experience of Twelve Less Developed Countries, 1973–1978', in *Comparative Development Perspectives*, Essays in Honor of Lloyd G. Reynolds (Gustave Rains, Robert L. West, Mark Leiserson, Cynthia Morris, eds). Boulder, Col. Westview Press, pp. 96–123.

Balassa, Bela (1984) 'Adjustment to External Shocks in Developing Countries', in *The Economics of Relative Prices* (Béla Csikós-Nagy, Douglas Hague, and Graham Hall eds). London, Macmillan, pp. 352–84.

15 · POLICY RESPONSES TO EXOGENOUS SHOCKS IN DEVELOPING COUNTRIES

This chapter reports on the results of research on the policy responses of developing countries to exogenous (external) shocks in the 1973–8 and 1978–83 periods. These shocks included terms-of-trade effects, associated largely with increases in oil prices; export volume effects, resulting from the recession-induced slowdown of world trade; and, in the second period, interest rate effects, due to increases in interest rates in world financial markets. Policy responses to external shocks took the form of additional net external financing, represented by increased borrowing compared with past trends; export promotion, reflected by increases in export market shares; import substitution expressed by decreases in the income elasticity of import demand; and deflationary macroeconomic policies, entailing a decline in the growth of demand for imports. (For a description of the methodology applied and results for earlier periods, see my 1985 paper.)

Table 15.1 provides summary data on the balance-of-payments effects of external shocks and of policy responses to these shocks in the two periods. Developing countries were classified as outward- and inward-oriented, depending on whether they provided similar incentives to exports and to import substitution or discriminated in favor of import substitution and against exports. Both groups include newly industrializing countries (NICs) and less developed countries (LDCs) although, to save space, only their combined results are reported in the table.

Among the NICs, Korea, Singapore and Taiwan adopted an outward-oriented development strategy in the early 1960s and continued with this strategy after 1973. In the mid-1970s they were joined by Chile and Uruguay, who had previously applied inward-oriented policies but turned outward in response to the external shocks. Conversely, Argentina, Brazil, Israel, Mexico,

This chapter was prepared while the author was at the Johns Hopkins University and the World Bank. Research assistance by Shigeru Akiyama is gratefully acknowledged. The author alone is responsible for the opinions expressed; they do not reflect the views of the World Bank. First published in *American Economic Review, Papers and Proceedings*, May 1986.

Table 15.1 Balance-of-payments effects of external shocks and of policy responses to these shocks[a]

	Outward-oriented countries		Inward-oriented countries	
	1974–8	1979–83	1974–8	1979–83
External shocks[b]				
Terms of trade effects	6.3	8.4	3.6	2.8
Export volume effects	2.4	4.9	0.9	0.4
Interest rate effects	—	1.7	—	1.6
Total	8.8	15.0	4.5	5.0
Policy responses[c]				
Additional net external financing	−26.4	−11.5	89.0	37.6
Export promotion	48.6	29.0	−14.9	11.5[d]
Import substitution	58.5	24.5	15.4	9.8
Effects of deflationary policy	19.4	58.0	10.5	41.1

Source: World Bank data base.
[a] For definitions, see text.
[b] Shown as percent of GNP.
[c] Shown as percent of external shocks.
[d] −2.3 excluding fuel exports.

Portugal, Turkey and Yugoslavia maintained, or reinforced, their inward-oriented stance. Among the LDCs, Kenya, Mauritius, Thailand and Tunisia were classified as having followed outward-oriented policies, and Egypt, India, Jamaica, Morocco, Peru, the Philippines, Tanzania and Zambia as having pursued inward-oriented policies.

The classification scheme was established for the first period of external shocks; for reasons of comparability, it was retained for the second period even though policy changes were made in several countries. In particular, Turkey undertook a far-reaching policy reform in January 1980, while Chile and Uruguay distorted the system of incentives by failing to adjust their exchange rates *pari passu* with domestic inflation.

EXTERNAL SHOCKS AND POLICY RESPONSES TO THE SHOCKS IN 1973–8 AND 1978–83

The results show that outward-oriented countries (OOCs) suffered substantially larger terms of trade losses and adverse export volume effects than inward-oriented countries (IOCs) during both periods of external shocks. This is explained by the larger share of foreign trade in their gross national product (28 percent of the OOCs, on average, in 1973 compared with 10 percent for the IOCs) that was only partially compensated by the favorable commodity composition of their exports.

One also observes considerable differences in policy responses to external shocks in the two groups of countries, when the sequencing of these responses is of further interest. In the first period of external shocks, the IOCs offset nearly the entire adverse balance-of-payments impact of external shocks by additional net external financing. This was done with a view to maintaining past economic growth rates, notwithstanding the deterioration of the external environment. They did not succeed in this effort, however, and the rate of growth of GNP declined during the period.

The lack of output-increasing (expenditure-switching) policies contributed in an important way to the deceleration of the rate of economic growth in the IOCs. Losses in export market shares practically offset import substitution in these countries, with their combined impact on the balance of payments and on domestic output being virtually nil. At the same time, losses in export market shares accentuated the effects of external borrowing on debt-service ratios, defined as the ratio of net interest payments and amortization to merchandise exports. This ratio nearly doubled in the space of five years, rising from 22 percent in 1973 to 43 percent in 1978, on the average.

The OOCs initially applied deflationary policies to limit reliance on external finance so that their debt-service ratio remained at slightly below 12 percent. The resulting decline in GNP growth rates remained temporary, however, as the OOCs adopted output-increasing policies of export promotion and import substitution that fully compensated for the adverse balance-of-payments effects of external shocks and led to the acceleration of economic growth.

The second period of external shocks thus found the IOCs (but not the OOCs) with considerable foreign indebtedness. Additional borrowing was possible for a while, except for Turkey which was practically bankrupt in 1979 and Yugoslavia which encountered borrowing limitations in 1980. However, with further increases in their debt-service ratios, the other IOCs also approached fiduciary limits and, following the August 1982 Mexican debt crisis, they ceased to be creditworthy for commercial bank loans.

Correspondingly, the IOCs made less use of additional net external financing in the second period of external shocks than in the first. They applied deflationary policies instead, leading to a decline in their economic growth rates. This result reflects the fact that the IOCs largely eschewed output-increasing policies of export promotion and import substitution.

In fact, the extent of import substitution in the IOCs declined during the second period of external shocks and discoveries of oil deposits in Mexico and Peru fully account for the observed increases in average export market shares. Thus, adjusting for the rise in petroleum exports, the IOCs again experienced losses in foreign markets. And although the losses were smaller than in the first period of external shocks, this was due to the improved performance of a few countries. The January 1980 policy reform, representing increased outward orientation, led to a near-doubling of Turkish exports between 1980 and 1983, while export subsidies contributed to the expansion of exports in Brazil. All other IOCs lost export market shares.

The OOCs also applied deflationary policies in response to the external shocks they suffered after 1978. But the resulting decline in GNP growth rates again remained temporary and the countries in question subsequently resumed higher rates of economic growth. This occurred as the OOCs continued to apply output-increasing policies, leading to increases in export market shares and import substitution, even though they had to rely to a greater extent on deflationary policies than during the first period, when the balance-of-payments effects of external shocks were much smaller.

At the same time, the OOCs continued to limit reliance on external finance, so that their average debt-service ratio remained below 14 percent notwithstanding increases in world interest rates. By contrast, debt-service ratios continued to rise in the IOCs, albeit at a slower rate than beforehand, reaching 53 percent in 1983.

THE POLICY MEASURES APPLIED AND THEIR ECONOMIC EFFECTS

In both periods, then, the OOCs made considerable gains in export market shares. In turn, the IOCs experienced losses in market shares, even though these losses were attenuated in the second period of external shocks by the export-promoting measures applied in a few countries. Providing similar incentives to exports and to import substitution in the OOCs, compared with the continued bias of the incentive system against exports in the IOCs, contributed in an important way to the observed differences in export performance.

Another contributing factor was exchange rate policy, with the adoption of realistic exchange rates in the OOCs and appreciation in real (inflation-adjusted) terms in most of the IOCs. Increased overvaluation in the IOCs was associated with foreign borrowing that obstructed adjustment in the exchange rate as the external financing of the balance-of-payments deficit permitted maintaining an overvalued currency.In turn, the OOCs did not use foreign borrowing to support the exchange rate.

The OOCs also experienced import substitution to a greater extent than the IOCs. This result may appear surprising since the bias against exports favored the replacement of imports by domestic production in the latter group of countries. Various factors contributed to this outcome.

To begin with, the adoption of realistic exchange rates contributed to import substitution parallel with export expansion in the OOCs, which was not the case in the IOCs. Export expansion in the OOCs also permitted simultaneous import substitution as the exploitation of economies of scale led to lower costs. Such efficient import substitution contrasted with inefficient import replacement in many of the IOCs, where net foreign exchange savings tended to decline as shifts occurred towards industries where the countries in question had a comparative disadvantage and increasingly encountered domestic market limitations.

Furthermore, the OOCs experienced import substitution in the primary sector as they provided similar incentives to primary and to manufacturing activities, while primary production suffered considerable discrimination in the IOCs. Finally, the former, but not the latter, group of countries encouraged energy savings, representing import substitution in fuels under the conventions adopted in this chapter, by increasing energy prices parallel with the rise in world market prices.

The lack of discrimination against exports and against primary activities raised the level of investment efficiency in the IOCs, thereby contributing to their economic growth. The liberalization of prices and the application of economic considerations in public investment projects also had a favorable impact on the efficiency of investment in these countries. Export expansion, too, had beneficial effects by permitting higher capacity utilization and the exploitation of economies of scale.

In turn, the bias of the incentive system against exports and against primary activities, together with the widespread application of price control, reduced the efficiency of investment in the IOCs. The situation was aggravated by the lack of sufficient attention given to economic considerations in the large public investment programs of these countries.

These considerations explain the observed differences in incremental capital–output ratios, taken to represent the level of investment efficiency notwithstanding the well-known limitations of these ratios. In the 1973–9 period, the ratios averaged 4.1 in the OOCs and 4.9 in the IOCs; the corresponding figures were 7.4 and 8.6 in the 1979–84 period, when the deflationary policies applied raised the ratios in both groups of countries.

The OOCs also exhibited higher domestic savings ratios than the IOCs. Between 1973 and 1979, these ratios averaged 25.6 percent in the former group of countries and 21.0 percent in the latter. The differences were maintained in the 1979–84 period, the average ratios being 25.7 percent in the OOCs and 20.9 percent in the IOCs.

These differences pertain equally to public and to private savings. While the IOCs practiced public dissaving as they incurred large budget deficits, the OOCs limited the size of these deficits. Also, real interest rates tended to be negative in the IOCs and positive in the OOCs, with corresponding effects on private savings.

Higher investment efficiency and higher domestic savings ratios in the OOCs were only partially offset by greater foreign borrowing in the IOCs. Correspondingly, rates of economic growth were considerably higher in the former than in the latter group of countries, with the differences increasing over time.

CONCLUSION

This chapter reviewed the adjustment experience of developing countries applying different policies in response to the external shocks of the 1973–8 and 1978–83 periods. Although outward-oriented countries suffered considerably larger external shocks than inward-oriented countries, these differences were offset several times as a result of the policies followed. Thus, while the OOCs accepted a temporary decline in GNP growth rates in both periods in order to limit reliance on foreign borrowing, their economic growth accelerated subsequently, owing to the output-increasing policies applied.

The IOCs relied practically exclusively on foreign borrowing in response to the external shocks of the first period. But, the bias of the incentive system against exports and primary activities, price control and the frequent choice of hight-cost public investment projects did not provide for the efficient use of these funds, and of investable funds in general, leading to lower economic growth rates and compromising their creditworthiness.

In eschewing output-increasing policies, limitations of external finance in the second period of external shocks led to the application of deflationary policies in the IOCs, further increasing differences in the growth performances of the two groups of countries. Between 1982 and 1984, GNP growth rates averaged 5.3 percent in the OOCs and 1.7 percent in the IOCs.

REFERENCE

Balassa, Bela (1985) 'Adjustment Policies in Developing Countries: A Reassessment', *World Development*, reprinted as Chapter 5 in *Change and Challenge in the World Economy*. London, Macmillan, pp. 89–101.

16 · EXPORT INCENTIVES AND EXPORT PERFORMANCE IN DEVELOPING COUNTRIES: A COMPARATIVE ANALYSIS

INTRODUCTION

This chapter provides a comparative evaluation of export incentives and their effects on exports and economic performance in 11 major developing countries that have already established an industrial base. The chapter concentrates largely on the experience of the 1966–73 period, when the export incentive schemes of the individual countries were by and large in full operation. 1973 was chosen as the terminal year because of the effects of the oil crisis in subsequent years.

The countries under consideration are Argentina, Brazil, Chile, Colombia, Mexico, Israel, Yugoslavia, India, Korea, Singapore and Taiwan. They have been classified in four groups, depending on the timing and the extent of their export promotion efforts. In 1973, these countries accounted for 68 percent of the exports of manufactured goods by the developing countries.[1] Another 16 percent came from Hong Kong which started exporting manufactures at an earlier date; no other developing country accounted for more than 3 percent of the total.

The countries of the first group, consisting of Korea, Singapore and Taiwan, adopted export-oriented policies following the completion of the first stage of import substitution which had entailed replacing the imports of non-durable consumer goods and their principal inputs by domestic production. These countries provided essentially a free trade regime for exports, with some additional subsidies.

This chapter was prepared in the framework of the Development Strategies in Semi-Industrial Countries, a research project undertaken at the World Bank and directed by the author. Successive versions were presented at the ECLA/IBRD Seminar on Export Promotion held in Santiago, Chile, on 5–7 November 1976, and at a seminar held at the World Bank on 28 January 1977. The author gratefully acknowledges the useful comments made by the participants at the two seminars, and in particular by Daniel Schydlowsky and Larry Westphal. Special thanks are due to Kishore Nadkarni who collected the data and performed the computations efficiently and with great care. First published in *Weltwirtschaftliches Archiv*, Band 114, Heft 1, 1978.

The second group of countries, comprising Argentina, Brazil, Colombia and Mexico, began their export promotion efforts after continued import substitution in the framework of national markets had encountered increasing difficulties. They provided various subsidies to exports, but by and large precluded the use of imported inputs in export production whenever domestic substitutes were available.

The countries of the third group (Israel and Yugoslavia) had started export promotion at an early date but their efforts slackened somewhat afterwards. Finally, India and Chile, classified in the fourth group, continued to pursue import substitution-oriented policies during the period under consideration.

In carrying out the comparative analysis, the author has utilized the findings of studies prepared under the auspices of the World Bank on Brazil, Chile and Mexico (Balassa *et al.* 1971) and on Argentina, Colombia, Israel, Korea, Singapore and Taiwan (*Development Strategies*). He has further made use of the results of studies on Argentina, Brazil, Colombia, Mexico, Israel, Yugoslavia, India and Korea, prepared for the ECLA/IBRD Seminar on Export Promotion, as well as the findings of other researchers.

The first section of the chapter briefly describes the export promotion efforts of the individual countries, the resulting changes in their incentive systems and the situation existing in 1973. In turn the second section evaluates the effects of these efforts on exports and economic growth, while the third section makes recommendations for an 'ideal' system of incentives for exports and for resource allocation in general. Finally, in drawing the conclusions of the chapter, consideration is given to future prospects for the exports of manufactured goods by the developing countries.

EXPORT INCENTIVES IN 11 MAJOR DEVELOPING COUNTRIES

Apart from the city-state of Hong Kong, where industrialization began in the framework of an open economy, export promotion policies generally followed some degree of import substitution in the protected domestic market. The sequencing of import substitution and export promotion varied among countries, depending on objective conditions and on the subjective evaluation of alternative possibilities by the policy makers. While *ex post facto* there is often a tendency to explain differences in the policies applied by reference to objective conditions, it will be apparent that governmental decision making has played an important role in the cases studied.

To begin with, it has been repeatedly claimed that objective conditions forced the two city-states, Hong Kong and Singapore, to orient their manufacturing industries towards export markets. In support of this proposition, it has been stated that 'Hong Kong and Singapore are almost totally lacking in natural resources. Unlike the developing nation-states of Asia,

Africa and Latin America, the two city-states do not have their own rural hinterlands. Nor do they have domestic markets large enough to serve as the initial base for industrialization' (Geiger, 1973, p.8).

Indeed, the lack of natural resources has made it necessary for Hong Kong to rely on exports of manufactured goods to earn foreign exchange. However, with a population of 2 million in 1950 and relatively high per capita incomes derived from trading activities, Hong Kong had a larger domestic market for manufactured goods than the majority of the developing countries, many of which nevertheless embarked on industrialization behind high protective barriers. In this connection, mention may be made of the experience of Tunisia which, with a home market smaller than that of Hong Kong, attempted to provide for domestic needs in small local plants that were to receive continued protection (cf. Aydalot, 1968).

Hong Kong, too, could have chosen a policy of complementing incomes derived from trading activities by the export of a few manufactured goods while relying on domestic markets for the establishment of a wide range of industries behind protection. The policy makers should thus be given their due for the choice of the policies applied, which led to export and income growth rates that were matched by no developing country practicing inward-oriented policies.

The other city-state, Singapore, went through an import-substitution phase aimed at establishing domestic industries serving the home market. According to an official report, 'In pursuance of the policy of providing protection to industries in Singapore, the import of a number of goods which were in various stages of manufacturing locally or which were likely to be manufactured in the near future, was made subject to quota restrictions' (*Annual Report*, 1968, p. 38). In contradistinction with most other developing countries, however, protection was considered temporary, with quotas to be superseded by tariffs that, in turn, were to be lowered and eventually eliminated (cf. *ibid.*, p.40). In fact, the number of commodities subject to quotas and tariffs was reduced to a considerable extent following the short import-substitution phase, which came to an end in the second half of the 1960s; by 1972, only three items remained under quota while tariffs were eliminated on a number of commodities and reduced on others.

Also, even during the import-substitution phase, rates of protection were much lower in Singapore than in other developing countries.[2] There was thus little discrimination against exports that enjoyed a free-trade regime as inputs used in export production were admitted duty free without any limitations. Exports have received additional incentives in the form of tax allowances on marketing expenditures abroad since 1965 and tax concessions on profits, royalties and interest on foreign loans since 1967.

Taiwan and Korea completed the first 'easy' stage of import substitution, entailing the replacement of the imports of non-durable consumer goods and their principal direct inputs, during the early 1960s. At that time, decisions were reached in the two countries to adopt outward-looking policies oriented towards the exportation of labor-intensive products (cf. Balassa, 1971). This was done with a view to accelerating economic growth in a situation where continued import substitution in the framework of national markets would have been increasingly costly.

Emphasis should be given to the element of conscious decision in taking these steps as Korea, with a population of 25 million, and Taiwan, with a population of 10 million, had domestic markets for manufactured goods larger than most developing countries, including countries such as Chile and Uruguay which continued with policies of import substitution beyond the first 'easy' stage. At the same time, while the availability of a well-educated labor force in Taiwan and Korea is said to have eased the transition to export orientation, Chile and Uruguay again provide examples of countries with even higher educational levels.

In both Taiwan and Korea, a free-trade regime was applied to exports, supplemented by some additional incentives. Exporters had the freedom to choose between domestic and imported inputs; they were exempted from indirect taxes on their output and inputs; and they paid no duty on imported inputs. The same privileges were extended to the producers of domestic inputs used in export production.

The application of these rules provided equal treatment to all export commodities in the two countries. The additional incentives provided to non-traditional exports did not introduce much differentiation among their export products. At the same time, the automatic application of the regulations and the favorable attitude taken by the two governments towards exports enhanced the effectiveness of the incentive measures.

In Korea, the subsidy equivalent of the export incentive measures, including generous wastage allowances, reductions in indirect taxes, credit preferences, and preferential electricity and railroad rates, amounted to 12.4 percent of value added in manufactured exports in 1968. By contrast, domestic sales of manufactured goods were subject to slightly negative effective protection.[3] Furthermore, unlike other industrializing countries, there was no discrimination against primary activities. The export incentive scheme underwent few modifications between 1968 and 1973 (cf. Balassa, 1977, Chapter 9).

In Taiwan, reductions in direct taxes, preferential credits, facilities for the rapid collection of export proceeds, and direct subsidies to the exports of several commodities provided a slight advantage to manufactured exports over import substitution in 1968 and there was little discrimination against primary activities. The incentive system remained practically unchanged in the following five years.

The second group of countries, comprising Argentina, Brazil, Colombia and Mexico, continued with import substitution beyond the completion of its first, easy stage. However, import substitution became increasingly costly as it was extended to industries that were highly capital intensive, required sophisticated technology, and could not produce at an efficient scale and/or use capacity fully because of the limited size of domestic markets.

At the same time, given the need for imported raw materials, intermediate products and machinery, the extent of *net* import substitution in these industries was rather small. The adverse effects on exports of the policies followed further aggravated the balance-of-payments situation in the countries of the second group. The resulting foreign exchange bottleneck limited the possibilities for economic growth and in some instances led to the application of stop-and-go policies.[4]

Exports offered a way to break the foreign exchange bottleneck by making possible the increased use of existing capacity, the application of large-scale production methods, and resource allocation according to comparative advantage. The desire to accelerate economic growth thus explains the adoption of export promotion policies in the countries in question. And, as foreign exchange receipts from exports increased, the need for the depreciation of the currency diminished, thereby reducing the protective effects of existing tariffs. Increases in foreign exchange earnings eventually also permitted reductions in tariffs and liberalization of import quotas.

Among the countries of the second group, the shift to export promotion started in Colombia in 1959 with the introduction of the Plan Vallejo that provided duty-free entry for imported inputs used in export production on a selective basis. The Plan Vallejo came into general application for manufactured exports in the mid-1960s, but it continued to be largely limited to inputs that were not available domestically. In turn, beginning in 1960, non-traditional exports (excluding coffee and petroleum) were exempted from taxes on profits presumed to equal 40 percent of export value. In 1967, this exemption was replaced by a transferable tax certificate equal to 15 percent of the value of non-traditional exports. Adjusted for the tax-free value of the certificates and the discount at which they were traded, the subsidy on export value was 18 percent. Exporters also had access to credits at preferential rates. Moreover, in 1967, the devaluation of the peso increased the domestic currency equivalent of foreign exchange receipts and, subsequently, the exchange rate was adjusted in small steps in accordance with the rate of domestic inflation (Hutcheson and Schydlowsky, 1982; Ffrench-Davis and Pinera Echenique, 1976).

However, exporters had to pay high prices for domestically produced inputs. Given further the protection provided to sales in the domestic market, in 1969 a bias against exports and in favor of import substitution obtained for intermediate products at higher levels of fabrication, consumer goods, machinery and transport equipment, although this was not the case for processed foods and lower-level intermediate products. Also, export subsidies expressed in relation to value added varied to a considerable extent among industries (Hutcheson and Schydlowsky, 1982).

While in Colombia the reforms undertaken in the mid-1960s represented an extension of the export promotion scheme introduced around 1960, in Brazil and Argentina major changes in the incentive system did not occur until the mid-1960s. Apart from the introduction of export incentives, both countries' also instituted frequent exchange rate adjustments *pari passu* with inflation that reduced uncertainty in foreign sales by keeping the real exchange rate constant.

In the period 1965–7, Brazil generalized indirect tax exemptions on processed exports (processed foods and minerals and manufactured products) and their inputs and duty drawbacks on imported inputs used in export production, both of which had been provided on a partial basis in the first half of the 1960s. While exemptions from indirect taxes do not represent 'genuine' subsidies, these measures increased incentives to exports *vis-à-vis* import substitution by re-establishing the equal tax treatment of production for foreign and for domestic markets.

Beginning in the late 1960s generous export subsidies were also granted in the form of tax credits, reductions in income taxes and preferential export financing. Excluding duty drawbacks and rebates of indirect taxes, in 1971 the subsidy equivalent of tax benefits averaged 20 percent on Brazilian exports of processed goods, to which 3 percent for the subsidy equivalent of preferential financing should be added (Garcia, 1976, pp. 105 ff.). Some additional incentives were introduced in 1972 and 1973.

Subsidies to export value varied to a considerable extent in Brazil, ranging from 6 percent on petroleum products to 38 percent on beverages, wood products and furniture, and 'miscellaneous' manufactures.[5] Variations in subsidies to value added in exports were even larger. Brazilian exporters did not generally have the choice between domestic and imported inputs; apart from some exceptions introduced in the early 1970s, they had access to duty-free imports only if a domestic 'similar' was not available. Subsidies to value added in exports thus varied with the input composition of export production and inter-commodity differences in input protection.

At the same time, notwithstanding reductions in tariffs after 1966, the average tariff on the imports of manufactured goods (48 percent in 1970) continued to exceed the average subsidy to exports (Garcia, 1976, p.105; Bergsman and Malan, 1971; Bergsman, 1971). This conclusion is not affected if we adjust for price comparisons for capital goods and intermediate products in order to take account of the effects of tariff redundancies and quantitative restrictions. Thus, on the average, there remained a bias against exports, albeit to a much lower extent than previously.

Furthermore, given the variability of subsidies on export value, as well as the existence of inter-industry differences in protection rates on inputs used in export production and on domestic final sales, relative incentives to exports and import substitution in the manufacturing sector varied greatly. And, while from the late 1960s Brazil promoted some agricultural exports, discrimination against other primary activities continued.

In Argentina a 12 percent subsidy was granted to non-traditional exports in 1967 while the export tax on grains, livestock and their derivatives was maintained at 10 percent. The 12 percent subsidy was provided in the form of a tax reimbursement and was not subject to income taxes, thereby raising its value to 17 percent on a pre-tax basis. An additional subsidy of 3 percent was provided in the form of income tax deductions. Furthermore, exporters received subsidies theoretically representing drawbacks for tariffs paid on imported inputs; such drawbacks were determined on an industry-by-industry basis. Finally, exporters had access to preferential credits.

However, in the case of most major industries, these subsidies did not suffice to offset the high cost of domestic inputs used in export production. Discrimination against exports was further augmented by the high protection accorded to import substitution. The resulting bias against exports was especially strong in the case of primary products. At the same time, similar to the case of Brazil, there were large inter-industry variations in the extent of export subsidies and of import protection on a value added basis (Berlinski and Schydlowsky, 1982). Finally, in both Argentina and Brazil, as well as with regard to the Plan Vallejo in Colombia, discretionary decision making on export incentives had a much greater role than in the countries of the first group.

In Mexico, border industries processing imported materials for re-export, principally to the United States, were accorded duty-free treatment beginning in the mid-1960s. In turn, there were few subsidies to domestic export industries until 1971 when a tax rebate scheme was introduced, together with a system of preferential export credits. In 1973, tax rebates amounted to 8.5 percent of the value of manufactured exports but, to a large extent, they represented rebates of indirect taxes paid at earlier stages of fabrication. In turn, the subsidy equivalent of preferential export credit amounted to 1.5 percent of export value (Balassa, 1977, Chapter 2). On a selective basis, exporters could also import inputs duty free, but this was in practice administratively difficult and did not apply to inputs that were produced domestically. Nor did the benefits provided extend to primary commodities.

The countries of the third group, Israel and Yugoslavia, were among the first to introduce export incentives. In Israel, the system of export incentives was unified in 1956, when a uniform subsidy was applied on value added in exports, other than the traditional export commodities (citrus and diamonds). Nevertheless, some additional subsidies remained, including the so-called branch funds for the textile industry, preferential credits and tax refunds on promotional expenditures.

In 1962, the across-the-board subsidies were transformed into a higher exchange rate, the effects of which wore off by 1965, so that there was a considerable degree of discrimination against exports and in favor of import substitution in that year (Sussman, 1982). In 1966, explicit export subsidies were again introduced but tariffs were generally higher than export subsidies and the protection of import substitution was raised further by the continued existence of import licensing on a variety of commodities. At the same time, exporters in Israel had to pay duties on their inputs and did not receive preference in the granting of import licenses (Sussman, 1982; Michaely, 1976, p. 24).

In Yugoslavia, retention quotas on foreign exchange earned through exporting and multiple exchange rates were used to provide incentives to exports until 1961; in 1957, the average exchange rate for exports was about 40 percent higher than that for imports. The multiple rate system was transformed into a system of export subsidies and import tariffs in 1961. Export subsidies were abolished in 1965, and benefits to exports were subsequently limited to foreign exchange retention quotas and to preferential export credits. However, the retention quotas amounted to only 1.8 percent of exports and, with the liberalization of import restrictions, they had negligible value. In turn, imports continued to benefit from tariff protection albeit to a reduced extent (cf. Dubey, 1976).

The fourth group of countries continued to follow policies of import substitution, entailing a considerable degree of discrimination against exports, during the period under consideration. In India, the 1966 devaluation of the rupee was supposed to benefit exports but, with reductions in export subsidies and increases in export taxes accompanying the devaluation, the bias of the incentive system in favor of import substitution and against exports increased rather than decreased (Bhagwati and Srinivasan, 1975, Chapter 6). The export incentive measures introduced subsequently, including cash subsidy, duty drawbacks, import replenishment licenses and preferential licensing for capacity expansion, were in general subject to complex procedures and considerable uncertainty as to their extent and availability. Also, the cash subsidy was apparently related to the excess variable costs of domestic production over export prices, so that high-cost exports received above-average subsidies while the lowest rates applied to exports that had relatively low domestic costs (cf. Wolf, 1976).

The situation was aggravated by restrictions on the transferability of import replenishment licenses and by the virtual exclusion of imported inputs that had domestic substitutes. The limitations imposed on firm size and on investments by large firms also militated against the development of manufactured exports. In turn, major primary exports and traditional manufactured export products were subject to export taxes.

Considering further the continued protection of manufacturing industries by the use of import prohibitions and qualitative restrictions, it would appear that India largely maintained its import-substitution orientation during the period under consideration. Changes occurred only at the end of the period, when India devalued the rupee *pari passu* with the depreciation of the British pound and export subsidies came into increased use.

Chile traditionally had the highest level of import protection in Latin America (Jeanneret, 1971). The high level of protection entailed considerable discrimination against exports and penalized the processing of domestic materials for exports in which Chile has a comparative advantage. The introduction of tax rebates on non-traditional exports and import liberalization in the late 1960s reduced this bias to some extent. However, the measures applied were largely reversed after the presidential election of 1970, when severe import restrictions and a greatly overvalued exchange rate discriminated against exports.

EXPORT PERFORMANCE AND ECONOMIC GROWTH

Export incentives and performance

There are few econometric studies of the effects of export incentives on export performance. This fact reflects the difficulties of establishing a statistical relationship between the two variables. In a time-series framework, the shortness of the time series, the difficulties involved in quantifying the effects of other influences on exports, as well as the lack of information on changes in incentives to import substitution that provides an alternative to exports, make estimation difficult. In turn, in a cross-section framework, the lack of stability of the incentive system and the existence of lags in the adjustment to incentives create problems for statistical estimation.

Nevertheless, studies for several of the countries under consideration show the existence of a positive relationship between export incentives and export growth. In a cross-section investigation of 91 sectors in Korea, Westphal and Kim (1982) have obtained correlation coefficients of 0.29 and 0.26 between export incentives in 1968 on the one hand, and the share of exports in output in 1968 and the growth contribution of exports between 1960 and 1968 on the other; the coefficients are significant at the 1 percent level. In turn, Ffrench-Davis and Pinera Echenique (1976, pp. 88 ff.) cite several time-series estimates for Colombia that indicate an elasticity of non-traditional exports with respect to incentives of 0.7 to 1.3, although the statistical significance of the estimates is low. Finally, an elasticity of 1.3 has been obtained in time-series studies on Israel by Halevi[6] and on Brazil by Tyler (1976, Chapter 8) and in pooling time-series and cross-section data for ten countries by Krueger.[7]

These estimates may be considered to provide lower limits of possible values, in part because of the downward bias resulting from the use of the least-squares method and in part because of the problems involved in capturing the lagged effects of the introduction of export incentives. Given the difficulties of statistical estimation, in the following we will rely on a comparative analysis of export trends in the four groups of countries covered in this chapter.

In the course of the discussion, distinction will be made between primary and manufactured exports and, within the former category, between traditional and non-traditional exports. Primary exports are defined to include SITC classes 0 to 4 as well as diamonds and unwrought non-ferrous metals. Primary commodities that accounted for at least 2 percent of the total exports of a particular country in 1953 have been considered traditional export products. For subsequent comparisons with data on agricultural production, the exports of agricultural goods, including livestock, fishery and forestry products, have further been distinguished.

Data on the rate of growth of exports for the above groups of commodities and for total exports are shown in Table 16.1 for the periods 1953–60, 1960–6 and 1966–73. In the discussion, we will concentrate on the experience of the period 1966–73, when the export incentive schemes of most of the countries concerned were in full operation. Attention will further be given to the 1960–6 period as several of the countries under consideration began their export production efforts in the early 1960s.

The rate of growth of exports is affected by the absolute value of exports in the base year. This is of particular importance for manufactured goods in the 1960–6 period, since the countries in question generally started from a low base. Correspondingly, we have also calculated the share of exports in manufactured output for the benchmark years, as well as incremental export–output ratios, defined as the ratio of the increment in manufactured exports to that in manufactured output (Table 16.2). For comparability with the trade data, manufactured output figures have been adjusted by deducting processed food (ISIC 311, 312), beverages (313), tobacco manufactures (314), refined petroleum (353), coal and petroleum products (354), unwrought non-ferrous basic metals (ex 372) and diamonds (ex 390) from the output figures reported according to the International Standard Industrial Classification.

Data expressed in the form of ratios have the further advantage that they are calculated using the prices of the same year. In turn, in estimating export growth rates, current price data have been used. This is because national price indices for the relevant product groups are not available in most of the developing countries under consideration.

We have seen that the first group of countries, comprising Korea, Singapore and Taiwan, adopted export-oriented policies following the completion of the first stage of import substitution. These policies entailed applying a free-trade regime to non-traditional exports, with additional incentives provided to manufactured exports largely on an across-the-board basis, and considerable stability in incentives assured over time. Also, on the average, incentives to exports were at the least comparable in magnitude to the incentives accorded to import substitution in manufacturing and there was little discrimination against primary activities.

Table 16.1 Growth of the value of exports and imports in selected developing countries (average annual growth rates)

	Argentina	Brazil	Chile	Colombia	India	Israel	Korea	Mexico	Singapore	Taiwan	Yugoslavia
Traditional primary products											
1953–60	0.7	−5.3	4.3	−4.5	2.4	16.8	−17.5	−0.3	—	−3.2	3.6
1960–6	6.7	2.0	9.5	−0.5	0.3	15.2	26.5	3.8	—	8.0	11.6
1966–73	6.9	7.6	5.1	6.5	0.2	16.7	16.9	1.7	—	1.2	12.5
Non-traditional primary products											
1953–60	−3.4	5.4	−5.6	11.9	5.6	47.0	7.1	12.2	n.a.	12.7	19.6
1960–6	3.6	9.6	11.3	5.9	9.2	16.8	22.5	10.3	29.5	36.5	2.3
1966–73	14.0	26.5	7.6	25.5	10.4	16.9	35.5	6.3	19.5	25.0	11.1
Primary products together											
1953–60	0.2	−3.1	2.5	−3.5	3.7	20.5	−5.4	3.8	n.a.	−1.2	12.4
1960–6	6.3	4.7	9.7	0.3	4.5	15.5	24.0	6.9	29.5	17.3	5.7
1966–73	7.8	17.0	5.5	10.7	6.5	16.8	26.0	4.3	19.5	17.0	9.8
Of which, agricultural goods											
1953–60	0.2	−3.5	−9.0	−4.8	3.9	18.3	−3.2	5.4	n.a.	−2.1	14.5
1960–6	6.2	4.5	22.5	1.0	3.7	9.5	25.2	7.7	2.9	15.6	6.7
1966–73	7.9	16.7	2.7	11.1	9.5	11.7	29.5	5.7	19.2	16.3	9.8
Manufactured goods											
1953–60	−11.7	9.9	3.2	0.0	1.3	18.0	14.0	5.6	n.a.	29.5	28.0
1960–6	14.6	27.5	15.6	35.0	6.7	15.3	80.0	12.7	24.5	36.5	21.5
1966–73	33.5	38.5	0.0	27.5	7.7	17.5	50.0	20.0 ʼ	42.0	47.0	14.9
Total exports											
1953–60	−0.6	−2.8	2.6	−3.4	2.6	19.6	−3.2	3.9	n.a.	2.2	17.2
1960–6	6.7	5.4	10.1	1.5	5.5	15.3	40.0	7.8	28.5	23.5	13.6
1966–73	10.8	19.9	5.3	12.7	7.0	17.0	44.0	8.1	28.5	35.5	13.8
Total imports											
1953–60	6.7	1.5	5.9	−3.6	9.8	8.5	0.0	5.6	n.a.	6.2	11.1
1960–6	−1.8	0.4	6.9	3.7	5.4	8.8	13.0	6.9	8.0	13.1	11.3
1966–73	10.3	24.5	5.7	6.7	−0.3	20.0	29.0	14.5	25.5	29.5	17.2
Purchasing power of exports[a]											
1960–6	4.0	4.0	8.8	0.2	4.2	13.0	38.0	6.5	26.5	22.5	12.9
1966–73	4.9	13.5	−0.6	6.7	1.2	10.2	36.5	2.3	21.5	28.5	7.7

Source: National and international trade statistics.
[a] Export values deflated by the unit value index for the manufactured goods exports of developed countries.

The early application of export-oriented policies by the countries of the first group may explain why they had the highest incremental export–output ratios in manufacturing during the period 1960–6. With the subsequent intensification of their export promotion efforts, all three countries further increased their incremental export–output ratios in the 1966–73 period and experienced the highest rates of growth of manufactured exports among the 11 countries under study. And although in Korea manufactured exports increased even more rapidly during the 1960–6 period, this had been attained starting from a base year figure of $5 million as compared to manufactured

Table 16.2 Exports, imports, manufactured output and GNP in selected developing countries[a] (percent)

	Argentina	Brazil	Chile	Colombia	India	Israel	Korea	Mexico	Singapore	Taiwan	Yugoslavia
Share of manufactured exports in manufactured output											
1960	0.8	0.4	3.0	0.7	9.7	7.9	0.9	2.6	11.2	8.6	10.8
1966	0.9	1.3	4.1	3.0	9.4	12.8	13.9	2.9	20.1	19.2	13.8
1973	3.0	4.4	2.5	7.5	8.6	14.1	40.5	4.4	42.6	49.9	16.9
Incremental ratio of manufactured exports to manufactured output											
1960–6	1.0	3.6	5.5	7.7	8.9	23.9	24.8	3.2	28.4	24.8	15.8
1966–73	6.5	5.6	0.0	11.4	7.7	14.9	45.7	5.5	47.5	56.4	19.5
Share of manufactured imports in total utilization of manufactured goods											
1960	14.6	10.8	26.3	30.8	19.3	28.5	24.4	19.6	56.2	28.5	22.0
1966	6.3	7.5	21.6	28.0	16.5	32.8	26.5	16.2	53.2	29.3	17.3
1973	5.4	13.0	17.5	21.5	9.5	41.2	35.9	15.2	64.3	38.9	24.0
Incremental ratio of manufactured imports to utilization of manufactured goods											
1960–6	−3.9	−3.0	14.1	20.5	10.4	42.5	31.9	11.7	49.2	30.5	13.6
1966–73	4.4	15.7	10.8	14.2	−0.4	45.1	40.4	14.4	67.0	42.2	29.4
Ratio of total exports to GNP											
1960	8.9	6.1	12.6	11.3	4.2	8.4	1.5	6.4	9.9	9.5	22.4
1966	7.3	7.1	15.7	9.5	4.2	12.8	6.5	5.4	26.6	17.1	14.2
1973	8.1	9.8	7.6	11.8	4.3	15.5	26.1	4.3	44.6	47.8	14.5
Incremental ratio of total exports to GNP											
1960–6	5.3	12.3	23.0	3.4	4.1	20.4	13.0	4.3	52.0	24.7	10.7
1966–73	9.0	11.5	3.3	14.5	4.3	17.4	34.8	3.3	52.0	63.3	14.8
Ratio of total imports to GNP											
1960	10.3	7.1	12.9	12.6	7.5	20.1	16.0	9.0	65.4	18.9	32.8
1966	5.2	6.1	13.5	12.6	7.4	21.2	18.7	7.2	62.5	19.9	18.3
1973	5.5	11.1	6.8	10.6	4.5	30.8	34.3	8.6	91.5	40.5	22.0
Incremental ratio of imports to GNP											
1960–6	−1.3	0.9	14.9	12.4	7.3	23.0	22.2	5.1	57.9	20.8	12.3
1966–73	6.0	14.2	2.4	8.4	−0.3	37.3	41.3	9.7	103.6	50.8	26.4

Source: Exports: national and international trade statistics. Manufactured output: UN *The Growth of World Industry*, various issues, and national statistics.
[a] The dollar values of manufactured output and GNP employed in calculating the ratios have been derived by converting data expressed in terms of national currencies by the use of exchange rates shown in the *World Tables, 1976*. An exception has been made in the case of Korea where the 1960 official exchange rate was adjusted for the devaluation undertaken in early 1961 and for wholesale price changes.

In the absence of manufactured output figures for 1960, these have been derived from the 1966 figures by utilizing growth rates of value added in manufacturing and inflation in prices of manufactured goods for the period 1960–6. The same method has been applied in cases where 1973 manufactured output figures are not available.

exports of $151 million in 1966. Correspondingly, the share of exports in manufacturing output tripled in Korea: from 13.9 percent in 1966 to 40.5 percent in 1973. In the same period, export–output ratios in manufacturing output rose from 20.1 to 42.6 percent in Singapore and from 19.2 to 49.9 percent in Taiwan.

The high, and increasing, share of manufactured exports in total exports did not adversely affect the exports of primary commodities in the three countries. In 1966–73, Korea showed the best performance in regard to traditional as well as non-traditional primary exports among the 11 countries under study. And, while shifts to higher-valued crops led to a decline in its traditional exports of rice and bananas, Taiwan was among the countries with the highest rate of growth of non-traditional primary exports. In the case of both countries, the relatively favorable treatment of primary activities helped exports; in turn, the rapid expansion of petroleum refineries led to a high rate of growth of primary exports from Singapore.

In contradistinction to the first group, the second group of countries began export-promoting efforts after import substitution had been extended to capital-intensive intermediate products, durable consumer goods and machinery. They also differ from the first group in that, with few exceptions, the use of imported inputs was limited to cases where comparable domestic inputs were not available. Correspondingly, subsidies to value added in exports varied to a considerable extent from industry to industry and, on the whole, the bias against exports and in favor of import substitution was reduced but not eliminated. Apart from Colombia and, in the case of a few products, Argentina and Brazil, the second group of countries also continued to discriminate against primary activities..

Within this group of Latin American countries, in the 1966–73 period manufactured export growth rates were the highest in Argentina and in Brazil, which introduced considerable export incentives at the beginning of the period. Apart from the increased use of existing capacity, these incentives gave impetus to the establishment of new facilities for export production whereas in the preceding period exports mostly took up the slack in domestic production.

As a result, between 1966 and 1973, the share of exports in manufactured output rose from 0.9 percent to 3.6 percent in Argentina and from 1.3 percent to 4.4 percent in Brazil. Nevertheless, in terms of both average and incremental export–output ratios in manufacturing, Argentina and Brazil were surpassed by Colombia which started export promotion at an earlier date; exports from Colombia accounted for 3.0 percent of manufacturing output in 1966 and 7.5 percent in 1973.

In Mexico's case, proximity to the United States may explain the 2.9 percent share of exports in manufactured output in 1966. The subsequent introduction of an export incentive scheme led to an increase in this share to 4.4 percent in 1973. However, given the relatively low level of these incentives, the rate of growth of manufactured exports and the incremental export–output ratio in manufacturing were lower in Mexico than in the other three countries of the group during the 1966–73 period.

These figures include only 'domestic' manufactured exports. Mexico's exports from the border area, which enjoyed a free trade regime, rose from practically nil in the mid-1960s to $651 million in 1973, of which $286 million was value added in Mexico. By comparison, domestic manufactured exports were $740 million in 1973.

Continued discrimination against primary activities may account for the relatively slow growth of traditional and non-traditional exports in Mexico. In the case of traditional exports, Mexico experienced a loss in market shares while non-traditional exports failed to develop as rapidly as in the countries of the group. The same conclusion applies to traditional exports and their derivatives in Argentina, where other non-traditional primary exports expanded in response to an export subsidy.

The course of traditional exports in Brazil and Colombia was determined largely by world market trends in coffee. At the same time, the selective policy of expansion concentrating on meat, sugar and soybeans in Brazil, and the extension of export incentives to all products other than coffee and petroleum in Colombia, led to rapid increases of non-traditional primary exports in the two countries.

The countries of the third group, Israel and Yugoslavia, started their export promotion efforts at an early date, although they did not accord free trade status to manufactured exports. By 1966, in terms of the share of exports in manufactured output, the two countries surpassed the second group of countries while falling behind the first. But, with a slackening in their export promotion efforts after the mid-1960s, the share of exports in manufactured output only increased from 12.8 percent to 14.1 percent in Israel and from 13.8 percent to 16.9 percent in Yugoslavia during the period 1966–73.

Correspondingly, by 1973, Israel's manufactured exports ($495 million) were exceeded by Argentina, Brazil and Singapore, while Yugoslavia ($2,031 million) was overtaken by Korea and Taiwan. Nevertheless, the average and the incremental shares of exports in manufactured output continued to be higher in the two countries than in the countries of the second group. Also, in the absence of substantial discrimination against primary exports, Israel was able to expand rapidly its exports of citrus fruit and diamonds and Yugoslavia its exports of meat and lumber.

We have seen that policies of import substitution continued in India and in Chile during the period under consideration. As a result, while India traditionally exported textile products, it lost ground in these exports and was slow to develop new manufactured exports. Correspondingly, its share in the manufactured exports of the 11 countries under consideration declined from 65.4 percent in 1953 to 50.7 percent in 1960, 31.2 percent in 1966, and 10.2 percent in 1973. In turn, the share of exports in India's manufactured output fell from 9.7 percent in 1960 to 9.4 percent in 1966 and 8.6 percent in 1973.

Following earlier increases in the exports of woodpulp, paper and fabricated copper products, manufactured exports remained at the 1966 level in 1973 in Chile. Correspondingly, Chile's share in the combined exports of manufactured goods of the 11 countries declined to 0.5 percent in 1973 as compared to 3.0 percent in 1953.

Given the continued discrimination against primary activities, the expansion of non-traditional primary exports was also relatively slow in both India and Chile. In turn, changes in world tea and copper exports, respectively, determined to a large extent the results shown for their traditional primary exports.

Exports and the growth of the manufacturing sector

The exports of manufactured goods provide advantages over import substitution inasmuch as they contribute to resource allocation according to comparative advantage, increased capacity utilization, the exploitation of economies of scale and improvements in technology stimulated by competition in foreign markets. To the extent that exports provide a more rapid increase in manufactured output than import substitution, the indirect effect of export growth, too, will also be larger in countries where resources are not fully utilized.

We cannot, however, expect to find a close correlation between exports and output growth since other factors, such as investment activity and the political climate, also influence the results. At the same time, the lack of data limits the possibility of introducing additional variables in the statistical analysis and some of the relevant variables are not even quantifiable.

Nevertheless, the data for the 11 countries under consideration tend to bear out our expectations as regards the existence of a positive correlation between exports and output growth in the manufacturing sector. Thus, in the 1960–6 period, Korea, Singapore, Taiwan, Israel and Yugoslavia had the highest incremental export–output ratios as well as the highest growth rates in manufacturing,[8] while Argentina and Brazil were placed at the bottom with regard to both variables. In the 11-country group, the Spearman rank correlation coefficient between incremental export–output ratios and the rate of growth of value added in manufacturing was 0.87 (for data, see Tables 16.2 and 16.3).[9]

In examining the data for the 1960–6 period, emphasis has been given to incremental ratios since, as noted above, growth rates of manufactured exports are affected to a considerable extent by absolute values in the initial year. This may explain the low correlation between the growth of exports and value added in manufacturing (0.40) during this period.

Growth rates of manufactured exports are more meaningful indicators of export performance in the 1966–73 period, when the volume of exports in the initial year was already substantial. The Spearman rank correlation coefficient between the growth of exports and that of value added in manufacturing was 0.85 in this period; the coefficient was 0.68 between incremental export–output ratios and growth of the manufacturing sector. These results are hardly affected if we exclude the direct effects of exports by deducting export values from the value of manufactured output. The corresponding

Table 16.3 Economic growth of selected developing countries (average annual growth rates)

	Argentina	Brazil	Chile	Colombia	India	Israel	Korea	Mexico	Singapore	Taiwan	Yugoslavia
Value added in agriculture											
1953–60	0.5	4.0	−0.3	3.3	2.5	10.0	2.3	5.7	n.a.	3.9	3.5
1960–6	3.2	3.8	2.7	2.7	−0.5	2.6	5.8	4.7	2.5	5.3	3.2
1966–73	0.7	5.9	−0.7	4.7	3.0	5.6	3.2	2.4	3.1	3.8	2.0
Manufacturing											
1953–60	5.8	10.1	2.8	6.6	4.8	10.3	13.6	8.5	n.a.	10.1	13.2
1960–6	5.3	4.5	7.2	5.7	6.2	8.0	13.0	9.7	10.3	12.3	9.9
1966–73	7.3	11.8	3.7	7.6	4.7	10.9	21.0	7.6	15.0	22.0	8.4
Gross National Product											
1953–60	3.2	6.3	2.8	4.3	3.5	10.0	5.6	6.5	n.a.	6.9	5.6
1960–6	3.6	4.1	5.1	4.7	2.8	8.4	7.3	7.1	7.3	9.4	5.8
1966–73	4.8	9.3	2.4	6.1	3.8	9.8	10.7	6.4	12.7	10.7	7.1
Per capita GNP											
1953–60	1.2	3.4	0.4	1.3	1.6	4.8	3.0	2.8	n.a.	3.2	4.4
1960–6	2.1	1.1	2.6	1.5	0.5	4.5	4.5	3.7	4.5	6.2	4.8
1966–73	3.3	6.4	0.2	2.9	1.5	7.0	8.8	2.9	10.9	7.9	6.0
Population											
1953–60	2.0	2.9	2.4	3.0	1.9	5.3	2.7	2.9	4.8	3.6	1.2
1960–6	1.5	2.9	2.6	3.3	2.3	3.9	2.7	3.4	2.8	3.2	1.0
1966–73	1.5	2.9	2.2	3.2	2.3	2.8	1.9	3.4	1.8	2.8	1.0

Source: UN, *Yearbook of National Accounts Statistics*, various issues. OECD.
National Accounts of Less-Developed Countries 1950–66. World Bank, *World Tables, 1976*.

Spearman rank correlation coefficients are 0.80 for export growth and 0.71 for incremental export–output ratios.

The data for the individual countries also show the effects of policy changes after 1966. With increased export orientation, the rate of growth of value added in manufacturing rose further in Korea, Singapore and Taiwan. In turn, with the slackening of export promotion efforts, Yugoslavia dropped out from the lead group. Yugoslavia, as well as the countries continuing with import substitution, India and Chile, also experienced a decline in the rate of growth of the manufacturing sector. Finally, the acceleration in the growth of this sector was particularly marked in Brazil where the shift to export promotion was the most pronounced.

Export orientation in manufacturing also has favorable effects for the national economy by saving capital. To begin with, an export-oriented strategy permits exploiting the comparative advantage of developing countries, which tends to lie in labor-intensive industries within the manufacturing sector. Also, increased capacity utilization through exports will lead to higher output without necessitating increases in the capital stock. Finally, exploiting economies of scale reduces capital costs per unit of output.

Savings in capital resulting from the expansion of manufacturing exports are indicated in Westphal's study (1976) on Korea. According to the estimates cited in this study, the average capacity utilization rate in the manufacturing sector, defined in terms of electricity usage and by taking three-shift operations as the norm, rose from 17.7 percent in 1962 to 31.8 percent in 1971. Westphal also finds that in the manufacturing sector labor–capital ratios are much higher for exports than for import substitution, with ratios for the direct use of labor and capital in the manufacturing process estimated at 3.55 for exports, 2.33 for imports and 2.64 for domestic manufacturing output in 1968.[10] Similar conclusions have been reached with regard to Taiwan by Riedel (1975, p. 492), who compared the factor intensity of exports and that of intermediate products that were purchased abroad in exchange for exports.

Colombian exports of manufactures also tend to be labor-intensive (Ffrench-Davis and Pinera Echenique, 1976, p.94) while labor requirements were estimated to be about 40 percent higher for manufactured exports than for imports in Brazil (Tyler, 1976, Chapter 6). Although comparable data for capital are not available for these countries, in case of equal profitability we would expect capital coefficients to be higher for imports than for exports.

Employment will benefit from the rapid growth of manufacturing output associated with export expansion and from the relative labor intensity of exports, while it will be adversely affected to the extent that export orientation leads to more rapid increases in productivity than would otherwise be the case. These influences have been analyzed with regard to Taiwan and India by Banerji and Riedel (1976). Their results indicate that the favorable effects of output growth on employment were enhanced by structural change through the shift of production in a labor-intensive direction associated with export expansion in Taiwan, while the shift towards capital-intensive production aggravated the effects of slow output growth in India.

Thus, in the period 1961–71, employment in Taiwanese manufacturing increased at an average annual rate of 10 percent, of which the output growth effect was responsible for approximately 18 percent, structural change through the greater labor intensity of production 4 percent, productivity change 4 percent, and the cross effects of these changes 8 percent. The corresponding estimates for India in the period 1960–9, when manufacturing employment increased at an average annual rate of 3 percent, were 11 percent for the output growth effect, 1 percent for structural change, 3 percent for productivity change, and 4 percent for their cross effects.[11]

The slow absorption of the labor force in the manufacturing sector has contributed to the increase in unemployment in India from 2.5 million in 1966 to 7.6 million in 1973, i.e., from 14.0 percent to 28.8 percent of the labor force. During the same period, unemployment in Taiwan fell from 3.1 to 1.5 percent of the labor force.[12] Unemployment declined also in Korea where manufacturing employment grew at an average annual rate of 12 percent between 1960 and 1973.[13]

Pari passu with the decline in unemployment, real wages increased to a considerable extent in the countries that pursued an export-oriented strategy. Real wages in manufacturing rose 20 percent a year between 1966 and 1973 in Korea and 6 percent a year between 1966 and 1972 in Taiwan. Increases in real wages were relatively rapid following increased orientation towards exports in Brazil, averaging 5 percent a year in the manufacturing sector between 1966 and 1972. By contrast, real wages in manufacturing remained unchanged between 1961 and 1968 in India and declined at a rate of 1 percent a year between 1966 and 1973 in Chile.[14]

Export expansion and economic performance

The influences described with regard to the manufacturing sector operate on the national economy level as well. To begin with, the direct effects of exports on output are observed in primary activities also. This is apparent from the high degree of correlation between the growth of agricultural exports and that of value added in agriculture: for the 11-country group, the Spearman rank correlation coefficient between the two variables was 0.57 in 1960–6 and 0.71 in 1966–73.

Furthermore, there are indirect effects operating in inter-sectoral relationships as manufacturing industries require primary inputs, primary producers purchase manufactured inputs and machinery, while higher incomes due to the expansion of exports, whether primary or manufactured, increase demand for the output of all sectors. Finally, export orientation leads to savings in capital and increases the availability of foreign exchange.

Apart from increased capacity utilization, the exploitation of economies of scale, and the relative labor intensity of exports in the manufacturing sector, export orientation may lead to savings in capital by reducing the bias against primary exports. Savings in capital, in turn, permit increasing output through greater employment in countries with unemployment or under-employment of labor. Also, increased foreign exchange earnings can contribute to the growth of the national economy by easing the foreign exchange bottleneck that has often been an obstacle to economic growth in the developing countries in limiting the importation of intermediate products and capital goods.

The impact of the increased availability of foreign exchange through higher exports is apparent in the continued rise of the share of imports in the gross national product in Korea, Singapore, Taiwan and Israel,[15] and in the reversal of the decline in this share in Argentina, Brazil, Mexico and Yugoslavia. By contrast, import shares declined to a considerable extent between 1966 and 1973 in both Chile and India. For the sample group as a whole, the Spearman rank correlation coefficient between incremental import–GNP rates and the growth of GNP was 0.91 in 1966–73.

The influences described are expected to lead to a positive relationship between export growth and the growth of GNP. The results for the countries under study tend to conform to these expectations. During the 1966–73 period, growth performance among the 11 developing countries was closely linked with export growth, except that the inflow of foreign private capital enabled Mexico to reach a higher rate of growth of GNP than expected on the basis of export figures. The relationship had been somewhat weaker during the 1960–6 period, when several of the countries concerned had started out with a low absolute export figure.

For the entire sample of countries, the Spearman rank correlation coefficient between the growth of exports and that of GNP was 0.82 for the 1960–6 period and 0.93 for the 1966–73 period. The estimated results are hardly affected if the rate of growth of exports is replaced by the incremental export–GNP ratio. For the 11 country group, the Spearman rank correlation coefficient between incremental export–GNP ratios and the rate of growth of GNP was 0.71 in 1960–6 and 0.86 in 1966–73.

It would appear, then, that trade orientation has been an important factor contributing to the inter-country differences in the growth of GNP. At the same time, income increments have been achieved at a substantially lower cost in terms of investment in countries that have followed a consistent policy of export orientation. Thus, taking the 1960–73 period as a whole, incremental capital–output ratios were 1.76 in Singapore, 2.10 in Korea and 2.44 in Taiwan. At the other extreme, these ratios were 5.49 in Chile and 5.72 in India.

In the same period, incremental capital–output ratios were between 3 and 5 in the countries of the second and the third group, with improvements shown over time in line with their increased export orientation. While figures for subperiods are subject to considerable error, it appears that the greatest improvement was experienced in Brazil following its pronounced policy change. Brazil's incremental capital–output ratio declined from 3.84 in 1960–6 to 2.06 in 1966–73, when the low figure for the second period presumably also reflects increased capacity utilization at higher export levels.[16]

The effectiveness of export incentives

We have examined available evidence regarding the effects of export incentives on export expansion and the effects of export expansion on the growth of the national economy. The results indicate that export orientation in the system of incentives had beneficial effects on economic growth in the countries concerned. For one thing, in an inter-country context, greater export orientation tends to be associated with higher export growth rates and better growth performance. For another, in the individual countries, the growth of exports and GNP generally accelerated following the introduction of export incentive schemes.

Also, we have provided evidence that export orientation has had beneficial effects on employment. These effects may in part explain that income distribution is much less unequal in countries such as Korea and Taiwan, which adopted an export-oriented strategy at an early date, than in countries where import substitution policies continued beyond the first stage.[17]

Export incentives include all measures that increase the profitability of exports by reducing costs or increasing revenue. In the first section of this chapter, note has been taken of measures that directly affect individual exporters, such as export exchange rates, subsidies to export value, tax and duty concessions, foreign exchange retention schemes and preferential credits. Automaticity in providing subsidies and governmental attitudes towards export promotion are further influences affecting exports. Finally, exporters may obtain benefits from direct government action in the form of government-sponsored market research and information services.

More generally, importance attaches to the general policy 'climate' in which the incentive scheme is applied and the removal of distortions in factor markets. The liberalization of economic policies has provided a boost to exports whereas continued constraints on investments and import allocation have mitigated the effects of export incentives as in India.

While export incentives provide inducement for increasing exports in a market economy, the question has been raised as to what role government interventions in the form of planning or programming may have played in inducing firms to export. A few of the successful exporting countries did prepare medium-term plans. However, the influence of these plans on resource allocation and on the composition of exports appears to have been minimal. At any rate, the plans were prepared on an aggregate level so that there was no direct link to the exports of specific commodities.

And, although Korea used export targets in a disaggregated framework, the application of a free trade regime to all exports was in no way related to the fulfillment or the non-fulfillment of these targets. Furthermore, preferential export credits were provided according to predetermined rules while wastage allowances were set on a product-by-product rather than on a firm-by-firm basis. Thus, by and large, the fulfillment of export targets did not modify the firm's access to incentives, although it has been reported that successful exporters enjoyed advantageous treatment in, e.g., pending tax cases. Note further that while the existence of export targets may have exerted pressure on some firms, most firms were exceeding their targets. A recent instance is the increase of Korean exports by two-thirds between the second quarter of 1975 and the second quarter of 1976 which exceeded expectations by a substantial margin.

In turn, there were no export targets in Hong Kong, Singapore and Taiwan that had an export performance comparable to that of Korea. And while in a few cases export obligations were imposed on firms in Latin America (e.g. automobiles in Mexico), programming or export targets hardly played a role in the expansion of exports in the countries of the second group. Thus, success in exporting and the acceleration of the rate of economic growth can in large part be ascribed to the incentives applied.

We come finally to the question of whether an import substitution phase is necessary for the subsequent expansion of exports and, if so, for how long and at what cost. The experience of Hong Kong indicates that exports may expand rapidly without a previous import substitution phase. Rather, with the increased sophistication of its industrial structure brought about by the expansion of exports, 'natural' import substitution has taken place in Hong Kong in several industries under free trade conditions (cf. Glassburner and Riedel, 1973, p. 638).

Also, the import substitution phase in non-durable consumer goods and their inputs was of short duration in the first group of countries. It lasted barely six years in Singapore while it covered largely the period of post-war reconstruction in Korea and Taiwan. Also, in all three countries, the bulk of their present exports, including plywood, wigs, synthetic textiles, electronics and ships did not go through an import substitution phase. Finally, the expansion of exports cum import substitution is envisaged in machinery where reliance on import substitution alone would not permit exploiting economies of scale and would raise costs for user industries.

It has been suggested that, without the preceding import substitution phase, export expansion in Latin America would not have occurred at the rates observed. At the same time, as we have seen, the rapid expansion of exports took place from a small base, and the absolute value of manufactured exports and share of exports in manufactured output remained relatively low in the countries concerned. This, in turn, may be explained by the establishment of high cost firms and by the lack of sufficient vertical specialization in the production of parts, components and accessories behind high protection. In particular, the lack of efficient industries producing inputs for export production was an obstacle to export expansion as the importation of substitutes was not generally permitted.

This is not to say that the manufacturing industries of developing countries would not need preferential treatment *vis-à-vis* primary activities. But the question is what is the desirable extent of such preferences and how exports and import substitution are to be treated. This, in turn, brings us to the consideration of 'ideal' trade policies in the developing countries.

'IDEAL' TRADE POLICIES FOR DEVELOPING COUNTRIES

Incentives to exports and to import substitution

An 'ideal' scheme of export incentives should aim at assuring that the expansion of exports, and resource allocation in general, conforms to the requirements of social profitability. It should further aim at minimizing the chances of retaliation on the part of the importing countries. Finally, the export promotion scheme should have an across-the-board character and should provide certainty and stability to exporters. These questions will be taken up in turn.

Social profitability considerations call for providing equal incentives to exports and to import substitution. For one thing, from the point of view of the national economy, a dollar earned in exporting is equivalent to a dollar saved through import substitution. For another, as noted above, equal incentives to production for domestic and export markets are necessary for exploiting economies of scale and for contributing to technical progress.

Similar considerations underlie the recommendations made by Ffrench-Davis and Pinera Echenique (1976) for 'equalizing-compensation'; i.e. for offsetting the discrimination against exports inherent in the protection of domestic markets by equivalent export subsidies. But Ffrench-Davis and Pinera Echenique (1976, p. 23) suggest that 'considering the fiscal restrictions with which the governments of developing countries are usually faced, it would seem advisable for the average level [of export subsidies] to be somewhat lower [than that of tariffs]'.

Fiscal limitations will not make, however, such exceptions necessary in most countries that have established an industrial base.[18] Thus, as we have seen, the 11 countries under study were able to provide substantial export subsidies. And, even if the levying and the collection of income taxes encounter difficulties, indirect taxes may be used to finance such subsidies.

It has also been suggested that tariffs should be set higher than export subsidies because of the danger of foreign dumping. However, in view of the paucity of cases of dumping, this argument cannot be used to countenance levying higher tariffs on imports in general. Considering further the need to avoid disincentives to exports, it would be desirable if, instead of tariffs, one relied on anti-dumping measures whenever the existence of dumping has been established.

Nor is the higher protection of luxury goods warranted on income distributional grounds. While luxury taxes are an appropriate device in most developing countries where income and profit taxation encounters difficulties, such taxes should also be levied on domestically produced luxury goods, since otherwise their home production would be encouraged as has indeed happened in a number of developing countries. Thus, an excise tax on luxury goods will be an appropriate measure; in the case of imports, this may be levied at a point of entry.

The application of tariffs at higher rates may be warranted, however, in cases when consumers have an irrational preference for foreign goods which involves a cost to the national economy as consumer goods are imported at a higher cost than they can be produced domestically. Such exceptions should be made sparingly, however, so as to avoid excessive protection of consumer goods industries leading to high cost, inefficient production.

It has also been suggested that higher tariffs should be applied to protect infant industries. But infant industry protection should apply to exports as well. In fact, it may be desirable to grant additional incentives to new export activities. For one thing, there are additional costs of entering foreign markets, including the cost of the collection of information and marketing; for another, the risk to individual exporters tends to be greater than to the national economy that has a diversified export structure. However, just like infant industry protection, additional incentives aimed at new exports should be given on a temporary basis until new markets have been established.

Differential treatment of particular sectors

Setting tariffs and export subsidies at equal rates on all products would be equivalent to free trade. This would not, however, be the appropriate policy in developing countries. For one thing, in the case of exports facing less than infinitely elastic foreign demand, one should apply optimum tariffs that equate the marginal revenue derived from the exportation of the commodity in question to marginal costs.[19] For another, the existence of externalities in the manufacturing sector warrants the preferential treatment of this sector in developing countries.

Manufacturing activities provide social benefits in the form of the 'production' of skilled labor and technological change that are not fully captured in the entrepreneur's profit calculation. There is a difference in this regard between manufacturing and agricultural activities as the latter generally use less skilled labor, and technological change is promoted chiefly by agricultural stations rather than by individual producers. At the same time, preferential treatment should be commensurate with the external economies manufacturing activities generate, which do not justify the high protection often observed in developing countries.

Ffrench-Davis and Pinera Echenique (1976) further suggest providing differential treatment to particular manufacturing industries. In their view (p. 73), 'it is necessary to discriminate deliberately between different items, since in practice the divergences between the social and private returns related with the nature of the production processes are not uniform in all activities.' But it is hardly possible to establish the extent to which social benefits vary among industries. For example, while at one time textile production was considered a vegetative industry in Latin America, it has had one of the best records of productivity improvement in recent years.

Given our ignorance as regards inter-industry differences in social benefits, it is suggested here that, infant industries apart, as a first approximation one should provide equal incentives to all manufacturing activities. This amounts to the application of the 'market principle' that will ensure that efficient activities will expand at the expense of inefficient ones. Exceptions from this rule should be made only in cases when it is well established that an industry generates substantially greater (lesser) external economies than the average. In so doing, one should avoid the use of 'tailor-made' tariffs benefiting a particular firm in response to pressures by special interest groups. In general, the burden of proof should be on those requesting special treatment.

At the same time, to the extent possible, exceptions should be made, and considerations other than economic efficiency introduced, in the form of direct measures rather than higher rates of protection.[20] Thus, in industries which show exceptional promise for technological improvements, the direct subsidization of research and development is preferable to additional protection that may lead to the establishment of high-cost firms. Also, measures taken to reduce the cost of labor will be a more appropriate way to encourage employment than the protection of labor-intensive industries that promotes the use of both labor and capital in these industries.[21]

Alternative incentive schemes

The proposed system of incentives may be implemented in various ways.[22] Under Alternative A, differential incentives are provided by applying the official exchange rate to exports facing less than infinitely elastic foreign demand (e.g. copper) and imposing import tariffs and export subsidies on other primary products as well as on manufactured goods, with higher rates applying in the latter case.[23]

Assume that, in the case described, optimum tariff considerations and external economies in the manufacturing sector warrant setting rates of import tariffs and export subsidies at 25 percent for primary products other than copper and at 40 percent for manufactured goods. Domestic prices and relative incentives as well as the allocation of resources and effects on the government budget will be the same if the official exchange rate is set 25 percent higher and is applied to primary products other than copper while a 20 percent export tax is levied on copper, and manufactured goods are subject to tariffs and export subsidies of 12 percent (Alternative B). Again, the economic effects will be the same but the official exchange rate will be 40 percent higher than under Alternative A if this rate is applied to manufactured goods, a 28.6 percent export tax is levied on copper, and a 10.7 percent export tax cum import subsidy on other primary products (Alternative C).

While the three alternatives described above have identical effects on trade, resource allocation and the government budget, they differ as to the chances of retaliation on the part of the importing countries, in particular the developed nations. This conclusion follows since tariffs and taxes are generally considered to be within the purview of every country but foreign nations may employ retaliatory measures in cases when export subsidies are granted. Indeed, in the United States, countervailing duties have been levied on several export products from developing countries and their application threatens all exporters who receive explicit subsidies.

The objective of avoiding retaliation thus favors Alternative B over Alternative A, and Alternative C will be superior to the other two since it does not involve explicit subsidies to exports.[24] Internal political considerations may, however, hinder the application of the third alternative. Primary producers may object to the use of (explicit) export taxes and a large devaluation may meet with general disapproval. Should this be the case, the use of explicit export subsidies could not be forgone. Developing countries could, then, minimize the chances of retaliation on the part of the developed nations by relying on measures that have not been traditionally considered export subsidies or have been used by the developed nations themselves.

To begin with, duty rebates on imported inputs used in export production are admissible under GATT.[25] Also, there are various institutional measures of export promotion that have been widely employed without inviting retaliation. They include services to exporters provided by governmental or quasi-governmental bodies in the form of the collection of information on export markets, the organization of trade fairs, export marketing institutions, quality control, labor training, etc.

Finally, the danger of retaliation is reduced if the developing countries utilize subsidy measures which have been employed by the developed nations, such as preferential export credits, credit insurance schemes and income tax deferrals. The application of such measures could not be recommended, however, on exports to the United States that have countervailed preferential export financing and schemes involving a delay of taxes payable on incomes derived from exports, although they are provided to US exports (Balassa and Sharpston, 1977, pp. 41 ff.).

Additional considerations on an 'ideal' incentive scheme

We have indicated the need for providing equal incentives to individual activities within the manufacturing sector. Uniformity should be understood in terms of effective rates of protection which express the margin of protection on value added rather than in terms of nominal rates of protection which relate to product price. The implications of these conclusions for export subsidization will next be indicated.

Value added in exporting equals net foreign exchange earnings, that is, the difference between the fob export price and the foreign exchange value of tradeable inputs. Providing equal subsidies on a value-added basis will thus ensure the expansion of efficient export activities; i.e. those where exports can be obtained at least domestic cost. Conversely, selectivity in export incentives based on differences in the international competitiveness of individual industries as suggested in the ECLA study on Mexico will tend to encourage high-cost, and discourage low-cost, exports (ECLA, 1976).

Nor is the proper objective of export policies to 'maximize their selective efficiency, in terms of sufficiently precise variable goals'.[26] To the extent that these goals are considered desirable, they would be more effectively served by measures that bear directly on the particular objective rather than by export subsidies that could not be appropriately used to pursue multiple objectives. Moreover, selectivity would impose a heavy administrative burden on the government bureaucracy and invite corruption.

Similar objections pertain to related proposals made for the planning and programming of exports.[27] Apart from the fact that firms are better able to discover export opportunities than a government bureaucracy, the responsibility for exports cannot be divided as firms have to take the risks involved in exporting and reap the rewards.

These conclusions are substantiated by the experience of the 11 countries reviewed above. They are also supported by the experience of Hungary, the country with the largest share of exports in GNP among the socialist states, which chose to decentralize decision making in the export sector, with firms responding to market signals. In fact, the Hungarian economic reform was to a large extent motivated by the difficulties encountered in planning an economy that relies to a considerable extent on foreign trade (Balassa, 1970). By contrast, India provides an example where investment, production and import controls applied in the process of planning compromised the effectiveness of export incentives and constrained the growth of the national economy.

To have the desired effects, the export incentive scheme – and the system of incentives in general – should also have the characteristics of stability and certainty. Frequent changes in the incentives tend to reduce their effectiveness. And while changes in the incentive system cannot be forgone, these should be carried out according to a predetermined timetable.

In this connection, it should be emphasized that the proposed incentive scheme could not be adopted overnight. Rather, it should be approached in steps generally involving the lowering and equalization of protection rates and the reduction of discrimination against exports over time. In this way, disruptions in production could be minimized.

In order to prepare firms for the prospective changes in incentives, these should be made known in advance. Infant industry protection, too, should be provided on a declining scale determined in advance. This would permit firms to take the necessary steps to reduce costs which was not the case in countries where protection was regarded as permanent.

Last but not least, exchange rate policy should aim at avoiding large shifts in export incentives that occur if inflation is offset by intermittent devaluations. Thus, in the event that domestic prices rise at a higher rate than abroad, the example of countries such as Brazil and Colombia should be followed in devaluing *pari passu* with inflation.

CONCLUSION

This chapter has provided evidence on the favorable effects of export incentives for the growth of exports and that of the national economy. It has been shown that, in an inter-country framework, greater export orientation tends to be associated with better growth performance. Also, in the individual countries, economic growth generally accelerated following the introduction of export promotion schemes.

It further appears that growth has been the most rapid in countries, such as Korea, Singapore and Taiwan, which most nearly conform to the 'ideal' system of incentives described in the third section of this chapter. The three countries provided a free trade regime for exports and ensured stability in the incentive system over time. They also granted comparable incentives to exports and to import substitution in manufacturing while there was little discrimination against primary activities.

The application of the proposed incentive scheme has been objected to on the grounds that the primary exports of developing countries encounter market limitations and their manufactured exports face high protection in the importing countries, in particular the developed nations. Experience shows that these objections have been much exaggerated.

Apart from tropical beverages, the factors limiting the expansion of primary exports by the developing countries have been on the supply rather than on the demand side. In turn, notwithstanding the application of tariffs and other restrictions in the developed nations, manufactured exports from the developing countries have risen much more rapidly than had been foreseen. Between 1960 and 1966, these exports increased at an average annual rate of 12 percent; they rose 25 percent a year between 1966 and 1973 as against an annual rate of increase of 17 percent for the manufactured exports of the developed nations.

The possibilities for the further expansion of manufactured exports from the developing countries are indicated by the fact that these countries account only for 7 percent of the imports of manufactured goods by the developed nations and for 1 percent of their domestic sales of manufactured goods. If the domestic market for manufactured goods in the developed nations were to increase at an average annual rate of 5 percent during a decade and the developing countries were to supply one-twentieth of this increment, they could increase their exports of manufactured goods to the developed nations from $16 billion in 1973 to over $61 billion (in 1973 prices) ten years later.

An increase of such a magnitude would, however, necessitate a considerable degree of diversification in the manufactured exports of the developing countries. Such a diversification is under way in Korea, Singapore and Taiwan with the upgrading of their existing exports and increased reliance on the exports of machinery and equipment. For other developing countries, such as Brazil, the exports of automobiles and steel may provide promise, Finally, developing countries may increase their participation in the international division of the production process by manufacturing parts, components and accessories of durable goods.

In a number of products, the developing countries could take over markets from countries which have recently become developed, such as Japan, whose comparative advantage is shifting to more advanced products. At the same time, the acceptability of manufactured imports from developing countries is greater if these replace imports from other developed countries rather than domestic production.

But possibilities exist for further expansion even in the exportation of textiles and clothing which is the single largest product group in developing country exports to the developed nations, amounting to 37 percent of the total. In this connection, note that the developing countries account for less than one-fourth of the imports and less than 4 percent of domestic sales of textiles and clothing in the developed nations.

Rather than market limitations, the main danger appears to be that, in response to adverse changes during the world recession of 1974–5, developing countries may again turn to import substitution. Yet the particularly severe recession reflected a confluence of circumstances – the quadrupling of oil prices together with the after-effects of the super-boom of 1972–3 – that cannot be expected to recur.

Aside from the resulting misallocation of resources, adopting an inward-looking policy would compromise chances for participation in the renewed growth of world trade. In fact, it appears that the policies followed have affected the success of the individual countries in resuming export growth following the recession. Thus, the exports of manufactured goods increased by two-thirds between the second quarter of 1975 and that of 1976 in Korea which maintained a policy of export orientation. In turn, increases were considerably smaller in Brazil, Colombia and Mexico which have adopted measures entailing increased discrimination against exports.

Apart from exporting to the developed countries, Korea and Taiwan have also been successful in the rapidly growing markets of the oil-exporting countries, particularly in the Middle East, whose total imports rose from $20 billion in 1973 to $55 billion in 1975. With the continuing rapid expansion of imports of the oil-exporting countries, the oil-importing developing countries could derive considerable benefit from efforts aimed at these markets.

In turn, the prospects for trade among the oil-importing developing countries appear modest. Countries which have established an industrial base have similar product specialization, while countries at lower levels of industrialization tend to protect the products of industries where the more advanced developing countries have export potential. At any rate, the combined manufactured imports of all the oil-importing developing countries have been less than the annual increment in the imports of manufactured goods by developed countries.

At the same time, the expansion of exports by developing countries to the developed nations would be greatly helped by reductions in existing barriers to trade, and the avoidance of the imposition of new barriers in the latter. The pursuit of such a policy is also of interest to the developed nations, in part because they benefit from the reallocation of resources according to comparative advantage, and in part because more rapid growth resulting from the application of export-oriented policies in the developing countries increased demand for the products of their technologically advanced industries.

NOTES

1. The developing country group has been defined to include the countries of Latin America, Africa (other than South Africa), Asia (other than Japan) and Yugoslavia.
2. In 1966, effective protection rates on domestic sales averaged 8.6 percent. Cf. Tan and Chin Hock (1982).
3. Westphal and Suk Kim, 1982. Wastage allowances were provided for the free importation of inputs in excess of the needs of export production.
4. According to Angel Monti (1976, pp.12), 'the four countries studied showed that there was instability, and in some cases, a chronic deficit in the balance of payments. This caused many adverse consequences. In Argentina, it was an important factor in causing the pattern of growth to show a typical "stop–go" behaviour. In Brazil it has already influenced the rate of growth. In Colombia, effects have been felt, including political effects. In Mexico it has caused a strong need for an inflow of foreign capital, thus aggravating the medium-term problem.'
5. Garcia (1976, p. 108). The figures exclude the subsidy value of credit preferences.
6. The study, published in Hebrew, is cited in Michaely (1976, p. 30).
7. Krueger, *Foreign Trade Regimes*, Chapter 9. In these studies, incentives to exports have been expressed by combining export exchange rates and export subsidies; using export exchange rates alone generally did not provide statistically significant results. Cf. Donges and Riedel (1977).
8. The Israel/Mexico comparison provides an exception, however, as despite its lower incremental export–output ratio Mexico had a higher manufacturing growth rate than Israel.
9. For 11 observations, levels of significance are 0.1 percent for a Spearman rank correlation of 0.82 or higher; 0.5 percent for coefficient values of 0.73 or higher, and 1 percent for coefficient values of 0.41 or higher.
10. While the differences in these ratios declined after 1968, labor–capital ratios for imports are understated since the data used refer only to import substitutes actually produced in Korea and do not include presumably highly capital-intensive machinery and intermediate products imported from developed countries, which are not produced in Korea.
11. In the case of Taiwan, the estimates of Banerji and Riedel (1976) for 1961–6 and 1966–71 have been combined in an approximative fashion.

12. *Ibid.*
13. *Korea Statistical Yearbook*, various issues.
14. Banerji and Riedel (1976). ILO, *Yearbook of Labour Statistics*. IMF, *International Financial Statistics*, various issues. Data for most of the other countries studied are not available.
15. In the case of Korea where the relevant data are available, we find that the results are little affected if we adjust for the import content of exports. Thus, while the share of imports in GNP increased from 18.7 percent in 1966 to 34.3 percent in 1973 in Korea, adjusting for the import needs of exports the relevant shares will be 16.0 percent in 1966 and 24.5 percent in 1973.
16. Additional calculations reported in Balassa (1978) indicate that exports had a considerable effect on economic growth even if we adjust for the contribution of domestic and foreign capital and labor.
17. These conclusions are unaffected by the choice of the indicators of income inequalities. For a compilation of the relevant estimates, see Jain (1975).
18. Nevertheless, budgetary considerations generally preclude the use of production subsidies in the place of tariffs and export subsidies in the developing countries. For a further discussion, see Balassa (1975, pp. 373 ff.). The paper also provides a further discussion of several of the issues considered in this section as well as references to the principal contributions in the relevant literature.
19. For the relevant formulas, cf. Johnson (1968).
20. This conclusion also applies if differences exist between the shadow and the market prices of productive factors.
21. For a discussion of the technological and employment arguments for protection, see Balassa (1977, Chapter 5).
22. These alternatives are discussed in Balassa and Sharpston (1977). The paper also describes actions taken by developed nations as regards export subsidization by developing countries.
23. Trade in intermediate goods is not considered here; their introduction necessitates relating incentives to value added rather than output value. On practical difficulties and possible solutions, see Balassa and Schydlowsky (1974).
24. These alternatives may be interpreted as variants of multiple exchange rates or, in the event of their application in replacing the existing system of protection, of a compensated devaluation. The latter has been first suggested in Balassa (1966) and Schydlowsky (1967).
25. Rebates of indirect taxes are also admissible and should be applied under all circumstances but, as noted above, they are not genuine export subsidies.
26. Monti (1976, pp. 61ff.). The stated goals are said to include 'value added, employment, distribution in general, net balance of foreign currency, technology-effect, structure of the power of decision, type of insertion in world trade, structure of trade by destination, induced structure of production by regional origin, etc.'
27. According to Monti (1976, p. 25), ' "promotion" policies as such should be abandoned in favor of designing selective "conduction" policies, with planning and participation, by activities, integrating production/substitution/exports in a single context in design and in operation.'

REFERENCES

Annual Report (1968) Department of Trade, Ministry of Finance, Singapore.
Aydalot, Philippe (1968) *Essai sur les problèmes de la stratégie de l'industrialisation en économie sous-développée: l'exemple tunisien*, Université de Tunis, Cahiers du CERES, Série Economique, 2, Tunis.

Balassa, Bela (1966) 'Integration and Resource Allocation in Latin America', paper prepared for the conference 'The Next Decade of Latin American Development', held in April 1966 at Cornell University; published in Spanish under the title 'Integracion regional y asignacion de recursos en America Latina', *Comercio Exterior*, Mexico City, September.

Balassa, Bela (1970) 'The Economic Reform in Hungary', *Economica*, NS, Vol. 37, London. pp. 1–22.

Balassa, Bela (1971) 'Industrial Policies in Taiwan and Korea', *Weltwirtschaftliches Archiv*, Vol. 106, I, pp. 55–77.

Balassa, Bela (1975) 'Reforming the System of Incentives in Developing Countries', *World Development*, Vol. 3, Oxford, pp. 365–82.

Balassa, Bela (1977) *Policy Reform in Developing Countries*, Oxford.

Balassa, Bela (1978) 'Exports and Economic Growth: Further Evidence', *Journal of Development Economics* (June), pp. 181–9. Reprinted as Chapter 17 in this volume.

Balassa, Bela, et al. (1971) *The Structure of Protection in Developing Countries*, Baltimore, Md., London.

Balassa, Bela, and Schydlowsky, Daniel M. (1974) 'Indicators of Protection and of Other Incentive Measures', in *The Role of the Computer in Economic and Social Research in Latin America*, edited by Nancy D. Ruggles, a conference report of the National Bureau of Economic Research, New York, London, pp. 331–46.

Balassa, Bela, and Sharpston, Michael (1977) 'Export Subsidies by Developing Countries: Issues of Policy', in *Commercial Policy Issues*, Geneva, No. 3.

Banerji, Ranadev, and Riedel, James, (1976) *Industrial Employment Expansion under Alternative Strategies: Some Empirical Evidence*, mimeo.

Bergsman, Joel (1971) *Foreign Trade Policy in Brazil*, February, mimeo.

Bergsman, Joel, and Malan, Pedro S. (1971) 'Brazil', in Bela Balassa et al., *The Structure of Protection in Developing Countries*, Baltimore, Md., London, pp. 103–36.

Berlinski, Julio, and Schydlowsky, Daniel M. (1982) 'Argentina', in *Development Strategies in Semi-Industrial Economies*, (Bela Belassa *et al.*), Baltimore, Md, The Johns Hopkins University Press, pp. 83–122.

Bhagwati, Jagdish, and Srinivasan, T.N. (1975) *Foreign Trade Regimes and Economic Development: India*, a special conference series on Foreign Trade Regimes and Economic Development, National Bureau of Economic Research, Vol. 6. New York, London.

Donges, Juergen B., and Riedel, James (1977) 'The Expansion of Manufactured Exports in Developing Countries: An Empirical Assessment of Supply and Demand Issues', *Weltwirtschaftliches Archiv*, Vol. 113. pp. 58–87.

Dubey, Vinod (1976) 'Yugoslavia: Commodity Exports and Export Policies', paper prepared for the ECLA/IBRD Seminar on Export Promotion Policies, Santiago, Chile, November.

ECLA (UN, Economic Commission for Latin America) (1976) 'The Export of Manufactures in Mexico and Its Promotion Policy', paper presented at the ECLA/IBRD Seminar on Export Promotion Policies, Santiago, Chile, November.

Ffrench-Davis, Ricardo, and Pinera Echenique, José (1976) 'Colombia Export Promotion Policy', paper prepared for the ECLA/IBRD Seminar on Export Promotion Policies, Santiago, Chile, November.

Garcia, Hector A. (1976) 'Brazil's Development Policy for Exports of Manufactures', paper prepared for the ECLA/IBRD Seminar on Export Promotion Policies, Santiago, Chile, November.

Geiger, Theodore (1973) *Tales of Two City-States: The Development Program of Hong Kong and Singapore*, Washington, DC.

Glassburner, Bruce, and Riedel, James (1973) 'Economic Development Lessons from

Hong Kong: A Reply', *The Economic Record*, Vol. 49, Melbourne, pp. 637–43.

Hutcheson, Thomas, and Schydlowsky, Daniel M. 'Colombia', in *Development Strategies in Semi-Industrial Economies* (Bela Balassa *et al.*), Baltimore, Md, The Johns Hopkins University Press, pp. 128–53.

ILO (International Labour Office), *Yearbook of Labour Statistics*, Geneva, various issues.

IMF (International Monetary Fund), *International Financial Statistics*, Washington, DC, various issues.

Jain, Shail (1975) *Size Distribution of Income, A Compilation of Data*, The World Bank, Washington, DC.

Jeanneret, Teresa (1971) 'The Structure of Protection in Chile', in Bela Balassa et al., *The Structure of Protection in Developing Countries*. Baltimore, Md, London, pp. 137–68.

Johnson, Harry G. (1968) 'Alternative Maximization Policies for Developing-Country Exports of Primary Products', *The Journal of Political Economy*, Vol. 76, Chicago, Ill., pp. 489–93.

Korea Statistical Yearbook, Seoul, various issues.

Krueger, Anne O. (1978) *Foreign Trade Regimes and Economic Development – Liberalization Attempts and Consequences*, New York, National Bureau of Economic Research.

Michaely, Michael (1976) 'Export Promotion Policies in Israel', paper prepared for the ECLA/IBRD Seminar on Export Promotion Policies, Santiago, Chile, November.

Monti, Angel (1976) 'Latin American Exports of Manufactures: Experiences and Problems', paper prepared for the ECLA/IBRD Seminar on Export Promotion Policies, Santiago, Chile, November.

OECD (Organization for Economic Cooperation and Development) *National Accounts of Less Developed Countries, 1950–1966*, Paris.

Riedel, James (1975) 'Factor Proportions and Linkages in the Open Developing Economy', *The Review of Economics and Statistics*, Vol. 57, Cambridge, Mass., pp. 487–94.

Schydlowsky, Daniel M. (1967) 'From Import Substitution to Export Promotion for Semi-Grown Up Industries: A Policy Proposal', *The Journal of Development Studies*, Vol. 3, London, pp. 405–13.

Sussman, Zvi (1982) 'Israel', in *Development Strategies in Semi-industrial Economies* (Bela Balassa *et al.*), Baltimore, Md, Johns Hopkins University Press, pp. 160–211.

Tan, Augustine, and Chin Hock, Ow (1982), 'Singapore', in *Development Strategies in Semi-industrial Economies* (Bela Balassa *et al.*), Baltimore, Md, Johns Hopkins University Press, pp. 280–309.

Tyler, William G. (1976) *Manufactured Export Expansion and Industrialization in Brazil*, Kieler Studien, 134, Tübingen.

UN (United Nations), *The Growth of World Industry*, New York, various issues.

UN, *Yearbook of National Accounts Statistics*, New York, various issues.

Westphal, Larry E. (1976) 'Korea's Experience with Export-Led Industrial Development', paper prepared for the ECLA/IBRD Seminar on Export Promotion Policies, Santiago, Chile, November.

Westphal, Larry E. and Suk Kim, Kwang (1982) 'Korea', in *Development Strategies in Semi-Industrial Economies* (Bela Balassa *et al.*), Baltimore, Md, Johns Hopkins University Press, pp, 280–309.

Wolf, Martin (1976) 'Indian Exports', paper presented at the ECLA/IBRD Seminar on Export Promotion Policies, Santiago, Chile, November.

World Bank (International Bank for Reconstruction and Development), *World Tables, 1976*, Baltimore, Md, London.

17 · EXPORTS AND ECONOMIC GROWTH: FURTHER EVIDENCE

CONCEPTUAL AND MEASUREMENT ISSUES

In examining the effects of exports on economic growth in countries which have established an industrial base, we test the hypothesis that export-oriented policies lead to better growth performance than policies favoring import substitution. This result is said to obtain because export-oriented policies, which provide similar incentives to sales in domestic and in foreign markets, lead to resource allocation according to comparative advantage, allow for greater capacity utilization, permit the exploitation of economies of scale, generate technological improvements in response to competition abroad and, in labor-surplus countries, contribute to increased employment.[1]

In turn, once the 'easy' stage of import substitution is over, substituting domestic production for imports entails rising costs due to the loss of economies of scale in small national markets and the relatively capital-intensive nature of the products involved. As a result, the domestic resource cost of saving foreign exchange through continued import substitution under protection will exceed the domestic resource cost of earning foreign exchange through exports and the difference will tend to increase over time.[2]

Inter-country differences in trade policies may be expressed in a variety of ways. Under one alternative, inter-country differences in the growth of exports are taken to reflect the extent of export orientation; i.e. the choice between using resources for exports as against import substitution under protection. Thus, *ceteris paribus*, different rates of export growth will be associated with differences in trade policies.[3]

It is of further interest to examine the relationship between export growth and the growth of GNP *net* of exports. In an inter-country context, the

This chapter was prepared in the framework of the Development Strategies in Semi-industrial Countries research project undertaken at the World Bank and directed by the author. He is indebted to Ian Little, Paul Streeten, Larry Westphal and an anonymous referee for helpful comments. First published in *Journal of Development Economics*, June 1978.

correlation between these variables may be taken to reflect the indirect effects of exports operating through changes in incomes and costs.[4] In turn, the correlation between export growth and GNP growth will provide an indication of the total (direct plus indirect) effects of exports on economic growth.

In the case of countries that started from a low base, export growth rates are sensitive to the choice of the initial year. Correspondingly, further interest attaches to relating the absolute increment in exports to the absolute increment in GNP, which is less sensitive to the choice of the base year. This measure, the so-called incremental export–GNP ratio, too, can be transformed so as to relate the increment in exports to that of GNP *net* of exports.

All these measures, as well as a variant of the measure proposed by Michaely,[5] have been used to investigate the relationship between export expansion and economic growth in an 11-country sample. The sample includes countries which have established an industrial base; within the constraints imposed by data availability, they have been chosen so as to provide representation of the principal tendencies as far as trade policies in developing countries are concerned.

Among the countries included in the sample, Korea, Singapore and Taiwan adopted export-oriented policies at an early stage; they provided essentially free-trade treatment to exports; and granted some additional subsidies which equalized, on the average, incentives to exports and to import substitution. Israel and Yugoslavia started early with export promotion but their efforts slackened somewhat afterwards. Argentina, Brazil, Colombia and Mexico continued further with import substitution and provided export incentives only from the mid-1960s onwards; at the same time, these countries did not generally ensure exporters free access to imported inputs. Finally, Chile and India pursued inward-oriented policies throughout the period under consideration, and their relatively weak export promotion efforts were frustrated by far-reaching controls on imports and investment.[6]

The period of investigation chosen is 1960–73. Since in a number of the countries included in the sample policy changes occurred in the mid-1960s calculations have also been made for the 1960–6 and 1966–73 subperiods. The estimates concern the relationship between total exports and GNP as well as that between manufactured exports and manufacturing output.

THE EMPIRICAL ESTIMATES

Table 17.1 shows the empirical results obtained by the use of the Spearman rank correlation coefficient, which has also been employed by Michaely. It is apparent that the statistical significance of the estimates generally improves between the first and the second subperiods. These differences in the subperiod results may be explained, at least in part, by the relatively low level of manufactured exports in several countries at the beginning of the period.

Table 17.1 Spearman rank correlation coefficients between exports and output growth in selected developing countries

	Manufacturing			Total		
	1960–6	1966–73	1960–73	1960–6	1966–73	1960–73
1. Export growth vs the growth of output	0.400 (0.112)	0.846 (0.001)	0.709 (0.008)	0.822 (0.001)	0.934 (0.001)	0.888 (0.001)
2. Export growth vs the growth of output net of exports	0.178 (0.301)	0.800 (0.002)	0.738 (0.005)	0.482 (0.067)	0.765 (0.004)	0.770 (0.003)
3. Incremental export–output ratios vs the growth of output	0.873 (0.001)	0.682 (0.011)	0.809 (0.002)	0.708 (0.008)	0.847 (0.001)	0.813 (0.002)
4. Incremental export–output ratios vs the growth of output net of exports	0.251 (0.229)	0.709 (0.008)	0.800 (0.002)	0.036 (0.458)	0.688 (0.010)	0.582 (0.031)
5. Increments in export–output ratios vs the growth of output	0.309 (0.178)	0.518 (0.052)	0.482 (0.067)	0.565 (0.035)	0.808 (0.002)	0.776 (0.003)
6. The average ratio of exports to output vs the growth of output	0.843 (0.001)	0.636 (0.018)	0.746 (0.005)	0.327 (0.163)	0.767 (0.003)	0.703 (0.008)

Notes:
1. Manufacturing exports have been related to the output of the manufacturing sector and total exports to GNP. The relevant export–output ratios are averages for the periods concerned.
2. Levels of significance are shown in parentheses.
3. Regression equations estimated by the inclusion of a constant term are not shown because of the lack of statistical significance of the constant.

Not surprisingly, a weaker relationship is obtained with regard to the indirect – as compared to the total – effects of exports. This is the case in particular for estimates made on the national economy level, where calculating indirect effects involves deducting the *value* of exports from GNP that is a *value added* concept. Nevertheless, the results for the entire period, and for the second subperiod, point to the importance of the indirect effects of exports.

With one exception, the observed correlations with regard to the total effects of exports are higher for GNP than for manufactured output. The opposite conclusion applies, however, to the indirect effects of exports, again reflecting the sensitivity of the estimates to deducting the value of exports from GNP.

Finally, the results obtained by the use of the Michaely measure for the entire period, as well as for the two subperiods, show a higher rank correlation than that obtained in Michaely's sample of 23 countries, with GNP per head exceeding $300 (0.523). The differences may be explained by reference to the heterogeneity of the sample used by Michaely that includes countries, such as Algeria, Guatemala and Paraguay, which rely chiefly on primary exports as well as countries, such as Cyprus, Malta and Panama, where service exports tend to dominate.[7] The greater homogeneity of our sample may also explain that we have obtained a relatively high correlation between export shares and the growth of GNP (0.703 for 1960–73) while Michaely found no such relationship.[8]

ADJUSTING FOR FACTOR INPUTS

Attempting to explain GNP growth in terms of export growth has the disadvantage of omitting other relevant variables. Michalopoulos and Jay (1973) attempted to remedy this deficiency by using domestic and foreign investment and labor as explanatory variables together with exports in an inter-country regression designed to explain inter-country differences in GNP growth rates. The inclusion of exports in a production function-type relationship is warranted on the grounds that exports tend to raise total factor productivity for reasons adduced in the introduction.

Using data for 39 developing countries in the period 1960–6, Michalopoulos and Jay found that inter-country differences in domestic and in foreign investment and in labor growth explained 53 percent of the inter-country variation in GNP growth rates, while adding an export variable raised the coefficient of determination to 0.71. These results are reproduced in equations (1) and (2) in Table 17.2.

We have applied the method utilized by Michalopoulos and Jay to the pooled data of ten out of the eleven countries under study for the periods 1960–6 and 1966–73; for lack of some of the relevant data, Singapore had to be excluded. The results shown in equations (3) and (4) indicate that adding the export variable in the regression equation raises the coefficient of determination from 0.58 to 0.77. At the same time, all regression coefficients are significant at the 5 percent level in both equations.

The regression coefficient of the export variable has the same value as in the Michalopoulos–Jay equation, indicating that a 1 percent increase in the rate of growth of exports is associated with a 0.04 of 1 percent increase in the rate of growth of GNP. In turn, the coefficients of the foreign capital and the labor variables are higher, and the coefficient of domestic capital is lower, than in the earlier study. The latter result may be explained by the fact that in most of the ten countries domestic investment was rising rapidly during the period under consideration and its effects were not yet fully absorbed in the national economy.

As shown in equations (5) and (6), the results are not substantially affected if the current dollar value of exports is replaced by the purchasing power of exports or by the incremental export–GNP ratio. In the latter case, a 1 percent increase in the rate of growth of exports appears to be associated with a 0.05 of 1 percent increase in the rate of growth of GNP.

Table 17.2 Inter-country regression analysis of the growth of GNP

Eq.	Dependent variable	Coefficients of independent variables						
		K_D	K_F	L	X	PPX	IXR	R^2
1	Y	0.25	0.20	0.66				0.53
		(7.81)	(3.35)	(2.44)				
2	Y	0.24	0.12	0.60	0.04			0.71
		(9.62)	(2.33)	(2.81)	(4.82)			
3	Y	0.18	0.30	1.09				0.58
		(3.23)	(2.42)	(1.74)				
4	Y	0.15	0.23	0.97	0.04			0.77
		(3.33)	(2.40)	(1.99)	(3.57)			
5	Y	0.16	0.24	0.92		0.05		0.75
		(3.59)	(2.44)	(1.82)		(3.34)		
6	Y	0.14	0.26	0.98			0.006	0.65
		(2.32)	(2.32)	(1.66)			(1.86)	

Notes:
Equations (1) and (2) have been taken from Michalopoulos and Jay (1973); equations (3) to (6) have been estimated for the pooled data of ten countries for 1960–66 and 1966–73. The gross national product (Y) and labor (L) have been expressed as the ratio of the absolute change between the initial and the terminal year divided by initial year values. The same procedure has been followed for exports, which have alternatively been expressed in terms of current dollar values (X) and in terms of their purchasing power (PPX), derived by deflating dollar values by the index of unit values of manufactured exports of the developed countries. IXR is the incremental export–GNP ratio as defined in the text. K_F is the average current account balance during the period in question, expressed as a proportion of initial year GNP, and K_D the average difference between gross fixed capital formation and current account balance, expressed as a proportion of initial year GNP. Data on labor refer to the labor force rather than employment.

The results obtained as regards the relationship between export and GNP growth may be compared to the estimate derived in a cross-section investigation of a partly overlapping group of ten countries by Anne Krueger (1977, Chapter XI) who found that an increase in the rate of growth of exports of 1 percent tends to raise the rate of growth of GNP by 0.06 of 1 percent. But while Krueger's estimates reflect an adjustment for a time trend, no adjustment has been made for changes in labor and capital.[9] At the same time, Krueger has found that, on the average, countries with liberalized regimes had a GNP growth rate 0.7 percent higher than others even after differences in export performance are taken into account.

IMPLICATIONS OF THE RESULTS

The next question concerns the implications of inter-country differences in export performance for the rate of economic growth. For this purpose, we have compared predicted values derived from equation (4), calculated by using *actual* export growth rates for the individual countries, with hypothetical values derived from the same equation on the assumption that each country had the *average* export growth rate calculated for the group as a whole. The calculations have been made for the period 1966–73.

According to the results thereby obtained, the increase in Korea's GNP would have been 37 percent smaller if its export growth rate equalled the average for the countries concerned. The corresponding proportion is 25 percent for Taiwan. At the other extreme, in Chile, India and Mexico, respectively, the increase in GNP would have been 14, 12 and 8 percent greater if these countries had average export growth rates. The corresponding estimates for the remaining countries of the group fall in the –6 to + 9 percent range (Table 17.3).

The differences are accentuated if the results are expressed in per capita terms. Thus, according to the calculations, increases in per capita incomes in Korea would have been 43 percent smaller and in Taiwan 33 percent smaller, if export growth rates in these countries had been identical to the average for the sample as a whole. Conversely, increases in per capita incomes in Chile, India and Mexico, respectively, would have been 21, 22 and 17 percent higher in such an eventuality.

As noted earlier, export growth rates are sensitive to the choice of the base year. This is the case, in particular, in Brazil where exports in 1966 were at a low level because of the adverse effects of import substitution policies. Correspondingly, we have also made estimates using incremental export–GNP ratios.[10] As shown in Table 17.3, the results by and large correspond to the estimates derived by the use of export growth rates.

These results point to the fact that trade orientation has been an important factor contributing to inter-country differences in the growth of incomes. It is further apparent that income increments have been achieved at a substantially lower cost in terms of investment in countries that have followed a consistent policy of export orientation. Thus, taking the 1960–73 period as a whole, incremental capital–output ratios were 1.76 in Singapore, 2.10 in Korea and 2.44 in Taiwan. At the other extreme, these ratios were 5.49 in Chile and 5.72 in India (World Bank, 1976).

During the same period, incremental capital–output ratios were between 3 and 5 in the remaining countries of the sample, with improvements shown over time in countries with increased export orientation. While figures for subperiods are subject to considerable error, it appears that the greatest improvement was experienced in Brazil following its pronounced policy change. Brazil's incremental capital–output ratio declined from 3.84 in 1960–6 to 2.06 in 1966–73, when the low figure for the second period presumably also reflects increased capacity utilization at higher export levels.

In indicating that export growth favorably affects the rate of economic growth over and above the contributions of domestic and foreign capital and

Table 17.3 Hypothetical gain or loss in the growth rates of GNP and per capita GNP assuming average export growth rates and incremental export–GNP ratios

	Export growth		Incremental export–GNP ratio	
	GNP	Per cap. GNP	GNP	Per cap. GNP
Argentina	+8.4	+11.9	+5.0	+7.0
Brazil	−5.3	−8.8	+0.8	+1.3
Chile	+13.7	+21.4	+11.9	+18.3
Colombia	+3.8	+7.0	−2.2	−3.7
India	+12.4	+21.8	+11.2	+20.2
Israel	−0.8	−1.2	−3.4	−4.8
Korea	−37.4	−42.5	−15.5	−18.3
Mexico	+8.4	+17.1	+9.9	+20.6
Taiwan	−25.1	−32.6	−31.3	−40.2
Yugoslavia	+2.8	+3.3	−3.0	−3.5

Note: Hypothetical growth rates have been calculated from equations (4) and (6), under the assumption that the country in question had the average growth rate of exports or average incremental export/GNP ratio calculated for the sample group as a whole. The difference between these hypothetical growth rates and the predicted growth rates from the same equations for the country concerned has been designated as the gain (+) or loss (−) in the growth rate of GNP and per capita GNP assuming average export growth and incremental export/GNP ratios.

labor, the estimates presented in this chapter provide evidence on the benefits of export orientation as compared to policies oriented towards import substitution. At the same time, the empirical results tend to underestimate the effects of export growth on the growth of GNP, since the method applied does not take account of the implications of export growth for the other variables included in the equation. Yet there is evidence that exports and domestic savings are positively correlated (Weisskopf, 1972). Also the improved balance-of-payments situation attendant on the expansion of exports may increase the attractiveness of the country concerned for foreign capital.

NOTES

1. Some of these factors (e.g. increases in employment) represent a once-for-all gain while others (e.g. technological change) will have a continuing effect. Furthermore, to the extent that marginal saving ratios exceed average ratios, the rate of economic growth will be permanently higher under export orientation as compared to import substitution under protection. As noted below, this conclusion also follows if increases in factor supplies are accompanied by a shift of existing resources from export industries into import substituting industries under protection.
2. An extreme case of import substitution under protection is that considered by Harry Johnson (1967), where increases in the capital stock bring about a shift of

labor into the protected capital-intensive industry that, in turn, gives rise to a decline in the economy's consumption possibilities. And, even if absolute impoverishment will not ensue, the shift of labor into the protected capital-intensive industry will adversely affect efficiency and growth.

3. This alternative has been objected to by Michaely on the grounds that 'since exports are themselves part of the national product, an autocorrelation is present; and a positive correlation of the two variables is almost inevitable, whatever their true relationship with each other' (1977, p. 50). However, import-replacing domestic production, too, is part of the national product, so that in an inter-country framework export growth rates reflect alternative uses of resources.

4. There will be indirect effects emanating from exports to the extent that the size of the stimulus will be larger than under import substitution, leading to multiplier effects if resources are not fully utilized. Also, exporting permits cost reductions for goods sold domestically through the exploitation of economies of scale in industries producing for domestic as well as for foreign markets.

5. While Michaely correlates the average size of the annual changes in the ratio of exports to GNP with the average annual change in per capita GNP, it is more appropriate to use the rate of growth of GNP as the variable affected by export growth. This adjustment, however, changes the results but little.

6. For a description of the policies applied, see Balassa (1977).

7. It will be observed that the relationship between exports and economic growth will not be invariant to the commodity composition of exports, as the possibilities of exploiting economies of scale and increased capacity use have relevance primarily for manufacturing industries.

8. Note further that the Michaely measure gives a somewhat lower correlation in export–GNP relationships than the measures proposed here, with larger differences shown for manufactured exports. These differences may be explained by the sensitivity of the Michaely measure to random factors resulting from the fact that it uses incremental export shares.

9. Regressing the GNP variable on the export variable alone, we have obtained elasticity values of 0.06 to 0.07.

10. It may be suggested that these ratios are affected by the size of the country. This is not the case, however, in our sample. Thus, the bottom group of countries includes Chile which has the smallest population after Israel. In turn, the group which experienced the least deviations between the two sets of calculated values includes countries with greatly different population size, such as Argentina, Brazil, Colombia, Israel and Yugoslavia. Finally, among countries in the first group, Korea had the third largest population in our country sample.

REFERENCES

Balassa, Bela (1978) 'Export Incentives and Export Performance in Developing Countries: A Comparative Analysis', *Weltwirtschaftliches Archiv*, Band 114, Heft 1, pp. 24–61. Reprinted as chapter 16 in this volume.

Krueger, Anne O. (1978) *Foreign Trade Regimes and Economic Development: Liberalization Attempts and Consequences*. New York, National Bureau of Economic Research.

Johnson, Harry G. (1967) 'The Possibility of Income Losses from Increased Efficiency or Factor Accumulation in the Presence of Tariffs', *Economic Journal* 77, pp. 151–3.

Michaely, Michael (1977) 'Exports and Growth: An Empirical Investigation,' *Journal of Development Economics* 4, pp. 49–54.

Michalopoulos, Constantine, and Jay, Keith (1973) 'Growth of Exports and Income in the Developing World: A Neoclassical View'. *AID Discussion Paper No. 28*, Agency for International Development, Washington, DC.

Weisskopf, Thomas E. (1972) 'The Impact of Foreign Capital Inflow on Domestic Savings in Underdeveloped Countries', *Journal of International Economics 2*, pp. 25–38.

World Bank (1976) *World Tables 1976*, Washington, DC.

18 · EXPORTS, POLICY CHOICES AND ECONOMIC GROWTH IN DEVELOPING COUNTRIES AFTER THE 1973 OIL SHOCK

INTRODUCTION

Following Michalopoulos and Jay (1973), the author estimated the effects of exports on economic growth in a production function-type framework for a sample of semi-industrial countries in the 1960–73 period (1978). The method applied involved introducing exports, in addition to capital and labor, in a cross-section equation used to explain inter-country differences in rates of economic growth. The same procedure was subsequently applied by Tyler (1981) to a larger group of middle-income countries for the period 1960–77.

The purpose of the inclusion of exports, together with capital and labor, in a production function-type framework was to test the hypothesis that export orientation raises total factor productivity through its favorable effects on the efficiency of resource allocation, capacity utilization, economies of scale and technological change. The results obtained in all three studies show that exports significantly contributed to the rate of economic growth in an inter-country relationship while raising the explanatory power of the estimating equations to a considerable extent.

Subsequently, Feder (1983) used an alternative formulation of the export variable and further separated the effects of exports on economic growth into two parts: productivity differentials due to differences between exports and non-exports and externalities generated by exports. Making estimates for broader as well as for narrower groups of semi-industrial countries for the 1964–73 period, Feder obtained highly significant results for both variables.

The author is greatly indebted to Kenneth Meyers, who has carried out the econometric work for this chapter, and has benefited from helpful comments made by Gershon Feder, Moshe Syrquin and Larry Westphal, as well as by participants at workshops held at the Johns Hopkins University and the World Bank. The author alone, however, is responsible for the opinions expressed in the chapter; they should not be assumed to represent the views of the World Bank. First published in *Journal of Development Economics*, May–June 1985.

The above studies investigated the relationship between exports and economic growth in the period preceding the quadrupling of oil prices of 1973–4 and the world recession of 1974–5.[1] It has been suggested, however, that while export orientation brought benefits during the period of rapid world economic growth, such would not be the case once the world economic environment deteriorated as higher export (and import) shares magnify the effects of external shocks.

This chapter has set out to examine the export–economic growth relationship in the period of external shocks after 1973. For this purpose, the equations utilized earlier have been re-estimated for the 1973–9 period. Furthermore, estimates made by the author on policy responses to external shocks (1981; 1984a, b, c) have been used to analyze the effects of alternative policies on economic growth. Finally, the procedures applied have been combined in a single estimating equation.

In contradistinction with the earlier studies, the present investigation covers the entire spectrum of developing countries from the least developed countries to the newly industrializing countries. In order to allow for the effects of the level of development on economic growth, per capita incomes in the initial year have been introduced as an additional variable in the estimating equations. The equations further include the share of manufactured goods in total exports as an indicator of the product composition of exports. The study covers 43 developing countries, all of which were adversely affected by external shocks after 1973.

EXPORTS AND ECONOMIC GROWTH, 1973–9

As in the author's earlier study, it has been attempted to explain inter-country differences in GNP growth rates in terms of differences in domestic and foreign saving shares, the growth of the labor force and the growth of exports. Estimates have been made by combining domestic and foreign savings that equal domestic investment, as well as by taking these sources of savings separately.[2] The results are reported in Table 18.1.

A comparison of equations (1) and (2) shows that the introduction of the export variable increases the explanatory power of the regression equation to a considerable extent. The export variable is statistically significant at the 1 percent level in a one-tail test; at the same time, its introduction reduces the level of significance of the capital (investment) and labor variables, although the former remains significant at the 2 percent level.

As shown in equation (3), adding the per capita income variable to represent the level of economic development further increases the explanatory power of the regression equation. The variable has a negative sign and it is statistically significant at the 5 percent level. This result indicates that, for given increments of capital, labor and exports, the rate of economic growth

Table 18.1 Savings, labor, exports and economic growth, 1973–9

Eq.	Constant	S_d/Y^a	S_f/Y^a	L/L	X/X	Y/P	X_m/X	R^2
1	−10.067	0.181	0.181	1.128				0.213
	(−0.721)	(3.458)	(3.458)	(1.625)				
2	−2.094	0.114	0.114	0.920	0.182			0.304
	(−0.154)	(2.013)	(2.013)	(1.394)	(2.457)			
3	8.005	0.100	0.100	0.683	0.216	−9.191		0.338
	(0.553)	(1.788)	(1.788)	(1.038)	(2.888)	(−1.723)		
4	4.148	0.117	0.117	0.614	0.161	−12.662	0.256	0.375
	(0.241)	(2.130)	(2.130)	(0.958)	(2.035)	(−2.289)	(1.800)	
5	−14.020	0.176	0.069	1.157				0.307
	(−1.058)	(3.573)	(1.042)	(1.771)				
6	−6.843	0.123	0.036	0.984	0.147			0.357
	(−5.165)	(2.251)	(0.537)	(1.548)	(2.009)			
7	5.075	0.106	0.070	0.694	0.184	−11.783		0.424
	(0.374)	(2.046)	(0.011)	(1.129)	(2.586)	(2.321)		
8	1.180	0.124	0.018	0.624	0.128	−15.288	0.258	0.465
	(0.089)	(2.437)	(0.287)	(1.052)	(1.721)	(−2.935)	(1.959)	

Sources: World Bank economic and social data bank.

Symbols: dependent variable: change in GNP between 1973 and 1979 as a percentage of 1973 GNP. Independent variables: L/L = change in labor force between 1973 and 1978 as a percentage of the 1973 value; X/X = change in merchandise exports between 1973 and 1978 as a percentage of the 1973 value; S_d/Y = sum of gross domestic investments less current account balances from 1973 to 1978 as a percentage of 1973 GNP; S_f/Y = sum of current account balances from 1973 to 1978 as a percentage of 1973 GNP; Y/P = 1973 GNP per capita; X_m/X = 1973 share of manufactured goods in total exports. All value data is in constant dollar terms.
[a] The coefficients for S_d/Y and S_f/Y are constrained to be equal in equations (1) to (4).

will be higher the lower the level of development. It thus conflicts with the oft-expressed view, according to which countries at lower levels of development have more limited possibilities for economic growth than middle income countries.

Introducing the share of manufactured exports in total exports in equation (4) further increases the explanatory power of the regression equation while raising the statistical significance of the per capita income variable. At the same time, the introduction of these two variables raises the level of significance of the capital variable but reduces that of the export and in particular the labor variable.

In fact, the t-value of the labor variable does not exceed 1. This result may be explained by the use of labor force rather than employment data and by the inclusion in the sample of developing countries with, as well as without, surplus labor. For lack of available information, however, adjustment could not be made on this count.

Disaggregating investment according to the sources of savings as in the author's earlier study provides statistically significant results for domestic savings but not for foreign savings. In fact, the t-value of the foreign savings variable approaches zero if per capita incomes and the share of manufactured exports are included in the regression equation. At the same time, the separation of domestic and foreign savings increases the explanatory power of the regression equation as well as the statistical significance of the per capita income and manufactured export share variables, while reducing that of the export variable. The relevant results are shown in equations (5) to (8).

Apart from its low level of significance, the regression coefficient of the foreign savings variable is considerably smaller than that of the domestic savings variable. This result contrasts with the author's findings for the earlier period that showed the regression coefficient to be higher for foreign savings than for domestic savings, with both being highly significant statistically.

A possible explanation for the results is that in the 1973–9 period foreign savings were 'gap-filling,' i.e. they were used to finance a balance-of-payments deficit generated by external shocks. This explanation, however, leaves out of account the policy element. As the author has shown in the papers on policy responses to external shocks cited above, in the 1973–9 period reliance on foreign borrowing was associated with inward-oriented policies, entailing relatively low capital productivity.[3]

Finally, the regression coefficients of the export growth variable are considerably higher in the present estimates (0.15 to 0.22) than in those for the earlier period (0.04), the difference being statistically significant at the 1 percent level. This result contrasts with the view according to which exports would have had less of an effect on economic growth after 1973.

It appears, then, that a 1 percentage point increase in the rate of growth of exports is associated with a 0.15–0.22 percentage point increase in the rate of growth of GNP. Comparing a country at the upper quartile of the distribution in terms of export growth rates (6.7 percent) with the median country (3.8 percent), there is a gain in GNP growth rates of 0.6–0.8 percentage points; in turn, a shortfall in GNP growth rates of 0.7–1.0 percentage points is shown if the lower quartile (− 4.0 percent) is compared to the median (the results are not fully symmetrical because of the lack of symmetry in the distribution of the data).

Instead of export growth, Feder (1983) employed the product of export growth and the ratio of exports to GNP to estimate the effects of exports on economic growth. This alternative has also been utilized in the present study. The results reported in Table 18.2 show a higher explanatory power of the regression equation and higher levels of significance for the capital (investment), export, per capita income, and manufactured export share variables, and lower significance levels for the labor variable, than in the comparable equations of Table 18.1.

Following Feder, his export variable has further been disaggregated into variables representing productivity differentials between export and non-export sectors and externalities associated with exports. The separation has, however, failed to improve the results. While the inter-sectoral shift variable is significantly different from zero at the 2 percent level, the level of significance

Table 18.2 Savings, labor, exports, export shares and economic growth, 1973–9

Eq.	Constant	S_d/T^a	S_f/Y^a	L/L	$(X/X)\cdot(X/Y)$	X/X	Y/P	X_m/X	R^2
9	−4.138 (−0.334)	0.151 (3.076)	0.151 (3.076)	0.775 (1.197)	0.691 (2.950)				0.343
10	7.800 (0.577)	0.142 (3.015)	0.142 (3.015)	0.440 (0.692)	0.866 (3.652)		−11.416 (−2.203)		0.402
11	5.272 (0.402)	0.145 (3.191)	0.145 (3.191)	0.379 (0.617)	0.073 (3.039)		−14.872 (−2.804)	0.253 (1.954)	0.444
12	−2.856 (−0.215)	0.135 (2.369)	0.135 (2.369)	0.778 (1.192)	0.550 (1.612)	0.060 (0.575)			0.332
13	9.626 (0.694)	0.123 (2.261)	0.123 (2.261)	0.440 (0.687)	0.707 (2.126)	0.069 (0.690)	−11.559 (−2.213)		0.394
14	5.880 (0.431)	0.139 (2.598)	0.139 (2.598)	0.381 (0.612)	0.007 (2.122)	0.020 (0.201)	−14.814 (−2.752)	0.246 (1.804)	0.429

Sources: World Bank economic and social data bank.

Symbols: as in Table 18.1; X/Y = the ratio of merchandise exports to GNP in 1973. All value data are in constant dollar terms.

^{a} The coefficients for S_d/Y and S_f/Y are constrained to be equal in all equations.

of the externalities variable is low, and the adjusted R^2 is slightly lower than in the previous case.[4]

It is apparent that, irrespective of the procedure applied, exports made an important contribution to economic growth in developing countries during the period of external shocks. At the same time, the results underestimate the effects of exports on economic growth as the method applied does not allow for the positive impact of exports on savings which has been shown by Weisskopf (1972).

The overall explanatory power of the regression equations estimated for the 1973–9 period is, however, lower than that of the estimates for the earlier period. Possible explanations are the greater heterogeneity of the country sample, the shortness of the time period and the effects of external shocks on economic growth. Interest attaches, therefore, to the results obtained when external shocks are explicitly introduced in the analysis. It is of further interest to introduce policy orientation directly rather than indirectly through the use of the export growth variable.

POLICY CHOICES AND ECONOMIC GROWTH

In the papers referred to earlier, the author estimated the balance-of-payments effects of external shocks due to the deterioration of the terms of trade, associated with the quadrupling of oil prices in 1973–4, and to the export shortfall, associated with the world recession of 1974–5 and the subsequent slow recovery. He also estimated the balance-of-payments effects of policy responses to external shocks in the form of additional net external financing, export promotion, import substitution and deflationary measures.

The statistical results were subsequently utilized to examine the relationship between development strategies and alternative policy responses to external shocks and to indicate the economic effects of the policies applied. This was done by distinguishing between outward-oriented and inward-oriented development strategies, classifying newly industrializing as well as less developed countries into two groups according to the strategy pursued, and comparing the character of policy responses expressed in the form of averages for these groups (Balassa, 1984b).

A broader classification scheme, based on the extent of market distortions, was used in a study of sub-Saharan Africa (Balassa, 1984c). In this study, regression analysis was used to examine the relationship between the choice of development strategies and policy responses to external shocks on the one hand, and the rate of economic growth on the other, in an inter-country relationship.

The classification of countries into groups according to the development strategy pursued necessarily involves a certain degree of arbitrariness. At the same time, the criteria used in establishing the classification scheme being largely qualitative, it would be difficult to subdivide these categories further for purposes of a statistical investigation.

In order to overcome these difficulties, quantitative criteria have been introduced in defining policy orientation in the present study. This has been done in respect to the trade orientation of the national economy, corresponding to the distinction made earlier between outward- and inward-orientation that was also the major element in defining market distortions in sub-Saharan African countries.

Trade orientation has been defined in terms of deviations of actual from hypothetical values of per capita exports. Hypothetical values have been derived from a regression equation that, in addition to the per capita income and population variables utilized in early work by Chenery (1960), includes a variable representing the availability of mineral resources. This is because of the expectation that, *ceteris paribus*, the availability of mineral resources will raise the amount a country exports.[5]

Mineral resource availability has been represented by the ratio of mineral exports to the gross domestic product,[6] which may be taken to provide an indication of the relative importance of mineral resources in the national economy. The results reported in equation (15) show that this variable, as well as the per capita income and population variables, has a high degree of statistical significance.[7]

$$X/P = 1.540 + 0.924 \, Y/P - 0.236 \, P + 0.026 \, X_m/Y, \quad R^2 = 0.837 \qquad (15)$$

$$(10.007) \quad (12.576) \qquad (4.511) \qquad (2.410)$$

Table 18.3 presents the statistical results obtained by utilizing the trade orientation variable, together with indicators of policy responses to external shocks, to explain inter-country differences in GNP growth rates in the 1973–8 period. Additional explanatory variables have been introduced to indicate the magnitude of external shocks, the level of economic development and the extent of reliance on manufactured exports.

As described in detail in the author's papers referred to earlier, external shocks have been defined to include changes in the terms of trade and the impact of the slowdown of the growth of world trade, calculated on the assumption of unchanged export market shares for the country concerned. In turn, the policy responses to external shocks introduced in the present estimates include additional net external financing, involving a net capital inflow over and above its trend value, as well as domestic adjustment policies in the form of export promotion, represented by increases in export market shares, and import substitution, represented by a decrease in the income elasticity of import demand.

For the purposes of the estimation, the balance-of-payments effects of policy responses to external shocks have been expressed as a percentage of the balance-of-payments effects of these shocks, thus indicating the relative

Table 18.3 Trade orientation, policy responses to external shocks and economic growth

Eq.	Constant	TO	EP/ES	IS/ES	ANEF/ES	ES/Y	Y/P	X_m/X	R^2
16	2.350	2.270	0.050	0.019	0.024				0.499
	(3.165)	(3.548)	(5.816)	(2.908)	(3.541)				
17	3.007	2.611	0.052	0.020	0.024	−0.085			0.501
	(3.164)	(3.683)	(5.931)	(2.924)	(3.542)	(−1.103)			
18	3.109	2.604	0.051	0.019	0.023	−0.084	−0.119		0.488
	(2.834)	(3.622)	(5.607)	(2.809)	(3.272)	(−1.080)	(−0.194)		
19	2.047	2.079	0.050	0.023	0.027	−0.068	−0.811	0.044	0.579
	(1.935)	(3.075)	(6.046)	(3.655)	(4.075)	(−0.958)	(−1.348)	(2.959)	

Sources: Balassa (1981; 1984a, b, c).
Symbols: dependent variable: GNP growth rate for the period. Independent variables: as in Table 18.1; *ES* = balance of payments effects of external shocks, averages for 1974 to 1978; *TO* = trade orientation; *EP* = balance-of-payments effects of export promotion, averages for 1974 to 1978; *IS* = balance-of-payments effects of import substitution, averages for 1974 to 1978; *ANEF* = balance-of-payments effects of additional net external financing, averages for 1974 to 1978. All value data are in constant dollar terms.

importance of alternative policies. In turn, the balance-of-payments effects of external shocks have been expressed as a percentage of the gross national product; the level of development has been represented by per capita incomes in the initial year; and the share of manufactured goods in total exports has been used to reflect reliance on manufactured exports.

The results reported in Table 18.3 show that trade orientation has significantly influenced the rate of economic growth in the 43 countries studied during the 1973–9 period. The export promotion, import substitution and additional net external financing variables exhibit a high degree of statistical significance and all regression coefficients have a positive sign.

It is noteworthy that both the trade orientation and the export promotion variables are highly significant statistically. Thus, economic growth in the 1973–9 period was favorably affected by the country's trade orientation in the initial year, represented by differences between actual and hypothetical values of per capita exports in 1973, as well as by export promotion in response to external shocks, represented by the relative importance of increases in export market shares in response to external shocks after 1973.

The impact of trade orientation on economic growth may be indicated by estimating differences in GNP growth rates between a country in the upper quartile of the distribution in terms of trade orientation, representing the median among outward-oriented countries, and the neutral case where the trade orientation variable takes a zero value. The results derived from equation (8) show a gain of 0.5 percentage points for the country concerned. In turn, a country in the lower quartile of the distribution, representing the median among inward-oriented countries, is shown to experience a shortfall of 0.5 percentage points in its GNP growth rate. *Ceteris paribus;* there is thus a difference in GNP growth rates of 1.0 percentage points between the median outward-oriented and the median inward-oriented country.

Furthermore, the regression coefficient of the export promotion variable exceeds that of the import substitution and the additional net external financing variables two to two and a half times, indicating that greater reliance on export promotion in response to external shocks permits reaching higher GNP growth rates. From equation (17), increasing export promotion by 10 percentage points at the expense of import substitution and additional net external financing would add 0.3 percentage points to the rate of economic growth. The gain is 0.7 percentage points if comparison is made between the upper quartile and the median in terms of reliance on export promotion, and a loss of 0.4 percentage points in GNP growth is shown if a country at the lower quartile of the distribution is compared to the median. Comparing the two quartiles, then, a gain of 1.2 percentage points is obtained which is additional to the gains associated with outward orientation at the beginning of the period.

It appears, then, that initial trade orientation and reliance on export promotion in response to external shocks explain a large proportion of inter-country differences in GNP growth rates; these growth rates averaged 5.0 percent in the 43 developing countries under consideration during the 1973–9 period, with an upper quartile of 6.5 percent and a lower quartile of 3.3 percent. At the same time, the level of significance of the per capita GNP variable is lower, and that of the share of manufactured goods in total exports higher, than in the production function framework.

Finally, the two approaches have been combined by introducing, in the same estimating equation, the variables from the production function and the variables representing initial trade orientation and policy responses to external shocks. This formulation is superior to the previous ones. For one thing, it separates the effects of the country's initial policy stance from those of policy responses to external shocks, and the variables in question are not subject to simultaneity bias. For another thing, it adjusts for the effects of changes in capital and labor on output growth.

The results reported in Table 18.4 confirm the conclusions obtained earlier. The combination of the two approaches does not materially affect the statistical significance of the individual variables, and the coefficient of the export promotion variable continues to be substantially higher than the additional net external financing and the import substitution variables. In fact, the estimated gains of outward orientation and export promotion are practically the same as those derived from equation (19).

CONCLUSION

Having earlier shown the favorable effects of exports on economic growth in semi-industrial countries during the 1960–73 period of rapid economic

Table .18.4 Savings, labor, trade orientation, policy response to external shocks and economic growth

Eq.	Constant	S_d/Y	S_f/Y	L/L	TO	EP/ES	IS/ES	$ANEF/ES$	ES/Y	Y/P	X_m/X	R^2
20	−6.286	0.079	0.079	0.308	12.348	0.366	0.194	0.205		−5.288	0.331	
	(−0.550)	(1.938)	(1.938)	(0.613)	(2.719)	(5.553)	(4.009)	(4.252)		(−1.212)	(3.081)	0.646
21	−7.131	0.082	0.022	0.389	10.317	0.330	0.185	0.185		−7.838	0.334	
	(−0.643)	(2.069)	(0.435)	(0.796)	(2.268)	(4.930)	(3.915)	(3.863)		(−1.755)	(3.198)	0.667
22	−4.764	0.078	0.078	0.284	12.941	0.369	0.195	0.205	−0.130	−5.234	0.329	
	(−0.362)	(1.868)	(1.868)	(0.549)	(2.490)	(5.415)	(3.958)	(4.197)	(−0.246)	(−1.182)	(3.014)	0.636
23	1.583	0.076	−0.010	0.285	12.971	0.334	0.183	0.179	−0.776	−8.619	0.323	
	(0.124)	(1.927)	(−0.175)	(0.582)	(2.641)	(5.050)	(3.915)	(3.744)	(−1.342)	(−1.936)	(3.129)	0.675

Sources: see Tables 18.1 and 18.3.
Symbols: dependent variable: changes in GNP between 1973 and 1979 as a percentage of 1973 GNP. Independent variables as in Tables 18.1 and 18.3. All value data are in constant dollar terms.

growth, the author has re-examined the validity of this proposition in the 1973–9 period of external shocks. Utilizing the same framework, and extending the scope of the investigation to countries at lower levels of development, he has found that the rate of growth of exports had an important effect on the rate of economic growth and that the numerical magnitude of this effect increased compared to the earlier period.

The rate of economic growth is further influenced by increases in the labor force and by domestic savings while, in contradistinction with the earlier results, foreign savings do not appear to have affected the outcome. At the same time, *ceteris paribus*, developing countries at lower levels of development have been better able to increase total factor productivity than countries at higher levels and a high share of manufactured exports was also positively associated with economic growth.

Estimates made by utilizing the product of export growth and the share of exports in GDP, instead of export growth alone, modify the results but little. Disaggregating the export variable into variables representing productivity differentials between export and non-export sectors and externalities associated with exports failed, however, to improve the results.

The introduction of an export variable in the production function-type framework aims at capturing the effects of exports on economic growth through improved resource allocation capacity utilization, economies of scale and technical change. Under the formulation utilized, inter-country differences in export growth rates, and in the share of exports to GDP, are considered to be a manifestation of the trade policies followed.

This approach introduces policy orientation only indirectly; it fails to adjust for the impact of the availability of natural resources on export shares; and it does not allow for the effects of external shocks on export growth. The described deficiencies have been remedied by introducing a trade orientation variable that adjusts for natural resource availabilities and by separating the effects of external shocks and of policy responses to external shocks on exports.

The results indicate the effects of trade orientation and those of policy responses to external shocks on economic growth. It is shown that the rate of GNP growth is the higher the greater the extent of outward orientation at the beginning of the period under consideration and the greater the extent of reliance on export promotion in response to the external shocks of the period. The results are cumulative and policy choices appear to account for a large proportion of inter-country differences in GNP growth rates during the 1973–9 period.

Combining the two approaches further reinforces the results of each. Thus, inter-country differences in the rate of economic growth appear to be affected by differences in investment rates and by the rate of growth of the labor force, by the initial trade policy stance and by the adjustment policies applied, as well as by the level of economic development and by the product composition of exports.

The results show that the policies adopted have had an important influence on the rate of economic growth in developing countries. In particular, an outward-oriented policy stance at the beginning of the period of external shocks, as well as reliance on export promotion in response to these shocks, appear to have affected growth performance favorably. The results further indicate the possibilities for low-income countries to accelerate their economic growth through the application of modern technology in an appropriate policy framework as well as the advantages of relying on manufactured exports.

APPENDIX

The countries included in this study, listed by their 1973 per capita incomes, are: Israel, Singapore, Argentina, Portugal, Yugoslavia, Jamaica, Uruguay, Mexico, Brazil, Chile, Costa Rica, Taiwan, Peru, Turkey, Guatemala, Tunisia, Zambia, Mauritius, Korea, Honduras, Morocco, Ghana, Senegal, the Philippines, Thailand, Cameroon, Egypt, Bolivia, Botswana, Togo, Kenya, Madagascar, Zaire, Sudan, Tanzania, Sri Lanka, India, Pakistan, Benin, Malawi, Bangladesh, Upper Volta and Mali.

NOTES

1. Tyler provides a partial exception, but the post-1973 years included in his investigation represent less than one-fifth of the period covered.
2. As noted in the author's earlier paper (1978), the export growth variable is taken to reflect alternative uses of resources as between exports and import substitution. It is further assumed that domestic saving shares are invariant with respect to rates of economic growth in an inter-country context.
3. As Gershon Feder noted in discussions with the author, attempting to explain differences in the regression coefficients for domestic and for foreign savings in terms of policy differences introduces an extraneous element in the estimation as, in a production function-type relationship, the expected coefficient of investment is the same irrespective of whether it is financed from domestic or from foreign savings. It should further be added that while the regression coefficients for the two variables show a similar pattern in all the estimating equations, the differences between them are not significant statistically.
4. In conformity with the procedure applied by Feder, however, domestic investment has not been disaggregated into domestic and foreign savings.
5. Consideration has further been given to including agricultural resources in the calculations, but no reliable index of agricultural resources could be established. At any rate, while mineral products are generally exported by developing countries, the availability of agricultural resources may lead to exports as well as to import substitution.
6. Data are for 1973; mineral exports are defined as the sum of exports for SITC classes 27, 283, 3, 51365 and 68.
7. While population appears in the terms shown on the two sides of the equation, just

as in Chenery's early formulation, this should not affect the appropriateness of using deviations from hypothetical values as an indication of trade orientation.

REFERENCES

Balassa, Bela (1978) 'Exports and Economic Growth: Further Evidence', *Journal of Development Economics*, June, pp. 181–9. Reprinted as Chapter 17 of this volume.

Balassa, Bela (1981) 'The Newly-Industrializing Developing Countries After the Oil Crisis', *Weltwirtschaftliches Archiv*, Band 117, Heft 1, pp. 142–94. Reprint No. 190, World Bank, Washington, DC.

Balassa, Bela (1984a) 'The Policy Experience of 12 Less Developed Countries, 1973–1978', in G. Ranis, R. L. West, M. Leierson, and C. C. Morris, eds, *Comparative Development Perspectives. Essays in Honor of Lloyd G. Reynolds*, Westview, Boulder, CO.

Balassa, Bela (1984b) 'Adjustment to External Shocks in Developing Countries', in B. Csikós-Nagy, D. Hague, and G. Hall, eds, *Economics of Relative Prices*, Macmillan, London.

Balassa, Bela (1984c) 'Adjustment Policies and Development Strategies in Sub-Saharan Africa, 1973–78', in M. Syrquin, L. Taylor, and L. W. Westphal, eds, *Economic Structure and Performance. Essays in Honor of Hollis B. Chenery*, Macmillan, New York.

Chenery, Hollis B. (1960) 'Patterns of Industrial Growth', *American Economic Review*, Sept., pp. 624–54.

Feder, Gershon (1983) 'On Exports and Economic Growth', *Journal of Development Economics*, Feb.–April, pp. 59–74.

Michalopoulos, Constantine, and Jay, Keith (1973) 'Growth of Exports and Income in the Developing World: A Neoclassical View', *Discussion Paper No. 28*, Agency for International Development, Washington, DC.

Tyler, William G. (1981) 'Growth and Export Expansion in Developing Countries: Some Empirical Evidence', *Journal of Development Economics*, Aug., pp. 121–30.

Weisskopf, Thomas E. (1972) 'The Impact of Foreign Capital Inflow on Domestic Savings in Underdeveloped Countries', *Journal of International Economics*, Feb., pp. 25–38.

INDEX